Inside Wellington's
Peninsular Army

Inside Wellington's Peninsular Army
1808–1814

Rory Muir, Robert Burnham, Howie Muir,
Ron McGuigan

Pen & Sword
MILITARY

First published in Great Britain in 2006 by
Pen & Sword Military
an imprint of
Pen & Sword Books Ltd
47 Church Street
Barnsley
South Yorkshire
S70 2AS

ISBN 1 84415 484 X

Typeset in Times New Roman by
Phoenix Typesetting, Auldgirth, Dumfriesshire

Printed and bound in England by
Biddles Ltd., King's Lynn

Pen & Sword Books Ltd incorporates the imprints of Pen & Sword Aviation, Pen &
Sword Maritime, Pen & Sword Military, Wharncliffe Local History, Pen &
Pen & Sword Select, Pen & Sword Military Classics and Leo Cooper.

For a complete list of Pen & Sword titles please contact
PEN & SWORD BOOKS LIMITED
47 Church Street, Barnsley, South Yorkshire, S70 2AS, England
E-mail: enquiries@pen-and-sword.co.uk
Website: www.pen-and-sword.co.uk

Contents

Introduction   vi

Chapter 1   Wellington and the Peninsular War:
             The Ingredients of Victory (Rory Muir)   1

Chapter 2   The Origin of Wellington's Peninsular Army
             June 1808–April 1809
             (Ron McGuigan)   39

Chapter 3   British Observing Officers of the Peninsular War
             (Robert Burnham)   71

Chapter 4   Order of Battle: Customary Battle-Array in
             Wellington's Peninsular Army (Howie Muir)   84

Chapter 5   Wellington's Generals in Portugal, Spain and
             France 1809–1814 (Ron McGuigan)   172

Chapter 6   Filling the Ranks: How Wellington Kept His
             Units up to Strength (Robert Burnham)   201

Chapter 7   British Bridging Operations in the Peninsula
             (Robert Burnham)   226

Appendix   British Memoirs of the Napoleonic Wars
             (Robert Burnham)   275

Select Bibliography   304

Acknowledgements   315

Index   318

Introduction

Ten years ago, when the internet was just catching on, the Napoleon Series (www.napoleon-series.org) was born. There, scholars and enthusiasts of the Napoleonic Era were able to meet people with similar interests from all over the world. For several years, Rory Muir, Ron McGuigan, Howie Muir, and I exchanged information and assisted each other with various research projects on the British Army. Each of us had developed our own area of expertise and resources, which we willingly shared. Ron McGuigan's ability to mine *Wellington's Dispatches* and the *British Army Lists* for information has constantly amazed me; while Howie Muir has always made his collection of regulations and period manuals available. Added to this was Rory Muir's encyclopaedic knowledge of Wellington and the Peninsular War, and my collection of British memoirs, diaries, and journals.

As our friendship grew, a proposal grew with it: that we combine our efforts and write this book about Wellington and his army. Although much has been written about the individual regiments and campaigns of the British Army, little has been written on why it was so successful. What was so special about Wellington and his army? How was this partnership able to beat the French year after year?

When we talked over the idea, we decided to use Sir Charles Oman's *Wellington's Army*, as our foundation. This study provided much valuable information, but since Oman published it in 1913, many fresh sources have become available. Exploiting these new sources, we have expanded some of Oman's ideas, while exploring areas that he did not cover. Although Oman looks closely at many aspects of the British Army, the present books attempts to be more focused. We examine in detail those aspects of Wellington's army that constituted the ingredients of its success: such as command relationships, tactical formations, intelligence operations, engineering, and how the Duke kept his forces up to strength. Finally we have included an appendix listing first hand accounts of the war for those who wish to delve further into the primary sources for themselves.

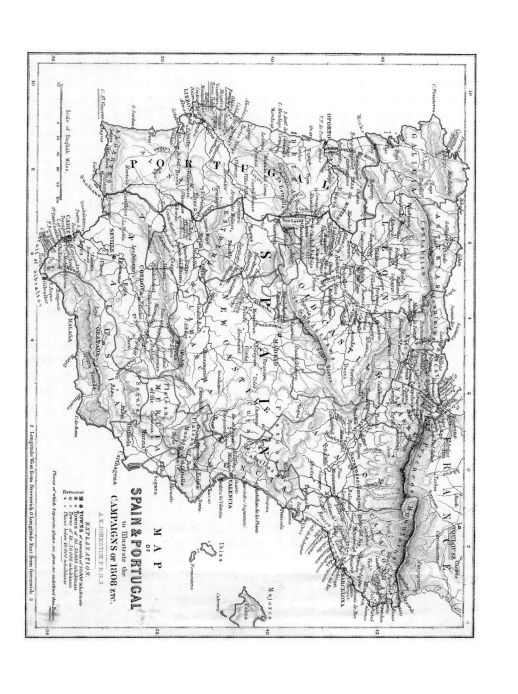

MAP
OF
SPAIN & PORTUGAL
to Illustrate the
CAMPAIGNS OF 1808 ETC.
A.K.JOHNSTON F.R.G.S.

EXPLANATION.
■ Cities of upwards of 10.000 inhabitants
■ TOWNS of upwards of 50.000 inhabitants
● Towns of 30..50.000 inhabitants
○ Towns of 10..30.000 inhabitants
+ Places below 10.000 inhabitants

Fortresses ☆ ✶ ✹

Places of which Separate plans are given are underlined thus Dublin

Scale of English Miles.

Longitude West from Greenwich ○ Longitude East from Greenwich

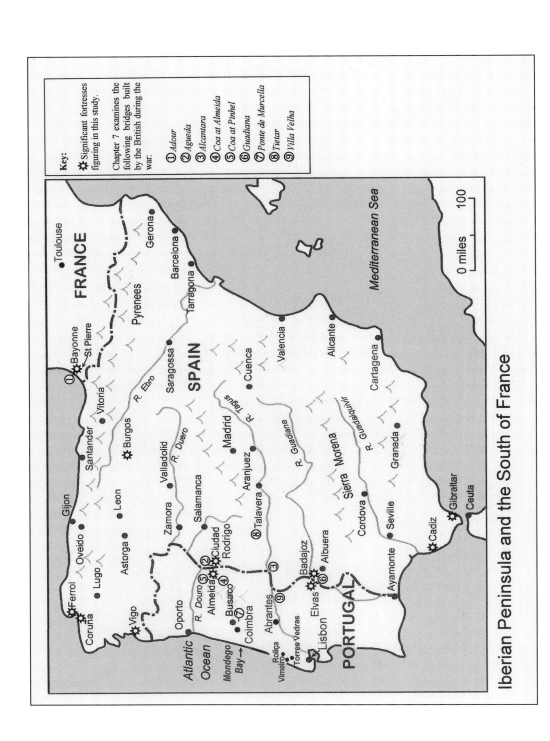

Key:

✹ Significant fortresses figuring in this study.

Chapter 7 examines the following bridges built by the British during the war:

① Adour
② Agueda
③ Alcantara
④ Coa at Almeida
⑤ Coa at Pinhel
⑥ Guadiana
⑦ Ponte de Murcella
⑧ Tietar
⑨ Villa Velha

Iberian Peninsula and the South of France

Chapter One
Wellington and the Peninsular War: The Ingredients of Victory

RORY MUIR

On the morning of 8 June 1808 a coach rattled into London from Falmouth, carrying a small party of Spanish notables. They had been sent by the ancient provincial assembly of the Principality of Asturias in northern Spain, with the news that their Principality had risen against French occupation, and was seeking British assistance. They were greeted with enormous enthusiasm and were lionized by London society and the press. The long war against Napoleon had not been going well, and a popular uprising in Spain was a completely new idea, untainted with previous failures, so that people of all shades of opinion in Britain could indulge in rose-tinted dreams of easy victories. Over the next few weeks the initial excitement was fed by fresh news from Spain, where province after province burst into insurrection and looked to Britain for arms, equipment and money. The optimistic forecasts and extravagant hopes that abounded seemed justified when, in the second week of August, accounts arrived of the capitulation of a French army at Bailen, the withdrawal of Bessières's army from Leon, and the flight of King Joseph and all the French from Madrid right back to the Ebro. The salvation of Spain seemed assured, and Lord Castlereagh, the Secretary of State for War and the Colonies, even dreamt of cutting off the French retreat at the foot of the Pyrenees and forcing their whole army to surrender.[1] In the heady days of the summer of 1808 nothing seemed impossible.

In this first phase of the war, the Spanish deputies did not ask for the assistance of a British army: they were full of confidence in the strength of their own people, while their recent experience of French betrayal made them wary of inviting more foreign troops into their land. Yet the British government was eager to do something to assist its new ally beyond providing them with huge quantities of arms and lavish amounts of money. The obvious solution, at least as a preliminary operation, was for the British to liberate Portugal, which had been occupied by the French since the previous November. A small expedition under Major General Brent Spencer was already off the coast of Spain, and a rather larger force, to be commanded by Wellington (then Lieutenant General Sir Arthur Wellesley),[2] was being prepared for overseas service at Cork. The most recent intelligence from Portugal suggested that if these two expeditions combined they would be more than sufficient, and on 30 June, Wellington was given his instructions. The convoy left Cork on 12 July, having been delayed for several days by adverse winds, and as soon as it cleared the Irish coast, Wellington sailed ahead to Coruña to get the latest news and to consult the Junta of Galicia. Having done so, he met the convoy off Cape Finisterre on 22 July, then again sailed ahead to Oporto, the centre of the Portuguese insurrection, and then further south to consult Admiral Cotton, who commanded the naval squadron blockading the Tagus. These meetings gave Wellington a good appreciation of the state of the war, both in Portugal and more widely in the Peninsula as a whole – even though the authorities at Coruña minimized the significance of their recent defeat at Medina del Rio Seco.

At Oporto, Wellington noted that while thousands of Portuguese peasants had joined the rising they were mostly without arms and equipment, and lacked a backbone of regular troops and experienced officers. At the same time, he was struck by the warmth of his welcome in Portugal and by the eagerness of the Portuguese to accept British help. These impressions were supplemented by his shipboard study of papers written by Lieutenant General Sir Charles Stuart and Lieutenant Colonel Richard Stewart, who had commanded previous British expeditions to Portugal in 1797 and 1803.[3] On 1 August, the same day that Wellington's army began landing at Mondego Bay, he wrote privately to Castlereagh, urging that the British government 'raise, organize, and pay an army in Portugal, consisting of 30,000 Portuguese troops . . . and 20,000 British, including 4,000 or 5,000 cavalry. The army might operate on the frontiers of Portugal in Spanish Estremadura, and it would serve as the link between the kingdoms of Galicia and Andalusia: it would give Great Britain the preponderance in the conduct of the war in the Peninsula; and whatever might be the result of the Spanish exertions, Portugal would be saved from the French grasp.'[4] Nothing came of this proposal at the time: Wellington found the actual experience of co-operating with the Portuguese more difficult than he expected, while the retreat of the French in Spain behind the Ebro made Portugal appear, for the moment, a strategic backwater. Nonetheless, it is remarkable that at this very early point in the war Wellington had identified one of the keys to his later success.

The British army in 1808 was not small: it had over 200,000 regulars plus a further 90,000 well-trained, full-time militia for home defence, but it had to provide garrisons for Britain's many colonies and for strategic points in the Mediterranean. Once these needs were met, the force available for active operations on the Continent was relatively modest: fewer than 40,000 men in the early years of war, then slowly rising, but never getting much above 70,000. This compared to a total French force in the Peninsula, which peaked at over 350,000 men, and was above 300,000 for several years. Consequently, the British army alone could not hope to be the dominant force in the war in the Peninsula. The solution that Wellington proposed in August 1808, and which was adopted six months later, was to supplement British troops with the Portuguese to make a powerful combined army under British command.

Those six months were full of disappointment. Wellington's early successes at Roliça and Vimeiro were followed by the arrival of reinforcements led by superior officers, and by the Convention of Cintra, which provoked such an outcry in Britain that his whole career was in jeopardy. Sir John Moore led the British Army into Spain, but long before it could reach the Ebro, Napoleon had launched a well-prepared offensive that overwhelmed the Spanish armies and recaptured Madrid. Moore risked everything to strike a blow that would divert Napoleon and give the Spaniards time to rally. He succeeded, but had to retreat headlong through the mountains of Galicia in midwinter: his army suffered dreadfully and its discipline collapsed under the strain. Turning at bay at Coruña, the British troops showed they were still happy to fight, and repulsed a French attack. The army was success-fully evacuated, although Moore was killed, but the campaign led to intense disillusionment with the Spanish cause in Britain. Nor was there much enthusiasm in the British government for Portugal, but George Canning, the Foreign Secretary, listened to Portuguese appeals for assistance, and in particular, for a British officer – preferably Wellington – to take command of their army and prepare it for action. The other ministers would not agree to send Wellington back to Portugal. Despite the furore over Cintra they had a very high opinion of his ability and felt that he would be wasted in Portugal, which they saw as an almost hopeless cause. But they did agree, in the middle of February, to lend the Portuguese Major General William Carr Beresford, and to allow him to take twenty-four junior officers with him as his assistants.[5]

Beresford proved an inspired choice. The full story of his labours to improve the Portuguese army has never been told (by far the best account in English is an unpublished thesis by Samuel E. Vichness),[6] but it is clear that no one initially appreciated the scale of the task or the time it would take. Beresford reached Lisbon at the beginning of March 1809 but did not take up his command for a fortnight – time spent in talks with the Portuguese regency, which was reluctant to concede the sweeping powers that he demanded. The Portuguese army was in a poor state: years of neglect and underfunding had been followed by the French invasion of 1807, when some of the best troops were sent off to France and the remainder allowed to disband. The insurrection against the French had been chaotic and subsequent attempts to reconstruct the army had been hampered by lack of funding, weapons and a strong commander. There was considerable suspi-cion of foreigners throughout the army, and an ingrained reluctance to change: officers and men alike were accustomed to a slow pace and little exertion in return for meagre rewards. If the army was to be of any use against the French, its whole approach to its work had to change, and the transition would not be easy. Beresford was not a subtle, nor a tactful man, and his harsh manners and insistence on strict discipline did nothing to lessen the resentment aroused by his reforms. He was careful, however, to divide his favour equally between British and Portuguese officers, and relied at least as much on Manoel de Brito Mosinho, his Adjutant General, as on Benjamin D'Urban his Quartermaster-General. Sensitive questions of personnel and promotion were handled by his military secretary Colonel Antonio de Lemos Pereira de Lacenda.[7] He seems to have chosen his staff well and – so far as we can tell – they served him loyally and with efficiency. One of his British aides, William Warre, wrote in a private letter home:

There exists not a more honourable, firm man, or a more zealous Patriot. His failings are mere foibles of a temper naturally warm and hasty, and a great zeal to have everything right, without much patience. Those who accuse him of severity are either those who have felt it because they deserved it, their friends, or people wilfully ignorant of the state in which he found the army. And of how much he has forborne, as to myself, I declare I do not know of one instance of severity, and do know of numberless ones of his mercy, and goodness of heart, where others would have been less lenient.[8]

But all Beresford's virtues would have counted for nothing if he had not been able to work well with the commander of the British forces in Portugal, or if the French had advanced in force on Lisbon before his reforms had had time to take effect.

The appointment of Beresford in February 1809 did not signal a firm British commitment to the defence of Portugal. A small British army, left over from 1808, remained in Lisbon, but its commander, Sir John Cradock, did not show much energy or confidence in his ability to hold his position – although he had been hamstrung by the need to detach a substantial part of his force on a wild-goose chase to Cadiz. Cradock's instructions from Castlereagh were desponding, being more concerned with the timing of his evacuation than measures to avoid the necessity.[9] But Canning was not willing to abandon Portugal without a struggle, and throughout the first three months of 1809 he continued to urge the Cabinet to reinforce the British army and to replace Cradock with Wellington. The other ministers were slow to respond: they were preoccupied with other business, notably the reaction to the Coruña campaign and the scandal that erupted over allegations that Mary Anne Clarke, the Duke of York's mistress, had taken bribes to procure commissions or promotions in the army. Castlereagh seems to have been particularly reluctant to send Wellington back to Portugal: they were old friends, and he had the highest opinion of Wellington's ability, but he probably feared that if Wellington returned to Portugal and was then forced to evacuate Lisbon, his reputation, which had suffered so much from Cintra, would be irretrievably damaged. Also, Wellington was Cradock's junior and his appointment would require Cradock's recall, which Castlereagh felt would be unfair, as Cradock had done nothing wrong, and not been given any chance to distinguish himself.

Wellington was asked to give his views on the prospects in Portugal and responded with a famous memorandum dated 7 March 1809. In this he expanded and elaborated on his ideas of the previous August, modifying the detail, but retaining the central insight that a close alliance with Portugal would enable Britain to play a much greater role in the war in the Peninsula. If the Portuguese regular army of 30,000 men was revived and made effective, and if it was supported by a militia of 40,000 men and by a British army of 30,000, (increased from 20,000 because so much time had been lost, and – although Wellington did not admit this – because the French had proved so much more formidable than anyone expected in August 1808), it would be able to defend Portugal and 'be highly useful to the Spaniards'. It might even decide the contest. However, the task would not be easy: it was obvious, Wellington declared, 'that the military establishments of Portugal could not be revived without very extensive pecuniary assistance and political support from this country,' which in practice meant that the Portuguese would have to accept continued British interference in all aspects of their government, not just their army, in return for a large subsidy. The British troops in Portugal would need to receive reinforcements, and Wellington specified 'some companies of British riflemen,' 3,000 British or German (King's German Legion) cavalry, and an increase of the artillery of the army so that it had thirty guns, including two batteries of 9-pounders, and that a siege-train of twenty brass 12-pounders be sent to Lisbon along with a large complement of engineers. Additional arms, uniforms and shoes for 30,000 men should be sent to assist the Portuguese, while Britain should undertake the commissariat service for the whole of the Allied army.[10]

Not all of these ideas proved practical, some needed to be modified with experience, and the commissariat in particular remained a difficult issue for years: the British Treasury was unwilling to undertake the whole responsibility for feeding the Portuguese army, and the British commissaries themselves did not perform very well in 1809, lacking the necessary experience and training; but the Portuguese commissariat proved particularly unreliable and gradually the British commissaries extended their responsibilities, at least when the army was on active service. But these details do nothing to obscure the remarkable insight Wellington displayed in the memorandum, for it laid the foundation of all Britain's subsequent success in the Peninsula.

Nonetheless, the Cabinet took its time to change its mind. On 12 March Castlereagh ordered Major General Rowland Hill out to Portugal with 4,500 reinforcements – six second battalions, not really fit to take the field, but the best that were available, for the good troops of Moore's army needed more time to rest and refit before they could be sent back into action. Six days later the Duke of York bowed to the inevitable and resigned, removing the issue that had preoccupied the ministers and dominated domestic politics since the beginning of February. Meanwhile, reports were beginning to reach London that Soult, having entered Coruña on 17 January and Ferrol on the 26th was moving south through Galicia towards northern Portugal. On 21 March Canning told the Prime Minister, 'Portugal is a source of constant, daily, and nightly uneasiness to me.'[11] Finally, on 26 March, the Cabinet agreed to transfer Cradock to Gibraltar and appoint Wellington in his place. The King, who thought Wellington too junior a lieutenant general to be given such an important command, reluctantly acquiesced on the following day. As Wellington was preparing to sail, news came that Soult had brushed aside a Portuguese army at Braga on 20 March and captured Oporto on the 29th. Wellington feared that the campaign might be over before he could arrive, or at least that Cradock might be engaged in active operations, but Castlereagh urged him on, and Wellington's ship sailed from Portsmouth on 15 April 1809.

After a quick passage Wellington landed at Lisbon on 22 April and found, to his relief, that the French were still at Oporto, and that while Cradock had moved his forces a little further forward, he had not begun a campaign. Wellington received an enthusiastic welcome from the Portuguese, who had been greatly impressed by his victories at Roliça and Vimeiro. Once ashore he lost little time in taking command of the army and making his plans. Although his instructions limited him to the defence of Portugal, he already had an eye on a campaign in Spain against Victor's army in Estremadura, but first he had to drive Soult from

Oporto. By early May Wellington had joined his army at Coimbra, halfway to Oporto. He had detached some 4,500 men to guard his eastern flank in case Victor should advance, and another brigade to assist a Portuguese force, which would attempt to cut Soult's line of retreat, but he still had some 16,000 British and 2,500 Portuguese troops with his main force. Given that Soult had more than 20,000 veterans under his command, and might choose either to advance against Wellington or withdraw behind the line of the River Douro, the result of the campaign seemed far from certain. But Wellington was confident, and the French army had lost momentum with the capture of Oporto – the men were tired after a gruelling winter campaign and not even Soult believed that the army was strong enough to take Lisbon without reinforcements or assistance from Victor. Faced with the sudden advance of the allies, Soult's thoughts turned not to a victory that would conquer the kingdom, but to an orderly retreat into Spain.

However, not even this proved possible. Soult detached Loison with 6,500 men to open the road east along the Douro and into Leon, for he had no wish ever to see the barren mountains and inhospitable peasants of Galicia again. Loison drove the Portuguese from the vital bridge over the Tamega at Amarante, but was then, on 10 May, repulsed from a strong position at Mezãofrio and fell back in disorder, abandoning even Amarante. Before Soult learnt of this disaster, the leading Allied troops had driven his advanced posts back to the Douro, and Wellington, in an act of remarkable boldness, had seized the bishop's seminary on the north bank. Thrown completely off balance the French struggled to mount an effective counter-attack, but the British position was naturally strong and well-supported by artillery fire from south of the river. The orderly retreat Soult had planned turned to flight. That night, camped halfway between Oporto and Amarante, Soult finally learnt of Loison's defeat two days before. The road east was blocked and the only hope of escape was to abandon all the army's artillery, wheeled transport and other heavy equipment, even the pay chests, and head north and north-east, crossing the mountains on goat tracks. Wellington pursued with vigour while Beresford tried to cut off the French, but Soult's men were great marchers and they escaped back into Galicia. Even so, it was a striking triumph. Less than a month after landing in Lisbon Wellington had avenged Coruña and driven the French forces that had sacked Oporto and threatened Lisbon back into Spain in a humiliating rout.[12]

The Portuguese army played an important role in the Oporto campaign. Silveira's success at Mezãofrio blocked Soult's preferred line of retreat, while the four battalions of infantry that served with Wellington's main army earned warm praise for their performance. Nonetheless, the action was premature, for the Portuguese were far from ready to take the field. Their troops suffered greatly in the pursuit of Soult, due to the bad weather, harsh terrain and lack of supplies, so that many units that had done well earlier were able to muster less than half their strength by the end of the campaign. Wellington recognized the problem and did not employ the Portuguese in his next campaign, preferring that they guard the frontier near Almeida. But the Portuguese commissariat could not supply even stationary troops in the barren frontier region, while a limited advance undertaken by Beresford in the hope of protecting Wellington's exposed northern flank greatly exacerbated the problem. Consequently, it was not until the early autumn of 1809, when the tattered troops were withdrawn deep into central Portugal, that Beresford's reforms had a chance to take much effect.

Beresford's most urgent task was to establish his authority and to force a large number of elderly or incompetent officers into retirement. He met considerable opposition on both fronts, but refused to compromise and eventually overcame the resistance. Discipline in the Portuguese army had been very slack – many officers took extended leave from their regiments without official sanction, while the poorly paid ordinary soldiers flouted orders and sold or pawned their equipment.[13] The existing form of court martial was slow, bureaucratic and ineffective. Beresford established a much simpler procedure with severe punishments. In the first case, on 20 April 1809, a soldier who disobeyed a direct order was sentenced to ten years' imprisonment, a result which produced a sensation.[14] Yet Beresford also abolished some forms of arbitrary and humiliating punishment, and while some corporal punishment was retained, it was much less severe than the flogging common in the British army. In June he enforced the execution of four deserters and ensured that subsequent executions attracted the maximum exposure by holding them, for example, in the main square of Oporto at noon on a market day. This enabled him to commute most sentences of death to imprisonment with hard labour without reducing the deterrent effect.[15]

Promotion in the old Portuguese army had been very slow for officers without influence, and regiments contained far too many middle-aged subalterns and elderly field officers – men whose courage may have been undiminished but who were too set in their ways to embrace new methods with enthusiasm. Beresford began cautiously, forcing the retirement of six officers in April. Again there was an outcry and the Portuguese government protested, but Beresford held firm and demanded that his authority be supported. He succeeded and established a precedent, which he immediately put to good effect. By midsummer over 100 officers had been removed, most of them captains and lieutenants, and on 14 July he doubled this number. The average age of the men on the July list was fifty-eight with thirty-nine years of service: the youngest was 47, the oldest, 75. These dismissals aroused considerable discontent, especially as many of the officers were dependent on their pay, and the government could not afford to give them adequate pensions. But Beresford disregarded the protests and used the vacancies to accelerate the promotion of promising officers and to appoint a whole generation of fresh subalterns. By the end of the year more than 350 officers had been forced into retirement and while some of those who remained were resentful others were embracing the new regime with growing enthusiasm.[16]

Beresford was assisted in his work by a number of British officers who were permitted to volunteer for service in the Portuguese army. The first group of these, the twenty-four appointed at the outset, were given one step of promotion in the British army and a further step in the Portuguese, so that overnight a captain became a British major and a Portuguese lieutenant colonel. Subsequently, officers received only the promotion in the Portuguese service, although the Commander-in-Chief promised to take account of their service wherever possible. This distinction naturally caused much discontent, while some British officers deeply resented the fact that a former subordinate might thus swiftly become their superior, and long-serving Portuguese officers questioned why they should defer to a much younger and less experienced man simply because he was British. Beresford's own position aroused similar resentment among the British generals whom he had leapfrogged: Major General John Murray went home in a huff over the issue, and throughout the war there was concern that if Wellington was killed or wounded, Beresford would assume command of the whole Allied army, at least temporarily, by virtue of his Portuguese rank.

The reform of the Portuguese army would not have succeeded without Wellington's steady, unwavering support. Privately he disagreed with some of Beresford's methods. He disliked the incentive given to British officers to serve in the Portuguese army and doubted the value of employing them scattered throughout the regiments, arguing that a smaller number of particularly able officers employed in a supervisory role would produce better results. But when Beresford was unconvinced by these arguments, Wellington gave way, recognizing that any attempt to interfere would simply cause muddle and confusion.[17] In public he was completely loyal in backing Beresford's authority: British officers who attempted to play one general off against the other retired discomfited, and he supported Beresford in all his tussles with the Portuguese regency. These culminated in December 1809 when Major Francisco de Mello informed Beresford of his intention to resign from the army. Beresford believed that de Mello, who came from an influential noble family, was not acting on private grounds, and that if his resignation was accepted it would rapidly be followed by many others. He brusquely informed de Mello that no officer had the right to resign without permission, and that permission would not be granted. Wellington gave his support to Beresford, and so, reluctantly, did the regency, and eventually the Regent, Prince João, in Brazil. De Mello remained in the army – where he was a good, brave officer – until he was killed at Salamanca in 1812. This symbolic triumph confirmed Beresford's authority and ensured that his reforms would be implemented.[18]

The real improvement in the Portuguese army began in September 1809 and proceeded all through the autumn, winter, and the following spring. Much of it arose from basic repetitive training: drill, drill, and yet more drill; weapons training, route marching and the occasional inspection day. Recruits were incorporated into the ranks, new officers got to know their men, and fresh arms and equipment were issued. Beresford appointed Major General John Hamilton as Inspector-General of the Infantry, and Hamilton proved full of energy, working tirelessly, supervising the training. In November the infantry were authorized to fire up to twenty rounds a day to practise their musketry – something that would not only improve their shooting, but also enhance their morale and sense of purpose. Beresford also argued strongly for an increase in the grossly inadequate pay of officers, and in February 1810 was able to almost double their salaries, with the greatest increase being for the most junior officers.[19]

Slowly the work bore fruit. In the middle of December Beresford inspected five line regiments, five battalions of *caçadores* (light infantry), and part of the artillery, and was sufficiently pleased with the result to grant fifteen days' leave to a number of men from each unit as a reward (five from each individual company).[20] At the end of the year, and in the first days of 1810, Wellington joined Beresford in a much more extensive series of inspections. Sixteen of the twenty-four regiments of line infantry, five of the six battalions of *caçadores*, and all the artillery were judged fit to take the field, although a good deal more work needed to be done on the cavalry. The next few months revealed that this judgement was rather too optimistic. Many problems remained to be overcome and months' more training were needed. But by the late spring of 1810 most of the Portuguese army was ready for action, although it was still inexperienced and it benefited greatly by the long delay in the opening of the campaign, and by Wellington's careful handling, which gave it the chance to gain confidence and experience in favourable conditions. It would not be until the spring of 1811 – two years after Beresford reached Lisbon – that it would be exposed to the full rough-and-tumble of active campaigning, and even then the Portuguese troops were mixed with the British – with the Portuguese typically amounting to between one-third and one-half of each division. Without the Portuguese, the British army would never have been strong enough to make a decisive impact on the war in the Peninsula; while without British help the Portuguese army would have remained incapable of facing the French. Portuguese co-operation was an indispensable element in all Wellington's operations after 1809.

Britain's alliance with Spain was much less close and intimate than her alliance with Portugal, but even more important. There would have been no Peninsular War if it had not been for the Spanish uprising of May–June 1808, and if the Spanish people had accepted defeat in November 1808 – which by every rational calculation they should have done – the war would have been over long before Wellington returned to Lisbon. The Spanish resistance came from below, not above. Napoleon had removed the royal family, and none of the local juntas that sprang up in the wake of the uprising, or the central governments that were eventually formed from them, had the power or legitimacy to make peace. Nor did Napoleon leave any room for a compromise settlement: he did not want concessions from Spain, he wanted the whole country, and its empire, under a subordinate government led by his brother. Unknown to his people, Prince Ferdinand had been craven in his assurances of loyalty to Napoleon, but the Emperor distrusted and despised him personally, and believed that Spain would be a more effective, as well as a more trustworthy, ally if its government, laws and society were modernized on French lines. The Spanish uprising was fuelled by patriotism and faith – devotion to the Crown and Church – and by many deep-seated social grievances and economic problems, which created an appetite for upheaval. But above all it was fed by resentment at the presence of French soldiers, who, even when well behaved, were overbearing, rude and foreign, and whose looting and harsh reprisals quickly established a cycle of atrocity and counter-atrocity.

The British public at the time – and many historians ever since – have been captivated by the image of the Spanish guerrilla. It appealed to the romantic spirit of the age: a time when Byron's 'The Corsair' was a popular bestseller, and it has continued to resonate ever since, as more and more wars are fought largely by irregular forces, and the distinction between combatants and civilians becomes less and less easy to locate. Guerrillas made good stories, and even their cruelty added piquancy when viewed from a comfortable distance. But in fact there was little romantic or even exciting about them, and the term itself is remarkably elastic. It covers a wide spectrum, from the Galician peasants who picked up whatever weapon was to hand, to defend their homes from the foraging parties of Soult's army in the winter of 1809, but who went back to their farming as soon as the French had disappeared over the mountains, to the disciplined battalions of Mina's army that dominated Navarre in the last year of French occupation. Some guerrillas were little more than thieves and bandits, while many more were deserters from the regular army. Not all the supplies, money and information they were given by the local population was offered voluntarily or with goodwill, although it is probably true that in general, bands that lacked local support did not survive very long.[21]

The Spanish regular armies seem dull in comparison. They generally made a poor impression on British observers and they were miserably unsuccessful in battle, achieving only four significant victories in six years of war, (Bailen, Alcaniz, Tamames and San Marcial). But to emphasize this is to miss the more important point that they kept fighting. No other country suffered so many defeats and disasters, lost so many men killed and so many prisoners, and still refused to yield. In 1805, a few months of campaigning drove Austria from the war; in 1806 a few weeks were enough to cripple Prussia: and yet they were both regarded as great powers, in a class above decadent Spain. But Spain maintained the war for six years with her capital and two-thirds of her provinces overrun by the enemy for most of that time. After every defeat fresh Spanish armies were formed and took the field, while every province that was 'conquered' required a large and permanent garrison to keep it quiet. Right up to the summer of 1812 the great majority of French troops in the Peninsula were not employed against Wellington and his Anglo-Portuguese army, but in holding down parts of Spain that had been overrun years before, where French rule was still not accepted, or in harrying small Spanish armies from one mountain retreat to another. The continuation of Spanish resistance was the essential prerequisite for all Wellington's campaigns.

The war in the Peninsula sapped Napoleon's strength but by itself it could not lead to his downfall. He might have been overthrown by a conspiracy, a coup, or an uprising in France, although that never seemed very likely. He might have been killed in action or died of natural causes, but no one could predict whether his death would lead to a return to revolutionary turmoil or a more pacific, less ener-getic, government. It was possible that if the war in Spain lasted long enough he might cut his losses and withdraw, accepting the loss of face as a price worth paying to retrieve his army from the quagmire. Such a move would have been popular in the country and the army, but there is no sign that he ever seriously considered it until his forces had already been driven back to the Pyrenees. By far the best hope of Allied victory in the Peninsula lay in conjunction with fresh campaigns in central Europe. The commitment to Spain had greatly weakened Napoleon's domination of the rest of the Continent, and if he was defeated there, he might be forced to withdraw his armies from Spain and even to negotiate a peace that would restore the balance of power in Europe.

The Habsburg court was alarmed by Napoleon's intervention in Spain – a long-standing French ally – and feared that Austria might be next. No one could foresee in the last months of 1808 that there would be no quick end to the war in Spain, and the Austrians decided that it would be better to strike while the bulk of Napoleon's army was still on the far side of the Pyrenees than to wait until he had consolidated his hold on Spain and was ready to move against them. They were not confident of victory, the Archduke Charles, commander of the Austrian army, was intimidated by Napoleon, and they had not been able to persuade Prussia or Russia to join them. Nonetheless, on 9 April 1809 the Austrian army invaded Bavaria and caught the French at a disadvantage.[22]

The implications of the Austrian war for the conflict in the Peninsula were immense, but not immediate. Napoleon did not recall any of his troops from Spain, although he ordered Mortier's corps to disengage from operations (it had taken part in the recently completed second siege of Saragossa) and to prepare to march north if needed. News of the Austrian action encouraged Wellington's plans for an offensive in Spain, but he was more influenced by the lopsided distribution of French forces in the Peninsula, which created a tempting opportunity. Overall, the French armies in Spain in the late spring of 1809 were far stronger than the Allies – there were nearly 300,000 French troops in the Peninsula, of whom almost 200,000 were present and fit for duty – the remainder including sick, garrisons and detachments[23] – but they had too many men in remote, strategically unimportant provinces like Galicia, and too few in central Spain. Wellington calculated that if he combined with General Cuesta's Spanish army he could drive Victor's corps back on Madrid and either force it to fight at a disadvantage, or to retreat at least to the Ebro. The sequel would depend on how the French reacted, and on the outcome of the fighting on the Danube, but Wellington was full of confidence in the ability of his troops to defeat the French, and in his own capacity to more than match the manoeuvres of the French generals.[24]

The British government was not enthusiastic about the prospect of another campaign in Spain. The ministers, including Canning, remained disillusioned by the defeat of the Spanish armies in 1808 and by the experiences of Moore's men, and had deliberately restricted Wellington's operations to the defence of Portugal. However, Wellington had scarcely arrived in Lisbon before he wrote home asking that his instructions be relaxed, and the ministers trusted him as they trusted no other general. The question was decided when news arrived of the victory at Oporto: Portugal was saved and the ministers felt that they had no choice but to let Wellington have his head, although their reluctance is palpable in the altered instructions that permitted him 'to extend your operations in Spain beyond the provinces immediately adjacent to the Portuguese frontier, provided you shall be of opinion that your doing so is material in a military point of view, to the success of your operations, and not inconsistent with the safety of Portugal'.[25] Wellington had already been promised the élite Light Brigade, although its departure was delayed for many weeks, first by the ill effects of the Coruña campaign, and then by contrary winds. Castlereagh now scratched around and found a further seven second battalions, which were ordered to sail before the end of May. As with the previous reinforcements, these were not particularly good units, and it is surprising that better battalions could not have been found four months after the army returned from Coruña. However, Castlereagh was also busy preparing for the Walcheren expedition, and it is possible that in this instance the army in Portugal suffered from the competition.[26]

Wellington was concerned to find that the discipline of his army deteriorated in the march south from Oporto to Abrantes, but few of the troops were yet seasoned or experienced, and the campaign against Soult, although brief and successful, had been very demanding. The army benefited from an extended halt at Abrantes, even though Wellington was maddened by the delay, which was caused by a shortage of money – cash to pay the troops, to buy supplies and to hire transport. The British government had been so open-handed in its generosity to the Spanish patriots in 1808 that it had exhausted its reserves, while the Austrian war increased the demand for ready money throughout Europe. The immediate problem was solved by the arrival of more than £200,000 in coin before the end of June, but it would recur throughout the war, leading to intemperate complaints from Wellington. Yet despite these problems, the essential point was that the British economy proved sufficiently robust to withstand the effects of Napoleon's Continental System, to finance the war in the Peninsula on an ever-increasing scale, and still to be able to grant huge subsidies to the Continental Powers in 1813–15. French propaganda always exaggerated the role of 'Pitt's gold' in bringing powers into the war, but money played a vital role in sustaining conflicts once they had begun. British subsidies to Portugal and Spain kept their armies in the field, while the shoes, uniforms and muskets carried by their troops were mostly made in Britain. In the long run, Wellington's operations were financed far more on credit – money raised in the Peninsula on bills drawn on London – than on shipments of cash, although the periodic injection of significant quantities of specie was important to keep the system operating reasonably smoothly. Credit, supported by the popularity of British and colonial exports, also paid for the importation of vast quantities of grain and other foodstuffs from north Africa and even America, which helped feed the Allied armies and the civilian population. Although the war was not primarily an economic or financial conflict, the strength and resilience of the British economy played a vital part in enabling Wellington's army to continue to take the field year after year.[27]

While Wellington fretted at Abrantes, Victor withdrew from his exposed position south of the Tagus to Talavera, not because he feared an Allied attack, but because his men had eaten out the country where they had been camped. This move made him more secure, but it also resolved differences between Wellington and Cuesta over their plan of campaign. The British army crossed the frontier into Spain on 3 July and Wellington met Cuesta at the Spanish headquarters on the 11th. Co-operation did not prove easy: Cuesta distrusted the British, while Wellington was soon complaining of a shortage of supplies. An excellent opportunity to attack Victor was lost on 23 July when Cuesta inexplicably refused to bring his army into action, and Wellington then announced that he would advance

mouths and there was much ill feeling towards their Spanish allies. The breakdown of the commissariat before Talavera, and the continuing severe shortage of supplies after the battle and throughout August were bitterly resented, while the misunderstood story of Cuesta's 'abandonment' of the British wounded when he retreated from Talavera was regarded as little short of calculated treachery. Wellington, now ennobled as Viscount Wellington, shared this disgust and refused to consider another campaign side by side with the Spaniards. He did not agree with his brothers (Lord Wellesley, ambassador to Spain in 1809, then Foreign Secretary 1809–12 and Henry Wellesley, ambassador to Spain 1810–21) who advocated much closer British involvement in the affairs of Spain, and he was guarded in his response to their idea that he be given command of the Spanish armies. In this Wellington was realistic: the alliance between Britain and Spain was essential to the struggle in the Peninsula, but attempts at close co-operation almost invariably produced friction and mutual irritation. The command of the Spanish armies proved a bone of contention for years, and when it was finally granted in late 1812 it led to more quarrels and only limited benefits. The alliance worked best when each country was able to operate in its own way, pulling in the same direction but not yoked tightly together.

For Wellington, the implications of the Austrian defeat were clear: Napoleon would be able to concentrate his efforts on the Peninsula, and the Allies should go on the defensive and prepare to ride out the storm. But the Spanish government lacked the authority and political strength to take the long view. It preferred to mount an autumn offensive in the hope of gaining a significant advantage before French armies could be reinforced. Predictably, this led to disaster, as one Spanish army was crushed at Ocaña (19 November 1809) and the other was defeated at Alba de Tormes (28 November 1809). The regular Spanish resistance never recovered from these defeats and in the following January Soult and King Joseph overran Andalusia, meeting little resistance, but narrowly failing to capture the great port of Cadiz. Throughout 1809 Andalusia had been the heartland of patriotic Spain and its fall signalled an important shift in the war, but the French paid a high price for their success, for although the conquest of Andalusia had been almost blood-less, it required a large French army – some 70,000 men – to retain it and to besiege Cadiz. There was an underlying dynamic to the war in the Peninsula, as the French expanded or contracted the area they occupied. At the beginning of 1809 they spent their resources in overrunning Galicia and northern Portugal and so lost the initia-tive. When they were driven out of Portugal and abandoned Galicia they gained a striking force, which enabled them to defeat Wellington's offensive in the summer and the Spanish autumn campaign, but they then used this force to conquer Andalusia. This would have again deprived them of the initiative if it had not been for the very large reinforcements Napoleon sent over the Pyrenees.

In the autumn of 1809 Wellington made his plans for the defence of Portugal. They were remarkable for their foresight and originality. The Lines of Torres Vedras, a chain of self-contained forts and redoubts stretched for almost 30 miles across the whole width of the Lisbon Peninsula from the Tagus to the sea, making the most of the naturally rugged terrain, which itself was strengthened by extensive excavations, escarping and inundations. The works were to be occupied, not by the main army, but by Portuguese militia and *ordenanza*, supported by some regular artillerymen, so that even if the French fought their way through the first Line, they would still have to face the whole Allied army. Steps were taken to strip and abandon the country in the path of a French invasion: civilians were ordered to flee, while large bodies of militia and *ordenanza* would harass the French flanks and rear. Fortresses were strengthened and supplied to withstand a siege, while strong positions were prepared along the most likely routes the French would take. Wellington provided the central direction, using Portuguese ideas and traditions wherever possible, but shaping them to his needs. The British also provided the money to pay the workmen and the engineers to design the works, but the great bulk of the burden fell on the Portuguese. It was they who served in the militia, or the *ordenanza*, and who toiled over the earthworks. It was their land that faced devastation, their livestock that would be carried off, their crops burnt, their homes abandoned. No European country in centuries had taken such systematic and extreme measures to avoid conquest, yet the Portuguese adopted Wellington's proposals with remarkable fidelity. Naturally there was a little grumbling, and a heartfelt wish that the invader could be repelled close to the frontier, but there was no serious opposition and no French party emerged. Indeed the greatest fear felt by all ranks of Portuguese was that when the crisis came the British would embark their army and abandon them to the French. This near universal determination to resist the French at any price was the sine qua non of Wellington's success in 1810–11, and he owed it to the actual experience of French rule, which the Portuguese had endured in the two previous invasions: Junot's in 1807–8 and Soult's in 1809.

Almost equally important to Wellington's success was the remarkable failure of French intelligence to discover anything of the extent or nature of Allied preparations until it was too late to be useful. Napoleon relied far too heavily on British newspapers: these were uncensored and full of letters written by officers in the army who did not hesitate to send sensitive military information to their friends at home. However, in late 1809, and to a lesser extent throughout the first half of 1810, the mood in Wellington's army was one of deep pessimism, and officers generally knew little and understood less of the preparations under way for the defence of Portugal. As a result the British press gave the impression that the Portuguese army was of little consequence and that Wellington simply waited for a decent excuse to embark his troops and quit Lisbon. As this confirmed his preconceptions, and as he seems to have had no direct source of information in Lisbon, Napoleon believed it and made his plans accordingly.

Nonetheless, he did not take success for granted. He appointed the most distinguished, experienced, and arguably the ablest of all his marshals, Andre Masséna, Prince d'Essling, to command the army of Portugal, and gave him authority over a large tract of north-western Spain as the base area for his campaign. Altogether, Masséna commanded an army of 140,000 men, although only half of these would be available for the actual invasion of Portugal. Given that Napoleon believed Wellington had fewer than 30,000 British troops, and that the Portuguese would not fight, this seemed more than enough, but Wellington had expected to face 100,000 men led by Napoleon in person.

Napoleon ordered Masséna to proceed slowly and methodically, and to wait for the harvest to advance much beyond the frontier. This was sensible in a way, but it gave the Allies several additional months in which to complete the Lines of Torres Vedras and improve the training of the Portuguese army. The French captured the Spanish frontier fortress of Ciudad Rodrigo in July, and its Portuguese counterpart of Almeida in August, but it was September before they began their march on Lisbon. The roads were poor, supplies hard to find, and the Portuguese population abandoned their farms and villages at the approach of the French, only to close in behind them, killing any stragglers, couriers or other isolated soldiers. The French, for their part, adopted the same harsh policies of pillaging and punishment that had done so much to sustain the guerrilla war in Spain. Wellington gave battle at Busaco, a few miles north of Coimbra, on 27 September 1810: his position was so strong that defeat was scarcely possible and he could hardly believe that the French would make a frontal assault. But Masséna was confident of victory and delighted at the prospect of a battle. The result was one-sided, as the French attacks were driven back with heavy losses – probably amounting to about 4,600 casualties – compared to 1,252 for the Allies, half of them Portuguese. The hard work of Beresford and his assistants was rewarded at Busaco, for the Portuguese troops generally fought well, and Wellington would not have had enough men to hold the position without them. However, the battle did not decide the campaign: and when Masséna found a way to turn the Allied flank, Wellington disengaged and withdrew to the Lines of Torres Vedras, where he expected to fight the decisive battle. Masséna followed slowly. His army was beset by logistical problems, and was disheartened by the loss of a large hospital at Coimbra, which was overrun and captured by Portuguese militia almost as soon as the main army had marched out of sight. The Lines came as a most unpleasant surprise, and Masséna was entitled to wonder how such extensive and well-planned works could have been kept so secret that he did not hear even a rumour of them until after he had left Coimbra. Thorough reconnaissance confirmed the first impression: the Lines were formidable and without any obvious vulnerable points. The French army had already suffered heavily in the campaign and it lacked a siege-train: it might have been able to storm the Lines, but if it did so it would be in no condition to fight the main Allied force. To attack would be folly, but that did not mean Masséna should retreat. His duty was plainly to maintain his position for as long as possible, while referring the problem to Napoleon, who alone could decide whether to order fresh armies in Masséna's wake to complete the conquest of Portugal, or to cut his losses and order the army to withdraw.

Wellington was disappointed at the refusal of the French to attack, for he had been confident of a complete victory followed by the rapid expulsion of their army from Portugal. He was puzzled by what they could hope to achieve by camping in front of the Lines, and blamed the Portuguese government for not thoroughly devastating the great tract of fertile country between the Tagus and the sea. He even toyed with the idea of attacking Masséna, but decided that while he could trust his Portuguese troops to defend a good position, they were not yet sufficiently experienced to be relied upon to manoeuvre coolly under heavy fire. There was no point in running such a risk when patience, however irksome, would be sure to bring victory in the long run.[29] After a month in front of the Lines, Masséna withdrew some 30 miles to a fresh tract of country around Santarem, and soon put his army into winter quarters.

Meanwhile, events in England threatened to upset all calculations. George III, who had been on the throne for half a century, suffered a recurrence of the porphyria that had afflicted him on several previous occasions. The disease was not then understood, and the King was assumed to suffer from insanity. His illness had serious political implications, for if he was incapacitated for long, a regency would need to be established with his son and heir, the Prince of Wales (later George IV) as regent. Moreover, the Prince had long-standing ties to the opposition Whigs and could be expected to dismiss the Perceval ministry and invite Lords Grenville and Grey to form a new administration. However, since the failure of Moore's campaign the Whigs had been pessimistic about the war in the Peninsula, and had shown themselves hostile to Wellington. No one could say for certain what effect a change of government in London would have on Britain's commitment to Portugal, but at the very least it would create doubt and uncertainty. The King's health fluctuated considerably during November and December: at times he seemed almost well but then would have a relapse, although his doctors remained full of confidence. Parliament deferred action for some time, but before the end of December it began to consider the government's proposals for a regency. January saw extended debates and much political speculation. Perceval had made no attempt to conciliate the Prince, and few observers expected that he would remain in office once the regency was established. But then the King's condition improved and he seemed well on the road to a full recovery. The Prince was embarrassed: it would be absurd for him to bring the Whigs into office only for the King to dismiss them again after a couple of weeks, but he did not wish to desert his old friends. Eventually, after much indecision, he confirmed Perceval in office, but did so as ungraciously as possible, and made it plain that if the King were not able to resume his powers, he would feel entitled to reconsider his decision.[30]

Wellington's relations with Perceval's government were not always harmonious. His private, confidential letters at this time were full of bitter, distrustful complaints against Lord Liverpool, who had succeeded Castlereagh at the War Department.[31] He was particularly upset at the government's weakness in Parliament, which meant that it might not be able to protect him if the campaign ended badly. Yet the government supported him loyally throughout 1810, despite the common opinion of senior officers both at home and in the army abroad, that Portugal could not be defended.

The Regency crisis was only one of four major political crises between the autumn of 1809 and the summer of 1812, any one of which could easily have led to a change of government. The successive Pittite ministries led by Portland, Perceval and Liverpool that governed Britain throughout the Peninsular War deserve a significant share of the credit for initiating the commitment to the Peninsula in 1808, renewing it in 1809, maintaining it in 1810, and then providing the resources that facilitated the successes of the later years of the war. Their contribution to Wellington's victories was no less important for being so often overlooked.[32]

Masséna held his ground at Santarem throughout the winter, although his army suffered greatly from disease and privation. At the end of the year he was re-inforced by Drouet with one division of the IX Corps and some convalescents, about 8,000 men in all, while a second division took up a position in northern Portugal, in a vain attempt to keep open the army's lines of communication. The new arrivals did not allow Masséna to resume the offensive, or even make up his losses, but they gave him just enough strength to hold his position until the spring. By the middle of February it was clear that Napoleon would not send the over-whelming reinforcements needed to take Lisbon. Soult had collected 20,000 men and was besieging Badajoz, but this brought no benefit to Masséna, for Soult's army was much too small to invade Portugal and join hands across the Tagus. Meanwhile, Wellington's troops were in fine condition, and he was waiting impa-tiently for the arrival of a convoy of reinforcements, which had been delayed by the winter gales, before going on the offensive.

Early in March 1811 Masséna finally bowed to the inevitable, abandoned Santarem, and began his retreat through Portugal. Wellington pursued the French with vigour and a number of hard-fought rearguard actions followed, which did nothing to alter the result of the campaign, but which filled the Allied forces with confidence and gave them valuable experience in manoeuvring under fire. On 8 April the French were finally driven across the frontier into Spain, after a campaign that had cost them 25,000 men killed or taken prisoner.[33] The magni-tude and completeness of the failure could not be disguised, and it gave comfort and inspiration to Napoleon's enemies across Europe. Wellington proceeded to blockade Almeida, having already detached Beresford, with 20,000 men, to recap-ture Badajoz, which had fallen to Soult on 11 March.

The French army recovered remarkably quickly from its ordeal. This was one of the most obvious differences between French and British forces in the Peninsula. The British were clearly superior in battle from the very outset of the war to its conclusion in 1814, even when facing French troops of the highest quality, as at Talavera. But the British army needed careful handling on campaign, and its strict discipline could deteriorate sharply in adverse conditions or in the relaxation that followed a victory. Wellington was haunted by the fate of Moore's army, which – with the exception of the rearguard and a few other regiments – had behaved badly in the retreat to Coruña: although the men had never been so demoralized that they were unwilling to fight. Wellington paid particular atten-tion to the army's provisions and to its discipline, but still faced significant problems on the march south after Oporto in 1809, on the final stages of the retreat from Burgos in late 1812, and in the aftermath of Vitoria in 1813. The French army, on the other hand, was used to privation and hard conditions, and its disci-pline was laxer, but still effective. Soult's corps in 1809, Masséna's army in 1811, and Marmont's army after Salamanca all rallied and returned to action sooner than Wellington expected; although repeated defeats at the hands of the British undermined French confidence and so further reduced their chances of success in battle.

At the beginning of May Masséna advanced in an attempt to relieve Almeida, whose garrison was running short of food. Wellington blocked his path at Fuentes de Oñoro on the frontier: there was a partial engagement on 3 May when French attempts to take the village of Fuentes were driven back after heavy fighting. The next day passed quietly, but on the 5th the French tried to turn the southern flank of the allies, bringing on heavy fighting. Wellington made one of his rare tactical errors when he detached the newly formed and still raw 7th Division to block the French advance, and then had to recall it, using the Light Division to help cover its retreat. The result was awkward and untidy, but the French were unable to exploit the mistake and their attacks were repulsed. The Allies lost just over 2,000 casualties in the two days of fighting; the French almost 3,000. A few days later the garrison of Almeida blew up part of the fortress and escaped through the Allied lines, so cheating Wellington of some of the fruits of his victory.

Beresford had meanwhile besieged Badajoz, but lacked a proper siege-train and had made only slow progress when Soult advanced from Seville to relieve it. The Allies, including a substantial Spanish contingent, gave battle at Albuera on 16 May. Their position was not strong and Soult succeeded in turning their right flank before a bloody battle of attrition developed near the centre. Three British battalions were cut to pieces when caught at a disadvantage by Soult's hussars and Polish lancers, but even this did not daunt the remaining British infantry, and after extremely heavy fighting the French finally withdrew. Some 40 per cent of Beresford's 10,000 British troops were casualties, while altogether the Allies lost nearly 6,000 casualties. The French probably lost rather more, from a smaller army.[34] Wellington had hurried south but arrived too late for the battle. He found Beresford on the verge of a nervous collapse or breakdown, which kept him out of action for months. Exactly what had happened is unclear, but it was said that Beresford had lost his head during the action and ordered the army to retreat, only for the situation to be saved by the initiative of his staff and subordinates.[35] Whatever the truth of this, the whole army was delighted that Wellington had assumed the command. The siege of Badajoz was resumed, but it continued to prove difficult and Marmont, who had replaced Masséna in command of the Army of Portugal, marched south and united with Soult. Wellington abandoned the siege and offered battle in a strong position behind the River Caya, but the French would not attack him, and were happy simply to have relieved the fortress. The armies then retired into cantonments through the worst of the summer heat. The initiative clearly lay with Wellington but he was thwarted in the second half of 1811, as several half-hearted attempts to blockade Ciudad Rodrigo proved fruitless.

Throughout most of 1810 and 1811 the French had about 350,000 men in the Peninsula, but they made little obvious progress in these two years towards bringing the war to an end. The weakening of the Spanish regular armies following the fall of Andalusia and other defeats was offset by the rise of the Anglo-Portuguese army, which from the spring of 1811, if not earlier, was the most powerful Allied force in the Peninsula. Could the French have won the war? Perhaps, but it would have taken an enormous effort and great patience. Some 100,000 reinforcements would have maintained the existing French armies in Spain and enabled them to overrun and occupy the remaining free provinces: Galicia, Valencia, Murcia and parts of Granada. Another 100,000, or perhaps

150,000, would have sufficed (combined with the existing Army of Portugal) to drive Wellington back to the Lines of Torres Vedras, occupy the provinces on both sides of the Tagus, capture Oporto, and maintain a chain of posts stretching back to the Spanish frontier. This might even have forced Wellington to evacuate Lisbon, although that is more doubtful. Would this occupation have suffocated the resistance, or would the increased number of French troops with their constant demand for supplies have encouraged the guerrilla war by adding to local grievances and resentment? No definite answer is possible, but the example of Navarre is instructive. It had been under firm French occupation since the outbreak of war, yet in late 1812 the simmering resistance erupted in a furious insurrection, which the French proved quite unable to quell, despite committing large forces to the task.

Napoleon could not send a further 250,000 men to the Peninsula and maintain them there indefinitely. The 350,000 men he had already committed to Spain stretched his resources, required increasingly unpopular conscription, and weakened his hold on Central Europe.[36] And even if he could find the men, he could not afford the money to pay them and to sustain the war. As it was, he found the financial burden almost unbearable; the pay of the soldiers fell many months in arrears, and from early 1810 he constantly tried to shift more and more of the cost of the war onto the Spanish people.[37] This naturally led to demands and exactions that drove many ordinary Spaniards from grumbling resentment at the French presence into passive or active support for the guerrillas.

In late 1810 there was a crisis in Franco-Russian relations, and in the first weeks of 1811 the Emperor Alexander toyed with the idea of sending his armies into Central Europe. He received no encouragement from the Prussians, Austrians or Poles and soon abandoned the scheme, resolving that if war came he would stand on the defensive. (His initial impulse may have been strengthened by the fear that the French were on the brink of success in Portugal, and his second thoughts aided by the news that Masséna's advance had been thwarted, although evidence for this is scanty.)[38] Napoleon was shocked by the possibility of war, for his forces in Central Europe were undermanned and in no position to take the field at short notice. He spent the rest of the year building them up, strengthening his alliances, and preparing for a war with Russia that now appeared close to inevitable in the medium term. The French armies in the Peninsula therefore received second priority in 1811 and towards the end of the year Napoleon withdrew 27,000 of his best men – Imperial Guards and Polish regiments – to take part in the Russian campaign; while in 1812 the steady supply of drafts and recruits needed to keep regiments up to strength dwindled, so that losses were not replaced, and by October 1812 total French strength in the Peninsula had fallen to 262,000.[39] Given this, Napoleon would have been wise to abandon some outlying territory in Spain so as to strengthen his hold on the centre of the country and to ensure that the army facing Wellington was strong enough to contain him. But he did exactly the opposite, ordering Suchet to undertake a campaign against the Spanish forces in Valencia, and requiring Marmont to detach troops to support him. As with Andalusia, the loss of Valencia was a great blow to the Spanish resistance, but both its conquest and its retention required substantial forces, which left the French over-extended and vulnerable in other parts of the Peninsula.

Wellington had learnt from his frustration in 1811 and had laid his plans with care, bringing a powerful new siege-train up to Almeida without the French discovering what was afoot. On 8 January 1812 the Allied army invested Ciudad Rodrigo; the batteries opened fire on the 14th; two practicable breaches had been made by the 19th, and the fortress was stormed that night with the loss of some 500 Allied casualties. The whole operation had been so swift and decisive that Marmont would have had no chance to intervene even if his army had been at full strength.

Wellington then shifted his attention to Badajoz, a much stronger fortress, with a garrison of 5,000 men, full of confidence after their success in resisting two sieges in 1811. Again Wellington made careful preparations, bringing up a proper siege-train and moving swiftly, although it seems that if Soult and Marmont had combined in an attempt to raise the siege, as they had done the previous summer, Wellington would have been happy to give them battle.[40] Badajoz was invested on 17 March, and the batteries opened fire on the 25th. Soult collected his men and marched from Seville, but Marmont had received orders from Napoleon not to join him, but rather to advance into northern Portugal in the hope that this would force Wellington to give up the siege. As Marmont lacked a siege-train with which to threaten Ciudad Rodrigo or Almeida, and as Wellington had no other important base of operation that the French could attack, this plan seems misguided, and the siege of Badajoz proceeded without interruption. On 5 April the engineers declared that the breaches were practicable but advised another day's battering to improve them, and Wellington agreed. At ten o'clock on the evening of 6 April Allied troops attempted to storm all three breaches, while making diversionary attacks on other parts of the walls. Unspeakable scenes of horror ensued as attack after attack on the breaches was repulsed with dreadful losses. Eventually one of the diversionary attacks succeeded in establishing a secure footing on the walls and at 6am on 7 April Badajoz surrendered. The Allied army suffered 3,713 casualties just in the storm, and 4,670 in the siege as a whole: more than in all but the bloodiest of its battles in the war so far. Wellington was shaken: witnesses report him to have been in tears during the night, and he sent home a strongly worded private letter to Lord Liverpool complaining of the lack of trained sappers and miners in the British army – rank and file men who specialized in the conduct of sieges and similar operations. He added that 'our Engineers, although well educated and brave, have never turned their minds to the mode of conducting a regular siege, as it is useless to think of that which it is impossible in our service to perform.' Without the skilled troops needed to proceed scientifically, Wellington had been forced to rely upon the gallantry of his troops, which had overcome every obstacle. 'But I anxiously hope that I shall never again be the instrument of putting them to such a test as that to which they were put last night.'[41]

The bloodshed at the storm of Badajoz, with the failed sieges of the previous year, the unsuccessful siege of Burgos later in 1812, and the prolonged and costly attack on San Sebastian in 1813, suggest that Wellington's army was less accomplished at siege warfare than at open battles. Some of the responsibility for this rests with Wellington: he undertook the 1811 sieges and that of Burgos without ensuring he had an effective siege-train. He may also have been at fault for pressing the 1812 siege of Badajoz too rapidly, but this is much more debatable: a longer bombardment would have improved the breaches but given the garrison more time to strengthen their interior defences, which cut the breaches off from the rest of the fortress. The choice of front to be attacked at both Badajoz and San Sebastian, and the whole conduct of operations at Burgos, can also be criticized on more technical grounds, although the blame here should probably fall more on the senior British engineer officers rather than on Wellington. They were also surely at fault for advising that the breaches at Badajoz were practicable on 5 April, and perhaps for not pressing for the construction of a new battery closer to the breach, as recommended by theory, although there is more than a hint of hindsight in these criticisms. Finally, one must wonder if more could not have been done to limit the misbehaviour of the troops – the pillaging, rape and murder – that followed the storm of both Badajoz and San Sebastian, ample warning having been given by the less prolonged outbreak of anarchy that occurred at Ciudad Rodrigo.

Some contemporaries and later writers have gone further and suggested that the conduct of Wellington's sieges was inept compared to the methodical professionalism of the French. Certainly the French had far more experience of siege warfare than the British. French engineers had conducted scores of sieges in every theatre of war since 1793, and had also frequently stood on the defensive. The British, on the other hand, had almost no relevant experience, in Europe at least, before the first operations against Badajoz in 1811, and it is clear that they underrated the difficulty of the task. Yet a comparison of the performance of the two armies is not wholly favourable to the French. Wellington's army took less than twelve days to capture Ciudad Rodrigo in 1812 at the cost of 500 casualties. Masséna's army in 1810 had taken thirty-eight days and had suffered almost 1,200 casualties, even though the fortress surrendered without having to be stormed.[42] Soult took six weeks to reduce Badajoz in 1811, although its garrison had been disheartened by the defeat of the Army of Estremadura at Gebora and the death of its energetic governor, General Menacho. Again the fortress capitulated without the need for a storm, but the French still lost almost 2,000 casualties.[43] Wellington took half the time and suffered more than twice the losses: a poor exchange, but the equation fails to take into account the difference in the quality and determination of the defence. If Menacho had lived, Badajoz would not have fallen so easily to Soult, and good as he was, Menacho was not equal to Phillipon, and nor was his garrison. Sieges against a determined opposition were not easy, and the French had more than their share of trouble with them in the Peninsula. The extraordinary resistance of Saragossa in its two sieges, and of Gerona, are only the most famous examples where French scientific methods failed to save lives or produce results. And then there is the siege of Cadiz, which occupied a whole French army for two and a half years without ever offering the slightest hope of success. What can be said is that the French knew how to defend a fortress with immense skill and determination, extracting every last advantage from its position, so that, with the possible exception of Ciudad Rodrigo, they gave Wellington no easy successes.[44]

Having secured his southern front by the capture of Badajoz, Wellington returned to northern Portugal and, in the middle of June, advanced against Marmont. The French withdrew, leaving garrisons in three fortified convents in Salamanca. It was almost three and a half years since the last British troops had been in Salamanca, and Wellington received a fine welcome, although the convents proved an awkward problem. Before they could be taken, Marmont returned to try to rescue the garrisons, even though he had not had time to collect his whole army. Wellington occupied a strong defensive position on the heights of San Cristobal just outside Salamanca, but neither general proved willing to attack the other. There was much murmuring in the Allied army at Wellington's caution – officers and men alike were confident of their ability to defeat the French, and Marmont's presumption in inviting battle with a weaker army was felt to deserve a thrashing. Wellington's motives are not completely clear, but it seems likely he was made more cautious by news from England that the government was on the brink of collapse, following the assassination of Spencer Perceval, the Prime Minister; and that he was worried that in the event of a defeat his retreat would be difficult because of the town and river close to his rear.[45] Whatever the reason, the opportunity was lost. Marmont's lagging divisions arrived and several days of delicate manoeuvring followed without producing a significant result. Then the convents were taken and Marmont executed a rapid and skilful retreat to a strong position some 40 miles north, behind the River Douro between Toro and Tordesillas. For a fortnight the two armies camped, facing each other, the troops glad to take their ease in the midsummer heat.

On 16 July operations resumed when Marmont stole a march on Wellington and went on the offensive. He would have been wiser to remain in position, for reinforcements from King Joseph's small central reserve were on the march to join him. But all the dispatches announcing this had been intercepted by the guerrillas and passed on to Wellington who, not for the first or last time, was better informed about French movements than were their own generals. Throughout the war in the Peninsula, but particularly from 1810 onwards, the Allies had an immense advantage thanks to their superior strategic intelligence gathering. This depended on the guerrillas and the support of the local population, but it was consciously developed by Wellington and his leading subordinates and staff officers. British officers, in uniform, were sent far ahead of the army to reconnoitre and watch for enemy movements; while Spanish civilians in strategically placed towns across the Peninsula reported the number of French troops who passed, the regiments they belonged to, and sometimes even their gossip. Guerrilla parties sent captured dispatches to the Allied army, usually being well paid for their trouble, while officers of the Quartermaster-General's Department busily surveyed the terrain both behind and in front of the army, and their reports were carefully collated. Like many other aspects of the army the system took time to evolve, but by the summer of 1812 it was working smoothly and yielding excellent results.[46]

Nonetheless, Wellington was caught by surprise by Marmont's advance and was forced to fall back as the French constantly threatened his flank. For two days the armies marched in close parallel and any mistake by either side would have invited immediate retribution. On 21 July the Allies were back at San Cristobal, while the French had swung a little to the east and were crossing the Tormes at the fords of Huerta and Encinas. This forced Wellington to bring most of his troops across the river as well, and as a thunderstorm broke that night, he knew that unless the campaign changed direction on the following day, he would be forced to abandon Salamanca and retire on Portugal: outmanoeuvred rather than outfought by an army that was marginally weaker than his own.

The French again took the initiative on the morning of 22 July, occupying the steep, isolated height of the Greater Arapile and using it as a pivot when shifting their march from south-west to west. The armies were now very close again: there was some skirmishing in the morning and exchanges of artillery fire. Around midday Wellington was tempted to attack but was dissuaded by Beresford. Nonetheless, the Allied troops were all close at hand and ready for action, although many of them were invisible from the French position. In the early afternoon Marmont pushed his leading division, that of Maucune, onto the rising ground south of the village of Los Arapiles. Maucune was an aggressive commander and may have advanced further than Marmont wanted: his skirmishers made an attack on the Allied troops holding the village, but were driven back and the guns on both sides resumed their fire. Marmont had no wish to bring on a battle, although he looked forward to landing a heavy blow or two on the Allied rearguard later in the day, and he needed to maintain pressure on the Allies to force Wellington to retreat, and to make that retreat as difficult as possible. But now things went badly wrong in the French army, although we do not know who was principally to blame or the exact sequence of events. The 7th Division, under Brigadier Thomières, should have remained in Maucune's rear, ready to support him; but instead it headed further west, becoming the leading division in the army. As a result the French left wing became dangerously overextended, for the divisions that should have been following Thomières (those of Clausel and Taupin) were lagging far behind. At about the same time, possibly as he was mounting his horse to ride to the left to take command in person, Marmont was badly wounded by a British shell. Messengers were dispatched to find Clausel, the second-in-command, only to find that he had, quite separately, been slightly wounded in the heel. The command devolved on General Bonnet, but he had no sooner assumed it than he too fell wounded. This extraordinary success of the British artillery left the French army leaderless for a crucial hour or more until Clausel, his wound dressed, was able to take charge.[47]

By then it was probably too late. Wellington had observed the French mistake and lost no time in seizing the opportunity to attack. Earlier in the day he had moved Pakenham's 3rd Division and D'Urban's brigade of Portuguese dragoons from the heights of San Cristobal on the northern side of the Tormes, across the river and behind the rest of the army to the village of Aldea Tejada, a mile or so to the west of the other Allied troops, effectively shifting from the far left to the far right of the line. Now Wellington galloped over to Pakenham and ordered him to march south until he was level with the French westward march, and then wheel to the east and roll up their line. While Pakenham turned the French flank, the main part of the Allied right wing, including Leith's 5th Division and Le Marchant's brigade of heavy cavalry, would attack Maucune and Thomières from the north. Further east, in the centre of the line, Cole's 4th Division would advance while Pack's independent Portuguese brigade protected its flank from the French troops clustered behind the Greater Arapile. Only on the left, where the French held a very strong position on the heights of Calvarrasa de Arriba, would the Allies not press forward.

The Allied troops were already in position and Wellington's orders were executed quickly and decisively, giving the French no chance to rearrange their forces to withstand the impending blow. Pakenham's men clambered up the steep hillside of Pico de Miranda and sent Thomières's leading regiment reeling in broken disorder. The French cavalry attempted a charge on the exposed southern flank of the division, but was beaten off by the British infantry after inflicting a little damage. The 5th Division, with Leith riding in front of the very centre of the line, advanced south over open ground and up the gentle slope of Monte de Azan to where Maucune's men were waiting, probably in two lines of battalion columns. When the Allies cleared the crest and saw the French infantry close at hand there was a momentary pause, then both sides fired: the British then cheered and charged, and the French broke before them. Among the Allied casualties were Leith and two of his aides, whose prominence made them an obvious target. The destruction of the French left was completed by a perfectly timed charge by Le Marchant's brigade of British heavy dragoons – probably the finest exploit of British cavalry in the whole war in the Peninsula. Two of the three regiments in Thomières's division were destroyed, each losing over 1,000 men as casualties or prisoners – more than three-quarters of their strength – while the flight of the remaining regiment, and of Maucune's division, was transformed into a rout. Even the leading regiment in Taupin's division, which was only now coming up to support the left, was caught up in the panic and cut to pieces. French accounts say that one battalion of this regiment, the *22e Ligne* (Line), had been detached, and that the remaining two battalions finished the day with only forty-seven men left in their ranks.[48]

Success did not come so easily for the Allies in the centre. Cole's 4th Division was rather overstretched, and was forced to advance in a single line of battalions with no second line able to provide immediate support. It occupied the gap between the village of Los Arapiles and the Lesser Arapile hill, and at first seemed destined to meet little resistance, for there were few French troops between Maucune's right and Bonnet's division at the Greater Arapile. However, Clausel's division filled this hole before the Allies could exploit it. There was heavy fighting between Clausel's leading brigade and the British fusiliers on Cole's right; the British gained the advantage, but were then broken when Clausel's second brigade attacked them before they could regain their order and composure. At the same time Bonnet's division attacked the exposed left flank of the Portuguese brigade, which made up Cole's centre and left, and the whole 4th Division crumbled. Just as this was happening, Pack's independent Portuguese brigade made a courageous but unsuccessful assault on the Greater Arapile, from which it was driven back in disorder. Bonnet's infantry led the counter-attack supported by three regiments of French dragoons, and for a moment it looked as if the French might be able to offset the disaster on their left and gain an unlikely victory. But only for a moment.

Wellington had strong reserves well placed to limit the damage done by the defeat of Cole. Already the 6th Division had been ordered forward, while the 1st and 7th Divisions were only a little further away. But the 6th Division, with some assistance from Spry's Portuguese brigade of Leith's division, was sufficient, and after heavy fighting the French counter-attack was snuffed out. The Allies now pushed forward in the centre: Bonnet's division was broken, the Greater Arapile abandoned, Boyer's dragoons withdrew, and Clausel's infantry gave way – probably after another round of fighting, for its losses were heavy, although the details are obscure.

The battle was now clearly lost and most of the French army was in flight, but the long summer day was finally drawing towards its close. It was important for the French that they gain time, so that the fugitives could escape, rally, and fight another day. Ferey's division in the centre took on the role of rearguard, occupying a long, low ridge facing north-west, about a mile south of the Greater Arapile. This position was assaulted by the 6th Division in the fading light, while an attempt was also made to turn its northern flank. But the French infantry were well-posted and inflicted heavy losses before finally giving way and following the flight of the rest of the army to Alba de Tormes to the south-east.

Salamanca was the greatest British victory on land since the days of Marlborough a century before. One-quarter of Marmont's army – some 12,500 men – were killed, wounded, or taken prisoner, and the remainder were thoroughly demoralized and broken. Foy's division, almost the only part of the army to escape the wreck unscathed, met with disaster the following day at Garcia Hernandez, adding another 1,100 casualties to the French total. The Allied army suffered 5,220 casualties in the battle, with Portuguese losses being slightly higher in proportion to their strength than those of the British. It was the first time Wellington had sent his army forward in a full-scale attack in open battle in the Peninsula, and the troops had fully repaid his trust.

The Allied success at Salamanca depended on the combination of Wellington's ability and the fighting qualities and confidence of his troops. Wellington's most obvious contribution to the victory was his recognition of the opportunity, and his courage in seizing it without hesitation. The plan of attack flowed naturally from the position of the two armies and the weakness of the French left, but it was not by chance that the Allied army was so well placed to go on the offensive with rapidity. The shift of Pakenham's division and D'Urban's dragoons from the extreme left to right was an unusual move that paid great dividends, but the placement of the other units was almost as important. The French left was vulnerable because its divisions were strung out and lacked reserves, while in the Allied army almost every division in the front line was well-supported. The importance of this was made clear with the breaking of Cole and Pack in the centre, when the 6th Division was in perfect position to contain the damage. A great deal of experience, skill and attention was required to achieve this result, not only during a battle, but whenever the army was close to the enemy. It seems obvious – so obvious that it is commonly taken for granted – but it was not easy to achieve, and even Wellington made some mistakes: at Salamanca, Cole's division was given too broad a front; at Talavera, there were insufficient reserves behind Sherbrooke's division in the centre; and at Busaco, too much ground was left lightly held between Lightburne's brigade and the main body of Picton's division. None of these were gross errors: they are only noticeable because these points came under pressure during the battle, and the French were able to take advantage of them – and in each case the problem was contained before it became too serious. Equally, Marmont's error at Salamanca might easily have passed unnoticed, or been regarded as nothing more than slight carelessness, if it had not opened the door to the destruction of his army. The French were beaten not just because Marmont slipped, but because Wellington was ready, watching, and waiting intently – and because his army was perfectly placed to exploit the opportunity when it came.

Wellington's record of battlefield victories in the Peninsula was extraordinary: from Vimeiro in 1808 to Toulouse in 1814 he fought a dozen full-scale battles and as many lesser actions with an unbroken record of success. He was equally expert at choosing a superb defensive position and holding it against superior numbers, and at boldly launching an unpremeditated attack. His crossing of the Douro in the face of Soult's army in 1809 remained one of the most remarkable feats of his entire career, while in terms of professional skill and daring, Salamanca was the finest of all his victories. Later campaigns in the Peninsula saw him almost invariably on the offensive, either maturing careful plans for attacks on strong positions, as at the crossing of the Bidassoa and the Nivelle, or throwing his army forward as soon as the enemy made a stand, as at Orthez. In action he was quick, decisive and sure, usually issuing his orders to subordinates in person and leaving little room for the sort of misunderstanding that contributed to so many military disasters. He filled all ranks of his army with confidence, and this itself was an important factor in his victories.

But the success of the British army in battle was not solely due to Wellington, and many of the features of its performance were well established by 1808. Like Napoleon, Wellington was not a great tactical innovator: rather he combined and improved existing methods and created the circumstances in which their full potential could be seen. British infantry seem to have adopted the two-deep line as their standard formation much earlier in the war.[49] Similarly, the other key elements of their tactics – the eagerness to close with the enemy and the emphasis on the cheer and charge to break an enemy quickly, rather than engage in a sustained firefight – can be traced back at least to Abercromby's campaign in Egypt in 1801, and possibly further. Such tactics were very effective, but they required good order, discipline, and confidence. British infantry did not succeed in the Peninsula simply because they manoeuvred and fought in line, they succeeded because they were good enough to manoeuvre and fight in line effectively. In other words, their underlying quality and discipline was at least as important as their formation, but each amplified the effect of the other. Consider Leith's advance at Salamanca. His division of some 6,700 men was formed in two lines (each two ranks deep) on a front about 900 yards wide, behind a thick belt of skirmishers. It advanced for nearly a mile across generally open ground (but even open ground has many minor obstacles and irregularities) under heavy fire. Leith rode at its head, as much to set the slow, steady pace and watch for enemy movements, as to inspire his men by his coolness. If the attack was to succeed, the infantry had to reach the French position in good order, unhurried or flustered, and full of confidence. It would have been very much quicker and easier to have advanced in two lines of battalion columns, which could keep roughly level with each other without constantly worrying about their alignment; but then, the division would have been forced either to fight in column or to attempt to deploy close to the enemy, both courses being full of risk. One of Leith's men wrote that as the division neared the French position, 'Captain Stewart of our company, stepping out of the ranks to the front, lays hold of Captain Glover and cries, "Glover did you ever see such a line?" I am pretty confident that in the Regiments which composed our lines there was not a man 6 inches out of his place.'[50] And Leith's ADC adds, 'A blank was no sooner made by the Enemy's fire but it was closed up as if nothing had happened, and as much attention was paid to dressing the Line, as if it had been a common Field day.'[51] Even allowing for some natural exaggeration, these comments reveal one of the secrets of the success of British infantry in battle in the period.

But not even Wellington's infantry at Salamanca could retain their perfect discipline and alignment after being heavily engaged. The most vulnerable moment for any troops was meeting a fresh enemy before order had been restored and composure regained after an initial encounter – hence the importance of close support and the frequent success of counter-attacks. This was how both Sherbrooke's division at Talavera and the fusilier brigade of Cole's division at Salamanca were broken. Fresh troops had a distinct advantage even over those who, having been successfully engaged, had then had time to rally and catch their breath. This may well be why the 6th Division failed to press home its attack on Ferey's division and instead became caught in a prolonged and costly firefight. Although the British use of line brought every musket to bear, giving them an advantage in most firefights, this was not their preferred means of deciding a contest. An experienced British officer wrote after Salamanca: 'The Charge of the Bayonet as usual carried everything, and it was owing to the 6th Division halting and firing at the Enemy that our loss was so great. Those Divisions who rushed upon the Enemy without hesitation not only did not lose nearly so many men, but did the business much better and nowhere did the French columns stand for an instant when fairly attacked with the Bayonet.'[52]

It was not only in close order infantry tactics that the British excelled: they equalled or surpassed the French in the use of light infantry, a speciality that the French had dominated since the early 1790s. British enthusiasm for light infantry dated back at least to the American War of Independence, and many of the brightest and most intelligent officers in the army became its advocates in the early years of the war. Despite some scepticism from conservatives in the Horse Guards, these innovators were given ample opportunity to develop and test their theories. The result included the famous camp at Shorncliffe, where the 43rd, 52nd and 95th Regiments were trained by Kenneth Mackenzie under the watchful eye of Sir John Moore.[53] As a result, by 1808 the British Army had an élite force of light infantry and many officers of all ranks with a particular interest in its employment.

Wellington was quite separate from these developments, having served in India from 1797 to 1805, but he was well aware of them. In Denmark in 1807 his brigade included the 43rd, 52nd and 95th Regiments (as well as the 92nd) and he had no sooner landed in Portugal than he issued instructions for the employment of light infantry in his small army, which shows that he was convinced of its importance.[54] In later campaigns he employed the Light Division not just to screen the army, and in other tasks traditionally associated with light troops, but as an élite spearhead in the forefront of battles and sieges. His confidence was justified, as the Light Division built up a superb record in the field and vindicated even the most extravagant claims of the proponents of light infantry, although Wellington has seldom been given the credit he deserves for his skilful use of the division, which brought its potential to fruition.

There were many light infantry in the army besides those in the Light Division, including two good battalions of the light infantry of the King's German Legion and several other British battalions, which had been trained as light infantry. Every British battalion had a light company, almost every Portuguese brigade had a battalion of *caçadores*, and Wellington distributed companies of the 5/60th and Brunswick-Oels throughout the army, attaching a company of these specialist skirmishers to most brigades of British infantry. As a result, a typical infantry division of Wellington's army could more than match any screen of skirmishers thrown out by the French. For example, the 6,700 men of Leith's division at Salamanca included almost 1,000 light infantry: light companies from the eight British line battalions, two companies of the Brunswick-Oels, and the whole of the 8th *Caçadores*.[55] These men were not as expert as the Light Division, but as the war went on they gained skill and confidence and were always able to perform their task effectively. There were few occasions in the whole war in the Peninsula on which the British line had to endure the sustained fire of enemy skirmishers preparing the way for a French attack; and many on which the French infantry, whether in attack or defence, had been considerably unsettled by the Allied light infantry before coming to grips with their main force. As in so many other aspects of tactics, the achievement was simple, even obvious, but difficult to consistently accomplish in practice.

Cavalry contributed much less than infantry to Wellington's victories in the Peninsula. Le Marchant's charge was the great exception, although mention must also be made of the remarkable success of the heavy dragoons of the King's German Legion at Garcia Hernandez on the following day. Several explanations have been given for this, ranging from the numerical superiority of the French cavalry in the early battles, to unsuitable terrain in the later campaigns. It is often suggested that British cavalry commanders were not particularly dashing or capable, and that Wellington lacked confidence in his cavalry – although whether this supposed lack of confidence was well founded or not tends to be passed over in silence. Several notorious incidents of British cavalry failing to halt and rally after successful charges in small combats (Campo Mayor in 1811, Maguilla in 1812) did great damage to its reputation, and have rather obscured success in other such affairs (Sahagun, Benavente, Usagre, Villagarcia). The Portuguese cavalry never equalled their infantry, while the Spanish had a remarkably bad record over the whole course of the war. The French cavalry achieved some extraordinary successes over Spanish armies, often deciding the course of a whole battle with a single charge, but its performance against the British was much less distinguished: the destruction of Colborne's brigade at Albuera was the only triumph of its kind, while at Fuentes de Oñoro and at El Bodon the French proved quite unable to take advantage of favourable circumstances. Even at Salamanca, Boyer's dragoons failed to exploit Cole's repulse, although they would appear to have been well placed to do so. Nor were the French cavalry ever able to gain clear dominance over their British counterparts in battle, even when they greatly outnumbered them.

Writing to the British government soon after the Battle of Salamanca, Wellington complained of the inferiority of his artillery to the French: 'I should wish also to be able to equip some more artillery, and of a larger calibre; as it is not agreeable to be cannonaded for hours together, and not to be able to answer with even one gun.'[56] This was clearly unfair, for the Allied artillery had a remarkable success in separately wounding the three most senior generals in the French army, producing a paralysis in command that probably made a significant contribution to the result of the day. By contrast, the French bombardment of the Allied lines appears to have been noisy but not particularly lethal – a comment that applies to many other battles in the Peninsula, with the exception of Talavera. In general, the Allied artillery seems to have provided good support to its infantry, often with rather limited means. It was crucial to Wellington's success at Oporto and prominent at Busaco. Some enthusiasts have criticized Wellington for dispersing his artillery across his army rather than concentrating it in grand batteries as Napoleon did, but this seems to be a triumph of theory over common sense: there were few, if any, occasions in Wellington's career when such a concentration would have suited his purposes.[57]

The success of the Allied army in the Peninsula depended upon its discipline and its confidence, and Wellington took great pains to foster both. He frequently upbraided regimental officers for neglecting their duty to their men both on campaign and in cantonments, and sacrificed easy popularity by his refusal to turn a blind eye to the misconduct of the troops, especially towards the local civilian population. Yet with the exception of a few incidents, which became notorious, he was not unreasonable, and never bothered his army about inessentials such as uniforms, or even the finer points of drill. The obedience he exacted from all ranks was required to maintain the health and efficiency of the army and enable it to continue its success against superior numbers of good troops in battle. In exchange, he worked very hard to keep the troops well supplied with food – although inevitably the commissariat still failed at times, especially in the early campaigns. And he tried never to ask too much of the army, especially in battle. Success bred success – failure would introduce doubts, which might persist. A deep-seated conviction that success would come, helps explain the extraordinary courage and persistence of the troops at Albuera and Badajoz. Not all the campaigns ended well, both 1809 and 1812 finished on a sour note, but this did little to undermine the confidence of the men that they would succeed if only they were allowed to fight. Wellington did not create this confidence – it is much in evidence in the Coruña campaign and in earlier operations – but he sustained and nurtured it through five long years of war, when it might quickly have been destroyed by disappointment and failure.

The aftermath of Salamanca revealed the limitations of the battlefield victories so consistently achieved by the Allied army. Wellington pursued Marmont's army to Valladolid, and then turned south to Madrid, which he entered in triumph on 12 August. But although the defeat at Salamanca had temporarily driven Marmont's army from the field, it had not transformed the overall balance of forces in the Peninsula. There remained some 260,000 French troops in Spain, while Wellington's main army had only 50,000 with a further 20,000 under Hill. The Allied victory forced the other French generals to put aside their immediate local concerns and deal with the common threat posed by Wellington. Peripheral campaigns and outlying posts were abandoned in order to concentrate forces ready to take the field, and Soult, with great reluctance, prepared to evacuate his entire vice-royalty of Andalusia and bring his whole army – with its immense train of baggage and plunder – north, lest he be completely cut off from France. In Madrid Wellington surveyed his options and found none of them promising. He considered marching south to force Soult to give battle, but the French forces in Andalusia were much stronger than Marmont's army, and the Allied troops were weary – and their sick lists were growing alarmingly. If he marched south, his flank and rear to the north and east would be exposed, while locals warned against embarking on a campaign in Andalusia in the heat of high summer. Besides, there was a chance that if he left Soult alone, the French marshal would remain quietly at Seville, at least for several months. So Wellington took part of his army north to confront the remnants of the Army of Portugal and elements of the Army of the North, who fell back before his advance. His objective was to find some way of securing this front so that he could return to Madrid and deal with the threats posed by Soult in the south and Suchet in the east. However, no obvious means of guarding the northern flank appeared, and he half-heartedly undertook the siege of Burgos without adequate means or preparation. The siege did not go well, but even if the castle had fallen quickly and a Spanish garrison had been installed, it is debatable whether it would have protected Wellington's flank: the French had collected sufficient troops in northern Spain both to besiege Burgos and advance against the Allies. In any case, repeated attempts to storm the fortress failed, and on 22 October Wellington abandoned the siege, having incurred 2,000 casualties in what was probably the least creditable operation of his entire career.

Meanwhile, Soult had moved: not directly on Madrid, but first to Valencia, where he united with King Joseph and Suchet, and from there had advanced on the capital from the east. At the same time the revived Army of Portugal, with strong support from the Army of the North, began pressing Wellington's positions in front of Burgos. The Allies had little choice but to retreat, for they were heavily outnumbered on both fronts, having received few reinforcements since the victory at Salamanca. (Although a large part of Spain had been liberated, this had not led to any significant increase in the Spanish armies – there had not been time to raise recruits, while the Spanish authorities showed little urgency or efficiency. Most of the guerrillas were reluctant to venture far from their accustomed haunts: when the French were driven from their home province they frequently reverted to their previous occupation, whether as peasant cultivators or thieves and vagabonds.) Hill's rearguard abandoned Madrid on 31 October, and by 8 November the Allied army was united behind the Tormes near Salamanca. Wellington offered battle but Soult, who commanded the combined French armies, would not risk an attack and avoided a repetition of the mistakes of 22 July, while still turning the Allied flank. This left Wellington with no choice but to retreat all the way back to the Portuguese frontier, and the last few days of the campaign were grim, with heavy rain, a failure of the commissariat, and exhaustion leading to a breakdown of discipline almost as bad as on the retreat to Coruña. Wellington issued a damning circular condemning the misconduct, which aroused such resentment that even decades later some veteran officers could not manage to forgive it. But Wellington, no less than the rest of the army, was intensely disappointed by the outcome of the campaign, and mentally and physically exhausted by an extremely demanding year.

Fortunately, the Allied army was able to rest for five months in winter quarters while its spirits were revived by news of Napoleon's defeat in Russia. This far eclipsed any of the events in the Peninsula in 1812. If Russia had been defeated, Napoleon would have been able to reinforce his armies in Spain, just as he had done after defeating Austria in 1809, and Wellington might even have been forced back to the Lines of Torres Vedras again, although the loss of Andalusia and Madrid had destroyed what little credibility and support King Joseph's regime had ever gained. The destruction of Napoleon's army in Russia and the spread of the war into Central Europe had equally important implications: no reinforcements would be heading south across the Pyrenees and soon orders arrived for the withdrawal of 20,000 veteran troops to strengthen the new armies Napoleon was forming. This was far fewer than might have been expected, and it should have left the remaining French armies, amounting to almost 200,000 men, secure in northern Spain with lightly held outposts stretching down beyond Madrid. However, when the Army of the North had relaxed its hold on the mountainous provinces of Navarre and Biscay, in order to concentrate against Wellington in the autumn of 1812, an insurrection had erupted across the whole region, which proved impossible to suppress all through the following winter and spring.

Wellington took the field in the middle of May 1813, launching a carefully planned advance that in only five weeks took his army from the Portuguese frontier to the foot of the Pyrenees. He caught the French off guard and turned the flank of every possible line of defence, including the Ebro. Finally, on 21 June, they offered battle at Vitoria, although with little confidence of success. The result was a crushing French defeat, even though Wellington's plans for a double-envelopment were not fully realized. Seldom in the whole war in the Peninsula did French troops fight with less spirit, for the army was very badly led. Having driven the French armies out of Spain (except for Suchet in Catalonia), Wellington settled down to besiege San Sebastian and blockade Pamplona. Napoleon sent Soult back to take command and he did a remarkable job of reviving the morale of the army. At the end of July Soult launched a bold offensive across the Pyrenees to try to relieve the two fortresses, and gained some surprising initial successes before being driven back after a series of engagements, including the two Battles of Sorauren.

A further attempt to relieve San Sebastian was defeated by the Spanish army at San Marcial at the end of August, and early in September the fortress was finally stormed. On 7 October Wellington forced Soult's position and crossed the French frontier on the River Bidassoa in a notably neat and well-planned operation, but limited his advance and did little to exploit the advantage he had gained. Pamplona finally surrendered on 31 October and Wellington made another limited advance, crossing the Nivelle on 10 November, but the end of the year still saw him in the Pyrenees, having defeated a French counter-attack in the Battles of the Nive (9–13 December).

Meanwhile, Napoleon had been fighting a losing campaign in Central Europe, where Russia had been joined by Prussia and then Austria in a grand coalition. However, the Allies were by no means united, and the Austrians at least hoped for a compromise peace that would preserve Napoleon's power as a counterweight to Russia. Unsuccessful peace negotiations alternated with active campaigning, and Wellington could never be sure that the Continental Powers would not agree to terms that Britain, Spain, and Portugal would find unacceptable. Of course, the fighting in Central Europe made Wellington's task much easier, for the French forces facing him were greatly reduced by the end of 1813 (Soult had some 75,000 men and Suchet 25,000), but it added a disconcerting element of unpredictability. Wellington was also reluctant to venture far into France in case an invasion triggered a patriotic surge of support for Napoleon's regime, a guerrilla war, or even a new French Revolution. All the Allies in 1813–14 were acutely aware of the precedent of 1792 and dreaded its repetition. Finally, there was the obvious risk that if he advanced deep into southern France while the Allies were still on the Elbe, Napoleon would feel obliged to drive him back to the Pyrenees.[58] So Wellington's operations in the last months of 1813 were restrained by the need to keep pace with the Allies, while in 1814 he clearly fell behind them: besieging Bayonne, entering Bordeaux, and fighting a battle at Toulouse when the other Allied armies were advancing on Paris. This was partly a matter of logistics (winter rains and deep mud in Gascony proved a greater impediment to operations than heavy snow in Champagne) and more of simple geography (Paris is much closer to the Rhine than to the Pyrenees), but it created the misleading impression that Wellington's operations were less significant in Napoleon's downfall than those of the other Allied generals. But the war in the Peninsula was never a separate, self-contained conflict: it was one aspect of the wider struggle against Napoleon's empire, and lasting success in the Peninsula could only be achieved as part of a greater victory.

There was nothing inevitable about the progress of the Allied army from Lisbon to Toulouse. The initial opportunity arose from the uprising of the Spanish people in 1808, and it was their refusal to accept defeat, despite Napoleon's victories and the occupation of so much of the country, that created the context for Wellington's campaigns. The wholehearted co-operation of the Portuguese people was equally important: they not only provided an essential part of the Allied army and suffered greatly from the devastation of war, but they gave the British an ideal base of operations. The British campaigns in the Peninsula all depended upon the Royal Navy's command of the sea, which protected the vital supply lines through which vast quantities of men, equipment, money, and food (from North Africa, the Mediterranean and North America, as well as Britain) were shipped. This in turn was underpinned by the strength of the British economy and the resilience of her commerce and finances in the face of Napoleon's Continental System. The advantages of the Peninsula as a theatre for British operations are much more obvious in retrospect than they were at the time, and in the wake of the Spanish defeats of late 1808 and Sir John Moore's retreat to Coruña many politicians and leading soldiers in Britain despaired of the cause. Nonetheless, the British government maintained its commitment to the Peninsula. The open-handed support given to the Spanish patriots in the summer helped keep the spirit of resistance alive in the dark days that followed. Canning's urgency ensured that Portugal was not forgotten, that reinforcements were sent to Lisbon, and that Beresford was dispatched to reform the Portuguese army. Crucially, the ministers entrusted Wellington with the command of the army and gave him broad discretion to act as he thought best, even though many of his own officers expected the campaign to end in another humiliating embarkation. Throughout the long years that followed, Wellington had the dominant voice in relations between Britain and her Peninsular allies, and he ensured that the underlying purpose they shared was not wholly submerged in the quarrels and mutual irritation produced by attempts at co-operation. He had the foresight to devise the plan that made the defence of Portugal possible in 1810, and the strength of character to implement it in the face of doubts and protests from allies and subordinates. As both a strategist and a tactician he showed a natural boldness, subdued when necessary by the need for caution. He nurtured his army, building its confidence, while looking after its material needs and preserving its discipline. He owed much of the fighting quality of the army, as well as its training and tactical system, to the hard work of scores of conscientious officers over a decade or more preceding 1808; to the inspiring leadership of generals such as Abercromby and Moore; and to the rigorous standards demanded by the Duke of York. But a fine blade can quickly lose its edge in clumsy hands, and Wellington showed great skill in handling his army both on and off the battlefield. The army in 1808 lacked the experience and practical knowledge needed for sustained campaigning on the Continent, and Wellington's attention to detail and wide-ranging expertise contributed greatly to the remarkable improvement of its general efficiency – in particular the work of the commissariat, the medical service, the staff, and subordinate commanders. On the battlefield he faced and defeated the finest French commanders of the day except Napoleon, despite frequently being outnumbered. At every turn, Wellington was present and his contribution was both personal and distinct. On the day after Waterloo he told a friend, 'By God! I don't think it would have done if I had not been there!'[59] and the remark is at least as true of the war in the Peninsula. Wellington was the final, indispensable, ingredient of victory.

NOTES

1 Castlereagh to Charles Stewart, 10 August 1808, Castlereagh Papers, PRONI D3030/Q2/2, p. 49.
2 To avoid confusion I have called him Wellington throughout this essay, even though he did not receive the title until 4 September 1809.

3   S. G. P. Ward, *Wellington's Headquarters: a Study of the Administrative Problems in the Peninsula, 1809–1814* (Oxford University Press, 1957), p. 163; Martin Robson, 'British Intervention in Portugal, 1793–1808', *Historical Research* vol. 76, 2003, pp. 97–8.

4   Wellington to Castlereagh, [Private], HMS *Donegal*, 1 August 1808, *Wellington's Dispatches* (all citations in this essay from the 'enlarged' edition in 8 vols, published by Parker, Furnivall and Parker in 1844), vol. 3, pp. 46–7.

5   Rory Muir, *Britain and the Defeat of Napoleon, 1807–1815* (New Haven, Yale University Press, 1996), pp. 84–5, citing Cabinet circulars by Canning and his private letters to Villiers, both from the Canning Papers, Bundles 41, 41A and 48, in the West Yorkshire Archive Service, Leeds.

6   Samuel E. Vichness 'Marshal of Portugal: the Military Career of William Carr Beresford, 1785–1814' (unpublished PhD thesis, Florida State University 1976).

7   Vichness, 'Marshal of Portugal', pp. 153–4.

8   Warre to his mother, Lisbon, 6 February 1810, *Letters from the Peninsula, 1808–1812* by Lieutenant-Gen Sir William Warre (Staplehurst, Spellmount, 1999), p. 69.

9   Castlereagh to Cradock, 28 January 1809, WO 1/232, pp. 287–91.

10   'Memorandum on the Defence of Portugal', London, 7 March 1809, *WD* (enlarged ed.), vol. 3, pp. 181–3.

11   Canning to Portland, 'Private & Secret', 21 March 1809, Canning Papers, Bundle 33A.

12   The best account of the Oporto campaign remains that in Oman, *History of the Peninsular War*, vol. 2, pp. 312–66.

13   Vichness 'Marshal of Portugal', pp. 155, 161.

14   Vichness 'Marshal of Portugal', p. 162.

15   Vichness 'Marshal of Portugal', pp. 240–4.

16   Vichness 'Marshal of Portugal', pp. 226–8, 276–7.

17   Wellington to Beresford, 26 August, 8 September and 15 November 1809 *WD* (enlarged ed.) vol. 3, pp. 454–5, 484–6, 588–90; Beresford to Wellington, 3 and 12 September, 2 October 1809, *Wellington's Supplementary Despatches* vol. 6, pp. 345–8, 361–3 and 384–5.

18   There is a good account of the affair in Vichness, 'Marshal of Portugal', pp. 279–81.

19   Vichness, 'Marshal of Portugal', pp. 281–6.

20   Vichness, 'Marshal of Portugal', p. 291.

21   See Charles J. Esdaile, *Fighting Napoleon: Guerrillas, Bandits and Adventurers in Spain, 1808–1814* (New Haven, Yale University Press, 2004), *passim* – an important and original work based on very detailed and extensive research.

22   For the Austrian decision to go to war see J. A. Vann, 'Habsburg Policy and the Austrian War of 1809', *Central European History* vol. 7, 1974, pp. 291–310; Paul W. Schroeder, *The Transformation of European Politics, 1763–1848* (Oxford, Clarendon Press, 1994), pp. 351–6.

23   Oman, *History of the Peninsular War* vol. 2, pp. 624–7.

24   See Wellington to Lieutenant Colonel Carroll, 19 June 1809 and to Lieutenant Colonel Bourke, 21 June 1809, *WD* (enlarged ed.) vol. 3, pp. 310–11.

25   Castlereagh to Wellington, 25 May 1809, *Castlereagh Correspondence* vol. 7, p. 71.

26   Castlereagh to Wellington, 26 May 1809, *Castlereagh Correspondence* vol. 7, pp. 71–72; Castlereagh to the King and reply, 25 and 26 May 1809, *Later Correspondence of King George III* vol. 5, pp. 284–5.

27   On this whole question see John M. Sherwig, *Guineas & Gunpowder: British Foreign Aid in the Wars with France, 1793–1815* (Harvard University Press, 1969) and T. M. O. Redgrave, 'Wellington's Logistical Arrangements in the Peninsular War, 1809–1814' (unpublished PhD thesis presented to the University of London, no date [c. 1979]).

28   Note by the editor in *A Series of Letters of the First Earl of Malmesbury, His Family and Friends, From 1745 to 1820*, edited by the Earl of Malmesbury, 2 vols (London, Richard Bentley, 1870), vol. 2, p. 129.

29   Wellington to Liverpool, 1 December 1810, *WD* (enlarged ed.) vol. 4, pp. 444–6.

30   The Prince of Wales to Perceval, 4 February 1811, *Correspondence of George, Prince of Wales*, edited by A. Aspinall, 8 vols (London, Cassell, 1963–71), vol. 7, pp. 200–201. See also pp. 124–38 for an excellent account of the Regency crisis.

31   For example, Wellington to William Wellesley-Pole, 11 January 1811, Raglan Papers, Wellington

A no. 39, Gwent Record Office, printed with extensive deletions in *Wellington's Supplementary Despatches* vol. 7, pp. 40–4.

32 See Muir, *Britain and the Defeat of Napoleon*, *passim.*

33 Oman, *History of the Peninsular War* vol. 4, p. 203.

34 Oman, *History of the Peninsular War* vol. 4, pp. 393–5.

35 William Wellesley-Pole to Wellington, London, 16 June 1811, Raglan Papers, Wellington B no. 114 states that this version of events was widely circulating around London, based on letters home from officers in Beresford's army. See also Vichness, 'Marshal of Portugal', pp. 422–5, 433–7.

36 It may be objected that Napoleon still found 600,000 men with which to invade Russia in 1812 while still maintaining his armies in Spain; however, about half the troops invading Russia came from Allied contingents (Austrians, Prussians, Poles, Germans from the Confederation of the Rhine, Swiss, Dutch and Italians) while most of the French part of the army had previously been employed in maintaining Napoleon's domination of Central Europe: i.e. keeping these 'allies' in a state of subordination. It would not have been possible for him to shift even the French half of this army to Spain, without relinquishing his hegemony over Central Europe, while few of these allies were willing to contribute large forces to the war in the Peninsula.

37 For example, see Napoleon to Berthier, 28 January 1810, *The Confidential Correspondence of Napoleon Bonaparte with his Brother Joseph*, 2 vols (New York, D. Appleton and Co., 1856), vol. 2, p. 102 – one of many letters on the cost of the war. See also Connelly, *Napoleon's Satellite Kingdoms* (New York, Free Press, 1965), pp. 241–2, 250–3.

38 Muir, *Britain and the Defeat of Napoleon*, pp. 182–3; Czartoryski, *Memoirs of Prince Adam Czartoryski* vol. 2, pp. 222–228; Palmer, *Alexander I*, pp. 199–203.

39 Oman, *History of the Peninsular War* vol. 5, pp. 82–84; vol. 6, pp. 741–5.

40 Wellington to Sir Henry Wellesley, 14 March 1812, *WD* (enlarged ed.) vol. 5, p. 550.

41 Wellington to Liverpool, [Private], Camp at Badajoz, 7 April 1812, *The Athenaeum*, no. 3209, 27 April 1889, p. 537. This letter is not included in the *Dispatches* or the *Supplementary Despatches*.

42 Figures from Oman, *History of the Peninsular War* vol. 3, p. 254 and Donald D. Horward, *Napoleon and Iberia: The Twin Sieges of Ciudad Rodrigo and Almeida, 1810* (Tallahassee, Florida State University, 1984), p. 182.

43 Oman, *History of the Peninsular War* vol. 4, p. 61.

44 No easy successes in sieges actually undertaken, but the capture by blockade of Almeida in 1811, and the French destruction of Burgos in 1813, both spared the Allies trouble, while the Retiro at Madrid should probably not have been garrisoned.

45 See Rory Muir, *Salamanca 1812*, pp. 7, 37–39, for further consideration of this question.

46 John S. Hyden, 'The Sources, Organization and Uses of Intelligence in the Anglo-Portuguese Army, 1808–1814' *J.S.A.H.R.*, vol. 62, no. 250 & 251, summer and autumn 1984, pp. 92–104, 169–175, gives an excellent introduction to the subject. Further studies by Mark Romans and Huw Davies will add greatly to our knowledge when they are published.

47 Rory Muir, *Salamanca, 1812* (New Haven, Yale University Press, 2001), pp. 47–83.

48 Castel, *Relation de la Bataille et Retraite des Arapiles*, pp. 19–20; Sarramon, *La Bataille des Arapiles*, p. 223 cited in Muir, *Salamanca*, p. 134.

49 It is surprisingly hard to find firm evidence for the introduction and spread of the two-deep line, but we know that it was in use as early as 1793, and although the drill manual continued to advocate forming in three ranks, it seems that the thinner formation was in general use well before 1808. For the use of two-deep line in 1793 see an order from Lord Moira to his troops dated Portsmouth, 29 November 1793, printed in R. M. Grazebrook, 'The Campaign in Flanders of 1793–1795: Journal of Lieutenant Charles Stewart, 28th Foot', *J.S.A.H.R.* vol. 117, no. 29, spring 1951, p. 4 (I am grateful to Howie Muir for drawing this to my attention). Wellington's General Order of 3 August 1808 in *WD* (enlarged ed.) vol. 3, p. 50 stipulates the use of the two-deep line almost in passing: it reads much more as the confirmation of an accepted norm than as the introduction of a significant innovation. When Wellington resumed command of the army in 1809 there was no mention of the subject at all.

50 Corporal John Douglas, *Douglas's Tale of the Peninsula and Waterloo*, edited by Stanley Monick (London, Leo Cooper, 1997), p. 45.

51 Andrew Leith Hay's manuscript narrative of the campaign of 1812 in the Leith Hay Papers, National Archives of Scotland, GD225 Box 40, and quoted in Muir, *Salamanca*, p. 109.

52 Andrew Leith Hay's manuscript narrative of the campaign of 1812 in the Leith Hay Papers, National Archives of Scotland, GD225 Box 40, and quoted in Muir, *Salamanca*, p. 191.

53 This rather over-simplifies a complex story, for the 95th had been formed and trained by Coote Manningham and William Stewart prior to the establishment of the camp at Shorncliffe, and many other regiments, besides the 43rd and 52nd were given light infantry training and status with mixed results. See David Gates, *The British Light Infantry Arm, c. 1790–1815* (London, Batsford, 1987), *passim* and especially pp. 105–7, 116–19.

54 GO 3 August 1808, *WD* (enlarged ed.) vol. 3, p. 50n.

55 It is also probable that the two regiments of Portuguese line infantry in Spry's brigade each contained a company of light infantry, but the evidence for this is strangely fragmentary, and it is not clear whether they were deployed as skirmishers on this occasion.

56 Wellington to Bathurst, 24 July 1812, *WD* (enlarged ed.) vol. 5, pp. 758–9.

57 For the criticism, see Captain Francis Duncan, *History of the Royal Regiment of Artillery*, 2 vols (London, John Murray, 1872), vol. 2, pp. 276–77.

58 On this, see Wellington to Bathurst, 19 September and 18 October 1813, *WD* (enlarged ed.) vol. 7, pp. 10, 71–72.

59 Reminiscences by Thomas Creevey written in 1822 and printed in *The Creevey Papers*, edited by Sir Herbert Maxwell (London, John Murray, 1923), p. 237.

Chapter Two

The Origin of Wellington's Peninsular Army, June 1808–April 1809

Ron McGuigan

By 1808 Great Britain had been at war with France for some fifteen years. Britain had not been able to sustain a campaign on the Continent and was left, for the most part, to conduct short ones against the possessions of France and its allies. All this was to change, however, when France became involved with the Iberian Peninsula.

In 1807 France conquered Portugal, and then in 1808, when Napoleon deposed Spain's sovereign and replaced him with Joseph Bonaparte, Spain exploded in rebellion and Portugal followed. When both countries appealed to Great Britain for assistance, Viscount Castlereagh, the Secretary of State for War, saw an opportunity of allowing the British army to return to the Continent and engage the French. But with all its overseas commitments, where was an army to be found? Lord Castlereagh had, with great foresight, prepared and maintained a disposable force, with shipping, ready to be used whenever an advantage presented itself. This chapter is about that force: the origin of the army Sir Arthur Wellesley, the future 1st Duke of Wellington, was to lead to victory in the Iberian Peninsula, liberating Portugal and Spain, and crossing the Pyrenees into southern France.

As will be seen, at its beginning, Wellington's command was not a homogeneous force but an army composed of different elements, commanded by different generals. But later, united under Wellington's leadership, it became: 'probably the most complete machine for its numbers now existing in Europe.' (Wellington, 21 November 1813.) Numbers shown below are for the rank and file, and an additional one-eighth must be added for officers, sergeants, etc. Neither have I included the Staff Corps or the Waggon Train, detachments of which served with the different forces. The lists of general officers given are arranged by army seniority. This chapter is primarily based on material published in Parliamentary Papers, Wellington's Dispatches, and *The Times* newspaper, as well as primary source General Orders issued.

During this time, Great Britain maintained garrisons in England, Ireland, Scotland, the Channel Islands, Africa, British North America, Cape of Good Hope, Ceylon, Gibraltar, Heligoland, India, Malta, New South Wales, Sicily, and the West Indies. Its regular force was made up of three regiments of household cavalry, seven regiments of dragoon guards, five regiments of dragoons, nineteen regiments of light dragoons, seven battalions (in three regiments) of foot guards and 175 battalions (in 103 numbered regiments) of infantry, with eight garrison battalions, twelve royal veteran battalions, four unnumbered regiments, and two garrison companies. In addition, it included the King's German Legion (consisting of two dragoon regiments, three light dragoon regiments, two light battalions, and eight line battalions, a depot company, a garrison company, two troops of horse artillery, and four companies foot artillery), ten foreign regiments, and fifteen colonial regiments. Other units included the Royal Regiment of Artillery, consisting of twelve troops of Royal Horse Artillery, 100 companies (in ten battalions) of foot artillery, twelve companies (in one battalion) of invalid artillery, the Corps of Royal Artillery Drivers (in eight troops), and the Royal Foreign Artillery (in four companies). Finally, the army was augmented by the Corps of Royal Engineers, the Corps of Royal Invalid Engineers, the Corps of Royal Military Artificers, the Royal Staff Corps, and the Royal Waggon Train.

The disposable force was mainly split between the Baltic Expedition (sent to assist the King of Sweden) and a projected South American Expedition. The former force consisted of approximately 11,346 rank and file, and the latter force some 8,319 rank and file. It was this latter force that was first earmarked for diversion to the Peninsula.

Disposable Force: the South American Expedition
In June 1808 units assembling at Cork, under the command of Lieutenant General Sir Arthur Wellesley, were available for immediate service in the Iberian Peninsula. This initial force was augmented by units assembled at Portsmouth, Ramsgate, Harwich, and Gibraltar.

CORK

1/5th Regiment (990)	1/9th Regiment (833)
1/38th Regiment (957)	1/40th Regiment (926)
5/60th Regiment (936)	1/71st Regiment (903)
1/91st Regiment (917)	2/95th Regiment (four companies = 400)
4th Royal Veteran Battalion (737)	

The headquarters staff included Major Generals Alexander Mackenzie and Rowland Hill, and Brigadier Generals Henry Fane and James Catlin Craufurd.

PORTSMOUTH

Royal Artillery (420)	20th Light Dragoons (300)

The artillery was commanded by Lieutenant Colonel William Robe and Major James Viney, and included Geary's Company (5th Battalion) and Raynsford's Company (8th Battalion) of five 9-pounders, ten 6-pounders, one 5½-inch heavy howitzer, and two 5½-inch light howitzers, all with limbers.

HARWICH
2nd Regiment (813)
20th Regiment (689)
1/95th Regiment (two companies = 180)
Crawford's Company (6th Battalion RA)
Tieling's 2nd Company (KGL) (Artillery = 430)

This force was under the orders of Brigadier General Wroth Palmer Acland.

RAMSGATE
2/9th Regiment (675)   2/43rd Regiment (861)
2/52nd Regiment (858)   97th Regiment (769)

This force was under the orders of Brigadier General Robert Anstruther.

GIBRALTAR
29th Regiment (863)   1/32nd Regiment (941)
1/50th Regiment (1019)   1/82nd Regiment (991)
Lawson's Half-Company (8th Battalion RA = 66).

This force was under the orders of Major General Brent Spencer and Brigadier General Miles Nightingall. (Note: the other half of Lawson's Company had gone to Sicily in May 1808.)

Disposable Force: the Baltic Expedition
Sent to Sweden in April 1808, had returned as its mission had failed and was now available. It was organized as:

Commanding the force: Lieutenant General Sir John Moore
Second-in-command: Lieutenant General John Hope
Adjutant General: Brigadier General Richard Stewart
Quartermaster-General: Lieutenant Colonel George Murray

1st Division: Lieutenant General Alexander Mackenzie Fraser

Clinton's Brigade: Brigadier General Henry Clinton
1/4th Regiment (971)
1/28th Regiment (1020)

Highland Brigade: Colonel Alan Cameron
1/79th Regiment(995)
1/92nd Regiment (934)

2nd Division: Major General John Murray

Langwerth's Brigade: Colonel Ernest Baron Langwerth
1st Line Battalion (725)
2nd Line Battalion (761)

Drieberg's Brigade: Colonel George de Drieberg
5th Line Battalion (753)
7th Line Battalion (679)

3rd Division or Reserve: Major General Edward Paget

1/52nd Regiment (951)
3 companies 1/95th Regiment (300)
3rd Light Dragoons KGL (570)
Garrison Company KGL (48)

Alten's Brigade: Colonel Charles Baron Alten
1st Light Battalion KGL (907)
2nd Light Battalion KGL (903)

Brigadier General John Sontag was attached to Moore's force.

Lieutenant Colonel George Wood commanding artillery (829) of Drummond's Company
3rd Battalion, and Wilmot's Company 3rd Battalion and Major Julius Hartmann
commanding the 1st Company (Gesenius) and 4th Company (Heise) KGL of four
medium 12-pounders, five heavy or long 6-pounders, sixteen light 6-pounders, two
8-inch howitzers, three 5½-inch heavy howitzers, four 5½-inch light howitzers, four
3-pounder mountain guns with two 10-inch iron mortars and six 5½-inch brass
mortars on beds. There were only limbers for five heavy or long 6-pounders, five
light 6-pounders, one 5½-inch heavy howitzer and one 5½-inch light howitzer.

The British Army in Portugal

On 14 June 1808, the Commander-in-Chief notified Wellesley that he was to
command the force being sent to either Portugal or Spain, as circumstances
warranted, and assigned Spencer's corps to Wellesley's force. The 4th Royal
Veteran Battalion was now destined for Gibraltar and A. Mackenzie was removed
from the staff of Wellesley's corps, being senior in army rank to Spencer. Major
General Ronald Ferguson, going out on the staff of Spencer's corps, was to serve
temporarily with Wellesley's force. Brevet Lieutenant Colonel James Bathurst the
Deputy Quartermaster-General and Brevet Lieutenant Colonel George Tucker
the Deputy Adjutant General serving with Spencer's corps were to both serve in
the same capacity with Wellesley's force. On 30 June, Wellesley was informed that
the 1/36th Regiment (647) and 1/45th Regiment (599) in garrison near Cork were
to join his command.

On 15 July, Lord Castlereagh informed Wellesley that the brigades at Harwich
and Ramsgate would be sent as reinforcements, that Moore's corps was being sent
to Portugal and that he was being superseded in command by Lieutenant Generals
Sir Hew Dalrymple (the Lieutenant Governor of Gibraltar) and Sir Harry Burrard
(from the Home Staff), the former as Commander-in-Chief and the latter as the
Second-in-Command.

The letter of service to Sir Hew Dalrymple of 21 July directed that the corps of
Moore, Spencer and Wellesley with reinforcements were to compose his army.
Burrard joined Moore's corps (which had left Sweden 4 July and arrived back at

Portsmouth by 21 July) at Portsmouth on 28 July and took command with Moore becoming the second-in-command of the corps. Sontag was removed to a political appointment in Portugal. Brevet Major Richard Fletcher joined 27 July to command the Royal Engineers.

Proposed staff for the army under Lieutenant General Sir Hew Dalrymple:

Lieutenant Generals
Sir Harry Burrard, Sir John Moore, John Hope, Alexander Mackenzie Fraser, Henry
    Lord Paget, and Sir Arthur Wellesley.

Major Generals
Lord William Bentinck, Edward Paget, Brent Spencer, Rowland Hill, John Murray and
    Ronald Ferguson.

Brigadier Generals
Wroth Palmer Acland, Miles Nightingall, Richard Stewart, Charles Stewart, Henry
    Fane, Robert Anstruther and James Catlin Craufurd.

The acting Adjutant General was Brigadier General Henry Clinton, and the acting
    Quartermaster-General was Lieutenant Colonel George Murray.

In that letter of service of 21 July was a memorandum of 20 July with the following suggested organization for the army:

Commander of the force: Lieutenant General Dalrymple
Second-in-command: Lieutenant General Burrard
Acting Adjutant General: Brigadier General Clinton
Acting Quartermaster-General: Lieutenant Colonel G. Murray

Reserve Division: Lieutenant General Moore and Major General E. Paget

C. Stewart's Brigade: Brigadier General C. Stewart
18th Light Dragoons
20th Light Dragoons
3rd Light Dragoons KGL

Anstruther's Brigade: Brigadier General Anstruther
1/52nd Regiment   2/52nd Regiment
1/95th Regiment (5 companies)   2/95th Regiment (4 companies)

R. Stewart's Brigade: Brigadier General R. Stewart
2/43rd Regiment   5/60th Regiment
1st Light Battalion KGL   2nd Light Battalion KGL

1st Division: Lieutenant General Hope

Acland's Brigade: Brigadier General Acland
2nd Regiment   1/4th Regiment
1/28th Regiment

Ferguson's Brigade: Major General Ferguson
1/79th Regiment   1/91st Regiment
1/92nd Regiment

2nd Division: Lieutenant General Lord Paget

Spencer's Brigade: Major General Spencer
1/6th Regiment   29th Regiment
1/32nd Regiment

Nightingall's Brigade: Brigadier General Nightingall
1/5th Regiment   1/50th Regiment
1/82nd Regiment

3rd Division: Lieutenant General Mackenzie Fraser

Hill's Brigade: Major General Hill
1/9th Regiment   2/9th Regiment
1/40th Regiment

Fane's Brigade: Brigadier General Fane
1/36th Regiment   1/45th Regiment
97th Regiment

4th Division: Lieutenant General Wellesley

Craufurd's Brigade: Brigadier General Catlin Craufurd
20th Regiment   1/38th Regiment
1/71st Regiment

Murray's Brigade: Major General J. Murray
1st, 2nd, 5th and 7th Line Battalions of the King's German Legion

It does not appear that this organization was ever put into effect. But it makes an interesting comment on the advice given by the Commander-in-Chief to a commander in the field.

Other units were being detailed to join the army. The 18th Light Dragoons (672), currently at Portsmouth, with Brigadier General Charles Stewart were to go with Moore's corps.

Also going with Moore's corps, both having missed sailing with Acland's Brigade, were Crawford's Company and the 2nd Company KGL of five medium 12-pounders, eleven light 6-pounders, one 5½-inch heavy howitzer and three 5½-inch light howitzers with limbers for five medium 12-pounders, five light 6-pounders, one 5½-inch heavy howitzer and one 5½-inch light howitzer.

The 1/42nd Regiment (943) was coming from Gibraltar. The 1/3rd Regiment (929) and Thornhill's Company RA (94) were coming from the garrison of Madeira with Major General William Beresford.

The Governor of Gibraltar had sent the 1/6th Regiment (966) under Brigadier

General Barnard Bowes with Spencer's corps. In July, Major General John Randoll Mackenzie received orders to join Spencer's corps and Brigadier General Alan Cameron was added to the staff of the army in Portugal.

On 23 June, Wellesley's force at Cork was organized as:

Commanding the force: Lieutenant General Wellesley
Second-in-command: Major General Hill

Hill's Brigade: Major General Ferguson (temporary)
1/5th Regiment   1/9th Regiment
1/38th Regiment

Light Brigade: Brigadier General Fane
5/60th Regiment   2/95th Regiment (4 companies)
4th Royal Veteran Battalion

Highland Brigade: Brigadier General Catlin Craufurd
1/40th Regiment   1/71st Regiment
1/91st Regiment

At Portsmouth were Lieutenant Colonel Robe, Geary's Company RA and Raynsford's
    Company RA with the 20th Light Dragoons.

Although Wellesley's troops at Cork went onto the transports 15–17 June, contrary winds kept them at Cork until they sailed 10/11 July. They had been joined by the transports carrying the 20th Light Dragoons and the artillery. They arrived off the coast of Portugal by 26 July and were landed beginning on 1 August at Mondego Bay. The 4th Royal Veteran Battalion remained aboard ship waiting to sail to Gibraltar.

Also sent in July were six 10-inch iron mortars and five 5½-inch brass mortars on beds. On 3 August, a howitzer and three pieces of artillery were attached to each brigade. The 9-pounders were attached to Ferguson's brigade and the remainder not allotted were to be in reserve. The 1/36th Regiment appears to have been assigned to Catlin Craufurd's brigade and the 1/45th Regiment appears to have been assigned to Fane's brigade. Spencer's corps arrived 6 August and landed over the next two days. Spencer's one artillery half-company came with four light 6-pounders and two 5½-inch light howitzers.

A General Order of 7 August reorganized the army as:

Commanding the force: Lieutenant General Wellesley
Second-in-command: Major General Spencer
Deputy Adjutant-General: Lieutenant Colonel Tucker
Deputy Quartermaster General: Lieutenant Colonel Bathurst
Artillery: Lieutenant Colonel Robe and Major Viney

1st Brigade: Major General Hill
1/5th Regiment   1/9th Regiment
1/38th Regiment

3rd Brigade: Brigadier General Nightingall
29th Regiment   1/82nd Regiment

5th Brigade: Brigadier General Catlin Craufurd
1/45th Regiment   1/50th Regiment
1/91st Regiment

4th Brigade: Brigadier General Bowes
1/6th Regiment   1/32nd Regiment

2nd Brigade: Major General Ferguson
36th Regiment   1/40th Regiment
1/71st Regiment

6th (or Light) Brigade: Brigadier General Fane
5/60th Regiment   4 companies 2/95th Regiment

Unbrigaded: 20th Light Dragoons

Artillery: Geary's Company (light 6-pounders), Raynsford's Company (9-pounders) and
    Lawson's Half-Company under Morrison (light 6-pounders). A half brigade
    (=battery) was attached to each infantry brigade and a howitzer to the 1st, 2nd, 5th
    and 6th Brigades and the 9-pounder brigade in reserve.

For an explanation of the infantry brigading sequence, see Chapter 4 – Order of
Battle.

On 8 August, Hill's brigade had two light 6-pounders and one 5½-inch light
howitzer under Raynsford, Ferguson's brigade had two light 6-pounders and one
5½-inch light howitzer under Locke, Nightingall's brigade had three light 6-
pounders under Graham, Bowes's brigade had three light 6-pounders under
Festing, C. Craufurd's brigade had two light 6-pounders and one 5½-inch light
howitzer under Morrison and Fane's brigade had two light 6-pounders and one
5½-inch light howitzer under Geary. Viney superintended the Reserve Half-
Brigades of three 9-pounders under Gardiner and two 9-pounders and one
5½-inch heavy howitzer under Eliot. This was the anticipated organization of the
artillery.

However, Robe was not able to horse all of the brigades and so three of
Lawson's guns were left aboard ship. After the army had advanced and reached
Leiria, Robe had to leave behind another three of Lawson's guns due to having to
consolidate the horses to draw Wellesley's original 18 guns.

On 14 August, Wellesley was reinforced by units of the Portuguese army under
Lieutenant Colonel Nicholas Trant:

6th Cavalry (104)   11th Cavalry (50)
12th Cavalry (104)   Cavalry of the police (41)
6th Caçadores (569)   12th Regiment (605)
21st Regiment (605)   24th Regiment (304)

On 18 August, a General Order assigned the 1/50th Regiment to the 6th Brigade
and assigned one company of the 5/60th Regiment to each of the five brigades

leaving five companies with the 6th Brigade. On 19 August, Anstruther's brigade arrived and was designated the 7th Brigade and on 20 August Acland's brigade arrived and was designated the 8th Brigade. On 20 August, Burrard arrived and assumed command of the army pending the arrival of Dalrymple. Also on 20 August, Moore's corps arrived at Mondego Bay and began to disembark. On the 22nd, it was re-embarked and ordered to Maceira Bay.

There had been a skirmish at Obidos 15 August, the Battle of Roliça fought 17 August (battle honour first awarded as Roleia) and the Battle of Vimeiro fought 21 August (battle honour awarded as Vimiera).

Wellesley's Corps at Vimeiro, 21 August, stood as:

Commanding the force: Lieutenant General Sir Arthur Wellesley
Second-in-command: Major General Brent Spencer
Deputy Adjutant General: Lieutenant Colonel George Tucker
Deputy Quartermaster-General: Lieutenant Colonel James Bathurst
Artillery: Lieutenant Colonel William Robe

1st Brigade: Major General Rowland Hill
1/5th Regiment   1/9th Regiment
1/38th Regiment   5/60th Regiment (1 company)

2nd Brigade: Major General Ronald Ferguson
36th Regiment   1/40th Regiment
1/71st Regiment   5/60th Regiment (1 company)

3rd Brigade: Brigadier General Miles Nightingall
29th Regiment   1/82nd Regiment
5/60th Regiment (1 company)

4th Brigade: Brigadier General Barnard Bowes
1/6th Regiment   1/32nd Regiment
5/60th Regiment (1 company)

5th Brigade: Brigadier General James Catlin Craufurd
1/45th Regiment   1/91st Regiment
5/60th Regiment (1 company)

6th (or Light) Brigade: Brigadier General Henry Fane
1/50th Regiment   5/60th Regiment (5 companies)
2/95th Regiment (4 companies)

7th Brigade: Brigadier General Robert Anstruther
2/9th Regiment   2/43rd Regiment
2/52nd Regiment   97th Regiment

8th Brigade: Brigadier General Wroth Palmer Acland
2nd Regiment   20th Regiment
1/95th Regiment (2 companies)

Unbrigaded: 20th Light Dragoons

A General Order of 21 August, issued after the Battle of Vimeiro, assigned the two companies of the 1/95th Regiment from the 8th Brigade to the 6th Brigade and assigned one company 5/60th Regiment each to the 7th and 8th Brigades, thus leaving only three companies with the 6th Brigade. On 21 August, Colonel John Harding arrived to command the artillery. A General Order of 22 August transferred the 97th Regiment to the 8th Brigade.

On 22 August, Dalrymple arrived and assumed command of the army. He immediately agreed to a suspension of hostilities and began to negotiate a convention for the withdrawal of French forces from Portugal, the Convention of Cintra. This was signed on 29/30 August. Also, on the 22nd, Dalrymple assigned most of the Vimeiro corps to Wellesley's command and the recently arrived reinforcements, with perhaps Acland's and Anstruther's Brigades to Moore's command. Charles Stewart arrived 23/24 August. Richard Fletcher took command of the Royal Engineers on 27 August.

Moore's corps arrived at Maceira Bay on 24 August and began landing on the 25th. The corps was ready to march by the 30th. Moore's original corps on landing stood as:

Lieutenant General Mackenzie Fraser's Division:
1/4th Regiment   1/28th Regiment
1/79th Regiment   1/92nd Regiment

Major General Murray's Division:
1st, 2nd, 5th and 7th Line Battalions, KGL

Major General E. Paget's Division:
1/52nd Regiment   1/95th Regiment (3 companies)
1st Light Battalion   2nd Light Battalion KGL
3rd Light Dragoons KGL   Garrison Company KGL

Artillery of Lieutenant Colonel George Wood and Major Julius Hartmann commanding the 2nd Company (Tieling's) KGL (originally part of Acland's brigade), 4th Company (Heise's) KGL, Drummond's Company, Wilmot's Company.

Arriving as reinforcements were the 18th Light Dragoons (arrived 1/2 September), Beresford with the 1/3rd Regiment and Thornhill's Company (from Madeira arrived 1/2 September) the 1/42nd Regiment, Skyring's Company 4th Battalion (120?) and Bredin's Company 8th Battalion (125) probably of four light 3-pounders and four 5½-inch light howitzers with 2 ammunition carts (from Gibraltar arrived 1/2 September). Crawford's Company (120?), originally part of Acland's brigade, arrived from Portsmouth 28 August. The 1st Company (Gesenius's) KGL only arrived at Lisbon on 8 September.

In a General Order of 5 September, Lieutenant General Dalrymple brigaded his army as:

Advanced Corps: Major General E. Paget

Anstruther's Brigade: Brigadier General Anstruther
2/9th Regiment   1/52nd Regiment
1/95th Regiment (5 companies)

Alten's Brigade: Colonel C. Baron Alten
1st Light Battalion KGL   2nd Light Battalion KGL

Cavalry Brigade: Brigadier General C. Stewart
18th Light Dragoons   20th Light Dragoons
3rd Light Dragoons KGL

1st Division: Lieutenant General Moore

Bentinck's Brigade: Major General Lord William Bentinck
1/4th Regiment   1/28th Regiment
1/42nd Regiment

R. Stewart's Brigade: Brigadier General R. Stewart
1/9th Regiment   2/43rd Regiment
2/52nd Regiment

5/60th Regiment (5 companies attached to the division)

2nd Division: Lieutenant General Hope

Ferguson's Brigade: Major General Ferguson
1/36th Regiment   1/71st Regiment
1/92nd Regiment

Acland's Brigade: Brigadier General Acland
2nd Regiment   20th Regiment
97th Regiment

5/60th Regiment (5 companies attached to the division)

3rd Division: Lieutenant General Mackenzie Fraser

Fane's Brigade: Brigadier General Fane
1/3rd Regiment   1/38th Regiment

Murray's Brigade: Major General Murray
1st Line Battalion   2nd Line Battalion
5th Line Battalion   7th Line Battalion KGL

4th Division: Lieutenant General Wellesley

Hill's Brigade: Major General Hill
1/5th Regiment   1/32nd Regiment
1/82nd Regiment

Beresford's Brigade: Major General Beresford
1/6th Regiment   1/45th Regiment
1/91st Regiment

Reserve: Major General Spencer

Nightingall's Brigade: Brigadier General Nightingall
29th Regiment   1/40th Regiment
1/50th Regiment

Cameron's Brigade: Brigadier General Cameron
1/79th Regiment   2/95th Regiment (4 companies)

Lieutenant General Lord Paget was to have overall command of the cavalry.

As early as 2 September, the Government designated another force to go to Portugal and Spain. This force was under the command of Lieutenant General Sir David Baird and was assembled in England and Ireland throughout September. It sailed from Falmouth on 8/9 October 1808 for Coruña.

During this time a number of general officers left the army to return home either on personal business or due to illness: Lord Paget (September) and Wellesley (20 September), Ferguson (20 September) and Spencer (October) and Nightingall (early October) and Bowes (back to Gibraltar?) were those who went. Brigadier General Cameron was appointed the Commandant of Lisbon.

When the news of the Convention reached Britain, it caused an uproar and a Board of Inquiry was established. This resulted in Dalrymple being recalled on 17 September and resigning the command on 3 October to Burrard. Dalrymple sailed on 5 October 1808 for Britain.

The British government then decided to assist the Spanish armies in the field and so separated their army in Portugal into two forces. One was to become a field army and advance into Spain and the other was to remain as the garrison of Portugal and provide assistance to the field army. On 25 September, Moore was notified that he was to command the field army and Burrard, that he was to command the Portugal Garrison. The change was announced in a General Order of 8 October.

At this point, the chapter will concentrate on Moore's army, then with the garrison remaining in Portugal and finish with Wellesley's army in April 1809.

Lieutenant General Sir John Moore's Army

In a General Order issued by Lieutenant General Burrard, on 8 October, the following were to serve on the staff of this army: Lieutenant Generals: Sir John Moore, John Hope and Alexander Mackenzie Fraser. Major Generals: Lord William Bentinck, Edward Paget, Brent Spencer, Rowland Hill and William Beresford. Brigadier Generals: Wroth Palmer Acland, Charles Stewart, Henry Fane, Robert Anstruther and James Catlin Craufurd. The commander of the Royal Artillery was Colonel John Harding. The Adjutant General was Brigadier General Henry Clinton and the Quartermaster-General was Lieutenant Colonel George Murray.

This list of general officers on the staff was later expanded to include:

Lieutenant Generals
Sir John Moore, Sir David Baird, John Hope, Alexander Mackenzie Fraser, Henry Lord
    Paget and Sir Arthur Wellesley.

Major Generals
Lord William Bentinck, Coote Manningham, Edward Paget, Rowland Hill, William
    Beresford, Ronald Ferguson, Henry Warde, James Leith and John Brodrick.

Brigadier Generals
John Slade, Moore Disney, Wroth Palmer Acland, Miles Nightingall, Charles Stewart,
    Henry Fane, Robert Anstruther and Charles Baron Alten.

Colonels
James Catlin Craufurd, Robert Craufurd and Robert Long.

J. C. Craufurd and R. Craufurd, although both Brigadier Generals with their
former commands, were only appointed as Colonels on the Staff of Moore's army.
No reason was given. Brevet Major Richard Fletcher was to accompany in
command of the Royal Engineers.

The units designated for Moore's corps were:

Cavalry Regiments:
18th Light Dragoons   3rd Light Dragoons KGL

Infantry Battalions:

1/4th	1/5th	1/6th
1/28th	1/32nd	1/36th
1/38th	1/42nd	2/43rd
1/52nd	2/52nd	5/60th
1/71st	1/79th	1/91st
1/92nd	1/95th (5 companies)	2/95th (4 companies)

1st and 2nd Light Battalions KGL

Due to the high number of sick in the regiments chosen to go into Spain, Burrard
added the 2nd, 1/9th and 20th from the Portugal Garrison to Moore's army.

On 8 October the army stood as:

Commanding the force: Lieutenant General Sir John Moore
Adjutant General: Brigadier General Henry Clinton
Quartermaster-General: Lieutenant Colonel George Murray
Royal Artillery: Colonel John Harding

Cavalry Brigade: Brigadier General Charles Stewart

18th Light Dragoons (672)
3rd Light Dragoons KGL (559)

Hope's Division: Lieutenant General John Hope

Craufurd's Brigade: Colonel James Catlin Craufurd

1/36th Regiment (871)	1/71st Regiment (864)
1/92nd Regiment (978)	5/60th Regiment (5 companies = 324)

Acland's Brigade: Brigadier General Wroth Palmer Acland
2nd Regiment (759)   1/6th Regiment (915)

Mackenzie Fraser's Division: Lieutenant General Alexander Mackenzie Fraser

Bentinck's Brigade: Lieutenant Colonel James Wynch (4th Regiment)
1/4th Regiment (962)   1/28th Regiment (1,037)
1/42nd Regiment (939)   5/60th Regiment (5 companies = 450)

Beresford's Brigade: Major General William Beresford
1/9th Regiment (945)   2/43rd Regiment (709)
2/52nd Regiment (623)

Paget's Division: Major General Edward Paget

Anstruther's Brigade: Lieutenant Colonel Robert Ross (20th Regiment)
20th Regiment (584)   1/52nd Regiment (874)
1/95th Regiment (5 companies = 495)

Alten's Brigade: Brigadier General Charles, Baron Alten
1st Light Battalion KGL (943)   2nd Light Battalion KGL (926)

Fane's Brigade: Brigadier General Henry Fane
1/38th Regiment (955)   1/79th Regiment (991)
2/95th Regiment (4 companies = 374)

Hill's Brigade: Major General Rowland Hill
1/5th Regiment (976)   1/32nd Regiment (876)
1/91st Regiment (900)

Artillery: Lieutenant Colonel George Wood, Major James Viney commanding
    Drummond's Company (light 6-pounders), Wilmot's Company (light 6-pounders),
    Carthew's Company (light 6-pounders), Crawford's Company (light 6-pounders),
    Raynsford's Company (9-pounders) with Thornhill's Company and Skyring's
    Company as the Park and Depot (686).

On 13 October, Burrard received orders to retain in Portugal only eight regiments, including four battalions of the King's German Legion, 20th Light Dragoons and artillery, the remainder were to go with Moore.

Before the advance into Spain, there already had occurred changes to the organisation of the army. On 7 September, Anstruther had been sent ahead to Almeida to provide information on the frontier and by 14 September Lord William Bentinck had been sent to Madrid on a diplomatic assignment, their brigades then being commanded by the senior battalion commanders in each. Acland returned on sick leave to Britain and his brigade was broken up with the 2nd Regiment posted to Catlin Craufurd's brigade and the 1/6th Regiment posted to garrison Almeida.

On 27 October as the army advanced into Spain, it stood as:

Mackenzie Fraser's Division: Lieutenant General Mackenzie Fraser

Bentinck's Brigade: Lieutenant Colonel Wynch

1/4th Regiment	1/28th Regiment
1/42nd Regiment	5/60th Regiment (5 companies)

Hill's Brigade: Major General Hill

1/5th Regiment	1/32nd Regiment
1/91st Regiment	

Wilmot's Company RA

This force, accompanied by Lieutenant General Moore, moved by Abrantes and Guarda to Salamanca.

Paget's Division: Major General E. Paget

Anstruther's Brigade: Lieutenant Colonel Ross

20th Regiment	1/52nd Regiment
1/95th Regiment (5 companies)	

Alten's Brigade: Brigadier General C. Baron Alten

1st Light Battalion KG	2nd Light Battalion KGL

This force moved by Elvas and Alcantara to Salamanca.

Hope's Division: Lieutenant General Hope

Cavalry Brigade: Brigadier General C. Stewart

18th Light Dragoons	3rd Light Dragoons, KGL

Craufurd's Brigade: Colonel Catlin Craufurd

2nd Regiment	1/36th Regiment
1/71st Regiment	1/92nd Regiment

Artillery: Colonel Harding, Lieutenant Colonel Wood, Major Viney with Drummond's Company, Carthew's Company, Crawford's Company, Raynsford's Company, Thornhill's Company and Skyring's Company.

This force moved by Badajoz and the Escurial to Salamanca.

Beresford's Brigade: Major General Beresford

1/9th Regiment	2/43rd Regiment
2/52nd Regiment	5/60th Regiment (5 companies)

Fane's Brigade: Brigadier General Fane

1/38th Regiment	1/79th Regiment
2/95th Regiment (4 companies)	

This force, under Beresford's temporary command, moved by Coimbra and Viseu to Salamanca.

As Moore's army advanced into Spain more changes occurred. By 22 October Moore had ordered the 1/3rd Regiment and the 1/50th Regiment to join his army. By 27 October, the 1/6th Regiment and 1/50th Regiment commanded by Brigadier General Moore Disney followed along the Abrantes–Guarda route. Disney, from the garrison of Sicily, had been on his way home to England and had stopped at Lisbon arriving 6 October. He was employed to reinforce Moore's army. The 1/3rd Regiment was escorting a waggon train of stores on the Abrantes–Guarda route.

On 13 November, five companies, 5/60th Regiment were ordered back to Portugal, but apparently only left at the end of November. The 1/3rd Regiment was then ordered to guard the sick and baggage train returning to Portugal. Its Grenadier Company remained with Moore's army attached to the 20th Regiment. The 1/82nd Regiment joined after 23 December. The regiment was the only one from a brigade (Alan Cameron, 1/45th Regiment; 1/82nd Regiment; 97th Regiment) sent to join Moore's army, that got through to it. This brigade had advanced from Oporto along the road to Zamora. The 1/6th Regiment joined on 22 December.

In a General Order of 17 November, Moore confirmed the appointment to serve on the staff of his army of Lieutenant Generals Sir David Baird, Henry, Lord Paget and Sir Arthur Wellesley, Major Generals Coote Manningham, Ronald Ferguson, John Brodrick, Henry Warde and James Leith, Brigadier Generals John Slade and Miles Nightingall with Colonel Robert Craufurd. However, Wellesley and Nightingall were not in orders to leave England after the Convention Inquiry ended (about 22 December) and then Wellesley returned to Ireland as the Chief Secretary and Nightingall was appointed to a different staff command. Ferguson only sailed for Spain in January 1809. Leith and Brodrick were placed on the staff for pay purposes as they were performing political assignments in Spain. They both later served in Moore's army.

The British government continued to look at reinforcing the army in Spain and the following were all reported as going on service: on 19 October, five cavalry brigades made up of Brigadier General Slade's with 7th and 10th Light Dragoons, Major General Cotton's with 14th and 16th Light Dragoons, Major General William Payne's with the 3rd Dragoon Guards and 4th Dragoons, Colonel John Dorrien's with the Royal Horse Guards, 2nd Dragoon Guards and 2nd Dragoons and another Light Cavalry Brigade; on 14 November, Moore was informed that two additional Horse Artillery Troops (Ross's A Troop and probably R. Macdonald's E Troop of 10 light 6-pounders and two 5½-inch light howitzers) and four regiments of cavalry would be embarked once the cavalry transports returned from Coruña; on 25 November the Horse Artillery Troops embarked on the transports; on 3 December, Payne's brigade embarked on the transports; on 7 December, Brigadier General Henry Campbell and the 2nd Brigade of Guards were reported as going on service. News that Moore and Baird were withdrawing from Spain, the first time, cancelled the cavalry and artillery embarkation.

On 1 December at Salamanca, Moore's army stood as:

Cavalry Brigade: Brigadier General C. Stewart
18th Light Dragoons   3rd Light Dragoons, KGL

Mackenzie Fraser's Division: Lieutenant General Mackenzie Fraser

Bentinck's Brigade: Major General Lord William Bentinck (rejoined 1 December)
1/4th Regiment   1/42nd Regiment
1/50th Regiment

Fane's Brigade: Brigadier General Fane
1/38th Regiment   1/79th Regiment

Hope's Division: Lieutenant General Hope

Hill's Brigade: Major General Hill
2nd Regiment   1/5th Regiment
1/32nd Regiment

Craufurd's Brigade: Colonel Catlin Craufurd
1/36th Regiment   1/71st Regiment
1/92nd Regiment

Paget's Division: Major General E. Paget

Anstruther's Brigade: Lieutenant Colonel Robert Ross
20th Regiment   1/52nd Regiment
1/95th Regiment (5 companies)

Disney's Brigade: Brigadier General Disney
1/28th Regiment   1/91st Regiment

Flank Brigade: Major General Beresford
1/9th Regiment   2/43rd Regiment
2/52nd Regiment   5/60th Regiment (5 companies)
2/95th Regiment (4 companies)

Flank Brigade: Brigadier General C. Baron Alten
1st Light Battalion KGL   2nd Light Battalion KGL

Unattached units: 1/6th Regiment   1/82nd Regiment

On 5 December the five companies, 5/60th Regiment were placed under Mackenzie Fraser's command and the next day they were ordered to return to Portugal escorting the heavy baggage, reserve ammunition and sick of Moore's army.

At Salamanca, Moore waited for the force sent from England. For the British government having decided to assist the Spanish armies, also decided to reinforce the army in Spain. This force, from the home garrisons, was under the command of Lieutenant General Baird.

At Cork on 12 September were Lieutenant General Sir David Baird with the 1st Brigade under Major General Coote Manningham of the 2/14th Regiment, 1/26th

Regiment, 2/31st Regiment and the 2nd Brigade under Brigadier General John Slade of the 3/1st Regiment, 2/23rd Regiment, 3/27th Regiment, 2/81st Regiment, Holcombe's Company 6th Battalion and Wall's Company 7th Battalion RA were at Cork. Collecting at Falmouth from Ramsgate, Harwich, Portsmouth and Jersey were a brigade of Guards under Major General Henry Warde and Colonel Robert Craufurd with the 1/43rd Regiment, 51st Regiment, 1/59th Regiment, 2/60th Regiment, 76th Regiment, 4 companies, 1/95th Regiment, 4 companies, 2/95th Regiment. Bean's Company and Truscott's Company both 3rd Battalion RA were at Falmouth.

On 22 September the force stood as:

Commanding the force: Lieutenant General Baird
Second-in-command: Major General Manningham
Artillery: Lieutenant Colonel John Sheldrake

Warde's Brigade: Major General Warde
1/1st Foot Guards (1356)	3/1st Foot Guards (1109)

Mackenzie's Brigade: Major General John Randoll Mackenzie (temporary)
51st Regiment (620)	2/59th Regiment (640)
2/60th Regiment (272)	76th Regiment (782)
2/81st Regiment (716)	

Slade's Brigade: Brigadier General Slade
3/1st Regiment (723)	1/26th Regiment (870)
3/27th Regiment (818)	2/31st Regiment (804)

Craufurd's Brigade: Colonel R. Craufurd
2/14th Regiment (630)	2/23rd Regiment (590)
1/43rd Regiment (912)	1/95th Regiment (4 companies = 367)
2/95th Regiment (4 companies = 405)	

Royal Artillery (402): Major Robert Beevor commanding Bean's Company, Truscott's Company, Holcombe's Company and Wall's Company of five 9-pounders, ten light 6-pounders, one 5½-inch heavy howitzer, two 5½-inch light howitzers, all with limbers and one 4 2/5-inch howitzer. Later, five 9-pounders, ten light 6-pounders, one 5½-inch heavy howitzer, two 5½-inch light howitzers, all with limbers and five 3-pounder mountain guns, on mountain carriages, were embarked for use with this force.

Changes however occurred almost immediately as Manningham took over Slade's Brigade. Slade was given command of a cavalry brigade:

7th Light Dragoons (eight troops = 672)
10th Light Dragoons (eight troops = 675)
15th Light Dragoons (eight troops = 674)

Lieutenant Colonel George Cookson RHA commanding Downman's B Troop and Evelegh's C Troop Royal Horse Artillery of ten light 6-pounders and two 5½-inch light howitzers (283).

This brigade, with Lieutenant General Henry Lord Paget, had been added to Baird's corps. The units were collecting at Portsmouth. Lord Paget was to command the cavalry of Moore's army. Mackenzie was placed on the staff at Lisbon but was to serve temporarily with Baird's corps. Major General Ronald Ferguson was on the staff of this corps, but due to being a witness at the Convention of Cintra Inquiry, did not immediately accompany it.

On 13 October, Baird's corps arrived off Coruña and on the 16th stood as:

Warde's Brigade: Major General Warde
1/1st Foot Guards   3/1st Foot Guards
Guards Flank Battalion (6 companies)

Mackenzie's Brigade: Major General Mackenzie (temporary)
51st Regiment   2/59th Regiment
2/60th Regiment   76th Regiment
2/81st Regiment

Manningham's Brigade: Major General Manningham
3/1st Regiment   1/26th Regiment
3/27th Regiment   2/31st Regiment

Craufurd's Brigade: Colonel R. Craufurd
2/14th Regiment   2/23rd Regiment
1/43rd Regiment   1/95th Regiment (4 companies)
2/95th Regiment (4 companies)

Baird's force began to land on 26 October. The 2/60th Regiment, being under strength, and Holcombe's Company were left as the Garrison of Coruña. Brodrick (being one of a number of officers used by Lord Castlereagh to report on the affairs in Spain) was appointed 25 September to superintend the landing and supplying of Baird's corps, but did not arrive at Coruña until 24 October. Baird appointed Brodrick the Commandant of Coruña by 4 November. The 3/27th and 2/31st Regiments did not arrive until 22 October and were sent on to Lisbon. They were to replace two regiments (1/3rd and 1/50th) from Portugal ordered forward by Moore. The 2/81st Regiment was transferred to Manningham's brigade.

By 19 November, Mackenzie was ordered to Lisbon by Burrard to take the command upon Burrard's departure and Leith (being one of a number of officers used by Lord Castlereagh to report on the affairs in Spain) was ordered by Moore for service with Baird's corps which was short of general officers.

The cavalry brigade with Lord Paget and Slade had not arrived in October. The 7th and 10th Light Dragoons arrived 7 November and the 15th Light Dragoons on 12 November. Cookson and Beevor with Downman's B Troop and Evelegh's C Troop arrived 8 November. In December, Baird was informed that the 14th Light Dragoons were to go first to Vigo and land there to join his corps if he thought necessary. (It went to Lisbon in late December.)

On Baird's advance to join Moore, he organized his corps about 19–23 November as:

Warde's Division: Major General Warde

Warde's Brigade: Colonel William Anson (1st Foot Guards)
1/1st Foot Guards   3/1st Foot Guards   Guards Flank Battalion (6 companies)

Craufurd's Brigade: Colonel Robert Craufurd
2/14th Regiment   2/23rd Regiment   1/43rd Regiment
1/95th Regiment (4 companies)   2/95th Regiment (4 companies)

Manningham's Division: Major General Manningham

Leith's Brigade: Colonel Robert Cheney (1st Foot Guards)
51st Regiment   2/59th Regiment   76th Regiment

Manningham's Brigade: Colonel Andrew Hay (1st Regiment)
3/1st Regiment   1/26th Regiment   2/81st Regiment

Cavalry: Lieutenant General Lord Paget and Brigadier General Slade
7th Light Dragoons   10th Light Dragoons
15th Light Dragoons

Lieutenant Colonel Cookson RHA with Downman's B Troop and Evelegh's C Troop

Artillery: Lieutenant Colonel Sheldrake and Major Beevor commanding Bean's
     Company, Truscott's Company, and Wall's Company which were attached to
     Warde's, R. Craufurd's and Manningham's brigades.

By 10 December, Leith was in temporary command of 3/1st Regiment, 1/26th
Regiment and 2/81st Regiment at Lugo. In December, left behind at Astorga were
Sheldrake(?) with Truscott's Company RA (light 6-pounders).
     On 20 December, Moore's Army and Baird's corps united at Mayorga and a
new organization was in orders:

1st Division: Lieutenant General Baird (Baird preferred an active command instead of
     being second-in-command)

Warde's Brigade: Major General Warde
1/1st Foot Guards   3/1st Foot Guards

Bentinck's Brigade: Major General Lord William Bentinck
1/4th Regiment   1/42nd Regiment   1/50th Regiment

Manningham's Brigade: Major General Manningham
3/1st Regiment   1/26th Regiment   2/81st Regiment

Bean's Company, RA

2nd Division: Lieutenant General Hope

Hill's Brigade: Major General Hill
2nd Regiment   1/5th Regiment   2/14th Regiment
1/32nd Regiment

Craufurd's Brigade: Colonel Catlin Craufurd
1/36th Regiment   1/71st Regiment   1/92nd Regiment

Leith's Brigade: Major General Leith (joined by 10 December)
51st Regiment   2/59th Regiment   76th Regiment

Drummond's Company, RA

3rd Division: Lieutenant General Mackenzie Fraser

Beresford's Brigade: Major General Beresford
1/6th Regiment   1/9th Regiment   2/23rd Regiment
2/43rd Regiment

Fane's Brigade: Brigadier General Fane
1/38th Regiment   1/79th Regiment   1/82nd Regiment

Wilmot's Company, RA

Reserve Division: Major General E. Paget

Disney's Brigade: Brigadier General Disney
1/28th Regiment   1/91st Regiment

Anstruther's Brigade: Brigadier General Anstruther (rejoined around 12–14 December)
20th Regiment   1/52nd Regiment   1/95th Regiment (9 companies)

Carthew's Company, RA

Flank Brigade: Colonel R. Craufurd
1/43rd Regiment   2/52nd Regiment   2/95th Regiment (8 companies)

Flank Brigade: Brigadier General Baron Alten
1st Light Battalion KGL   2nd Light Battalion KGL

Cavalry: Lieutenant General Lord Paget

Slade's Brigade: Brigadier General Slade
10th Light Dragoons   15th Light Dragoons

Stewart's Brigade: Brigadier General Stewart
7th Light Dragoons   18th Light Dragoons
3rd Light Dragoons, KGL   B Troop
C Troop, RHA

Reserve Artillery: Colonel Harding commanding Crawford's Company, Wall's
        Company, Raynsford's Company, Thornhill's Company and Skyring's Company.

By 25 December, the artillery was organized as: Harding with Cookson commanding Evelegh's C Troop RHA (light 6-pounders), Bean's Company (light 6-pounders) and Wilmot's Company (light 6-pounders) and Wood commanding Downman's B Troop RHA (light 6-pounders), Drummond's Company (light 6-pounders) and Carthew's Company (light 6-pounders). Viney commanding the reserve of Crawford's Company (light 6-pounders), Wall's Company (light 6-pounders), Raynsford's Company (9-pounders), and Brevet Major Robert Thornhill commanding both his company which acted as the park and Skyring's Company which acted as the advanced depot.

On 11 January 1809, Moore was informed that should he retire on the Tagus, Lieutenant General Cradock, who had succeeded Burrard, would be recalled from Portugal and the entire British Force in Spain and Portugal would be united under his command.

This then was the army which conducted the final campaign, with cavalry actions at Sahagun, 21 December 1808 and Benavente, 29 December 1808, ending in the Battle of Coruña, 16 January 1809, and evacuation of the army from Spain, which was completed on the 18th. Battle Honours were awarded for the cavalry action at Sahagun and for Coruña. Changes which occurred included Anstruther ill (died 14 January) and his brigade commanded by Lieutenant Colonel Robert Ross, 20th Regiment, Moore, mortally wounded and Baird severely wounded, 16 January. Command of the army devolved upon John Hope. Lord William Bentinck succeeded to the command of the 1st Division and his brigade was perhaps commanded by Lieutenant Colonel James Stirling, 1/42nd Regiment. Hill succeeded to the command of the 2nd Division and his brigade was perhaps commanded by Lieutenant Colonel Samuel Hinde, 1/32nd Regiment. Colonel Robert Long only arrived off of Coruña on 15 January.

Embarked by 15 January were the cavalry and all of the artillery except for seven light 6-pounders and one 5½-inch light howitzer, along with four Spanish 8-pounders, which were manned by Major Viney with Truscott's and Wilmot's Companies and fought at the Battle of Coruña. On the 17th, Major Beevor assisted by Brevet Major Thornhill with Thornhill's Company, Bean's Company and Truscott's Company helped man the land defences of Coruña with the Spanish to cover the evacuation. Viney's guns could not be embarked due to severe weather and were destroyed. Hill's Brigade and Beresford's Brigade formed the rearguard under Beresford's command.

By this time, the artillery had embarked from Portugal or Spain a total of 82 guns to England of fifteen 9-pounders with ten limbers, fifty-three light 6-pounders with nine limbers, three 5½-inch heavy howitzers with two limbers and eleven 5½-inch light howitzers with three limbers.

The British government continued to look at reinforcing the army in Spain and confirmed for foreign service on 14 December were the 1st, 3rd and 4th Dragoon Guards, 1st, 3rd and 4th Dragoons, 14th and 16th Light Dragoons, 1st and 2nd Light Dragoons KGL, 2nd Brigade of Foot Guards, 2/83rd, 2/87th and 1/88th Regiments with a staff to command the cavalry of Lieutenant General William Cartwright, Major General James Erskine and Brigadier General Fane (as Henry

Fane was already commanding a brigade in Spain, I believe, this may be an error for Major General Payne) and Major Generals Christopher Tilson and William Dyott for the infantry.

They had ordered out more reinforcements in December 1808, two brigades under Major General John Sherbrooke, for Spain (they sailed 15 January 1809). They were to support Baird's corps, if Baird could not join Moore's army and had remained in Galicia or they were to join Moore's army if they could. They eventually arrived at Lisbon by 13 March 1809. Meantime the Government had also tried to reinforce Baird's corps with a force under Ronald Ferguson and William Dyott. They sailed from Portsmouth in January 1809 for Coruña with detachments for the following regiments; 1st, 9th, 29th, 43rd, 50th and others. They sailed back to Britain in the convoy carrying the flank brigades of Craufurd and Alten from Vigo.

The British Garrison in Portugal

The garrison in Portugal on 26 September 1808, was to consist of:

Commanding the force: Lieutenant General Sir Harry Burrard
Appointed to the Staff:

Major Generals
John Murray and John Randoll Mackenzie

Brigadier Generals
Richard Stewart, George de Drieberg, Ernest Baron Langwerth and Alan Cameron

Deputy Adjutant General
Lieutenant Colonel Thomas Carey

Deputy Quartermaster-General
Colonel Rufane Donkin

Carey and Donkin had served as the Deputies of these departments with Burrard's force in July and August, 1808.

The units designated for the garrison were:

Cavalry:
20th Light Dragoons (four troops = 327)
3rd Light Dragoons KGL (detachment =145)

Infantry:

2nd (771)	1/3rd (940)	1/9th (925)
2/9th (644)	20th (578)	29th (777)
1/40th (926)	1/45th (872)	1/50th Regiment (937)
1/82nd (932)	97th (695)	1st Line Battalion (930)
2nd Line Battalion (756)	5th Line Battalion (745)	7th Line Battalion (671)
Garrison Company KGL (49)		

Artillery was under Lieutenant Colonel William Robe and Major Julius Hartmann with Bredin's Company, Lawson's half-company, 1st Company (Gesenius), 2nd Company (Tieling) and 4th Company (Heise), KGL Artillery. The guns of which were five brigades of spare guns consisting of one brigade of 12-pounders, three brigades of light 6-pounders and one brigade of 3-pounders with some howitzers.

Due to the high number of sick in the regiments chosen to go into Spain, Burrard added the 2nd, 1/9th and 20th to Moore's army. On 13 October, Burrard received orders to retain in Portugal eight regiments (including four battalions of the King's German Legion), 20th Light Dragoons and artillery, the remainder to go with Moore's force. On 18 October, Brigadier John Sontag (being one of a number of officers used by Lord Castlereagh to report on the affairs in Portugal) was left in Lisbon to look after the sick and forward supplies to the army in Spain. By 22 October Moore had ordered the 1/3rd and the 1/50th Regiments to join his army.

Burrard was recalled home by 1 November. He resigned the command and left Lisbon on 18 November. R. Stewart was in temporary command in Portugal as Murray was not in Portugal at this time and Mackenzie was serving with Baird's corps. Mackenzie having been ordered to Lisbon, arrived to take command by 29 November. Lieutenant General Sir John Cradock was appointed to the command in early November. He sailed for Portugal on 3 December 1808.

The 3/27th and 2/31st Regiments from Baird's corps arrived at Lisbon on 1 November. On 20 November, an order was received to send two weak battalions (3/27th and 2/31st) to Gibraltar in exchange for the 1/48th and 1/61st Regiments which were to join Moore's army and Cradock was informed that another cavalry regiment was being sent out and that the detachment of the 20th Light Dragoons could be sent to join their regiment in Sicily.

On 1 November, Lieutenant Colonel Robe reported the artillery in Portugal as nine light 6-pounders and three 5½-inch light howitzers in two brigades (originally landed with Wellesley's force); five medium 12-pounders, five heavy or long 6-pounders and two 5½-inch heavy howitzers in two brigades which were still aboard ship, never having been landed; four medium 12-pounders, twelve light 6-pounders, two 5½-inch heavy howitzers and two 5½-inch light howitzers in three brigades for the KGL artillery and four light 3-pounders and two (actually four) 5½-inch light howitzers in one brigade from Gibraltar. This made a total of 52 guns available to be horsed and sent forward to Moore's army, if requested by Colonel Harding as he had thought that he might require the heavy guns sent forward.

On 14 November the stations of the garrison were reported as:

Lisbon:

2/9th Regiment	3/27th Regiment
29th Regiment	2/31st Regiment
1st Line Battalion	2nd Line Battalion
5th Line Battalion	7th Line Battalion

Garrison Company, KGL with the 20th Light Dragoons and detachment 3rd Light
    Dragoons KGL and Bredin's Company, Lawson's Half-Company, 2nd and 4th
    Company KGL

Oporto:

1/45th Regiment	1/82nd Regiment
97th Regiment	1st Artillery Company KGL

Elvas:

1/40th Regiment	4th Artillery Company (Heise), KGL

When Cradock assumed command on 14 December 1808, the garrison consisted
of:

Appointed to the Staff:

Major Generals
John Murray, John Leveson Gower and John Randoll Mackenzie

Brigadier Generals
Richard Stewart, John Sontag, George de Drieberg, Ernest Baron Langwerth and Alan
    Cameron

Deputy Quartermaster-General
Colonel Rufane Donkin

Deputy Adjutant General
Brevet Lieutenant Colonel Duncan Darroch

Cavalry:
20th Light Dragoons
3rd Light Dragoons KGL (detachment)

Infantry:

2/9th	29th
1/40th	1/45th
97th	1st Line Battalion
2nd Line Battalion	5th Line Battalion
7th Line Battalion	Garrison Company KGL

Major Generals Murray and Leveson Gower were not in Portugal at this time.
Other units in the garrison included the 1/3rd and 5/60th Regiments arrived from
Spain and the 3/27th and 2/31st Regiments from Baird's corps. Major General
Stapleton Cotton and eight troops 14th Light Dragoons (672) from England
arrived on 21/22 December. On 24 December, six light 3-pounders with limbers
were embarked in England for service in Portugal.

The stations of the Portuguese Garrison on 6 January 1809 were:

Lisbon:

Lieutenant General Cradock; Major General Cotton; Brigadier Generals Sontag and
Baron Langwerth. Units: one-half of the 20th Light Dragoons; one-half of the 14th
Light Dragoons with detachment 3rd Light Dragoons, KGL attached; 29th
Regiment; 5 companies 5/60th Regiment; 1st Line Battalion; 2nd Line Battalion
and a Garrison Company KGL. Artillery was under Lieutenant Colonel William
Robe and Major Julius Hartmann with Bredin's Company, Lawson's Half-
Company, 1st Company (Gesenius) and 2nd Company (Tieling) KGL.

Almeida:

Brigadier General Cameron and units: 1/3rd Regiment; 1/45th Regiment; 97th Regiment.

Santarem:

Brigadier Generals Stewart and Drieberg and units: one-half 20th Light Dragoons; 2/31st
Regiment; 5th Line Battalion and 7th Line Battalion KGL;
Sacavem: Major General Mackenzie and units: one-half 14th Light Dragoons; 2/9th
Regiment; 3/27th Regiment; 5 companies 5/60th Regiment.

Elvas:

Colonel James Kemmis, 1/40th Regiment; 4th Artillery Company (Heise) KGL.

Cradock had tried to reinforce Moore's army in early December by sending
Cameron with the 1/45th, 1/82nd and 97th Regiments. Only the 1/82nd Regiment
got through and the others turned back. 26–29 December, R. Stewart and
Drieberg with 29th Regiment, 2/31st Regiment, 5th Line Battalion and 7th Line
Battalion KGL and half-brigades of light 6-pounders under Lawson and Rettberg
were sent to reinforce Moore's army; however, they only reached Castello Branco
and on 8 January they turned back to Abrantès. On 5 January, Cameron, with
1/45th Regiment, 97th Regiment and the convalescents of Moore's army,
advanced again into Spain, but on 9 January news of Moore's retreat caused him
to return. Cradock, on 14 January, ordered a brigade (probably commanded by
Mackenzie) of 14th Light Dragoons, 2/9th Regiment and 3/27th Regiment to
embark for Vigo and try to reach Moore's army from there. While still in the
Tagus, news of Moore's retreat caused them to disembark.

In February 1809, Mackenzie was dispatched to Cadiz with the 2/9th, 29th and
3/27th Regiments and Major Hartmann with Bredin's Company RA and the 4th
Company (Heise) KGL Artillery. They were again refused permission to land and
returned 11 March. Kemmis with the 1/40th Regiment was sent to garrison Seville.

In January and February 1809, Cameron had organized two battalions of
detachments from soldiers of Moore's army be left behind when that army went
to Spain. Later more of the sick and the stragglers from Moore's army in Spain
were added. On 6 February, they numbered about 1,463 rank and file. See Chapter
6 'Filling the Ranks'.

Reinforcements continued to arrive. On 4 March, more Royal Artillery landed
of May's Company 1st Battalion (127), Glubb's Company 5th Battalion (93) and
Sillery's Company 7th Battalion (120).

The Government had ordered out more reinforcements in December 1808 for

Spain (they sailed 15 January 1809). With news of Coruña, they were sent to Cadiz instead. Refused admittance they went to Lisbon, arriving by 13 March 1809. The force consisted of:

Commanding the force: Major General John Sherbrooke with Brigadier General Henry Campbell, 1/2nd (Coldstream) Foot Guards (1120); 1/3rd Foot Guards (1361) and Major General Christopher Tilson, 2/87th Regiment (710); 1/88th Regiment (758). The 2/83rd Regiment was also ordered, but did not embark with the other units. May's Company RA had been sent, from Lisbon, to meet this force at Cadiz and returned with it in March.

On 18 March the British garrison in Portugal stood as:

Commanding the force: Lieutenant General Cradock
Second-in-command: Major General Sherbrooke

Brigades of Major General Cotton and Brigadier General R. Stewart
14th Light Dragoons	3rd Light Dragoons KGL (detachment)
2/9th Regiment	29th Regiment
5/60th Regiment (5 companies)	97th Regiment

Guards Brigade: Brigadier General H. Campbell
1/2nd (Coldstream) Foot Guards	1/3rd Foot Guards

Brigades of Major General J. R. Mackenzie and Brigadier-General A. Cameron
3/27th Regiment	2/31st Regiment
1/45th Regiment	5/60th Regiment (5 companies)
1st Battalion of Detachments	

King's German Legion: Major General J. Murray with Brigadier Generals Drieberg and Langwerth
1st Line Battalion	2nd Line Battalion
5th Line Battalion	7th Line Battalion
Light Battalions and Garrison Company (detachments)	

Brigades of Major General Tilson and Brigadier General Sontag
20th Light Dragoons	1/3rd Regiment
2/87th Regiment	1/88 Regiment
2nd Battalion of Detachments	

At Seville: 1/40th Regiment

On 23 March, the artillery consisted of Robe and Hartmann commanding May's Company (light 6-pounders with the Guards), Glubb's Company (in Cascaes), Sillery's Company (light 6-pounders), Bredin's Company (reserve 6-pounders in Lisbon), Lawson's Company (light 3-pounders with the cavalry), 1st Company (Gesenius at Fort St Julian), 2nd Company (Tieling of light 6-pounders) and 4th Company (Heise of either heavy guns or position artillery as required).

The garrison continued to be reinforced as the British were reluctant to give up Portugal. On 2 April Colonel Edward Howorth arrived to command the artillery and with him came local Lieutenant Colonel Richard Fletcher to command the Royal Engineers. Also on 2 April, Lieutenant Colonels Hoylet Framingham and George Fisher of the artillery arrived. On 5 April reinforcements from Cork arrived under Major General Rowland Hill and Brigadier General Alexander Campbell with the 2/7th, 2/30th, 2/48th, 2/53rd, 2/66th and 2/83rd Regiments.

The force in Portugal was reorganized 6 April as:

First Line:
King's German Legion: Major General J. Murray with Brigadier Generals Drieberg and
       Langwerth
1st Line Battalion (748)   2nd Line Battalion (801)
5th Line Battalion (765)   7th Line Battalion (721)
Garrison Company (49)   detachment Light Battalions KGL (144)

Guards Brigade: Brigadier General H. Campbell
1/2nd (Coldstream) Foot Guards (1198)
1/3rd Foot Guards (1229)

Mackenzie's Brigade: Major General J. R. Mackenzie
3/27th Regiment (811)   2/31st Regiment (784)
1/45th Regiment (856)

Tilson's Brigade: Major General Tilson
1/3rd Regiment (856)   2/87th Regiment (710)
1/88 Regiment (758)

Stewart's Brigade: Brigadier General R. Stewart
29th Regiment (726)   1st Battalion of Detachments (828)

Second Line:
Sontag's Brigade: Brigadier General Sontag
97th Regiment (660)   2nd Battalion of Detachments (731)

Campbell's Brigade: Brigadier General A. Campbell
2/7th Regiment (576)   2/53rd Regiment (699)

Cameron's Brigade: Brigadier General Cameron
2/30th Regiment (630)   2/83rd Regiment (850)

Reserve:
Cavalry Brigade: Major General Cotton
14th Light Dragoons (8 Troops = 672)
3rd Light Dragoons KGL (detachment = 123)
20th Light Dragoons (4 Troops = 304)

Hill's Brigade: Major General Hill
2/48th Regiment (717)   5/60th Regiment (838)
2/66th Regiment (667)

In Lisbon were the 2/9th Regiment (645) and at Seville the 1/40th Regiment (871).

On 10 April, the artillery (949) was organized as: Colonel Howorth, Lieutenant Colonel Framingham, Lieutenant Colonel Robe, Lieutenant Colonel Fisher and Major Hartmann: consisting of May's Company (under Baynes) of five light 6-pounders and one 5½-inch howitzer, Sillery's Company (under Lane) of four light 6-pounders and two 5½-inch howitzers, Lawson's Company of six light 3-pounders, 2nd Company (Tieling's under Rettberg) of five light 6-pounders and one 5½-inch howitzer and 4th Company (Heise's) of five heavy or long 6-pounders and one 5½-inch howitzer. Glubb's Company, Bredin's Company and 1st Company (Gesenius's) garrisoned the Lisbon forts.

On 15 April, 8 troops 16th Light Dragoons (672) from Falmouth arrived at Lisbon.

When the British government finally decided not to evacuate Portugal, but to continue the struggle, they chose Lieutenant General Sir Arthur Wellesley once again to command. He was to supersede Sir John Cradock as the Commander-in-Chief in Portugal. Cradock was appointed to the staff at Gibraltar. Wellesley was informed of his appointment on 2 April 1809. He arrived in Lisbon on 22 April.

Lieutenant General Sir Arthur Wellesley's Army

Wellesley assumed command of the army at Lisbon on 27 April 1809. It consisted of:

Appointed to the staff: Lieutenant Generals John Sherbrooke, William Payne, Lord William Bentinck and Edward Paget. Major Generals Stapleton Cotton, Rowland Hill, John Murray, James Erskine, John Randoll Mackenzie and Christopher Tilson. Brigadier Generals Alexander Campbell, Henry Campbell, Richard Stewart, Alan Cameron, Henry Fane, George de Drieberg, Ernest Baron Langwerth and Colonel Rufane Donkin. Its Adjutant General was Brigadier General Charles Stewart and its Quartermaster-General was Colonel George Murray.

The units were those already in Portugal and the following embarked or under orders to proceed there:

Eight troops, 3rd Dragoon Guards (Portsmouth) (672)
Eight troops, 1st Dragoons (Cork) (672)
Eight troops, 4th Dragoons (Portsmouth) (672)
1st Light Dragoons KGL (Ipswich) (606)
2/24th Regiment (Jersey) (780)

When Wellesley assumed command on 27 April, the army was organized from 22 April, or in orders as:

Commanding the force: Lieutenant General Wellesley
Second-in-command: Lieutenant General Sherbrooke
Adjutant General: Brigadier General C. Stewart
Quartermaster-General: Colonel G. Murray

Cotton's Brigade: Major General Cotton
14th Light Dragoons 3rd Light Dragoons KGL (detachment)
16th Light Dragoons 20th Light Dragoons (2 squadrons)

Fane's Brigade: Brigadier General Fane
3rd Dragoon Guards 4th Dragoons

Guards Brigade: Brigadier General H. Campbell
1/2nd (Coldstream) Foot Guards 1/3rd Foot Guards

1st Brigade: Major General Hill
1/3rd Regiment 2/48th Regiment
2/66th Regiment

2nd Brigade: Major General Mackenzie
3/27th Regiment 2/31st Regiment
1/45th Regiment

3rd Brigade: Major General Tilson
5/60th Regiment 2/87th Regiment
1/88th Regiment

4th Brigade: Brigadier General Sontag
97th Regiment 2nd Battalion of Detachments

5th Brigade: Brigadier General A. Campbell
2/7th Regiment 2/53rd Regiment

6th Brigade: Brigadier General R. Stewart
29th Regiment 1st Battalion of Detachments

7th Brigade: Brigadier General Cameron
2/9th Regiment 2/83rd Regiment

King's German Legion: Major General J. Murray

1st Brigade: Brigadier General Langwerth
1st Line Battalion 2nd Line Battalion
Light Battalions (detachment)

2nd Brigade: Brigadier General Drieberg
5th Line Battalion 7th Line Battalion

Unbrigaded:
2/24th Regiment 2/30th Regiment
1/40th Regiment Garrison Coy, KGL

The artillery was still organized under the command of Colonel Howorth as it had been on 10 April.

The 16th Light Dragoons were on the march to join Wellesley's army. The

2/24th Regiment (at Lisbon 24 April), 3rd Dragoon Guards and 4th Dragoons (at Lisbon 27/28 April) had just landed. These three units were instructed to join Mackenzie's force. Mackenzie with his brigade, Fane's Cavalry Brigade and May's Company RA under Baynes (light 6-pounders) were to remain on the line of the Tagus river and guard Abrantes to Santarem. The 1/40th Regiment remained with the garrison in Seville, although arrangements were being made to have it join the main army.

Left in Lisbon were the Town Major, Brevet Lieutenant Colonel Anthony Walsh with the 2/30th Regiment; Garrison Company KGL; and Lieutenant Colonel Fisher RA with Glubb's Company, Bredin's Company and 1st Company (Gesenius) KGL in the Lisbon forts.

Not joined until May were E. Paget, Payne and J. Erskine. Expected to arrive were the 1st Light Dragoons KGL and the 23rd Light Dragoons (672?) to form a brigade under Erskine. Payne was to command the cavalry. Lord William Bentinck declined his staff appointment with the army. Apparently in April, Wellesley knew that the Light Brigade (Brigadier General Robert Craufurd with the 1/43rd, 1/52nd, and 1/95th Regiments) and Horse Artillery (probably Ross's A Troop and Bull's I Troop) were to be ordered to Portugal and requested that they be sent as soon as possible. Although Sontag was with the army in Portugal, he was not confirmed in orders to be placed upon the staff until early May.

In April, Marshal William Beresford now commanding the Portuguese army organized a portion of it to operate under Wellesley's command.

Two regiments, the 10th Regiment of two battalions and the 16th Regiment of two battalions (with a unit known as the 1st Portuguese Grenadiers formed from the Grenadier Coys of the 1/6th & 2/6th and the 2/18th Regiments) were to be integrated into British Brigades with Wellesley's army.

Under Marshal Beresford's immediate command to join the main army were:

1st Cavalry Regiment (3 squadrons)

Blunt's Brigade: Brigadier Richard Blunt
2/1st Regiment	1/7th Regiment
2/7th Regiment	1/19th Regiment
2/19th Regiment	

Artillery of 3 Portuguese Batteries perhaps under Major Victor von Arentschildt of 6-pounders, light 3-pounders and English 3-pounder mountain guns manned by companies of the 4th Artillery Regiment.

Beresford was to also incorporate the following under his command:

Bacellar's Brigade: Major General Manoel Bacellar
1/9th Regiment	1/11th Regiment
2/11th Regiment	
6th and 12th Cavalry Regts (two squadrons)	

Sousa's Brigade: Major General José Lopes de Sousa
1/2nd Regiment   2/2nd Regiment
1/14th Regiment   2/14th Regiment

Silveira's Brigade: Brigadier Francisco da Silveira
1/12th Regiment   2/12th Regiment
1/24th Regiment   2/24th Regiment
Militia of the Bragança and Moncorvo Regiments

Wilson's Brigade: Brigadier Sir Robert Wilson
3rd *Caçadores*   6th *Caçadores*

Mousinho's Brigade: Brigadier Brito Mousinho
Militia of the Miranda   Vila Real and Chaves Regiments

To be assigned to Major General Mackenzie's command on the line of the Tagus river:

Cavalry Brigade: Brigadier Manuel de Lusignano, Conde de Sampaio
4th Regiment   7th Regiment (5 squadrons)

Campbell's Brigade: Brigadier William Campbell
1/1st Regiment   1/3rd Regiment
1/4th Regiment   2/4th Regiment
1/13th Regiment   2/13th Regiment
1/15th Regiment

Lecor's Brigade: Colonel Carlos Lecor
1st *Caçadores*   4th *Caçadores*
5th *Caçadores*

Militia from the garrison of Abrantes of the Santarem, Thomar and Covilhã Regiments
      under a Colonel Leça.

Artillery of three Portuguese Batteries perhaps of 6-pounders and 3-pounders.

On 27 April 1809, Wellesley issued instructions to Sherbrooke to begin the advance of the army on 29 April. This then was the beginning of the Peninsular Army's journey down that long road to the final victory and forever being known as Wellington's Army.

Chapter Three

British Observing Officers of the Peninsular War

Robert Burnham

'Sir, the loss of a brigade could scarcely have been more felt by me; I am quite in the dark about the movements of the enemy and as to the reinforcements which they expected.'

Wellington on Major Colquhoun Grant's capture[1]

One of the enduring legends of the Peninsula War is that of the British Observing Officer. This officer, at great risk to himself, would range far ahead of Wellington's army, gathering vital information on the enemy. The French often would know of his whereabouts but could never catch him, because he was mounted on a superb English thoroughbred horse that could easily outrun his pursuers. The information he sent back to Wellington was so critical that the war would have been lost without him. But despite their near mythical adventures, very little has been written on the Observing Officers. Little is know about who they were, what their mission was, how they transmitted information back to Wellington, or even their more notable exploits.

The Setting

Neither the French nor the British were prepared for conducting operations in the Iberian Peninsula. In many ways, Spain and Portugal were alien environments for them. Few officers had ever been there, and little was known about terrain or road networks. Maps and guidebooks were outdated, often inaccurate, or would only show major roads and terrain features. S.G.P. Ward states that: 'The best description of Portugal was P. Joao de Castro's *Roteiro Terrestre de Portugal*, published sixty years previously . . . For Spain great use was made of what is always referred to as 'the Spanish Road-Book.' This may have been one of several in existence: Campomane's *Itinerário* of 1761, Bernardo Espinalt's *Guia General* of 1804, or Juan Muñoz Escribano's *Guia Genera* of 1796. But whichever it was, it was found to be untrustworthy at an early stage in the war, and it does not appear to have been used except for determining halts on well-established routes. In fact, none of these books could be of very great value to a commander in the field.' [2]

Compounding the problem was the fact that – even when guides or local liaison officers were available – they frequently had little knowledge to offer. For the French this was particularly critical, due to the general hostility of the local populace, which made reconnaissance dangerous.

Organization

The British Army had no intelligence branch from which officers were drawn for duty. Instead, their senior commanders tasked officers on an ad hoc basis. The information requested by these commanders was commonly of three distinct types: topographical information, intelligence on the enemy, and local political conditions. Many times these missions overlapped, but just as often they did not.

For topographical intelligence, Wellington made great use of his trained engineers, who were tasked to map those areas of Portugal and Spain where the British Army would be operating. But engineers were not the only ones sent. According to S.G.P. Ward, during the planning for the 1813 Campaign that would advance into the northern part of Spain, Wellington's Quartermaster General, George Murray:

> sent two officers from each of three British cavalry brigades, and one from two of the divisions to examine the roads as far as the frontier; one D.A.Q.M.G. (Bainbrigge[3]) to examine the Trás-os-Montes between the Sabor and the Douro, a second (Broke[4]) in the country between the Sabor and the Tua, and a third officer (Mitchell) to examine the region north of the Douro from its junction with the Esla to Benavente. Four officers were also sent to examine the passages of the Douro. Within five weeks, the information collected by these men had been collated; the routes were issued; and before another fortnight had passed, the troops had moved from their cantonments to the assembly area and had crossed two large rivers with the loss of only half a dozen men, a few horses, and two waggons, without losing any of the time allowed. This achievement (a complete surprise to the French, as it proved), by which over 50,000 men with artillery, countless horses, baggage animals, and bullocks were moved punctually over 150 miles of roads, upon none of which Wellington nor any of his principal staff officers had ever set eyes, is sufficient testimony of the experience these men had acquired and of the reliance that could be placed upon them in default of other information.[5]

For intelligence on the enemy and on the local political situation, Wellington employed what is best known as the Observing or Scouting Officers. According to Sir Charles Oman, these officers 'were all good horsemen, good linguists in Spanish, French, and Portuguese, and noted for resourcefulness and cool heads.' Captain Rees Gronow, of the 1st Foot Guards, left the following description of Lieutenant Colonel John Waters, one of the most famous of the observing officers:

> He was one of those extraordinary persons that seem created by kind nature for particular purposes; and without using the word in an offensive sense, he was the most admirable spy that was ever attached to an army. One would almost have thought that the Spanish war was entered upon and carried on in order to display his remarkable qualities. He could assume the character of Spaniards of every degree and station, so as to deceive the most acute of those whom he delighted to imitate. In the posada of the village he was hailed

by the contrabandist or the muleteer as one of their own race; in the gay assemblies he was an accomplished *hidalgo*; at the bullfight the toreador received his congratulations as from one who had encountered the *toro* in the arena; in the church he would converse with the friar upon the number of Ave Marias and Paternosters which lay a ghost, or tell him the history of every one who had perished by the flame of the Inquisition, relating his crime, whether carnal or anti-Catholic; and he could join in the *sequadilla* or in the *guaracha*.

But what rendered him more efficient than all was his wonderful power of observation and accurate description, which made the information he gave so reliable and valuable to the Duke of Wellington. Nothing escaped him. When amidst a group of persons, he would minutely watch the movement, attitude, and expression of every individual that composed it; in the scenery by which he was surrounded he would carefully mark every object: not a tree, not a bush, not a large stone, escaped his observation; and it was said that in a cottage he noted every piece of crockery on the shelf, every domestic utensil, and even the number of knives and forks that were got ready for use at dinner.

His acquaintance with the Spanish language was marvellous; from the finest works of Calderon to the ballads in the patois of every province he could quote, to the infinite delight of those with whom he associated. He could assume any character that he pleased; he could be the Castilian, haughty and reserved; the Asturian, stupid and plodding; the Catalonian, intriguing and cunning; the Andalusian, laughing and merry; in short, he was all things to all men. Nor was he incapable of passing off, when occasion required, for a Frenchman; but as he spoke the language with a strong German accent, he called himself an Alsatian. He maintained that character with the utmost nicety; and as there is a strong feeling of fellowship, almost equal to that which exists in Scotland, amongst all those who are born in the departments of France bordering on the Rhine, and who maintain their Teutonic originality, he always found friends and supporters in every regiment in the French service.[6]

Another contemporary description of an Observing or 'Exploring' Officer was that of Captain Colquhoun Grant. It was written by his brother-in-law, Sir James McGrigor, who was Wellington's Surgeon General:

Colquhoun Grant had a singular talent, not only for the acquisition of languages, but of the different dialects of languages. He was a proficient in those of all the provinces of Spain; was intimately acquainted with their customs, their songs, their music, and with all their habits and prejudices. He was, moreover, an enthusiastic admirer of the Spanish character; was well read in all their popular works; he danced even their national dances most admirably. With such qualifications and predilections so flattering to the national sentiment of the Spaniards, in union with a character of the most rigid morality, it will not be surprising that he was a favourite with them; particularly with their priests and peasantry, who spread his name and character so widely, and were so devotedly attached to him that in most critical situations, and when surrounded by posts of the French Army, he was at all times secure.[7]

Their Numbers

The exact numbers of these intelligence-gathering officers is open to debate. Oman states that there were only four, while John Fortescue states there were six. Ward says there at least fifteen British officers.[8] The ones that have been identified are:

Lieutenant Colonel John Grant, 4th Foot & Loyal Lusitanian Legion (Granto Malo)
Lieutenant Colonel John Waters, 1st Foot (Royal Scots)
Major Colquhoun Grant, 11th Foot (Granto Bueno)
Captain Henry S. Blanckley, 23rd Foot
Captain John Burrows, 57th Foot
Captain Charles Cocks, 16th Light Dragoons
Captain Andrew Leith Hay, 29th Foot
Captain James Jones, 87th Foot
Captain Lewis Rumann, 97th Foot
Lieutenant John Alyling, 40th Foot
Lieutenant Samuel C. Grey, 71st Foot
Lieutenant George Hillier, 29th Foot
Lieutenant Henry Mellish, 87th Foot

Ward also identified two Portuguese officers and four Spanish officers who served as Observing Officers:

Captain José Clemente Pereira (Portuguese Army)
Captain Beirimhof Daubrawa (Portuguese Army)
Major Pierre Baradiu (Spanish Army)
Captain José O'Ryan (Spanish Army)
Captain Tomás Connolly (Spanish Army)
Lieutenant Ange Auberge (Spanish Army)

Mode of Operations

One of the myths surrounding the Observing Officers was that they travelled by themselves on fast steeds that could quickly outdistance any French pursuit. This picture is not totally accurate. John Grant usually did travel alone. However, Captain Charles Cocks many times had a troop or squadron of light dragoons as an escort. Captain Leith Hay usually only travelled with an English groom; while Colquhoun Grant had an escort of Spanish guerrillas.

The Observing Officer usually would find a safe haven to operate from, leaving his entourage and spare horses there. He would go out alone or with one or two companions, sometimes for days, returning to his base for rest and replenishment of his supplies. Often these bases gave only the illusion of safety. In one case, Colquhoun Grant avoided being captured in 1810 by jumping out of a window, but was forced to leave all of his kit, papers, and horses behind! Leith Hay was not so fortunate. In 1813, a peasant revealed to the French where he was staying and:

About two o'clock, a violent knocking was heard at the outer gateway, which speedily gave way before the force applied to break it down, and soon after the court was filled with French infantry. The house, although spacious, was but of one storey in height; the windows were slightly elevated from the court, which, of considerable extent, was surrounded by a lofty wall. There could not for an instant be a doubt as to what had happened; the enemy's troops had succeeded in surprising me, and a last but hopeless effort at escape was the sole alternative. Extinguishing the lamp which burnt in my room, I locked the door, retiring into a chamber to the back of the house, the entrance to which I also secured, and attempted to force through a window, the only one in the apartment, which I had not previously inspected, but which proved to be closely grated with iron bars. No other egress presenting itself, my fate became inevitable . . . I walked forward, surrendering to Captain Acoste . . .[9]

Obtaining Information

The type of information that the Observing Officer obtained included what he personally saw and what others reported to him. The better officers would set up networks of informers throughout an area, who would brief him on those items of military activity that occurred while he was gone. Those people who provided information to the Observing Officers ranged from local guerrilla leaders and village headmen to smugglers and farmers. In many cases, the French had so abused the local populace that most were willing to provide information to the British (but sometimes for a price). In 1808, a key of piece of information that was vital to the safety of the British expeditionary force under Sir John Moore, was obtained by John Waters, then a captain. According to Edward Fraser:

Captain Waters, acting as an aide-de-camp with the cavalry, was scouting by himself far in advance of the army. While so doing, at the village of Valdestillos, near Sahagun, to the north of Valladolid, he intercepted a dispatch of the utmost urgency from Marshal Berthier, Napoleon's Chief of the Staff, to marshal Soult. It announced that the Spanish armies Sir John Moore was marching to join had been defeated and scattered, and that Madrid had surrendered, and had been in the complete possession of the French for the past ten days. Napoleon himself, the dispatch stated, was rapidly moving at the head of greatly superior forces to attack Moore's Army, and orders had been sent to the other French armies in Northern Spain to concentrate and close round the British so as to hold them fast, enormously outnumbered, as in a net. Soult was to push across so as to cut off Moore's retreat and bar him from reaching the coast.

The dispatch fell into Captain Waters' hands by a strange chance. It had been sent in the care of a young French staff officer, riding very imprudently, without an escort. He had ridden safely for over 150 miles until he reached Valdestillos, where he halted at the posting-house – the village inn – to get a fresh horse. The villagers, as it befell, were celebrating a local festival on that day and holding revel, and dancing in front of the inn at the moment the French officer rode up. In a loud and arrogant tone he called for the innkeeper. The man was dancing among the rest, and shouted back to the officer that he would have to wait: he was going to finish his dance first. The French Captain lost his temper, swore at the Spaniard, swung himself out of his saddle, and striding in hot anger into the middle of the dancers, roughly laid hold of the innkeeper and tried to drag him away to go and get the horse. The man resisted, and the girl he had been dancing with joined in the scuffle. She freed her partner, shoving back the officer, who in a fury shouted in her face a brutal insult. Whipping out a knife from her garter for answer, the girl stabbed the young Frenchman to the heart then and there. The dead man's valise was searched and the dispatch was found. As that took place Captain Waters came riding up.

The document was of little use to the Spanish peasants, who had no idea of its importance, nor thought of the British General in the matter. They would, however, not part with it. Captain Waters had to use all his arts of cajolery to get them to give it up to him. The innkeeper refused to let it go for less than twenty dollars.[10]

Andrew Leith Hay cultivated extensive contacts among partisan leaders, *alcaldes*, magistrates, as well as peasants and local nobles. Often the information was provided freely, but other times with reluctance. Leith Hay records in 1813 that:

On the forenoon of the former day, after ascertaining the departure of the enemy's troops from Ciudad Real, I passed the Guadiana, and entered that town. I was received with a restraint and ill-dissembled reluctance that convinced me the French were not far distant; and to the Spaniard who accompanied me it was explained, that receiving a British officer with cordiality would be reported by the persons in their interest immediately on the return of the enemy, which was confidently expected, and would produce, under these circumstances, effects of a ruinous character to them and their families.[11]

Missions

The type of information the Observing Officer sought would vary, depending on what he had been tasked to look for, and where he was sent. Officers did not just report on the French, but also provided topographical information and intelligence on local political and economic situations. Records of some of their missions still survive. For example, in late 1809, Captain Charles Cocks – a British officer assigned to the 16th Light Dragoons – was sent into southern Spain to observe what he could on the local situation. It was a fortuitous move, for at this time, the French were moving into Andalusia to seize Seville and Cadiz.

On 20 September 1810 Wellington informed his cavalry commander:

You see that the enemy have all crossed the Mondego and I propose that you should cross tomorrow . . . Be so kind as to leave on this side of the Mondego an intelligent officer, either Krauchenberg or Cordemann or Cocks, with about a squadron to observe the enemy's movements between the Dao and the Mondego, and do take care to keep up communication with him.

Captain Cocks had been on the right flank of the British Army with a squadron of light cavalry since early summer, with orders to provide early warning of French movements along the southern route towards Guarda. His new orders were basically a continuation of the orders he was already carrying out. By the time he was back with the main force of the British Army, Captain Cocks had been in front of the French Army for three months, as the British retreated from Almeida to Busaco. There he rejoined his regiment, which was part of the cavalry force screening the British retreat to the Lines of Torres Vedras.[12]

And then, in 1812 Major Colquhoun Grant was sent to determine the exact location of the French divisions in the Army of Portugal, and whether they would make an attempt to retake Cuidad Rodrigo. While the following year, Captain Andrew Leith Hay was sent to the vicinity of Toledo to observe the military and political situation in the area.

Reports

Very few of the reports Observing Officers sent back survive today. Fortunately, Captain Cocks kept a detailed diary, containing copies of his reports to Wellington. It is a gold mine of information on French military activities, Spanish forces, road conditions, the size of towns, and the attitude of local populations towards the French. The following letter is dated 21 January 1810, and was written in the town of Cabeza del Buey, which is located in south-eastern Estramadura, about 150 kilometres from Seville:

My Lord,
    In compliance with the wishes of Colonel Roche,[13] in a letter from whom I have the honour to enclose, and my own earnest desire to render myself of any use to the service that lay in my power, I left Carolina the 16th ult, and passing the Spanish cordon, crossed the route pursued by the French corps which has entered Andalusia.
    The Sierra Morena to the west of Almoden branches off into various ramifications, diverging from each other. The most northern passes in nearly a direct line to Santa Marta, on the road between Badajoz and Sevilla, the most southern inclines to the Guadalquivir and follows the course of that river. Between these and the intermediate ranges of mountains are plains, some leagues in width and producing considerable supplies.
    In the northern branch of the mountain is situated Almoden del Roque, a point of union to most of the communication between Estramadura and La Mancha on the one hand and Andalusia on the other. This was the extreme of the Spanish line and occupied by General Serain. His division

consisted nominally of 3 or 5,000 men but, in reality, was composed of only a few hundred, ill-armed and worse clothed.

From Almoden proceed two carriage roads to the south, one by Cordoba, the other by Llerena and Monasterio to Sevilla. From Cordoba to Almoden is 22 leagues and from Sevilla 39. Both these roads are bad, particularly that to Cordoba, but both practicable for artillery. The road to Sevilla is called the Camino de los Plate and is the route by which the quicksilver is transported from the mines of Almoden. Besides these, there are other routes practicable to cavalry both to Cordoba and Sevilla.

The advanced guard of the enemy entered Almoden on the 16th ult having marched by Abenojar and Zazuela. General Serain fell back without resistance to Campo Alto, a pass 4 leagues to the north of Cordoba, and where he has been reinforced by troops from that and the adjacent cities.

On the 17th the 1st Division of French infantry occupied Almoden, the cavalry were pushed forward to Alamillo and Santa Euphemia, it was, in fact, dispersed in every direction. I believe it may be estimated at 4,000 and the infantry at 5,000, with 30 pieces of artillery. Passports opened from Almoden were signed by Pilgash Chef de l'Etat, Major du Premier Corps d'Armée.

The 2nd Division, said to be commanded by Soult, marched the same day from Abenojar. On the 19th, after a day's halt, the advanced cavalry, crossing the second range of mountains, entered the plains where Los Suit Villas or Los Pedroches de Cordoba are situated; these are seven towns each distant a league from the other. Puerto Blano, which is the principal, contains near 2,000 inhabitants; 2,000 cavalry are encamped at Torre Camp, about 8 leagues from Almoden and the remainder were cantoned in the other towns. One division of infantry followed the cavalry, the remainder without the artillery pursued the carriage road by Santa Euphemia and Puerto Blano.

During the 16, 17, 18, 19th, they put almost every town in requisition within the distance of 5 or 6 leagues; on the 20th the cavalry were again en route.

I feel mortified that I cannot give your Lordship more certain accounts of the number of enemy, but no dependence can be placed on the flying rumours in circulation and the Spanish officers whom I have seen, although pushed forward for the express purpose of reconnoitring, are too torpid or too cautious to gain information.

Comparing, however, the various accounts I have received in the different towns where the enemy has passed, I do not think his force on the 20th, south of Almoden, exceeded 20,000 and on that day he had no troops either in Almoden or Alamillo. Had I fortunately left Carolina two days sooner I might have concealed myself 3 leagues from Almoden in a point which commands the road and seen the whole of his left column defile at the distance of 400 yards.

It will scarcely seem probable to your Lordship that, with this movement only, the enemy thinks of penetrating Sevilla but perhaps he expects that his movement on the left of the Spaniards will compel the latter to abandon their present position and, in that case, another column will pour down through Despena Perros and Almoden del Roque and will then be the point of reunion.

This project will answer the double purpose of facilitating his subsistence and of rendering every position between Carolina and Cordoba untenable. In the event, too, of a sudden and hurried retreat from Carolina it will be impossible to collect the Army of the Centre. 6,000 of their best troops are at Montezon, 11 leagues east of Carolina and 2 leagues from Villa Manriques; the remainder is dispersed in corps of one, two and three thousand men between Montezon, and Mestanza, a distance of 28 mountain leagues and without any facilities of communication.

The Duc of Albuquerque is marching by Maquilla and Guadalcanal towards Cordoba. I understand that he has 10,000 infantry and 12,000 cavalry. He has sent his guns, etc. to Llerena. There is a road practicable for infantry and cavalry by Guadalcanal to Cordoba, which is distant 15 leagues and in Cordoba he will find a sufficiency of artillery.

As your Lordship may possibly wish to receive further information of the enemy's movements in this interesting moment, I shall overtake the Duke of Albuquerque's army and, in case I meet no other British officer, remain with it until I receive your Lordship's orders. As the British Army is now in cantonments and as I speak and write Spanish, I should be most happy should your Lordship think to continue me upon this service.

The peasantry of the Sierra Morena are bold, active and intelligent and there are among them men who might be made extremely useful in gaining accurate information.

I fear some time will elapse before your Lordship will receive this letter, there being no regular post from here.[14]

The Transmission of Intelligence
Collecting information on the enemy was often the easiest part of the mission. Once it was obtained, the officer had to find a way to send it back to headquarters in a timely manner. No easy feat for someone hundreds of miles behind the enemy lines. Unfortunately, the officers rarely mentioned how they did it. In 1813, Andrew Leith Hay, deployed in the vicinity of Toledo, found that King Joseph had fled Madrid to Valladolid. He states in his memoirs that he 'sent an express direct to Lord Wellington with the intelligence'. What an 'express' is, he does not state.[15]

But generally speaking, several methods were employed for the transmission of intelligence. For those Observing Officers deployed with an escort, two or three riders might be returned back to friendly lines with a dispatch. This could permit the officer to remain on reconnaissance indefinitely – or until he no longer had an escort.

On the rare occasions when the postal service was working, the officer might make use of it to send a copy of his report – perhaps not the most secure method!

But the most common method of chanelling intelligence back to headquarters was via trusted peasants, smugglers, or guerrillas. In 1812 Colquhoun Grant was tasked to find out if the French would try to retake Ciudad Rodrigo. When he was informed that the French were seen moving towards the fortress with scaling-ladders and siege artillery, he entrusted the message to Manrico el Barbado, a bearded guerrilla, who 'sprang out of the rocks and saluted Grant, who was known and loved by all those wild hillmen. Manrico hid the note beneath his beard, swore he would reach Wellington with it, and vanished'.[16]

Finally, if the information was important enough, the Observing Officer would deliver it himself.

Accomplishments

Since few of their actual reports survived, an air of secrecy surrounds the information Observing Officers sent back to headquarters. In addition to Colonel Waters obtaining the vital dispatch that saved the British Army in 1808, there are a few other accomplishments that are known. In 1809, Wellington made a surprise march to northern Portugal to recapture Oporto from Marshal Soult. Oporto stood on the northern bank of the Douro and the French had moved all boats to their side of the river. Waters was able to find a barber who knew of four unattended wine barges on the north bank. He crossed the river with four or five Portuguese peasants, and got the barges back across the river without being noticed by the French picquet. In the process, Waters was able to observe that the large seminary, which overlooked the river, was unoccupied. Based on this information, Wellington ordered a force to cross the river on the barges and seize the seminary. Almost a complete regiment was across before the French realized what had happened. By that time, it was too late, and the French were forced to abandon Oporto and retreat precipitously to Spain.

In January 1810, Captain John Grant was able to intercept Napoleon's private correspondence to King Joseph. Grant was fluent in Portuguese and operated in the Tagus valley. He acquired the nickname 'Granto el Malo' from the Spanish. As often as not, he travelled in disguise and quickly established a reputation among both the British and the French. When Major Colquhoun Grant was captured by the French, Marshal Marmont mistook him for John Grant and told him that 'he should be very grateful for the redcoat on his back: but for that he would have suffered the penalty of a spy – a gallows 20 feet high.'[17]

In 1812 Major Colquhoun Grant – nicknamed 'Granto el Bueno' – was ordered to discover the intentions of the French Army of Portugal, commanded by Marshal Marmont. Specifically, would Marmont try to retake Ciudad Rodrigo while the main force of the British Army was besieging Badajoz? If not, what would the French do? According to Napier, Grant:

> obtained exact information of Marmont's object, and more especially of his preparations of provisions and scaling-ladders, notes of which he sent to Lord Wellington from day-to-day by Spanish agents . . . Grant had already ascertained that the means of storming Ciudad Rodrigo were prepared, and that the French officers openly talked of doing so, but he desired still further to test this project, and to discover if the march of the enemy might not finally

be directed by the pass of Perales, towards the Tagus; he wished also to ascertain more correctly their real numbers and therefore placed himself on a wooded hill, near Tamames, where the road branches off to the passes, and to Ciudad Rodrigo. Here lying perdue, until the whole French Army had passed by in march, he noted every battalion and gun, and finding that all were directed towards Ciudad, entered Tamames after they had passed and discovered that they had left the greatest part of their scaling-ladders behind, which clearly proved that the intention of storming Ciudad Rodrigo was not real.[18]

Major Grant quickly passed the information back to Wellington and continued to observe the French, to determine whether they would attack Guarda or Castello Branco. It was here that he was captured.

Although Captain Leith Hay was captured in May 1813, he still was able to provide valuable intelligence to Wellington. After spending over a month as a prisoner, Leith Hay was at Vitoria on 19 June when arrangements were made for him to be exchanged. While he was being escorted to French headquarters, the Colonel who accompanied him made no effort to keep his side's preparations for battle a secret. Furthermore, not only was Leith Hay not blindfolded, he was actually taken past the French artillery reserves:

> In point of number I had never seen so many pierces of field artillery assembled, nor can I conceive any thing more regular, beautifully arranged, or in better order, than was this very imposing display of cannon. The French Colonel particularly called my attention to this sight, and, as if determined it should be my last impression of the imperial army, ordered my eyes to be bound up immediately after.[19]

Leith Hay duly arrived at French headquarters, where he met Colonel Alexander Gordon. He also met General Gazan and his wife. The latter requested Leith Hay that, in the case of her capture by the British, he might exert his good offices 'to obtain for her a favourable reception'.[20] Shortly afterwards, Captain Leith Hay and Colonel Gordon were escorted to the British lines:

> I was immediately received by Lord Wellington, and, with delight, communicated to him the information derived from a residence with the imperial troops. The important fact of the French Generals being determined to make a stand in their present position, from every circumstance I considered perfectly decided, and adduced reasons for that opinion.
>
> Having marched with the different armies, obtained information from each, and learned probably more than was intended of their relative situations and numerical strength, my observation, although defective, carried with it a certainty of authenticity seldom to be derived by a commander-in-chief on the eve of fighting a general action.[21]

Casualties

The observing officers spent weeks and sometimes months behind enemy lines. Amazingly, there is no record of any of them being killed while on these missions. However, at least three officers were captured:

Lieutenant Colonel John Waters on 3 April 1811
Major Colquhoun Grant in 1812
Captain Andrew Leith Hay on 17 May 1813

Wellington wrote to Marshal Beresford about Waters' capture:

> You will be concerned to hear that Waters is at last taken prisoner. He crossed the Coa alone, I believed, yesterday morning, and was looking at the enemy through a spying glass, when four hussars pounced upon him. Nobody has seen him since yesterday morning; and we have the account from the prisoners, who tell the story of an officer attached to the Staff, a Lieutenant Colonel, *blond*, with a *petit chapeau*. They saw him with Regnier.[22]

Two other officers were killed while serving with their units:

Lieutenant John Ayling killed at the storming of Badajoz in 1812
Major Charles Cocks at the Siege of Burgos in 1813

Four officers were wounded while serving with their units:

Colonel John Grant, wounded three times during his six years in the Peninsula
Captain John Burrows, in the Battle of the Pyrenees in 1813
Captain Andrew Leith Hay, at Salamanca in 1812
Lieutenant Colonel John Waters, in the Battle of the Pyrenees in 1813

Finally, one officer – Henry Mellish of the 87th Foot – in spite of numerous accomplishments, was sent home by Wellington, due to a gambling problem.

Conclusion

The impact of the Observing Officers on the Peninsula War has been underestimated. Although their numbers were never large and their deeds were probably exaggerated with each retelling, nevertheless, their contributions are immeasurable. The worth of these officers must be measured, not by the dangers they endured, but by the quality of the information they provided. These officers had the training and the experience to provide critical information that a civilian spy could not. What might be unimportant to a civilian could be a key piece of information to a trained soldier – although the opposite also could be true. The Observing Officers knew what to look for because they were soldiers with experienced eyes, and could put what they saw and heard into context. For example, they could determine if a road was passable to artillery and supply waggons, or if an area could support troops on the march. The Duke of

Wellington summed up their contributions when he said: 'No army in the world ever produced the like.'

NOTES

1 McGrigor, James, *The Scalpel and the Sword: the Autobiography of the Father of Army Medicine*, Mary McGrigor (ed.) Dalkeith, Scottish Cultural Press, 2000, p. 191.

2 Ward, S.G.P., *Wellington's Headquarters: A Study of the Administrative Problems in the Peninsula 1809–1814*, Oxford, Oxford University Press, 1957, pp. 105–106.

3 Major Philip Bainbrigge 93rd Foot; on the Army Staff as Deputy Assistant Quartermaster-General; lieutenant general on 20 June 1854. Stephen, Leslie and Sidney Lee (editors), *The Dictionary of National Biography*, vol. i; Oxford, Oxford University Press, 1960, pp. 908–909.

4 Lieutenant Colonel Charles Broke. He changed his name to Charles Broke Vere in 1822 and is known for his pamphlet, *Marches, Movements and Operations of the 4th Division*.

5 Ward, p. 111.

6 Hibbert, Christopher (editor), *Captain Gronow: His Reminiscences of Regency and Victorian Life 1810–60*. London, Kyle Cathie, 1991, pp. 53–55.

7 McGrigor, p. 189.

8 Ward, p. 117.

9 Hay, Andrew, *A Narrative of the Peninsular War*, London, John Hearse, 1850, pp. 318–319.

10 Fraser, Edward, *The Soldiers whom Wellington Led*, London, Methuen, 1913, pp. 97–98.

11 Leith Hay, p. 305.

12 Page, Julia, *Intelligence Officer in the Peninsula: Letters & Diaries of Major the Hon. Edward Charles Cocks: 1796–1812*, New York, Hippocrene Books, 1986, p. 79.

13 Philip Keating Roche, a lieutenant colonel in the British Army, left them initially to serve with the Portuguese but went to the Spanish Army instead and rose to be a Marechal de Campo and commanded a division on the East Coast of Spain.

14 Page, pp. 48–50.

15 Leith Hay, p. 310.

16 Bell, Douglas, *Wellington's Officers*, London, Collins, 1938, pp. 36–37.

17 McGrigor, p. 190.

18 Napier, Wiliam, *History of the War in the Peninsula and in the South of France from A.D. 1807 to A.D. 1814*, vol. III, New York, W.J. Widdleton, 1862, pp. 397–398.

19 Leith Hay, p. 350.

20 Ibid, p. 351. In fact, Madame Gazan was captured the next day!

21 Ibid, p. 353.

22 Wellington to Marshal Beresford, 4 April 1811, in *Wellington's Dispatches* (New Edition), London, John Murray, 1838, vol. vii, p. 416.

Chapter Four

Order of Battle: Customary Battle-Array in Wellington's Peninsular Army

Howie Muir

BATTLE-ARRAY, the order in which an army is drawn up, and called a line of battle.
— Simes, *MILITARY DICTIONARY* (1768)

Battle Order, *the arrangement, or disposition of things in their proper place; custom, or manner, rule, or discipline; as order of march, &c.*
— James, *MILITARY DICTIONARY* (1810)

TACTICS, a word derived from the Greek, signifying order, or the distribution of things by mechanical arrangement, so as to make them subservient to the higher principles of military science: i.e. of Strategy.
— James, *MILITARY DICTIONARY* (1810)

As Wellington looked out from the knoll of Pujade, north-east of Toulouse, on the morning of 10 April 1814, elements of the Anglo-Allied army were still manœuvring into position for the final pitched battle of the Peninsular War. South, to his front-left, the divisional columns of Marshal Beresford's corps laboured southward along the sodden west bank of the Ers River, perhaps a half-mile away. Their destination, the far end of Mount Rave, lay some 2½ miles beyond. When, later, its divisions fronted to the right for the assault upon the French positions, their near, right flank would be some 2 miles distant from Wellington's position. A Spanish corps of two more divisions stood immediately below him to the west waiting to deploy and commence an attack upon the left of the French positions on Mount Rave, nearly three-quarters of a mile away. Beyond them, about half a mile, lay the left flank of the Light Division, taking up its position. A mile and a half west, beyond the Light Division, began the left flank of the 3rd Division, whose front covered yet another 1½ miles.[1]

At such distances, even with a telescope, it was impossible to see the distinguishing colour of regimental flags, let alone the colour of uniform facings. Yet Wellington could confidently chart the progress and position of each division, each brigade, and each regiment of his army. His subordinate commanders could do likewise. In fact, so could every soldier in his army, even without a telescope. They all shared a common understanding of 'the key' to deciphering the shadows that moved across the far fields and distant slopes. They were all familiar with the customary pattern of the battle-array the army had employed since the Peninsular campaigns began in 1808. This same basic pattern shaped all of Britain's armies during the French Revolutionary and Napoleonic Wars, as it had formed British armies throughout the eighteenth century. The pattern's essential elements were, in fact, a common military heritage across Europe, the origins of which lay in antiquity.

Battle-Array: Pattern and Purpose

'Custom is king of all.'
                        – HERODOTUS, *THE HISTORY* (FIFTH CENTURY B.C.)[2]

How did Wellington array his troops for battle? This chapter explores the enduring pattern employed by the Anglo-Allied army to arrange and manage its regiments, brigades, and divisions on the battlefields of the Peninsular War. At the core of this pattern is a set of principles that is little discussed, rarely examined, and now largely forgotten – but the pattern remains visible still, reflected in treatises, memoirs, and battle reports.

'Order of battle' describes a concept that has diversified into various meanings with the passage of time, and the development of military sophistication. The meaning likely to be its oldest and most forgotten pertains to a sense of the 'proper place' of units and commands in an army deployed on the battlefield. In other words, an 'order of battle' was, among other things, an order or *sequence* in which soldiers, units, and commands stood in line of battle. The concept lies at the heart of the evolution, management, and discipline of soldiers employing close order drill; it was critical to manipulation of armies in an age when runners or horsemen were the principal methods of battlefield communication, supplemented by the wave of a hat or sword, the sound of the drum or bugle, or the firing of cannon. Order *in* battle was a foundational component of 'tactics'.

Order is an important attribute, distinguishing an army from a mob. It establishes identity and creates the means to accomplish collective goals. It is even the directing impulse given to military action (i.e. 'to give an order'). Order creates pattern, a sequence imposed on matter or ideas. In an army, ordered pattern includes the physical arrangement of troops and the formulation of concepts as a doctrine, or system, to guide and sustain them. While necessary in any army, patterned order was central to the functioning of a close order army, in which men marched and fought shoulder-to-shoulder. Without a high degree of order, close order warfare was simply impossible.

The Peninsular army shared with every other close order army a need for pattern. In particular, it shared elements of an ancient pattern that encompassed principles for sequencing each body of troops at every level of the organisational hierarchy, from the file, to the company or troop, up to an army division and above. Its elements reflected the fundamental importance of precedence, as expressed through seniority and rank.

This pattern of battle-array was founded upon the inherited primacy of the right (flank) as the first 'post of honour' – an elemental precept whose lineage traces a direct path back to ancient Rome and Greece. It resonates in Homer's epic, *The*

Iliad, at the far edge of the West's recorded military history: Achilles, the warrior archetype, had stood on the right of Agamemnon's array at Troy.[3] The right was the post of honour for the city states of Classical Greece, the Foot and Mounted Companions of Alexander the Great, the senior legion of Republican and Imperial Roman armies, and for the senior command and chief subordinate general of an army through the 17th and 18th centuries. All close order armies, across the millennia, shared the same fundamental challenges of organisation and control. The legacy of the Greek quest for decisive combat had fed Rome's further development of the means to accomplish it, leaving patterns upon which Europe drew heavily and purposefully in the formation of its armies and its military thought.[4] The primacy of the right endured as common legacy throughout all of Enlightenment Europe's contemporary military establishments, persisting to the present day, deeply embedded in the protocol and visual imagery of Western civil and military society.

From this ancient primary precept flowed others, which shaped the form in which Wellington and the rest of Europe arrayed troops for battle. The 'second post of honour' was that upon the left (flank). The centre remained a lesser post of dignity. Naturally, honourable posts were to be occupied by those deserving of them. By the eighteenth century, that was determined by rank and seniority. This precedence of spatial position – right, left, centre – was a generally iterative pattern at each level of organisational hierarchy: the junior element taking the left of the senior, additional junior elements following the same principle to the inside flanks of the two most senior elements, and trending toward the centre (e.g., 2–4–5–3–1). This pattern was not only an intellectual prism through which Wellington and his officers viewed the organisational world, but serving as a vital, practical tool for imposing and sustaining order, it literally shaped physical dispositions on the battlefield. This chapter seeks to illuminate briefly these patterns and meta patterns in the dispositions Wellington and his officers made for battle during the Peninsular War. This study focuses on the infantry, which was the fighting core of the army.

Awareness of the existence and purposes of Britain's deployment pattern has slipped away from current military history. The pattern was not an overt matter of written regulation beyond the level of the battalion or squadron, nor often the subject of correspondence or instructions. Rather, its principles were transmitted and its application governed by more a powerful influence: 'custom of the service'. As the gentleman-compiler of 'A Complete System of Camp Discipline' (1694) admonished regimental quartermasters with respect to their responsibilities, because 'there are a great many things belonging to this Employ which cannot be recited here, and that happen without Rule, ancient Custom, and the Custom of War, must be followed.'[5] A treatise in 1791 expressed a similar sentiment in its definition of 'military discipline' as having three parts, such that:

> the third part of discipline consists in the laws and institutions of war (which are, first, the act of parliament for the government of the army, then the articles of war framed by his Majesty, as well as other regulations established by him; and, lastly, the unwritten law, or custom of war) . . .[6]

With the nineteenth century's later evolution from close order warfare to dispersed-order in the face of the increasing lethality of weapons, and with the invention of new, technological methods for communication, the need for and employment of the customary patterns of battle-array faded, as did memory of them.

Although space denies an opportunity for an extensive study of the evolution of battle-array or of its application in all of Wellington's Peninsular engagements, this chapter attempts to offer an appreciation for rank and seniority, precedence and customary battle-array sufficient to provide explanatory and analytical tools to the historian or enthusiast with which to explore the Peninsular War.

Precedence: Rank & Seniority in the Peninsular Army

> *In all duties, whether with or without arms, picquets, or courts martial, the tour of duty shall be from the eldest downwards.*
> — GENERAL REGULATIONS (1804 & 1811)[7]

This first sentence of Britain's *General Regulations* established the fundamental relationship of rank to seniority, with precedence accorded to the senior, or 'eldest', in rank. Within the regimental home, the organisational bedrock of the army, this principle applied in a specific manner, rooted in a more elemental authority: the *Articles of War*, the principles of which could be traced back to ancient Rome.[8] In the British army, there were *two* ranks, *two* seniority-tracks: 'regimental' and 'army' (usually referred to as 'brevet') rank. With regard to rank, the *Articles of War* stated:

> Officers having Brevets, or Commissions of a prior Date to those of the Regiment in which they now serve, may take place in Courts Martial, and on Detachments, when composed of different corps, according to the Rank given them in their Brevets, or Dates of their former Commissions, but in the Regiment, Troop, or Company, to which such Brevet Officers, and those who have Commissions of a prior Date, do belong, they shall do Duty, and take Rank, both in Courts Martial and on Detachments which shall be composed of only their own corps, according to the Commissions by which they are mustered in the said corps.[9]

For the implications and applications of this structure to become coherent, it is helpful to recall the distinctive attribute of the regimental nature and proprietary origins of the British army.[10] The regiment was an officer's home. Although commissions were issued by the Crown,[11] line and field officers were commissioned in a specific regiment. Within the regiment, officers ranked 'according to the Commissions by which they are mustered in the said corps'. In other words, within a regiment, date of entry into it at a given rank accorded precedence within that rank, not the officer's earlier commission at that rank in *another* regiment. The regiment was the organisation in which the officer was substantively promoted up through the rank of lieutenant colonel, and through which he was paid;[12]

regimental rank was the basis for calculating the pay of a general officer not employed on staff, and an unemployed officer's half-pay.

As an officer's regimental seniority within a given grade was based on his commission in his regiment, a newly arrived officer (by transfer or exchange) automatically became the regiment's most junior officer in that grade, regardless of his prior length of service at that rank in another corps. So, too, did a newly promoted officer become the junior in his new rank. In two-battalion regiments, the 1st Battalion was senior to the 2nd, and the junior officers of each grade were posted to the 2nd Battalion. Thus, advancing seniority would progress an officer from the 2nd to the 1st Battalion, while promotion would usually cycle him back to the 2nd Battalion as the most junior of his grade. The same principle applied proportionally in regiments with more battalions. This was relevant to battle-array because the captain's relative regimental seniority was the basis of a battalion company's position in the battalion's line of battle, as is discussed in the following section.[13]

Outside the regiment, the officer's rank and seniority in the *army* was the basis of his station. The Crown bestowed 'brevets', from French for 'commission' or 'appointment'. In the case of British brevets, though, the term carried two related meanings. First, 'brevet rank', awarded for merit, valour, or through influence, was:

a rank in the army higher than that for which pay is received. It gives precedence (when corps are brigaded) according to the date of the brevet commission.[14]

In other words, when occasion arose for duties outside one's regimental responsibility, an officer's army rank applied. Brevet rank only garnered pay when the officer received a staff appointment with that rank,[15] it provided no basis for half-pay retirement, and it could not be sold. Brevet rank was also important for determining who assumed a vacant command, or was available for command and staff assignments. Second, 'the brevet', was simply 'a term used to express general promotion, by which a given number of officers are raised from the rank of captain, upwards, without any additional pay'[16] – in other words, the general promotion itself.

Unless he held a brevet to a higher rank, an officer's regimental rank was also his army rank. An officer's seniority in the army dated to his first commission or brevet at his grade. Thus might a regimental major with a brevet to lieutenant colonel assume command of a brigade containing his regiment over the head of his own regimental commander, if the latter's army rank or seniority was junior to his.

Army rank governed eligibility for army commands, such as those of brigades and divisions, and general officers were just that: generally available for posting to any part of the army.[17] General officers retained their regimental rank, but, beginning with 'major general', rose substantively on their army rank. The appointed rank of 'brigadier general' was a sort of transitional step. Originally, 'colonel of brigade' in the late 17th century, 'brigadier general' was not a substantive rank or commission, but a wartime staff appointment specific to a particular force, the seniority of which rested on the holder's underlying rank in the army (usually that of a senior colonel).[18] Rank and seniority carried privileges (allowances and staff)[19] and opportunity (for command). Rank and seniority were as jealously monitored by officers of all grades in Wellington's army as they were in any army, in any age. The annual *Army List*, referenced even by Wellington,[20] provided a regular review of every officer's standing, while official announcements in the *Gazette* of promotions, exchanges, and deaths were avidly read by all. In such a necessarily hierarchical organisation, rank had a natural precedence. Seniority of rank correlated to seniority of command. Throughout the eighteenth century, British custom had distributed regiments to brigades[21] based on seniority of the regiment, creating an inherent brigade seniority and to which commanders were assigned according to *their* seniority. By 1799, however, this practice had withered in the face of competing manpower demands for different operations and the increasing tendency to form expeditions by incremental reinforcement and transfers as troops became available. The assignment of brigadiers (a term, in this chapter, denoting any rank commanding a 'brigade') continued to reflect a correlation of seniority, rank and command with numbered brigades in descending order of seniority and number.

To appreciate the underlying influences that manifested themselves in the grand tactical battle-array of the Peninsular army, it is necessary to examine an obscure detail of an officer's tenure of command. Although distinguishing between the natures of different manners of holding command may seem appallingly arcane to the civilian mind, such nuances remain of abiding and practical interest to military officers in all ages, and tenure of command had a fundamental and practical impact upon the army's order of battle. The terms applied below are not contemporary, for the period seems to have lacked established vocabulary for these distinctions, though its officers understood them well. Briefly put, an *incumbent* commander, whose army appointment usually appeared in General Orders, had full authority over his command, which he, his superiors, and his subordinates expected he would exercise for the long-term. His brigade or divisional command took its precedence from his seniority.

While the army appointment of an *interim* commander also normally appeared in General Orders, his command was expected to be of relatively short duration. Its temporary nature was usually signalled in orders by phrases such as 'during the time' of some indisposition or absence of the incumbent, or 'until further orders'. The appointment, however, did make available relevant allowances and personal staff for the duty assigned. An important variant of this status was command 'under the orders of' a superior officer, to lead a brigade (or division) on behalf of the incumbent while that officer undertook higher command responsibilities – this was the case for the 2nd Division's commander 'under' Hill,[22] and for the two colonels on staff appointed, in 1810, to command Picton's and Cole's brigades of the 3rd and 4th Divisions, respectively. Interim command did not affect the previously established precedence of brigades and divisions.

Lastly, an *assumptive* commander was one who had merely assumed command as the next senior officer available upon the absence, incapacitation, or death of the officer commanding. Such officers did not ordinarily appear in orders or in the reported 'States' of the army, division, or brigade, as their transitory and contingent elevation to higher command was dependent upon a negative, the non-presence of the appointed commanding officer, rather than upon a positive act of assignment. An assumed army command was the pure product of on-the-spot *army*, not regimental, rank and seniority. For example, at Albuera (16 May 1811), when Major General Lumley, commanding the 2nd Brigade of the 2nd Division, was placed in command of the Allied cavalry on the morning of the battle, Lieutenant Colonel Abercromby (2/28th Foot) *assumed* command of the 2nd Brigade as the brigade's senior officer present – the brigade remained, however, Lumley's. While this issue was usually relevant only for brigades (or smaller detachments composed of more than one regimental element), it affected divisions from time to time, owing to shortages of, or casualties among, general officers. Assumptive commanders also did not affect the command's pre-existing precedence.

The *Army List* and orders assigning general officers to expeditions and commands, usually listed them in descending order of seniority. Similarly, the army's reporting 'states' usually listed the divisions in numerical descending order, and their brigades in descending order by seniority of their incumbent and interim commanders. Officers who had assumed command – and were, by definition, *not* 'in orders' – were not normally listed. Both nuances, of brigade seniority and tenure of command, have frequently been lost on later historians. As an example, for March 1811, so eminent and knowledgeable a historian as John Fortescue, author of the seminal work, *A History of the British Army*, listed two of the army divisions operating under Field Marshal Beresford as follows:[23]

Second Division. Maj.-Gen. W. Stewart
Colborne's brigade
Hoghton's brigade
Lumley's brigade
Fourth Division. Maj.-Gen. Cole
Myers' brigade
Kemmis' brigade
Harvey's brigade

Lost from his presentation of the order of battle is the information that W. Stewart was only an interim divisional commander 'under' Hill, and that Lieutenant Colonel Colborne only had assumptive command of W. Stewart's brigade. Furthermore, Fortescue's sequence implied an incorrect order of seniority, for Lumley's (2nd) brigade was senior to Hoghton's (3rd). The possibility that Fortescue intentionally listed the brigades in their *tactical* order is contradicted by the sequence in which Fortescue presented the 4th Division's brigades. Lieutenant Colonel Myers' brigade appears above Brigadier General Kemmis', implying the reverse of the actual relative precedence of the two brigades, and Harvey's Portuguese brigade was the junior of the three. Myers held assumptive command of the 2nd Brigade following Major General Houston's transfer on 5 March, and Kemmis commanded the 1st Brigade on an interim basis on behalf of its official incumbent, Major General Cole, while the latter had charge of the division. The relative precedence of the two brigades was based on the status of their incumbent commanders: Houston, whose prior incumbency still gave the 2nd Brigade its seniority until the assignment of a new incumbent commander, was junior to Cole.

Wellington frequently shaped the leadership of his divisions and brigades through active manipulations of incumbent, interim, and assumptive commands. Natural military obsession with precedence made numerical associations with seniority inevitable, thereby imposing an almost necessary correlation between the numerically identified brigades (and divisions), and the seniority of their commanders. All concerned unquestioningly assumed – nay, expected – that the senior general had the 1st Brigade (or Division), with his juniors assigned to the remaining army commands in descending order of seniority of rank and numerical sequence of organisations. This implicit relationship created administrative challenges for Wellington throughout the war, only worsening with time, the army's growth, and the fluctuations of available general officers.

The traditional association of seniority of rank with numerical order had evolved in a world where British military expeditions were comparatively short or seasonally organised, or rarely large enough to require brigades to be numbered. As the Peninsular War lengthened, it demanded the longest sustained existence of what became the largest British army on active operations in its history to date. The persistent association between seniority and organisational numbers, however, proved increasingly difficult to sustain as generals were incapacitated, died, or resigned, and others arrived or sought to fill their places, always with an eye to their personal and hierarchical standing. It is likely to have been one reason that, with the June 1809 shift to a divisional organisation, Wellington completely and abruptly halted the practice of numbering brigades. Instead, he referred to brigades either by the name of their (incumbent or interim) commander or by listing out their constituent regiments – the latter practice was most awkward, but precise.

Wellington worked ceaselessly and artfully to reconcile rank, self-importance and self-esteem, army politics, social considerations, existing organisational precedence, and operational needs in his appointments. He performed this task masterfully, and it deserves a full study of its own – which is to say there is inadequate space here to address the subject as it deserves.

These idiosyncrasies of British rank and seniority, and such nuances of command, are important to comprehending and exploring the manifestation of precedence in the Peninsular army's battle-array.

Precedence as Order

The military science has been defined the SCIENCE OF ORDER.
   – WILLIAMSON, *THE ELEMENTS OF MILITARY ARRANGEMENT* (1791)[24]

In 1826, Wellington was recorded to have observed, with regard to managing an army, that:

One must understand the mechanism and power of the individual soldier; then that of a company, a battalion, or brigade, and so on, before one can venture to group divisions and move an army. I believe I owe most of my success to the attention I always paid to the inferior part of tactics as a regimental officer.[25]

Implicitly included was appreciation for, and application of, the customary principles governing battle-array.

At the foundation of the physical arrangement of soldiers, was the rank and file:

by *file* is meant the line of soldiers standing one behind the other, which makes the depth of the battalion; and is thus distinguished from the rank, which is a line of soldiers drawn up side by side, forming the length of the battalion. A file is 2 or 3 deep; hence a battalion or regiment drawn up, consists of 2 or 3 ranks, and of as many files as there are men in a rank.[26]

Rank and file was the essential military architecture of close order warfare. Its depth and breadth had varied with the nature of weaponry and numbers available, but rank and file constituted the matrix into which the individual soldier was firmly webbed. Giving him his 'place', it created the order by which he and his comrades were arranged and, by arrangement, could be manipulated for action. Even the soldier's person was 'ordered' – e.g., his body was to be carried 'square to the front' – and his movement cadenced by mastering the pace's length and various rates. His complete immersion in the regularity of the whole was vital, 'for one aukward [sic] man, imperfect in his march, or whose person is distorted, will derange his division, and of course operate on the battalion and line in a still more consequential manner'.[27]

When a British recruit had been trained in the movements of rank and file, and the management of his weapon, Part II of the 1792 *Rules and Regulations for the Formations, Field-Exercise, and Movements of His Majesty's Forces*, issued 'to order and establish one uniform and complete system' for the army, placed him in a platoon, the equivalent of a company.[28] The company, the primary division of the battalion, was divided into two equalized 'subdivisions'[29] or into as many as four 'subsections', each 'never . . . less than five files'.[30] The soldier occupied a mere 22 inches' width, about the same space as allowed in the aisle of a modern airliner, with 30 inches between ranks. This was 'close order', 'the chief and primary order, which with the battalion and its parts at all times assemble and form'.[31] The soldier was guided by the touch of elbows to each side, without turning the head to look, an action which would derange his 'squareness' in the rank and the movement of his neighbours. These were some of the necessary components of close order drill, manœuvre, and combat, the means by which the individual soldier was woven into the greater whole, made an organic part of the machine, his place established in the greater battle-array. (See Fig. 1)[32]

Though the company was 'always to be sized from the flanks to the centre',[33] during training, 'the four best trained soldiers' were 'placed in the front rank, on the right and left of each subdivision'.[34] This practical placement helped govern

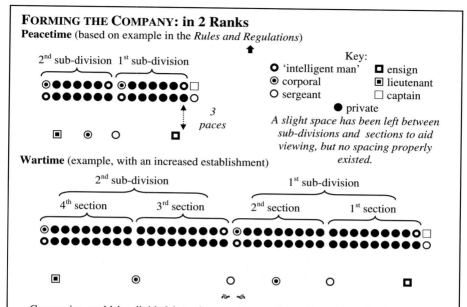

Fig. 1

speed and regularity of movement and to anchor pivots for wheeling; after training, these posts were also those of corporals and 'intelligent men'. In training and in the field, the flanks were crucial for steering, changing formations, and controlling bodies of troops, so was where key officers and non-commissioned officers (NCOs) were posted:

> When the company is singly formed; the captain is on the right, and the ensign on the left, of the front rank, each covered by a serjeant in the rear rank. [. . .]

> The left of the front rank of each subdivision is marked by a corporal. The right of the left subdivision may be marked by the other corporal.

> When necessary, the places of absent officers may be supplied by serjeants, those of serjeants by corporals, and those of corporals by intelligent men.[35]

The remaining officers and NCOs formed a final supernumerary rank to the rear, the 'essential use' of which was 'to keep the others close up to the front during the attack, and to prevent any break beginning in the rear . . .'[36] The senior company officer, the captain, was in the first post of honour, on the right, another officer in the second post of honour, on the left (though when formed in battalion, 'the ensign and his covering serjeant quit the flank' to join the supernumerary rank). Corporals were the chosen men to anchor the 'pivot' (left) flanks of the internal subdivisions.[37] The supernumeraries augmented control and a succession was clearly established to replace fallen superiors as needed.

In this way, the company contained within it the first iterative layers of precedence, seniority and rank distributed to the flanks in each organisational layer. At the lowest level, of section and subdivision, the merit and capability of corporals (or 'intelligent men') took the laurels of precedence; at the next step, the company, commissioned rank asserted itself as the basis of spatial precedence, again with priority to the right flank, where the company's commander took station. This distributive pattern of precedence, with variation, continued up through the entire military structure. It was the organisation's reference point. It underpinned the physical manifestation of order, created conceptual order, and made possible the direction of masses of men with precision and purpose. The company was the first organisational step of infantry's battle-array.

The next major step on the organisational ladder was the battalion. 'The battalion is ten companies', composed of, '1 Grenadier, 8 Battalion, 1 Light'.[38] The Grenadier company stood on the right, in the first post of honour, as it had since grenadiers were introduced into British regiments in the late 17th century.[39] The light company, also considered élite stood on the left, the second post of honour – a flank position from which it was conveniently detached for skirmishing and independent operation. In between, tactically numbered in sequence right to left, the battalion companies stood in an underlying order dependent upon the relative regimental seniority of their captains.[40] (See Fig. 2)

The sequence of a battalion's grand divisions (paired companies), based on the eldest captain in each pair, was a variant of the customary principles of battle-array, dating back to antiquity, resulting in a more balanced order of seniority: 2–3–4–1. This sequence equalized the 'martial temper' of each battalion 'wing', or pair of grand divisions (each wing's seniority summed to '5'), and while maintaining the priority of the flanks, reversed the alternation of the junior, centre elements, therein differing from the typical pattern of British battle-array (2–4–3–1) at higher organisational levels. The sequencing of companies accomplished the same result, with the captains' seniority in each grand division's pair of companies summing to '9'.

The sequence of the infantry companies in a battalion was fixed by custom, practical efficiencies, and the *Rules and Regulations*, based on the incumbent captain's, not the company's, seniority. Its precedence was retained regardless of the incumbent's absence, whether temporary (due to sickness, wounds, detachment) or permanent (due to death, exchange, transfer, or resignation), until a new incumbent captain was appointed. When a new captain arrived to replace a permanently absent incumbent, not only did he become the battalion's most junior

FORMATION OF THE BATTALION

The companies will draw up as follows from right to left: — grenadiers; — 1st captain and major; — 4th and 5th captain; — 3d and 6th captain; — 2d captain and lieutenant-colonel; — light company. — The colonel's company takes place according to the rank of its captain: — the four eldest captains are on the right of the grand divisions: — officers commanding companies or platoons, are all on the right of the front rank of their respective ones.

~War Office, *Rules and Regulations*, (1808 printing) Part III, p. 66.

Mapping the Distribution of Companies in an Infantry Battalion:

Light   LtC - 2nd Capt   6th Capt-3rd Capt   5th Capt-4th Capt   Maj-1st Capt   Gren.

Though the above language of the *Rules & Regulations* did not reflect it, from May 1803, the number of captains in a battalion was augmented to 10. As one result, the colonel's (previously commanded by a captain-lieutenant, ranking as the junior captain), lieutenant colonel's, and major's former companies were now commanded by captains. As observed in 1804: 'Regiments were long deprived of their necessary officers by allowing Field Officers to hold companies, but since the hint given of this inconvenience […] much to the good of the service, the ideas of improvement were embraced, the suggested plan completely adopted, and each regiment now has ten captains.' (Hood, *Elements of War*, p. 126)

The resulting sequence of battalion companies based on the regimental seniority of their captains (the 'eldest' of the pairs in **bold**) was:

	7th - **2nd**	6th - **3rd**	5th - **4th**	8th - **1st**
	Capt Capt	Capt Capt	Capt Capt	Capt Capt
Sum of seniorities =	'9'	'9'	'9'	'9'

Reide, in his 1795 explanation of drill, described the pairings: 'The eight battalion companies form four grand divisions to be commanded by the four eldest captains.' (Reide, *Treatise*, p.107) The purpose of the distribution seems to have been to spread seniority's presumed benefits of knowledge and experience evenly throughout the battalion's battle-line. Thus, each 'grand-division' of two neighbouring platoons contained the same notional 'martial temper', a quality equalized through the line.

This arrangement is distinct from the tactical numbering of the battalion companies for manœuvre. 'The battalion companies will be numbered from the right to the left, 1.2.3.4.5.6.7.8.' (*Rules and Regulations*, p.67) Thus, the battle-array's tactical sequence would have the following numbered pattern for centre companies:

Seniority:	7th - **2nd**	6th - **3rd**	5th - **4th**	8th - **1st**
	Capt Capt	Capt Capt	Capt Capt	Capt Capt
	□ □	□ □	□ □	□ □
Tactical No.:	8 - 7	6 - 5	4 - 3	2 - 1

Fig. 2

captain, conformable to the *Articles of War*, but the vacated company that fell to him followed him to become the most junior company, conformable to the *Rules and Regulations*. This entailed a physical relocation of the company within the battalion in order to remain consistent to the *Rules and Regulations*. Since no reasonable officer would wish to jeopardize the crucial advantages of well rehearsed drill with the existing sequence of companies during an active campaigning season, it is likely, in practice, that the actual re-sequencing of the companies was delayed until there was adequate time and opportunity to re-drill the battalion with the companies in their new sequence. The most logical time to revise company order was between campaigning seasons, usually during the winter.[41] A similar dynamic would later apply to brigades' positions in divisions.

Another, more worrisome event that could change a battalion's order of battle was an internal re-sequencing that good sense and the regulations advised against unless necessary: inversion. 'Although in general the INVERSION of all bodies in line is to be avoided, yet there are situations where this rule must be dispensed with, and the quickest formation to a particular front thereby obtained.'[42] 'Natural' order was the sequence of companies and their components as laid out by the *Rules and Regulations*. 'Inversion' reversed the sequence of companies or, even more seriously, of the sections and subdivisions of which the companies were composed. (See Fig. 3)[43]

In theory, all well-drilled troops were capable of executing evolutions with inverted sub-units, but a unit's inherent vulnerability to confusion increased. If it had to move or manœuvre with inverted sub-units, the battalion faced much greater risk of falling into potentially fatal confusion and disarray. Even well drilled troops were unlikely to accomplish inverted manœuvres with their usual facility, and would habitually sacrifice time to avoid the serious risk of disorder by inverted operation. Rallying an inverted battalion could prove exceedingly difficult, as harried soldiers attempted to interpret reassembly in an inverted orientation. The *Rules and Regulations* provided a number of counter-marches (e.g., Sections 53, 97–103, and 143) as tools to avoid the problems inversion created. Even inversion of greater bodies, brigades or larger commands, was not casually resorted to. The planned *reversal* of the order of regiments of a brigade, and brigades of a division, however, was customary for the army's far left-flank command: the priority of the left as a second post of honour imposed an obligation to sequence precedence from the left of that command.

The relative order of a battalion's companies was fixed by regulation and generally maintained. The sequence of regiments in a brigade was a matter of long tradition, a time-hallowed custom of the service, but was more flexible in practice. Nevertheless, precedence among regiments was fixed in the *General Regulations*:

> His majesty's lifeguards have the precedence of all other corps. On parades, the horse artillery, whether mounted or dismounted, take the right of all other cavalry. The cavalry, whether mounted or dismounted, take the right of the line, the royal artillery have the precedence of other infantry; the foot guards are the next in rank, then regiments of the line, according to their number and order of precedence; the militia regiments take rank after those

NATURAL ORDER & INVERSION

1. '**Natural**' order, with sub-units regularly sequenced from right to left:

8 7 6 5 4 3 2 1

2. '**Inversion**' of the 'natural' order of sub-units:

1 2 3 4 5 6 7 8

If facing about in place, the question of inversion hinged on the unit's purpose. If to retrograde away from the enemy, this was *not* an 'inversion', for the sub-units were still in their 'natural' order, but simply a 'rear-front' while in motion and ready to 'front' again. Yet, the same event became an 'inversion' if the about-face was to engage an enemy to the rear:

8 ㄥ 9 � � Ɛ ᄅ Ɩ

3. Example. Inversion of the constituent sub-units would occur when forming line to the 'reverse' flank of an open column. This sample column leads by the *right*, ready to **A**) wheel to the left in natural order; but if the sub-units **B**) wheel to the right, each sub-unit would remain in natural internal order, but put the sub-units themselves into inverted order. Inversion could be avoided by **C**) progressive, sequential wheels of sub-units, after each passed behind the preceding sub-unit to form on its farther flank, thereby still forming line to the reverse flank – at the cost of greater time to complete the evolution (see *Rules & Regulations*, Sec. 62).

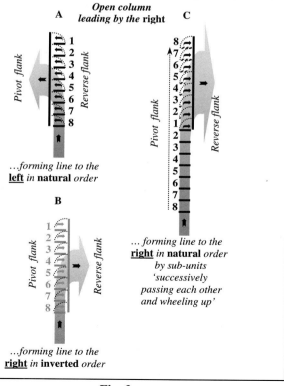

Open column leading by the **right**

A

Pivot flank — *Reverse flank*

1 2 3 4 5 6 7 8

…forming line to the **left** *in* **natural** *order*

B

Pivot flank — *Reverse flank*

1 2 3 4 5 6 7 8

…forming line to the **right** *in* **inverted** *order*

C

Pivot flank — *Reverse flank*

8 7 6 5 4 3 2 1 2 3 4 5 6 7 8

… forming line to the **right** *in* **natural** *order by sub-units 'successively passing each other and wheeling up'*

Fig. 3

of the line, according to their respective numbers; but it is to be clearly under-stood, that this regulation refers merely to circumstances of parade: on all other occasions corps are to be distributed, and drawn up, in the mode which the General, or other Officer commanding, may judge most convenient and best adapted to the purpose of the service.[44]

The terminating disclaimer served to underscore that regulation, embodying long-established traditions of precedence, did not set the arrangement of a field army's order of battle. Rather, battle-array was outside regulation, subject to a commanding general's discretion – though subject to the army's unwritten customs. Notwithstanding the disclaimer, precedence had a practical impact on array beyond the merely ceremonial.

By taking precedence of the line, the Guards stood outside the seniority pattern of the line, with an unchallengeable claim to the post of honour on the right. In the Peninsula, the Guards Brigade(s) would be consistently found on the right of the 1st Division. Not mentioned here, but evidenced by any *Army List*, foreign corps took precedence after British (e.g., see Fig. 4).[45] The King's German Legion, from the British monarch's Hanoverian Electorate, was privileged to stand first among foreign corps, and uniquely served as a body whenever possible, standing outside the internal British sequence of the divisional line of battle, but in the subordinate, junior position, on the left.

Customs that have endured the tests of time and practicality acquire a power on par with regulation. Lieutenant Colonel, and later Lieutenant General, Humphrey Bland conveyed the eighteenth century's customary spatial precedence in *A Treatise of Military Discipline*. It was a precedence still actively current in military thinking of the early nineteenth century.[46]

The Battalions draw up in Brigade thus:

The eldest Battalion is placed on the Right of the Brigade, the second Battalion on the Left of it, and the two youngest in the Center, the third Battalion being on the Right of the fourth. This Rule, of placing the eldest Battalion on the Right of the Brigade, is only observed by the Brigades which are posted in the Right Wing; but those in the Left draw up the Reverse, the eldest Battalion being posted on the Left of the Brigade, and the second Battalion on the Right of it, and so from Left to Right.[47]

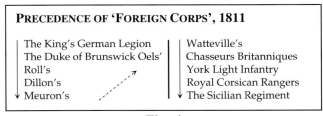

PRECEDENCE OF 'FOREIGN CORPS', 1811

The King's German Legion	Watteville's
The Duke of Brunswick Oels'	Chasseurs Britanniques
Roll's	York Light Infantry
Dillon's	Royal Corsican Rangers
↓ Meuron's	↓ The Sicilian Regiment

Fig. 4

Bland's eighteenth-century treatise, printed in nine editions from 1727 to 1762, and capturing in print much that constituted unwritten 'customs of the service', was extraordinarily widely read among Britain's officer corps.[48]

James' *Military Dictionary* (1810) sustained this explanation of practice eighty-three years later:

> *POST of honour*, the advanced guard is a post of honour; the right of the two lines is a post of honour, and is always given to the eldest regiment: the left is the next post, and is given to the next eldest, and so on. The centre of the lines is the post the least honourable, and is given to the youngest regiments.[49]

Under 'Seniority', both Simes' dictionary (1768) and James' (1810) described in identical language how regiments' numerical identity, reflecting precedence, translated into battle-array: 'All regiments take place according to seniority in numerical order', thereby twining unit seniority with spatial placement in the order of battle. Brigades, too, applied the same principle: 'The eldest brigade takes the right of the first line, [. . .] the youngest always possessing the center.'[50] The notoriously vulnerable flanks of a close order line of battle, positions of heightened danger, required men of the highest standing to hold them, and custom had institutionalized 'honour' in correlation with seniority: the senior body of troops was posted on the right, and the second eldest on the left of the line, with the junior in the centre.

While captains' regimental rank shaped the tactical array within battalions, and the numerical seniority of regiments dictated their array within brigades, the army ('brevet') rank of commanding officers was the basis of precedence for the grand tactical relationship of brigades. Regiments were the highest level of permanent organisation in the army – with the exception of the brigades formed by the Foot Guards since 1803. Broader organisations, brigades and 'columns', were transient creatures of passing need and convenience, usually formed for a season of campaigning, and lacking any enduring identity beyond that which coalesced temporarily around its composition or commander. Thus, during the eighteenth century, brigades had been variously identified by their senior regiment, the name of their commander, and then by a numeral reflecting seniority within the field army. That seniority was based upon the rank and seniority of the brigadier.

The placement of brigades in the line of battle was also guided by custom, as described by Bland:

> When the Brigades are formed, they are divided into two Lines, as follows:
> The first and second Brigades are posted on the Flanks of the Front Line; and the third and fourth Brigades on the Flanks of the Rear Line.
> The fifth and sixth Brigades are placed in the Front Line, on the Inside of the first and second; and the seventh and eighth Brigades are placed in the Rear Line, on the Inside of the third and fourth; and so on in this manner 'till they are all formed in both Lines, the youngest Brigades drawing up in the Center: For as the Flanks of the Lines are more liable to the Attacks of an Enemy, than the Center, by their lying open, they are esteemed the Posts of Honour, and therefore belong to the eldest Brigades; but as the Front Line

is the more exposed than the Rear, since it begins the Attack, while the other only Sustains it, the Left Flanks of the Front Line is, undoubtedly, the second Post of Honour, and therefore belongs to the second Brigade; so that the Right Flank of the Rear Line can only be looked upon as the third Post of Honour, and the Left Flanks of the said Line as the Fourth.'[51]

This customary array of the 'Lines' inevitably influenced the array within later army divisions, as well as of the divisions themselves.

The organisational level of the 'army division' as an alternative to the simple 'Line' had only recently evolved. Britain's *Rules and Regulations* had, since 1792, defined an army's structure as British military men had viewed it for over a century, by dividing it into 'one or more lines' 'divided into right and left wings', 'each composed of one, two, or more divisions', themselves constituted 'of one or more brigades', each 'formed of two, three, or four battalions'.[52] Here, the word 'division' denoted simply a portion of a larger whole. By June 1811, an article on the 'Elements of the Art of War' in the *Royal Military Chronicle* could comfortably include army divisions and army corps in the organisational matrix, noting that: 'a division is one of the greater component parts of an army in the field, and usually consists of from 3 to 8 or 10,000 men; a corps is a smaller army acting subordinately to a greater one, and ordinarily consists of from 16 to 26,000.' However, a conservative discomfort with such changes was evident: 'They are more usual in the French than the English service.'[53]

Britain's employment of her army required expensive sea transportation, which tended to limit the size of her expeditions. Consequently, her land forces rarely had had need for organisational structures larger than the brigade. In British usage, the organisational structure of an 'army division' seems to have made one of its earliest appearances under Lieutenant General Sir Ralph Abercromby, in the Mediterranean, in 1800.[54] Although Abercromby did not use the structure in his Egyptian campaign the following year, British organisation by army division increased, appearing in Hanover (1805), Denmark (1807), the Baltic (1808) and in the army that became Sir John Moore's for his Spanish campaign (1808–09). Wellesley formed his Peninsular army into divisions in June 1809, first of two, and later three (occasionally four), brigades; from 1810, one Portuguese brigade was in most divisions – only the 1st Division would not receive one, while the Light Division's Portuguese troops were not separately brigaded, but integrated into British brigades. Supported with a battery of artillery, divisions were commanded by lieutenant generals, when available, otherwise a major general or, in a few instances, a brigadier general as an interim or assumptive commander when superior officers were unavailable or, in Robert Craufurd's case, because of certain talents Wellington valued. A divisional commander in the Peninsula was supported by roughly two dozen staff.[55] Just as brigades had come to be known by a numerical tag correlated to the seniority of their commanders, so did divisions.

With the establishment of a divisional structure, brigades were no longer sequenced with reference to the army as a whole, but to the smaller world within the army division. Brigade precedence continued to be based upon the incumbent commander, with the senior general's brigade on the right, the next senior's on the left, and the junior's in the middle (a sequence typically reversed when the division was on the army's left flank). A similar pattern applied more loosely to the placement of divisions for battle, absent reasons for posting a division otherwise. As with brigades, the numerical identification of divisions established an organic sequence of seniority: the 1st Division was inherently the senior, and the natural assignment for the anointed second-in-command, Wellington's senior subordinate. The 1st Division generally remained the Peninsular army's numerically strongest (sometimes rivalled by the 2nd, after it gained a Portuguese brigade), and was always home to the Foot Guards. Until the autumn of 1810, the divisional commands correlated the division's number with the commander's seniority; later command assignments to divisions formed subsequently were subject to availability (and appropriateness) of general officers and did not, could not, continue the correlation. By this time, however (later 1810–early 1811), divisional identities had taken firm root and asserted a loose pattern of precedence based upon their own (numerical) seniority – established in no small degree by the original correlation of numerical tag and seniority of commander.

At the upper end of the operational organisational scale were the grand columns, army wings, and proto- and *de facto* army corps (*corps d'armée*) composed of more than one army division, roughly corresponding to what earlier military thought had inclusively described as 'the Line' (though this was a term of no fixed dimension). Inevitably, these organisations were characterized by an even more transient existence and identity, making them harder to define. Nevertheless, Wellington did use such structures, or their functional equivalent. Gurwood, the compiler and editor of Wellington's general orders and dispatches, described this level of organisation thus:

> When two or more divisions were placed under the second in command, or other Officer of high rank, to act as a corps, a similar Staff [to that of the division] was attached to the corps to assist him in the command of it. One or more brigades [i.e. batteries] of artillery were in general attached to the corps in addition to the artillery of the divisions; as also a force of cavalry in proportion to the service and duties required of the corps.[56]

Wellington's first creation on this scale was his arrangement for Hill's semi-independent command from the end of 1809, the core of which was composed, for the remainder of the war, of the 2nd and Portuguese Divisions.[57] More transient commands of this sort included Major General W. Erskine's 'advance guard' in March–April 1811, and then the 'northern corps' of four divisions in May–July 1811 (1st, 5th, 6th, and Light Divisions), and again in March–April 1812 (1st, 5th 6th, and 7th Divisions), occasions when Wellington shifted his active operations southwards against Badajoz. The senior officer assuming command of the northern corps was, quite naturally, the commander of the 1st Division: Lieutenant General Spencer in 1811, and Lieutenant General Graham in 1812. By 1813, a curious reversal of operational array evolved from Hill's customary employment on the army's southern, or right, flank. The column with the 1st

Division (Graham's) operated on the army's left in the 1813 campaign. As more substantial versions of army corps emerged from the initial 'columns' of this campaign, to become army 'wings' (among other terms used) in the Pyrenees, their commanders were to be found in reversed order of precedence, so that the senior wing commander was on the left (Lieutenant General Sir John Hope), the next senior on the right (Lieutenant General Hill), and the junior (in British rank) in the centre (Marshal Beresford).

These, then, were the organisational forms, shaped by customs of precedence based on a mix of rank and seniority, which together created the customary battle-array of the Peninsular army.

Space naturally precludes a succession of even modest battle studies across the six-year span of the Peninsular War. Instead, what follows is a series of sketches of the initial dispositions adopted for the Anglo-Allied army at a number of the war's engagements, large and small. Several schematics accompany the text to help the reader visualize battle-array's spatial relationships. These do not purport to provide scale, distance, or even detailed orientation, but merely to depict general relative relationships, usually on the cusp of the critical commitment to battle. The key for all of these schematics is given in Fig. 5.

Battles are difficult things to pin down. To quote Wellington's famous remark in the wake of the battle at Waterloo:

> The history of a battle is not unlike the history of a ball. Some individuals may recollect all the little events, of which the great result is the battle won or lost; but no individual can recollect the order in which, or the exact moment at which, they occurred, which makes all the difference as to their value or importance.[58]

Based as it must be upon the observations and memories of whichever participants recorded them, and conveyed by reports, letters, and memoirs, some written at the time of the event, others after the passage of many years, and still others lost, the information available to posterity for any battle is necessarily partial, always incomplete, and peppered with apparent contradictions. The schematics appearing here are subject to the information available. Yet, patchy information also offers the opportunity to use the principles of customary battle-array to illuminate these obscure gaps in the historical data. In the figures, units and commands appearing in normal print are those whose placement or arrangement is reasonably supported by available data, while those indicated in italics are *conjectural*, based upon British battle-array's customary principles.

The schematics, therefore, both reflect the historical application of customary battle-array by the Anglo-Allied army and employ those principles to illustrate how gaps in our knowledge might be bridged or some contradictions resolved with a degree of confidence. Their purpose is to show how Wellington and his commanders arranged their forces and prepared for battle. The schematics thus endeavour to represent an outline of 'the moment before' the battle began, the last opportunity at which a commander had reasonably untrammelled power to position or direct his forces as he thought best.

GENERAL KEY TO REMAINING FIGURES:

The schematic figures represent general dispositions of troops relative to one another, and are not generally intended to reflect details of ground-scale, relative frontage, tactical formation, or individual facing.

italics = conjectural positions within or of the command.

bold unit no. = senior regiment in the brigade.

① or ❶ = indicates an officer's relative seniority within a subordinate chain of command; dark or light to distinguish between different steps in those chains of command.

Bgde (**4**th) = Parenthetical numbers for Portuguese brigades indicate the official number assigned in August 1813, though in earlier informal use, as an aid to facilitating identification through the war.

Ḍ = infantry/combined-arms unit ⎫ *these sizes usually represent approximately*
Ⓩ = cavalry unit ⎬ *a battalion or regiment; larger icons*
🄰🄱 = infantry/cavalry detachment ⎭ *represent larger commands.*

Ħ = artillery
🛒 = baggage
Ḍ = when icon is grayed, position from/to which unit displaced
⋮⋮ = when icon is dashed, unit's alternative position
■ = 'foreign' infantry is partially or wholly solid
⋯⋯ = skirmishers, or deployed as skirmishers
⬆ = direction to front

12th = unit's numeric designation, usually related to its seniority
2/12th = battalion/regiment: 2nd Battalion of the 12th Regiment
C = 'caçadores' (Portuguese light infantry)
co / cos = 'company' / 'companies'
det = 'detachment/s'
D / DG = 'dragoons' / 'dragoon guards'
Gren or Gr = 'grenadiers'
Gds = 'Guards'
Hus = 'hussars'
LD = 'light dragoons'
Lts = 'light infantry'
P = 'Portuguese Line'

Ranks

FM / M = Field Marshal / Marshal	Col = Colonel
(F)G = (Full) General	LtC = Lieutenant Colonel
LG = Lieutenant General	Maj = Major
MG = Major General	Capt. = Captain
BG = Brigadier General	Lt = Lieutenant

for = assumptive or interim command on behalf of…
vice = succeeding to incumbent command after…

Fig. 5

At War's Beginning: 1808 – 'One of Our Most Important Affairs'[59]

The expeditionary force assembling around Cork, Ireland, in June 1808, under Lieutenant General Sir Arthur Wellesley's command, was under the immediate superintendence of his senior subordinate, Major General Rowland Hill. It was provisionally organised in three brigades, with the expectation that the brigade under Major General Ronald Ferguson[60] would become Hill's command:

Brigadier General Henry Fane: 5/60th and 95th Foot (the 'Light brigade')
Major General Ronald Ferguson: 5th, 9th, and 38th Foot
Brigadier General Catlin Craufurd: 40th, 71st, and 91st Foot (the 'Highlanders')[61]

The 36th and 45th Regiments, added to the expedition before it departed Cork,[62] appear to have been temporarily united with Fane's small brigade for the voyage.[63] Debarkation at Mondego Bay began on 1 August, and on the 3rd, Wellesley issued the General Order by which he revised the provisional brigading, shaping the little army into its first order of battle (see Fig. 6).[64]

Consistent with custom, the pattern positioned the brigade of the senior commander (Major General Ferguson) on the right flank, the 'post of honour', and the junior line brigade (Brigadier General C. Craufurd's) to its left. The brigade commanded by Fane was comprised of light infantry. 'Light' infantry stood, by definition, *outside* the line of battle and therefore outside the sequence established for the 'line' regiments and brigades. The customary notional place for

---

GENERAL ORDER: **Initial Battle-Array**

Lavos, 3rd Aug., 1808

The order of battle of the army is to be two deep, and as follows, beginning with the right:—

Major-General Ferguson's brigade.
Brigadier-General Catlin Craufurd's ditto.
Brigadier-General Fane's ditto, on the left.

There is to be a howitzer and three pieces of cannon attached to each of the brigades of infantry. The 9-pounder brigade with that under Major-General Ferguson, and the remainder of the artillery not allotted, will be in reserve.

[…] When the army shall move from its left, the 95th and 5th battalion 60th will lead the column in the ordinary course. When the army shall move from its right, the 95th and 5th battalion 60th must form the advanced guard, and lead the column from the right of the two corps with the howitzer and 6-pounders attached to General Fane's brigade.

[…] The cavalry is to be in reserve; and its position as well in the column of the line of march, will be pointed out in the orders of the day. […]

Fig. 6

light infantry, pending a specific tactical or operational assignment, was on the left, mimicking at a higher organisational level the position of the battalion light infantry company. It was a flexible relationship to the line of battle, as clarified in Wellesley's second paragraph stipulating that regardless of the flank by which the force advanced, Fane's light brigade was to lead.

The order included Wellesley's explicit direction to employ the tactical formation that his army would make famous during the Peninsular War: the two-rank line. Though in contradistinction to the three ranks generally deemed the proper formation of a battalion in line of battle by the *Rules and Regulations*, there had been a long history of customary use, and it was a shallow formation not unfamiliar among Continental armies.[65]

GENERAL ORDER: Revised Battle-Array

Lavos, 7th Aug., 1808

Major-General Spencer's corps having joined the army, the regiments will be brigaded as follows, from the right:

1st brigade	5th regiment / 9th " / 38th "	Major-General Hill
3rd brigade	29th " / 82nd "	Brigadier-General Nightingall
5th brigade	45th " / 50th " / 91st "	Brigadier-General Catlin Craufurd
4th brigade	6th " / 32nd "	Brigadier-General Bowes
2nd brigade	36th " / 40th " / 71st "	Major-General Ferguson
6th, or light brigade	2nd batt. 95th / 5th batt. 60th	Brigadier-General Fane

The foregoing will be the general formation of the brigades in one line, excepting that the light brigade will be ordered to take post in front or in rear, or on either flank, according to circumstances. The cavalry will be in reserve, and posted as may be necessary. A half brigade of artillery will be attached to each brigade of infantry. Howitzers will be attached to the 1st, 2nd, 5th, and 6th brigades, and the 9-pounder brigade will be in reserve.

Major-General Spencer being second in command, is not to be put on duty as a General Officer. [...]

Fig. 7

On 5 August, Major General Spencer arrived from Gibraltar, and Wellesley arranged a 'new modelled'[66] order of battle incorporating the three additional general officers, five new regiments, and the artillery that followed him (see Fig. 7).[67]

Spencer, senior to Hill, took up the anticipated role as second-in-command, without a specific brigade command, thereby permitting Hill to claim his promised brigade, numbered the '1st' as the next most senior major general. The remaining general officers were assigned brigade numbers in the order of their respective seniority. Four of Spencer's five regiments remained under the two brigadiers, Miles Nightingall and Barnard Bowes, who had accompanied them, while the fifth regiment, the 50th, was allocated to Catlin Craufurd. Meanwhile, some of the troops from Cork had been redistributed to create a brigade under Ferguson, the third-ranking major general. Craufurd surrendered the 40th and 71st, which with the unassigned 36th, formed Ferguson's brigade, while Craufurd retained the 91st, received the 50th from Spencer's force, and was assigned the orphan 45th.[68]

For this study, the most noteworthy aspect of this general order is to observe that the brigades were listed not in numerical order (typical of an administrative inventory), but in the sequence in which they were to stand in the line of battle (which may be considered a 'tactical' rather than 'administrative' order). The five line brigades took precedence, and were numbered, in the order of their commanders' respective seniority. The senior brigade stood on the right, in the 'post of honour', the second most senior on the left, and the remainder were distributed in alternating order to each inside flank, with the most junior command in the centre, reflecting over a century of British customary battle-array. The light brigade, numbered 6th, stood nominally on the far left, outside the sequence. Although not apparent from the *administrative* numerical sequencing in this general order, the infantry regiments in each brigade stood in a similar sequence in the brigade's tactical battle order: the senior regiment, or lowest numbered, on the right, the next senior on the left, and the junior in the centre. Thus, Wellesley's battle-array, as he prepared for what would be his first skirmishes on 15–16 August and his first engagement, at Roliça on 17 August, would notionally stand in line of battle as in Fig. 8.

When considered visually, Wellesley's order of battle reveals several elegant symmetries. The alternating right-left distributive pattern, trending to the centre – of regiments within brigades, and of brigades within the army's line of battle – is evident. The 6th (the 'light infantry') brigade, composed entirely of rifle companies and some 1,500 strong,[69] was outside the main array, nominally on the left. According to custom, left-most brigade contained the exception to the right flank's primacy for the sequence of regiments within a brigade; in this 'second post of honour', the proper sequence of regiments in the 2nd Brigade was in reverse, with the eldest on the left extremity.

The two brigades commanded by major generals were, through the alternating, seniority-based distributive pattern, posted on each flank of the battle line, while commands of the brigadier generals were in the centre. As it happened, the two brigades from Spencer's force,[70] both composed of two regiments, fell symmetri-

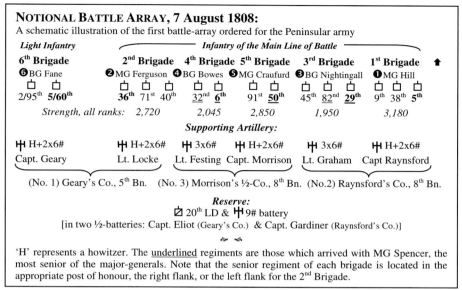

Fig. 8

cally into the right-centre and left-centre positions, by virtue of their commanders' seniority. They were buttressed to each flank by the brigades from Cork, each of three regiments. Their relative manpower was also rhythmically sequenced. Wellesley proved equally successful in melding the comparatively weak late-comers, the 36th and 45th Regiments (with strengths of roughly 660 and 750, respectively), smoothly into the distribution. The allocation of greater strength to the 1st Brigade reflected a tendency that would manifest itself throughout the Peninsular War: that of making the army's 1st Division the numerically strongest subordinate element.

How did this 'order of battle', as laid out as in this normative general instruction, compare to the battle-array Wellesley actually employed at Roliça just 10 days later? With remarkable consistency.

Following the skirmishes at Caldas and Obidos, Wellesley issued an 'After General Order' (A.G.O.), on 16 August, to prepare for the following day's expected engagement with the French, under General Delaborde:

> The army will move off from their present ground at half-past four o'clock tomorrow morning, and assemble in contiguous columns of brigades, right in front, in the plain on this side of the castle of Obidos.[71]

The very phrase, 'right in front', assumed a normal sequence of a command's internal components. The instruction meant the brigade was to march with its regiments ordered so that the right-most regiment in the brigade's line of battle led the column and the left-most regiment brought up the tail. This was regarded as the 'natural order' of march for a column; 'left in front', of course, reversed this sequence (see Fig. 9). Moreover, all the constituent units of a column normally led by the same flank as the column they constituted. The sequence implicit when marching by the left or right had broad consequences. 'When the army marches from its left, every regiment [in that column] marches from its left; and when the army marches from its right, every regiment marches from its right' was the accepted and practical wisdom.[72] The decision about whether to lead by the right or left flank was contingent upon the commander's expectation regarding the flank (or direction) to which he expected to form his command, whether by wheeling units' components 90° to face one side of his axis of advance, or by 'deploying' ('prolonging' or stretching out his troops from column into line to that side, perpendicular to the axis of advance) still facing the original direction of march.

Wellesley assembled his army before determining upon his final disposition. Having studied the French position, Wellesley revised the battle-array so that the two right-most brigades confronted the enemy, the centre brigade acting as their reserve – leading by the right, it was natural that Craufurd followed Nightingall's brigade – while the two left-most line brigades marched as a column under Ferguson's command, to turn the French right (as a Portuguese column, under Colonel Trant, turned the enemy's left). Meanwhile, Fane's brigade, light infantry with no fixed place in a line of battle (and of only 11 companies, after detachments), extended to provide a link between the left column and the main body, while pressing the French right. Schematically, these dispositions for Roliça (Fig. 10)[73] closely mirrored the order of battle laid out in his general order ten days previously (Figs. 7 and 8).[74]

This close correlation offers an example of how historians have often missed implicit information about an order of battle's sequence, or simply refused to believe that it was relevant. Captain Lewis Butler in his two-volume study, *Wellington's Operations* (based on Napier's famous *History of the Peninsular War*), and published ten years before the World War of 1914–18, reproduced a table of organisation based on Wellesley's General Order of 7 August. Not only did Butler alter the sequence of brigades to present them in numerical order, but

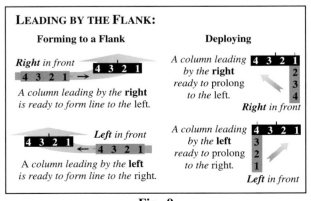

Fig. 9

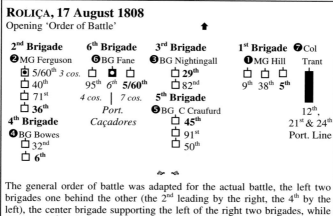

Fig. 10

he opined that the sequence Wellesley had stipulated was merely intended for 'parade purposes'. Here, just a century after the event, the imperatives of customary close order battle-array were not only forgotten, but denied by a serving British military author. He erred. The pattern of customary battle-array was a very real and practical tool for battle.

One significant change from Wellesley's initial arrangements to march 'right in front' was found on the left flank. Ferguson's brigade led Bowes', forming a grand column led by the left brigade – but Bowes' brigade appears to have marched *left* in front while Ferguson's marched by the right. The disposition of the left-most brigade leading the flanking march under Ferguson was, of course, a natural product of the senior general leading the advance. Put another way, the ordinary sequence of the two left-most brigades, marching out to the left to embark on a flanking movement, naturally led with the brigade on the far left. Ferguson's brigade was, like the others, already disposed right in front; Bowes' brigade, however, if Fortescue and Verner interpreted their unnamed sources correctly,[75] would have had to counter-march to change the flanks by which the regiments were marching and reversed their order of march. This sequence of the two brigades marching by opposite flanks in the same grand column was unusual. It reflected, however, Wellesley's objectives and priorities for this flanking column: to turn his opponent's right flank while preventing possible intervention from outside reinforcements.

While both brigades could form line of battle to their front easily enough, Bowes' 4th Brigade of two battalions, advancing by its left, was disposed to expedite formation of a line of battle facing to its right and towards the enemy it was to outflank; Ferguson's three-battalion 2nd Brigade, leading with its right, was ready to form line of battle facing to its *left*, away from Delaborde's French and in the direction from which French General Loison could be expected to arrive or be found. Wellesley thereby hedged his bets, his objective to outflank one enemy while fending off another force was mirrored in his battle-array.

It was not the last time that Wellesley would arrange his manœuvre elements in contrary fashion. He would make a related disposition on a grander operational scale for the advance to surround Salamanca in mid-June 1812. At that time, two columns, respectively under Graham and Beresford, marched in parallel around Salamanca to the east while Picton's column surrounded it to the west. Graham's column (with the 1st and 7th Divisions) moved by its right while parallel and to its right, Beresford's column (with the 5th and 4th Divisions) marched by its left (as did Picton's, to the west). In this way, Graham's command was prepared to face to the left against Salamanca in order of battle while Beresford's column was prepared to face to its right, also in order of battle, ready to shield British operations against French-occupied forts inside the city from intervention by Marmont's troops to the north-east.[76] (See Fig. 11)[77]

At Roliça, although the two brigades of Ferguson's column remained unengaged during the battle (for Loison had marched to Torres Vedras),[78] Wellesley was content that they had served their dual purpose. Roliça had been fought with a battle-array built upon the order of battle that he had developed in the General Orders of 3 and 7 August. Together, those orders exemplified and embodied the structuring principles of a customary battle-array that the Anglo-Allied army

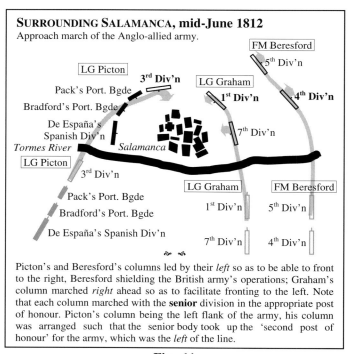

SURROUNDING SALAMANCA, mid-June 1812
Approach march of the Anglo-allied army.

Picton's and Beresford's columns led by their *left* so as to be able to front to the right, Beresford shielding the British army's operations; Graham's column marched *right* ahead so as to facilitate fronting to the left. Note that each column marched with the **senior** division in the appropriate post of honour. Picton's column being the left flank of the army, his column was arranged such that the senior body took up the 'second post of honour' for the army, which was the *left* of the line.

Fig. 11

would employ and build upon throughout the nearly six years it would contest the Peninsular War. There was little in his order of battle that Wellesley's military colleagues would not have recognised at any time during the preceding century or more, or for over half a century afterwards. The principles of an alternating distributive pattern by rank and seniority were 'customary' in so far as they were not to be found in official regulations, or in either general or specific orders from

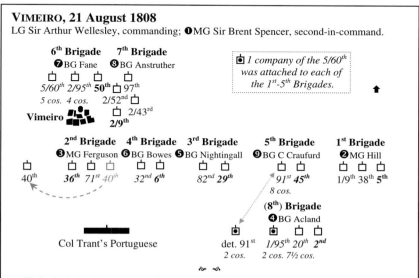

VIMEIRO, 21 August 1808
LG Sir Arthur Wellesley, commanding; ❶MG Sir Brent Spencer, second-in-command.

Wellesley's battle-array accorded closely with that described in his General Order of 7 August (Fig. 8), except that the 5th and 3rd Brigades had exchanged places. The 6th Brigade, being light infantry, stood literally outside the sequence of the main line of battle. To support the army's pickets on the far left, Ferguson apparently chose to reposition his *right* battalion (the brigade's array being reversed in the second post of honour). This was to have an effect on the later battle-array that materialized against the French turning movement farther left.

Anstruther's Brigade had joined only the previous day, and Acland's landed only on the morning of the battle (and was not actually denominated '8th' until after the battle). Anstruther's Brigade, half of his regiments being light infantry well known to Wellesley from Denmark, was placed with Fane's Brigade at the key forward post. Acland was directed into a supporting position for the main line. The order of their arrival accounts for their brigade numbers not corresponding with their or others' relative seniority.

Anstruther's deployment, notionally should have been: 2/43rd – 2/52nd – 97th – 2/9th. Challenging though it is, it may be rationalized if viewed as though the exterior battalions were folded back to supporting positions, and then the 2/52nd echeloned back as well. The 2/9th Foot was apparently a pretty raw battalion and was never committed to the fight. During the battle, the 2/52nd moved across the rear of the 97th and out from the right flank, while the 2/43rd was marched leftwards to defend Vimeiro village.

Craufurd's brigade moved rearwards to the left, in a deep arc, picking up Trant's Portuguese brigade along the way, to guard against any French move against the British rear. This left Hill's Brigade to relocate leftwards along the ridgeline to support Fane and Anstruther's right.

As a harbinger of future practice, on 18 August, Wellesley distributed 5 companies of the 5/60th to augment the light infantry capabilities of his line brigades.

Fig. 12

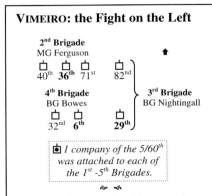

VIMEIRO: the Fight on the Left

2nd Brigade
MG Ferguson

40th 36th 71st   82nd

4th Brigade   3rd Brigade
BG Bowes   BG Nightingall

32nd 6th   29th

*1 company of the 5/60th
was attached to each of
the 1st -5th Brigades.*

The battle-array for this part of the engagement has been troublesome for several subsequent histories. Appreciation for customary battle-array illuminates the actual sequence employed. When Ferguson hurried his brigade to the left, the 36th Foot led the column – but the 40th had already been posted across the river farther leftwards, and so either moved ahead of the brigade, or waited for the brigade to reach it. Either way, the 40th thus wound up at the head, or left, of the brigade when it was arrayed for battle. Bowes' Brigade was next to join, naturally having marched by its left. Nightingall's Brigade arrived last, also marching naturally by its left, in which orientation it moved onto the right of the existing dispositions, having the effect of extending the British line to its right in the face of the French advance. Acland's Brigade, following, halted to support the fight at Vimeiro from the heights to the village's left (north).

Fig. 13

superior authority; in fact, there does not appear to exist any written evidence requiring their application above the regiment, but the principles were well-established, widely shared, and regularly applied.

Vimeiro was Wellesley's second and last battle of his tidy little 1808 campaign, fought just four days after Roliça (Fig. 12).[79] Observe that his battle-array was again closely consistent with his order of battle as conceived at Lavos, two weeks earlier. Neither Oman nor Fortescue were able to unravel the British dispositions made for the fight on the far left of the battle; but, as an example of battle-array's utility as an analytical tool, a review of the sources, viewed through the prism of customary battle-array, makes clearer how the British line of battle was formed there (Fig. 13).[80]

Wellesley had made, on 18 August, one noteworthy alteration to his order of battle: 'One company of the 60th to be attached to each of the following brigades: the 1st, 2nd, 3rd, 4th, and 5th; and to join them as soon as possible.'[81] Wellesley thereby introduced a rifle-armed light infantry component into each of his line brigades, an arrangement he would reinstitute immediately upon resuming command in 1809 and sustain throughout the war.[82]

Introducing Divisions: Reconstructing the Peninsular Army, 1809

The evolution of the army's initial organisation is explored in greater depth in Chapter 2 on 'The Origin of Wellington's Peninsular Army' and a cursory glance at Moore's final battle at Coruña reveals the principles of British customary battle-array fully applied, even after a debilitating retreat through the rains and snows of a Galician winter (Fig. 14).[83] With the enlargement of the Peninsular army immediately after Vimeiro, Moore had formed it into army divisions. While the new divisions acquired numbers or labels (e.g., 'Reserve'), the brigades reverted to the older practice of identification by the name of the brigadier. This seems to have also applied to the brigades left behind in Portugal under Lieutenant General Cradock, an army that only took on an operational shape, arrayed in three lines, with his General Order of 6 April.[84]

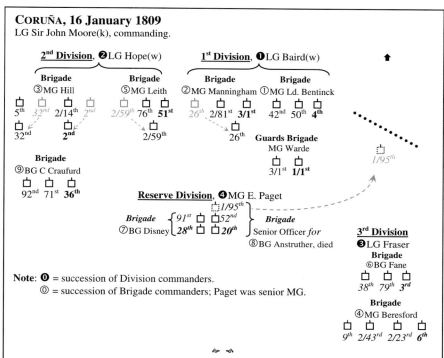

CORUÑA, 16 January 1809
LG Sir John Moore(k), commanding.

2nd Division, ❷LG Hope(w)   **1st Division**, ❶LG Baird(w)

Brigade   **Brigade**   **Brigade**   **Brigade**
③MG Hill   ⑤MG Leith   ②MG Manningham   ①MG Ld. Bentinck

5th *32nd* 2/14th *2nd*   2/59th 76th **51st**   *26th* 2/81st **3/1st**   42nd 50th **4th**

32nd   **2nd**   2/59th   26th   **Guards Brigade**
MG Warde

3/1st **1/1st**

Brigade
⑨BG C Craufurd

92nd 71st **36th**   **Reserve Division**, ❹MG E. Paget

1/95th

Brigade {91st 52nd   **Brigade**
⑦BG Disney {**28th** **20th**   Senior Officer *for*
⑧BG Anstruther, died

3rd Division
❸LG Fraser

Brigade
⑥BG Fane

38th 79th **3rd**

Note: ❶ = succession of Division commanders.
⑩ = succession of Brigade commanders; Paget was senior MG.

Brigade
④MG Beresford

9th 2/43rd 2/23rd **6th**

1/95th

    It seems that when the line brigades were placed within a divisional structure, the naming convention reverted to the earlier practice of identification by their commanders' names. Divisions were numbered, except for the 'Reserve'. The Reserve Division was no larger than the 'reserve' Moore had commanded in Egypt – in fact, it also contained the 28th Foot, which had been commanded in Egypt by Paget, and who, in Spain, now commanded the Reserve.
    The disposition of the Reserve Division is mysterious, and contradictorily mapped by a number of sources. The Reserve had, however, been marching en route to embark when the battle began. Sources are unclear about whether it counter-marched its companies, battalions, entire column or simply faced about to return to its reserve position – in light of the sense of urgency, it seems likely it countermarched by companies, thereby reversing the natural order of the battalions and putting the columns left in front. Arriving back at its position, it is again unclear how it arranged its parts – represented here is the assumption that both brigades were placed abreast. This would facilitate the order in which its parts appear to have been subsequently committed to battle. Whether the 95th had remained behind or subsequently resumed its extended post to Baird's right, is also murky. Further, with Anstruther's death (of dysentery) the day before, the Reserve was shorn of one brigadier, and that may explain the disassociation of battalions from a brigade structure during the ensuing battle – but that would have been very much in the tradition of 'Reserves' over the past decade.
    All of the brigade battle-arrays exhibit the application of the customary principles, except for C Craufurd's, and the sources shed little light on the reasons for its sequence. It may be worth considering that both the 92nd and 71st were Highland regiments: the former with a long history of use as light infantry, the latter about to be officially designated 'light infantry' later in 1809. In fact, a detachment from the 92nd was forward of Hill's line (see Gardyne, Verner). As for Hill's, Leith's, and Manningham's brigades, which all formed brigade reserves, the relationship between the nominal order of battle and the supported array actually adopted is shown using grayed icons for the nominal position.
    Although the brigades were not numbered, one can see that they were disposed within each division consistent with customary battle-array. While the Guards were in support, the senior line brigade (commander) held the right of the 1st Division, and the left of the 2nd Division, while the 3rd Division was placed left in front, appropriately for its position on the field.

Fig. 14

Then, in the course of just over six weeks, from 4 May to 18 June 1809, in a fascinatingly telescoped example of a military version of epigenesis, the order of battle of Britain's Peninsular army underwent a rapid succession of organisational changes that mirrored the conceptual evolution of battle-array during the previous century of European military history. The biological concept, epigenesis, 'stresses the fact that every embryological step is an act of *becoming* (Greek *genesis*) which must [build] upon (Greek *epi*) the immediate status quo ante'.[85] Just as the developing embryo moves through stages of form and development that resemble the progressive steps in the species' evolutionary past, so the birth of Wellesley's army in 1809 embodied the organisational forms of the military institutions and conceptual world that had preceded it. In a month and a half, the army evolved from a single unitary line (4 May),[86] to an army articulated in two wings (8 May), to an informal use of three, more flexible proto-army divisions (in the Oporto campaign of later May), and finally to a formal reorganisation into four army divisions (18 June).

Shortly after Wellesley's return in April 1809, to resume command in the Peninsula, the brigades were again numbered and given a new order of battle (see Fig. 15).[87] Just as brigades had normally been in previous British expeditions, and were in 1808, so were they now numbered in correlation with the commanding officers' relative seniority. With respect to the expression and sequence of battle-array, it was similar to that which Wellesley had established in early August 1808 (see Figs. 6 and 7). The version given here is that which Lieutenant Dickson (who would rise to become Wellington's artillery chief in 1813) recorded in his journal.

The array had symmetry. Wellesley equalized the halves of the line of battle with five brigades each (counting the KGL as two); the right half's line brigades were odd-numbered and the left even-numbered; and there was a simple alternation of seniority from right to left, toward the centre, with the KGL standing on the far left outside the British sequence, and the Guards standing outside on the right. Wellesley maintained that balance when selecting two brigades, Mackenzie's and Tilson's, for detached service: he drew one from each half of the army.

Wellesley's new battle-array introduced the Foot Guards to his command. This contingent was the 2nd Guards Brigade. From 1803, the three regiments of Foot Guards appear to have been organised into three brigades: the 1st Brigade, composed of the 1st and 3rd Battalions of the 1st Foot Guards; the 2nd Brigade, of the 1st Battalions of the Coldstream and 3rd Foot Guards; while the 3rd Brigade was composed of all three regiments' 2nd Battalions, acting as a grand depot.[88] The Guards were never numbered in sequence with the Line brigades, not least, because they stood outside the order of the line of battle, taking precedence on the right. Moreover, the Guards claimed the privilege of being commanded by none but guardsmen. Therefore, their brigadier also stood outside the usual seniority that informed other command assignments – the same applied to the Household cavalry.

This battle-array also introduced the unique element of the King's German Legion to Wellesley's command and was destined to form an enduring partnership with the army's senior element, the Guards, throughout the rest of the Peninsular War. The KGL infantry battalions formed part of a single, unregimented corps. Though unregimented, they had been brigaded, from the Legion's

ORDER OF BATTLE, as of 4 May 1809

A unitary army

General Order, Head Quarters, May 4, 1809

The Army will be Brigaded and will stand in Line from the Right as follows until Further orders.

❶ M. Gen. Stapleton Cotton	14th Light Dragoons		
	20th " "		2 Squadrons
	3rd " "	K.G.L.	1 Squadron
	16th " "		

③ Brig. Gen Henry Fredrick Campbell	Guards – two battalions	⎫	Coldstream, 1st Battalion
		⎬	3rd Foot Guards, 1st Battalion
	1 Company, 5th Battalion, 60th		

1st Brigade.

❷ M. Gen. Rowland Hill	3rd or Buffs	1st Battalion
	66th Regiment	2nd Battalion
	48th "	2nd Battalion

3rd Brigade.

❺ M. Gen. Christopher Tilson	5 companies, 5th Battalion, 60th	
	88th Regiment	1st Battalion
	Portuguese Grenadiers	1st "
	87th Regiment	2nd "

5th Brigade.

② Brig. Gen Alexander Campbell	7th Regiment	2nd Battalion
	10th Portuguese	1st Battalion
	53rd Regiment	2nd Battalion
	1 Company, 5th Battalion, 60th	

7th Brigade.

⑦ Brig. Gen. Alan Cameron	9th Regiment	2nd Battalion
	10th Portuguese	2nd Battalion
	83rd Regiment	2nd Battalion
	1 Company, 5th Battalion, 60th	

6th Brigade.

④ Brig. Gen. Richard Stewart	1st Battalion, Detachments	
	16th Portuguese	1st Battalion
	29th Regiment	

4th Brigade.

① Brig. Gen. John Sontag	Detachments	2nd Battalion
	16th Portuguese	2nd "
	97th Regiment	
	1 Company, 5th Battalion, 60th	

2nd Brigade.

❹ M. Gen. John [Randoll] Mackenzie	27th Regiment	3rd Battalion
	45th "	1st Battalion
	31st "	2nd Battalion

Kings German Legion

Two Brigades under
❸ M. Gen. John Murray

⑤ Brig. Gen. George de Drieberg	5th Line Battalion	
	7th " "	

⑥ Brig. Gen. Ernest Baron Langwerth	2nd Line Battalion	
	1st " "	

> **Note:**
> Seniority tags added:
> ❶ = seniority of MGs
> ① = seniority of BGs

At Lisbon

	24th Foot	2nd Battalion
	30th "	2nd "
	Independent Light Company, K.G.L.	

⑧ Brig. Henry Fane	3rd Dragoon Guards	Formed into a Brigade and
	4th Dragoons	employed in the
		neighbourhood of the Tagus.

Fig. 15

inception, by pairing battalions to form a Light Brigade of two light battalions, and the 1st through 4th Line Brigades by progressively pairing the 1st through 8th Line Battalions as they were completed.[89] The actual operational brigading of the line battalions for the Peninsular War, however, may have been largely the consequence of the winter gales that struck the fleet returning from the Danish expedition in December 1807. The 3rd, 4th, 6th, and 8th Line Battalions, delayed at sea, were still mostly embarked when additional troops were needed to join Spencer's expedition to the Tagus River. These battalions were attached to him, and eventually went on to Sicily, leaving the 1st, 2nd, 5th, and 7th Line Battalions, in two brigades, to join Cradock in Portugal a year later.[90] In the Peninsula, the brigading of pairs of KGL battalions resulted, through October 1809, and again in December 1813–April 1814 (when the brigade of light battalions joined their colleagues of the line), in the peculiar arrangement of a KGL 'brigade' composed of constituent brigades.

It appears that some aspects of precedence in Hanoverian customary practice differed from those of their British colleagues. Hanoverian practice posted brigades by seniority of commands rather than commanders. Brigadier General Langwerth's 1st KGL Line Brigade took precedence of position over his senior's, Brigadier General Drieberg's, 2nd KGL Line Brigade. Being placed within a separate command permitted Hanoverian practice to work itself out within a suprabrigade, and may have been one reason for the creation of this peculiar organisational superstructure. Interestingly, Dickson's version of the General Order listed Langwerth's senior brigade at the bottom (equating to the left of the line of battle), and in reverse order. He was not alone in supposing the KGL, though standing outside the British line of battle, and thus on the left and junior to its British brethren, would reverse its internal order in light of its position on the left.[91] As it happens, this was *not* an arrangement the KGL followed.[92]

Wellesley's General Order for 4 May 1809 continued with further instructions for his battle-array (Fig. 16).[93] Paragraph two made explicit that the order of battle laid out in these instructions was a point of departure, a default arrangement unless otherwise directed, or unless other imperatives necessitated different dispositions. In other words, the battle-array was not set in stone, but was a flexible springboard for battle.

Paragraph three redeveloped the instructions for light infantry that Wellesley had given on 3 August 1808 (see Fig. 6), and supplemented on 18 and 21 August. Upon his return to Portugal, the Peninsular army possessed proportionally even less light infantry than at Vimeiro: only one battalion, the 5/60th Foot, plus fragments of the 43rd, 52nd, and 95th Regiments gathered in the 1st Battalion of Detachments and similar fragments of the KGL light battalions in another detachment. He valued the riflemen's capabilities from his earlier experience in Denmark and Portugal. In his 7 March 1809 'Memorandum on the Defence of Portugal' he had specifically noted the need to augment the forces there with 'riflemen and other good infantry'.[94]

In his dispatch to Castlereagh, written just two days after arriving in Lisbon, Wellesley referred to the expected arrival of a 'light brigade', and his instructions attempting to anticipate its rendezvous with the army reflected some degree of

---

(G.O., 4 May 1809, cont.)

2. Although this is to be the order of the line of battle, circumstances of ground and situation may render a deviation from it necessary.

3. The light infantry companies belonging to, and the riflemen attached to each brigade of infantry, are to be formed together, on the left of the brigade, under the command of a Field officer or Captain of light infantry of the brigade, and to be fixed upon by the Officer who commands it. Upon all occasions, in which the brigade may be formed in line, or in column, when the brigade shall be formed for the purpose of opposing an enemy, the light infantry companies and riflemen will be of course in front, flanks, or rear, according to the circumstances of the ground, and the nature of the operation to be performed. On all other occasions, the light infantry companies are to be considered as attached to their battalions, with which they are to be quartered or encamped, and solely under the command of the Commanding Officer of the battalion to which they belong.

Fig. 16

anxiety for its earliest arrival.[95] That brigade, however, would not drop anchor at Lisbon until June, under Robert Craufurd, and would miss the battle at Talavera by just a day. Meanwhile, Wellesley had to make judicious use of his line regiments' light infantry companies. He invoked an established, pre-existing practice: combining the light companies from each battalion in a brigade into an ad hoc light battalion (battalions being a body of two or more companies) under the central command of a senior light infantry or field officer. The practice of grouping light companies was long-established, as reflected in a 1795 treatise:

> In time of war, light companies are always taken from their respective regiments, and formed into battalions.
>
> Their manœuvres are nearly on the same principles as regiments, the officers taking post in the same manner.[96]

This improvised grouping was distinct, however, from the past (and occasionally continued) practice of stripping off the élite flank (light and grenadier) companies from regiments to form flank battalions for separate operations.[97] Wellington was much opposed to this, as he noted in a letter to Major General W. Stewart in March 1810: 'I disapprove of detaching flank companies from the battalion to which they belong, and I have not allowed of such detachments in this army.'[98] These light battalions were to remain with their parent brigades, in battle and on campaign.

Wellesley's unique twist to the ad hoc light infantry battalion was to reinstitute his 1808 distribution to the various brigades of a company of riflemen, detached from the specialist 5/60th. As before, he began by detaching only half of the

5/60th's companies, later detaching three more to various brigades as the war progressed, supplemented still later by three rifle companies from the Brunswick-Oels Jägers. The KGL line brigades had no need of outside rifle companies, for every battalion company already had as many as ten rifle-armed sharpshooters (*Scharfschützen*) available to support their own light companies.[99] The KGL light battalions (which returned to the Peninsula in 1811) and the Portuguese light infantry (*caçador*) battalions also carried a significant number of rifles in a proportion that rose during the course of the war.[100]

The result was a potent skirmishing asset for each brigade. Wellesley's General Order, just two days later, specifically noted that:

> The Commander of the Forces recommends the Companies of the 5th Battalion of the 60th Regiment, to the particular care and attention of the General Officers commanding the brigades of Infantry, to which they are attached; they will find them to be most useful, active, and brave troops in the field, and that they will add essentially to the strength of their brigades.[101]

The result of this combination of the brigade's light companies and a rifle company was a small ad hoc 'light battalion' (sometimes referred to in memoirs as a 'brigade') that operated in conformance to the parent brigade's movements. It was an effective organisational and tactical practice that endured throughout the war.

Wellesley's order identified the left of the brigade as the post for its light infantry battalion when not skirmishing. This was merely an iteration, at a higher scale, of the customary position of a battalion's light infantry company. The systematization of a holding-space pending the unit's deployment was reflected in the contemporary written formats, which normally listed the attached rifle company last in orders of battle. It has consequently been adopted in this examination's schematics as the default post for light infantry. The schematics, however, generally omit to show each brigade's ad hoc light infantry battalion, though the brigade assignments of the detached rifle companies are noted.

A grand review was held at Coimbra on 6 May on the eve of the advance north to eject Marshal Soult's French forces from Oporto: 'The regiments having formed a line (reaching above 2 miles), wheeled into column, marched past, and filed to their quarters.'[102] Doubtless, one by-product of such a review was to practice the newly established sequencing, accustoming commanders and regiments to their new spatial relationships.

Just two days later, on 8 May, Wellesley made a final revision of his order of battle in light of the new organisational potential offered by the arrival of needed lieutenant generals (Fig. 17).[103] The line of battle was formally divided into two 'wings', leaving the sequence of brigades and regiments unchanged. Although not specifically noted in the orders, the implication was that, while Lieutenant General Payne commanded the cavalry, the other two available lieutenant generals, Sherbrooke and Edward Paget, would command the Right and Left Wings, respectively – Sherbrooke being senior to Paget having customary claim to the right. The three lieutenant generals even received the beginnings of staff when members of the Adjutant General's Department were assigned to them.[104] The preparation of Wellesley's order of battle was in complete harmony with traditional practice, as recorded by the prolific military writer, Thomas Simes, forty years earlier, who noted regarding 'Of the Rendezvous of an Army': 'When the encampment is to be formed, the General Officers, &c. are appointed to their several posts and stations; and the army divided into brigades, columns, wings, or lines.'[105] Wellesley also reiterated that this battle order was not immutable, but

---

ORDER OF BATTLE, from 8 May 1809
The army in transition: divided into two wings.

A.G.O.   Coimbra, 8th May, 1809.

    1. Lieutenant General Paget being arrived to-day, the Army is to be divided as follows, till the other Lieutenant Generals attached to it will join:

      Guards...................................
      Major-General Hill's...................
      Brigadier-General A. Campbell's... } Right Wing
      Brigadier-General Cameron's........

with a brigade of heavy 6 pounders, and a brigade of light 6 pounders.

    2. The King's German Legion..........
      Brigadier-General Sontag's............ } Left Wing
      Brigadier-General R. Stewart's......

with one brigade of six pounders, and one brigade of three pounders.

    3. These wings will be formed into two or more lines, as circumstances may require, and brigades will be detached from them according to circumstances, to form advanced guards and reserves: there is to be no alteration in the orders of march to-morrow.

                 *   *

    Note that the brigades of the Right Wing were listed in the sequence of the order of battle (compare with Fig. 15), allowing for Tilson's detachment (3rd Brigade) on a separate mission. The Right Wing was composed of the odd-numbered brigades (1st, 5th, and 7th) plus the Guards. Allowing for Mackenzie's independent command (with the 2nd Brigade), the Left Wing was composed of the even-numbered brigades (4th and 6th), plus the KGL. Both wings totaled 4 infantry brigades. While the Right Wing was sequenced from the right, the Left Wing was given in the orders as sequenced from the left, thereby placing the KGL on the outside of the left flank – for although in the King's service, it stood outside and junior to the order of battle of the British line brigades, yet senior to all other foreign corps serving the crown, a pattern that continued throughout the war.

Fig. 17

subject to alteration 'according to circumstances'. As it happens, this order of battle immediately vanished out the proverbial window as the army advanced on Oporto, and Wellesley instead operated with three proto-divisions, rather than simply two wings.

Even as the army's battle-array evolved, the evolution of Wellesley's (and other contemporaries') use of the term 'division' was in flux, fraught with multiple meanings entirely dependent upon context. Wellesley's General Order of 9 May contained instructions that: 'The division under General Sherbrooke, General Cotton, General Murray, General Hill, and General Cameron, will march tomorrow . . .'[106] Here, 'division' corresponded to the entire 'Left Column', which was constituted of most of the British army, save Tilson's and Mackenzie's infantry (and Fane's cavalry) brigades detached on separate service. Yet, Wellesley's terminology in his dispatch to Castlereagh three days later was very different, resonating a more modern sense of the term:

> The infantry of the army was formed into three divisions for this expedition, of which two, the advanced guard, consisting of the King's German Legion, and Brigadier General R. Stewart's brigade, with a brigade of 6-pounders, and a brigade of 3-pounders, under Lieutenant General Paget; and the cavalry under Lieutenant General Payne; and the brigade of Guards, Brigadier General Campbell's and Brigadier General Sontag's brigades of infantry, with a brigade of 6-pounders, under Lieutenant General Sherbrooke, moved by the high road from Coimbra to Oporto: and one, composed of Major General Hill's and Brigadier General Cameron's brigades of infantry, and a brigade of 6-pounders, under the command of Major General Hill, by the road from Coimbra to Aveiro.[107]

There had been no formal reorganisation, however, just a *de facto* evolution of operational structure and usage. With the evolution toward a more flexible battlefield management tool, using columns or proto-divisions, and then fully realized army divisions, the principles of customary battle-array that had heretofore manifested themselves on the basis of the entire force in the field, were reapplied to work themselves out within divisional confines. The principles would be expressed less formally and less consistently in the arrangement of divisions, particularly as the war progressed, but their influence would not entirely disappear.

Wellesley was certainly alive to the effects and demands that the changes of organisational scale in the Peninsular army imposed. The day before he reorganised the army into divisions, he wrote to Castlereagh about the challenges of maintaining discipline and order:

> You will say, probably, in answer to all this, that British armies have been in the field before, and that these complaints, at least to the same extent, have not existed; to which I answer—first, that the armies are now larger, their operations more extended, and the exertions required greater than they were in former periods; and that the mode of carrying on war is different from what it was.[108]

ORDER OF BATTLE, as of 18 June 1809
Formally initiating a Divisional structure

G.O.   Abrantes, 18th June, 1809

3. Colonel Low, of the King's German Legion, is appointed to act as Brigadier General till his Majesty's pleasure is known, and is to command the brigade of the Legion, consisting of the 5th and 7th battalions of the line. Brigadier General Low will be pleased to recommend an Officer as his Brigade Major.

4. As the weather will now admit of the troops hutting, and they can therefore move together in large bodies, brigades are to be formed into divisions as follows:

Guards . . . .⎫
Brigadier Cameron's brigade . . ⎬ 1st Division
Hanoverian Legion . . . .⎭
Major Gen. Hill's brigade . . . .⎫ 2nd Division
Brig. Gen. R. Stewarts's ditto . .⎭
Major Gen. M'Kenzie's brigade. .⎫ 3rd Division
Colonel Donkin's ditto . . . . .⎭
Brig. Gen. A. Campbell's brigade .⎫ 4th Division
Colonel Peacocke's ditto. . . . .⎭

Lieutenant General Sherbrooke will take the command of the 1st Division; the senior General Officers of brigades will respectively take the command of the division in which their brigades are placed, till the other Lieutenant Generals will join the army. The brigades in divisions are to be formed from the right, as placed in this order:*

The divisions will stand in one or more lines, in respect to each other, as will be ordered at the time.

An Assistant Adjutant General will be attached to the Officer commanding the division; an Assistant Provost will also be attached to each division.

☙ ☙

Note. On 14 June Col. Donkin had replaced MG Tilson and Col. Peacocke had replaced BG Sontag (by the AGO of 14 June 1809).
* Unfortunately for posterity, the published General Order omitted the language describing the sequence!

Fig. 18

SEQUENCING THE BRIGADES

1ˢᵗ Division: ①LG Sherbrooke

KGL   KGL   BG Cameron   Guards

2ⁿᵈ Division: (②MG Hill)

❷BG R. Stewart   ❶MG Hill

3ʳᵈ Division: (③MG Mackenzie)

❷Col Donkin   ❶MG Mackenzie

4ᵗʰ Division: (④BG Campbell)

❷Col Peacock   ❶BG A. Campbell

The command of the 2ⁿᵈ to 4ᵗʰ Divisions was *assumed* by the senior brigadier in each division.

Fig. 19

On 18 June 1809, as the army waited on the Portuguese frontier, triumphant after the Oporto campaign, preparing to carry the offensive into Spain, Wellesley issued orders organising the army into four divisions, thereby completing a rapid organisational metamorphosis from an 18th to an early nineteenth century army (Figs. 18 and 19).[109] The dispositions developed in the Oporto campaign harboured associations that influenced the basis for reorganisation into army divisions. The 2nd Division comprised Hill's and R. Stewart's brigades (the latter whose brigade, from Paget's column, had been sent across the Douro to support Hill at the seminary); the other infantry brigades in Hill's and Paget's columns, respectively Cameron's and Murray's KGL, were grouped with the Guards brigade (from Sherbrooke's column) to form the 1st Division; the remainder of Sherbrooke's column, A. Campbell's and Sontag's brigades, formed the 4th Division. Mackenzie and Tilson, both of whom had been detached from the main army on separate missions, combined to form the 3rd Division. When Major General Murray resigned from the Peninsular army in May, the unique arrangement of the KGL suprabrigade vanished, leaving the Legion in two closely associated, but separate brigades.

In the British army, 'major general' was the grade normal for the command of brigades, and 'lieutenant general' the rank for command of a group of brigades, to include army divisions. Sherbrooke, the senior lieutenant general below Wellington, and the formally stipulated second-in-command, naturally acceded to the senior division, the '1st'. The other available lieutenant general, Payne, retained the command of all the cavalry brigades; Paget, Wellesley's third subordinate lieutenant general, had returned home after being severely wounded at Oporto. The command of the remaining divisions, therefore, was *assumptive*; that is, it was *assumed* by the senior brigade commander. Hill, however, who initially assumed command of the 2nd Division as its senior brigadier, ceded command of his brigade five days later (23 June) to Major General Tilson. Hill and Major General Cotton, Hill's senior, were both nominated by Wellesley for rank of 'local' lieutenant general[110] (granted in August), which made Hill a candidate for divisional command as an incumbent.

In mid-July, the army underwent another, minor internal reorganisation at Placentia, largely involving the incorporation of reinforcements and redistribution of some regiments among brigades.[111] Brigadier General G. Anson, who had replaced Colonel Peacocke on 22 June (sent to 'command the British troops in garrison at Lisbon'), was shifted to command of Major General W. Erskine's cavalry brigade during the latter's 'indisposition' and Colonel Kemmis (40th Foot) was placed upon the Staff and in command of Anson's former brigade in the 4th Division, his recently arrived regiment being transferred from Cameron's brigade with him. This transfer reflected Wellesley's determination to keep regiments belonging to colonels on staff and appointed to brigade command, in the same brigade. The practical reason for this was that such commanders were unlikely to hold their post for long, having usually to yield them as soon as general officers arrived and became available for commands.[112]

The Battle of Talavera offered the redesigned Peninsular army its first, nearly set-piece battle; it was the last for Wellesley under that name: he would earn a peerage as Viscount Wellington of Talavera for his victory there – a victory perhaps more closely won than Wellesley's after-action dispatch acknowledged. His dispositions for the battle proved to be inelegant, perhaps partly owing to the operational awkwardness of 23–27 July. The sudden and unpredictable vacillations of his Spanish ally, General Cuesta, left Wellesley straddling offensive and defensive modes after the initial success at Talavera on 22 July, so that, though Wellesley had a previously considered defensive position in mind, when the time came to occupy it on 27 July, he was compelled to do so while retreating under enemy pressure.

There was also a collective learning curve with respect to managing the new command arrangements and the army's size. Captain Stothert, adjutant in the 3rd Foot Guards, would note of the army's advance to Talavera on 22 July:

> This morning the combined army was in motion before daybreak, and advanced along the extensive plain towards Talavera. Few officers had ever previously seen so large a body acting as if by one impulse, and marching in one direction. It was in truth a sublime and magnificent spectacle, and the occasion was calculated to excite the most exalted ideas in a soldier's bosom.[113]

Though he had commanded large forces in India, this was the first time Wellesley had commanded so large a European force on a battlefield. It was also his first occasion for managing the army in battle through its new divisional structure. Sensibly, the *Rules and Regulations* introduced management of the 'Movements of the Line' with the admonishment that:

> The movements and manœuvres of a considerable line are similar to, and derived from the same general principles as those of the single battalion; they will be compounded, varied, and applied, according to circumstances, ground, and the intentions of the commanding officer; but their modes of execution remain unchangeable, and known to all. The greater the body, the fewer and more simple ought to be the manœuvres required of it.[114]

The divisional structure, however, introduced a more flexible and more complex nuance than the simple management of 'the Line'. As Wellesley and his subordinates worked out their modes of collective operation, principles of customary battle-array would provide a solid backstop for guiding conduct amidst war's fog.

Allied cooperation was fraught with many difficulties, but the junction of the two armies provided an opportunity for a review, the day before the advance to Talavera, as well as a chance to illustrate here the connection between battle-array and the order of march. Battle-array shaped not only battlefield dispositions; it also had a formative impact on two other aspects of military activity: the order of march and 'castrametation',[115] or the arrangement of camps. Indeed, these three aspects of military dispositions were so fundamentally intertwined as to be inseparable. Polybius, a Greek general, historian, and close observer of Republican Roman military institutions and practices in the second century B.C., had noted this interrelationship:

> I think therefore that it will be in place here to try to make my readers understand, as far as words can do so, the Roman tactics in regard to the march (*agmen*), the camp (*castorum metatio*), and the line of battle (*acies*). I cannot imagine any one so indifferent to things noble and great, as to refuse to take some little extra trouble to understand things like these; for if he has once heard them, he will be acquainted with one of those things genuinely worth observation and knowledge.[116]

The order of battle upon the field was inevitably a product, to a great degree, of the order in which units and commands marched onto the field.

Almost a century after the Peninsular War, Colonel Furse's full-length study, *The Art of Marching* (1901), made the same correlation:

> The leading principle in all marches is that the army always moves in that formation from which it can most readily assume the order of battle. From this it naturally follows that everything in the column should be arranged in the order in which it is likely to be wanted.[117]

The preparation and commencement of any march was naturally facilitated by encamping in the order in which units and commands were to move, and an army frequently moved off from camp by one or the other of its flanks. Perhaps more importantly, with respect to an army's camp, especially in proximity to the enemy, was the necessity to consider the encampment itself as a potential battlefield upon which the enemy might descend, for as Bland's eighteenth-century treatise had noted:

> Troops always Incamp in the same Order in which they Draw up in the Line, that, if the Enemy, by a sudden March, should endeavour to Surprise you in your Camp, you may be ready to enter upon Action as soon as you are Formed at the Head of your Incampment.[118]

A similar admonishment opened John Williamson's 1791 treatise on *The Elements of Military Arrangement*: 'An army encamps in the same order and disposition with that in which it draws up for action . . .'[119]

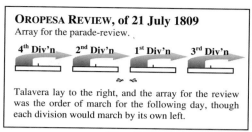

Fig. 20

For the 21 July review, Captain Hawker, 14th Light Dragoons, recorded: 'Having passed Oropesa, the whole British army was drawn up, for General Cuesta's inspection, and afterwards picquetted in the contiguous fields'[120] (see Fig. 20).[121] At 5 p.m., the British drew up on the south side of the main road in what was, in fact, to be their order of march the following day (see Fig. 21). From Hawker's comment, it appears inevitable that the army was encamped in that same order. An order of march was normally calculated to bring an army into action in an efficient and (quite literally) orderly fashion.

As a national force on the left of the line, the post of honour for British troops was the left flank. Bland's treatise had noted the protocol from Flanders, almost 100 years earlier. When an army consisted:

> of Troops of several Nations, every Nation had a distinct Post in the Line; so that the first or eldest Nation had all their troops on the Right; the second Nation had all theirs on the Left; and the third had theirs on the Left of the first; the Fourth on the Right of the second, and the fifth (if they consisted of so many Nations) had all theirs in the Center. And tho' this may seem, at first View, contrary to the foregoing Rule [for distributing the brigades in the line], yet, by looking on every Nation only as a Brigade (which must be done in this Case) it will be found, in every Respect, conformable to it.
>
> The Troops of each Nation are generally divided in both Lines, that those in the first may be sustained by their own troops, as also that each Nation may share equally of the Danger . . .
>
> The first Nation posts their eldest Brigade on the Right of the Front line, and their second Brigade on the Right of the Rear Line. Their third and fourth Brigade are placed on the Left of the first and second Brigades, and so on by Seniority till the two youngest Brigades are draw up on the Left of their own Troops in both Lines, the youngest Posts being those which lie nearest the Center.
>
> The second Nation draws up their two eldest Brigades on the Left Flank of both Lines . . .[122]

This international protocol of precedence would express itself at several Peninsular battles at which the host-nation's army of an Allied force took the post of honour on the right when on its home soil. At Talavera (1809), and again at

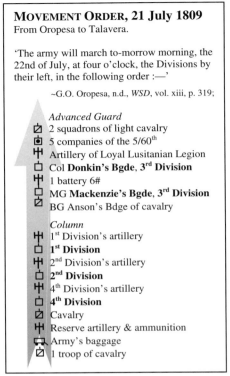

Fig. 21

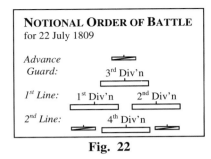

Fig. 22

Albuera (1811), both battles in Spain in which allied Spanish troops fought alongside an Anglo-Portuguese army as a separate national force, without a formally integrated command, the Spanish occupied the right of the Allied line; in Portugal, the Portuguese had had the honour of the right at Roliça (1808), the operational right in the Oporto campaign (1809), and the honour was extended again at Busaco (1810), for what was regarded as Portugal's national battle-test.[123]

For the approach march to Talavera, Wellesley's divisions led by their left, in anticipation of moving against the French right flank[124] (see Fig. 21).[125] Mackenzie's 3rd Division, as the advance guard, had the lead.[126] The order of march appears to have been arranged so as to place the 1st Division on the left of a front line (consistent with the principles Bland described), the other component of which would be the 2nd Division, following it, with the 4th Division and cavalry in support (see Fig. 22).

In the event, Cuesta did not press his contact with the French rearguard, which after a game display, was turned out of its position by the British threat to outflank it. When the allies finally managed to coordinate their onward movement two days later, Wellesley advanced his two leading divisions (the 3rd Division, with the 1st Division coming up on its left, the flank consistent with precedence for the left-wing nation), while the two rearward divisions (2nd and 4th) remained in the vicinity of Talavera.

Unconvinced of the wisdom of this advance, Wellesley had naturally considered the defensive position he suspected would prove necessary. Unfortunately, the record he left of his thinking is not particularly clear – possibly the result of his having to prepare for multiple eventualities, leaving him settled firmly on none. His Adjutant General, a man one might suspect to be relatively close to the commander's thinking on such matters, seems to have believed Wellesley had a disposition in mind for Talavera as of 26–27 July (Fig. 23).[127] Londonderry's insistence on the clarity and 'perspicuity' of Wellesley's dispositions is not entirely borne out by the evidence. Napier, as historian, possibly interpreted Wellesley's intended array through hindsight, for the anticipated disposition Napier described was very close to the one achieved (Fig. 24).[128]

Wellesley's own correspondence leaves a more nuanced impression – nevertheless, it is possible that his description incorporates a degree of *ex post facto* readjustment of his intentions (Fig. 25).[129] On 27 July, Campbell's 4th Division, already in place on what would become the Spanish left, provided the only existing anchor to the anticipated position. Wellesley ordered Sherbrooke's 1st Division

---

TALAVERA, morning of 27 July 1809
Intended battle-array?

| 2nd Div'n | 3rd Div'n | 1st Div'n | 4th Div'n |

'Sir Arthur Wellesley had, for some time, been examining with an eagle's glance, the country about Talavera, and he suddenly selected ground, of which no one except himself had taken notice, but to the excellence of which future events bore ample testimony. Here he determined to draw up the armies; and he took his measures with such promptitude, and issued his orders with so much coolness and perspicuity, that every battalion, Spanish as well as English, stepped into the very spot which his admirable foresight had marked out for it. The following is a sketch of the dispositions which were thus effected...' [...]

'Upon that height our right [...] leaned. A strong redoubt had been begun, for the purpose of increasing its defensibility; but it was not yet sufficiently advanced to add much to the security of the troops who happened to be in position there. These consisted of the fourth division under General Campbell, next to whom came the guards; which, again, were succeeded in the alignment by General Cameron's brigade and the Germans, as these were by General Mackenzie's and General Hill's. The last-named division held the extreme left of all.'

~ Londonderry

≈ ∙∾

Thus effused Londonderry in 1828, who as Charles Stewart, was Wellesley's Adjutant-General in 1809. His chronology is hard to pin down, but appears to relate to Wellesley's initial thinking between 26 and 27 April, prior to his conducting the retirement on the afternoon of 27 April. The sequence of British divisions Londonderry describes was not at all the array in which the army took up its positions in the late afternoon. Londonderry does, however, clearly hint at the suddenness of Wellesley's decision about the position.

Although this sequence failed to place the 1st Division in the (left) post of honour, the relationship of the divisions in this pattern is interesting in that each wing of two division sums to the same quotient of seniority (here, '5') – an even distribution of 'martial temper'?

Fig. 23

TALAVERA:
Another alternative intention?

	1st Div'n	

2nd Div'n	3rd Div'n	4th Div'n

'The front of battle was prolonged by the British infantry. Campbell's division, formed in two lines, touched the Spanish left, and Sherbrooke's division stood next to Campbell's, but arranged on one line only, because Mackenzie's division, destined to form the second line, was then near the Alberche. It was intended that Hill's division should close the left of the British, by taking post on the highest hill in the chain before mentioned, as bounding the flat and woody country; but, from some cause unknown, the summit of this height was not immediately occupied.'

~Napier

Fig. 24

TALAVERA:
Development of an alternative plan?

	1st Div'n	

3rd Div'n	4th Div'n

2nd Div'n

'The position taken up by the troops at Talavera extended rather more than two miles: the ground was open upon the left, where the British army was stationed, and it was commanded by a height, on which was placed en echelon, as the second line, a division of infantry under the orders of Major General Hill.'

~Wellesley to Castlereagh

'The German Legion were on the left of the position in the first line. I had intended this part for the Guards; but I was unfortunately out, employed in bringing in General Mackenzie's advanced guard when the troops took up their ground.'

~'Memorandum upon the Battle of Talavera'

Could Wellesley's intention have been to reverse the 1st Division, as was customary for the command closing the left flank?

Fig. 25

to retire from Cebolla midmorning[130] to the new line at Talavera, where it was to prolong the British lines leftwards from Campbell's position. Wellesley evidently anticipated placing Mackenzie's 3rd Division in support, to the rear, after falling back from its advance guard-turned-rearguard duties, while Hill's 2nd Division would take up a rearwards position, echeloned to cover the open left.

These judicious arrangements, though, seem to have fallen victim to problems of communication, some more critical than others. From Wellesley's own words it appears that he had meant to reverse the order of the 1st Division, placing the Guards on the left of the line, the British post of honour, thereby closing the left of the Allied line of battle. The 2nd Division's intended position, covering the left rear, would place it in the Allied left wing's next post of honour; indeed, Fortescue noted Wellesley's intention to place 'the Guards in the post of danger on the extreme left, and Hill's division in second line', thereby hinting at the historian's appreciation for the principles of spatial precedence.[131] Wellesley's expectation of closing the left with the 1st Division was consistent with his dispatch's reference to 'Lieutenant General Sherbrooke's division, which was in the left and centre of the first line of the British army'.[132] But in the hurly-burly of personally managing the retirement of the 3rd Division, it appears that the message to Sherbrooke was either never sent, never received, or never followed up. That Sherbrooke deployed in 'natural' order hints at the possibility that he expected *another* division to close his left. Yet, this miscarriage was minor compared to the apparent failure of communication with Hill. All three of the above-mentioned battle-arrays presumed the presence of the 2nd Division on the left, either in the front line or echeloned to the left rear. Hill and his division, however, were on the far right of the Allied position through most of 27 July, in and around the town of Talavera . . . 2 miles away.

Generally, historical analysis has not spent much time considering the dispositions of the two divisions Wellesley left behind when he advanced the other half of his army across the Alberche. Intriguingly, the senior of the pair of remaining divisions was posted to the right of the junior – happenstance or customary precedence of position? (See Fig. 26)[133]. While Wellesley and others may have nurtured expectations that the 2nd Division would take post somewhere on the left, it does not appear that anyone had told Hill.[134] If Wellesley had a plan, Hill did not know of it. Hill's division was not moved out of Talavera until late afternoon (Fig. 27, point A), and then without his knowledge or even presence. It then spent a considerable period awaiting further directions in a position behind the 4th Division (Fig. 27, point B), where Hill found it as dusk approached. Hill had no clear idea of the ground he was expected to occupy, underscoring how disconnected the situation had become. He led his division onward to the left and fortuitously, as dusk deepened, into the combat that developed in the wake of the French attack upon the Cerro de Medellin (Fig. 27, point C). Hill, unaware even of the enemy's presence, could easily have arrived too late – Talavera was a 'close-run thing' six years before Waterloo.

The main schematic for the battle presents Hill's division just after it resumed its dusky journey leftwards from its halt behind the centre (see Fig. 28a–b).[135] Marching naturally by the left, Stewart's junior brigade led the divisional column.

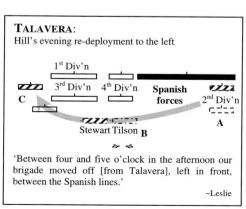

TALAVERA:
Actual battle-array, morning of 27 July

4th Div'n   Spanish   2nd Div'n

Hill's 2nd Division is usually shown, on most maps of the battle, as behind the army's centre, or already on its left. In point of fact, it was on the far right of the allied army, around Talavera, until very late afternoon.

Fig. 26

TALAVERA:
Hill's evening re-deployment to the left

1st Div'n

C   3rd Div'n   4th Div'n   Spanish forces   2nd Div'n

Stewart Tilson B   A

'Between four and five o'clock in the afternoon our brigade moved off [from Talavera], left in front, between the Spanish lines.'

~Leslie

Fig. 27

The division's location and movement seems to be an aspect of the battle that eluded both Oman and Fortescue, though Oman is validated in having placed Stewart on the division's left and Tilson on the right, an order to which Fortescue had objected – an objection based on his understanding that the left was 'the place of precedence in the division of the extreme left' and thus where Tilson's senior brigade should have been found.[136] It marvellously demonstrates that he understood aspects of British customary battle-array and used it as a tool of analysis. Here, however, he was waylaid by having not understood from where the division was moving nor that Hill was unacquainted with the expectation that it would stand on the left of the battle line and, so, had not reversed its order.

Evidence for command confusion goes further. Sherbrooke seems to have lost track of half of his division as he brought it into the front line that afternoon. The KGL moved an hour's march west of Talavera, where it started to camp before

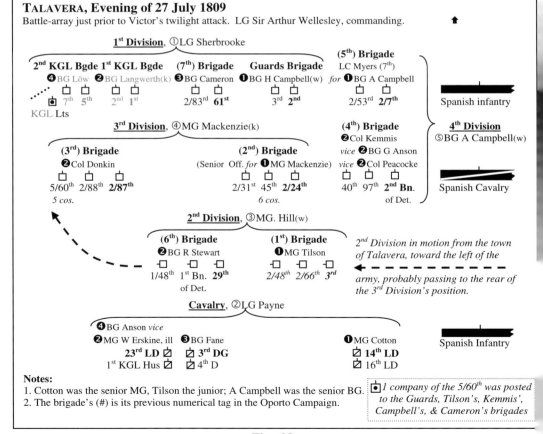

Fig. 28a

being found and summoned back to battle line, arriving about dusk.[137] The sequence of the KGL's array, according to the commander of the 7th Battalion, von Berger, was 'in the order of their numbers'[138] thereby imposing immediate work on the 7th and 5th Battalions when the French evening attack struck. Meanwhile, Colonel Donkin seems to have been left largely to his own devices when Mackenzie's 3rd Division finally shook off its pursuers and entered the position. Commanding the junior brigade, his natural position was on the division's left, and he fortuitously selected the open hill of the Cerro de Medellin, though Wellesley's laconic dispatch to Castlereagh implies that a superior may have had a hand in the choosing:

General Mackenzie continued to fall back gradually upon the left of the position of the combined armies, where he was placed in the second line in

---

TALAVERA, Evening of 27 July 1809

On 27 April, '…General Cuesta having consented to take up this position on the morning of the 27th, I ordered General Sherbrooke to retire with his corps to its station in the line , leaving General Mackenzie with a division of infantry…as an advanced post…on the right of the Alberche….' […]

'In the centre, between the two armies [British and Spanish], there was a commanding spot of ground, on which we had commenced to construct a redoubt, with some open ground in its rear. Brig. General Alexander Campbell was posted at this spot with a division of infantry, supported in his rear by General Cotton's brigade of dragoons and some Spanish cavalry.

'At about 2 o'clock on the 27th, the enemy appeared in strength on the left bank of the Alberche, and manifested an intention to attack General Mackenzie's division.' […]

'As the day advanced, the enemy appeared in larger numbers on the right of the Alberche, and it was obvious that he was advancing to a general attack upon the combined armies. General Mackenzie continued to fall back gradually upon the left of the position of the combined armies, where he was placed in the second line in the rear of the Guards, Colonel Donkin being placed in the same situation farther upon the left, in the rear of the King's German Legion.'

~ Wellesley to Castlereagh

The KGL battalions are grayed, to note that they, having been initially separated from the division and marched well west of Talavera before being brought back into line just before dusk (Beamish, vol. i, p. 207). Unlike as often portrayed on many later maps, Hill's 2nd Division did *not* start from behind the left flank, but was actually far to the right, around the town of Talavera until late in the day. It made its way leftwards, haltingly, and initially without Hill even present to direct it. Hill appears not to have been where Wellesley had either expected or desired him to be. It is thus little wonder that the French thought the British left vulnerable to an early evening attack.

The initial dispositions of brigades and divisions seem to have been widely consistent with the principles of customary battle-array, with the senior brigade and regiment on the right. The regiments of Kemmis' brigade offers one anomaly: the 2nd Battalion of Detachments seems to have taken precedence, perhaps based on its senior constituent regiment (2nd Foot). Its sister 1st Battalion of Detachments occupied the junior position in R Stewart's Brigade. Although Capt Hawker's 1810 map shows the 2nd Battalion of Detachments in the *centre* (junior position) of Kemmis' Brigade, Londonderry has probably mapped it correctly, making the spatial relationship of the later advance by the 40th Foot from Kemmis' *left* to support Campbell's *left* more logical (see Oman, vol. ii, p. 534). Lieutenant Wood's account supports this pattern; Wood was with the detachment of the 82nd forming part of the Battalion.

The British army, being the junior partner in Spain, ceded the right flank to the Spanish army – fortunately, a practical arrangement for other reasons.

Fig. 28b

the rear of the Guards, Colonel Donkin being placed in the same situation farther upon the left, in the rear of the King's German Legion.[139]

The dispositions for battle on 27 July seem to have lacked the anticipatory planning and efficiency of direction that the Peninsular army would steadily acquire under Wellesley's guidance. Supervision by senior officers appears to have been particularly weak, whether by Sherbrooke (who lost his KGL brigades), Mackenzie (who seems not to have guided Donkin's placement), or Hill (who seems to have been surprisingly out of touch with events and his own division until almost too late). Wellesley's own oversight seems to have been distracted, perhaps overwhelmed with a multitude of demands engendered by international co-ordination and cooperation. After leading Mackenzie's closely pressed division into the battle lines in the late afternoon, Wellesley spent much of the following time among his Spanish allies. Only the sound of fighting on the Cerro de Medellin finally brought Wellesley to the left to see the key to his position for himself.[140] Nevertheless, Wellesley and his subordinates proved adept at picking up the proverbial pieces under pressure, and the underlying framework of customary battle-array served the army well, demonstrating the value of a 'default' or normative guide for dispositions.

In fact, such was the power of this norm, that over the course of the night and the following morning, the 2nd Division altered its dispositions, so that, in the end, it largely conformed to the customary principles of battle-array. Having been committed to the left of the army, Hill's division actually reversed, by stages, its order of battle. The division's two brigades initially concluded their evening combat atop the Cerro de Medellin, with Tilson's brigade coming up on the right of R. Stewart's, the left-to-right sequence of the former having become reversed in its advance: 29th – 1st Battalion of Detachments – 1/48th.[141] It was thus the 1/48th, and not the 29th, to which Wellesley would turn to send down the slopes later the next morning to cover the retreat of the Guards. Interestingly, Leslie (29th Foot) claims that Wellesley first called upon the 29th, 'but as the regiment had suffered so much during the previous attack, the 48th was sent instead'.[142] This might indicate that Wellesley had not realized that the brigade had reversed its order, simply sending for the battalion he assumed was on the brigade's right. After all, customary array for the left flank did not ordinarily reverse the internal sequence of the junior brigade's regiments, but normally switched the division's brigades and then reversed the senior brigade's regiments.

Sir Charles Oman cited this arrangement in language revealing that he, too, appreciated that battle-array had a customary sequence and a use as an analytical tool:

> The troops occupying it [the hill] were rearranged, as far as was possible, in the dark. The front line on its left and highest part was now formed by Richard Stewart's brigade, ranged, not in its proper order of seniority, but with the 29th on the left, the 1st Battalion of Detachments in the centre, and the 1/48th on the right. Tilson's brigade, the other half of Hill's division, was to the south of Stewart, continuing his line along the crest.[143]

In response to this assertion, posterity is blessed with an example of the Peninsular War's other great historian, the Hon. J.W. Fortescue, gently quibbling over the interpretation of the principles of customary battle-array as applied by his colleague to R. Stewart's brigade:

> Mr. Oman observes that this was not the proper order of the brigade in respect of seniority. He may be right, but in the left brigade of a division, the left was the place of honour.[144]

The reason for this difference of opinion may have lain in the phasing of the division's adjustments to its unexpected positioning on the left of the line, something to which both Oman and Fortescue had paid scant attention.

When the 2nd Division moved from Talavera, it had done so in its 'natural' order, left in front, with the result that the senior brigade (Tilson's) had followed R. Stewart's junior brigade and had not been much involved in the evening's action, though it was evidently brought up on R. Stewart's right afterwards. During the following morning most of Tilson's brigade was relocated to R. Stewart's left and rear, to face the valley north of the Cerro de Medellín. This shift was by no means a complete one, but seems to have involved a kind of temporary exchange of regiments between the two brigades. Although Wyld's *Atlas* (1845) does not provide much specific insight, both Londonderry's (1828) and Hawker's (1810) maps do note this shift, though neither is clear about the time of day represented nor is in perfect agreement about the regiments involved (Fig. 29).[145] On the whole, it does appear likely that the 29th Foot was at the corner of an arrangement *en potence*, that R. Stewart's brigade stayed in position facing east, probably with the 66th remaining behind from Tilson's brigade, and that Tilson moved to take up the post customary for a senior brigade of the army's left-most division, duly reversing the sequence of his regiments' order of battle. Tilson's troops would witness the famous charge by the 23rd Light Dragoons and KGL's 1st Hussars down the valley to their north – the cavalry also arrayed conformably to customary precedence: the 23rd Light Dragoons on the right, and KGL Hussars on the left.

Talavera was the last major fight in which Wellington's Peninsular army engaged as a purely national entity.[146] And a last major reorganisation by Wellesley, who became Lord Wellington after Talavera, awaited it. The battle at Talavera had tested the army's new structure, and proved it resilient, if not yet entirely mastered. Wellesley, though, was to continue to prove, as Lord Wellington, that he remained a fast and adaptive learner. By July 1811, Captain Cocks, one of Wellington's favourites, would perceptively note to his brother, Wellington's growth: 'Lord Wellington is worth fifty Sir Arthur Wellesleys.'[147] The Peninsular army's grasp of the divisional concept would continue to mature as it steadily mastered the flexibility of its new divisional structure.

Final Reconfiguration: A New Divisional Framework, 1810

Seven months after Talavera, contemplating how to orchestrate British and Portuguese forces, Wellington opted for substantial, but not total, integration of

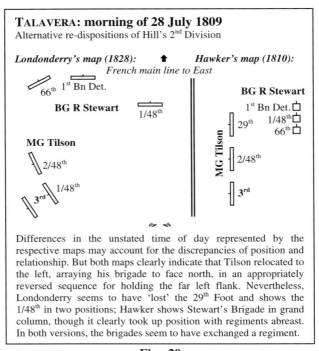

Fig. 29

the two nations' field armies. A fifth division, Portuguese, had been formed in late 1809, partnering with the 2nd Division to form Hill's corps until the end of the war (though Wellington, it seems, had originally intended to add a British brigade to it), and its record proved dependable and successful, if unsung. On 22 February 1810, however, Wellington began to integrate the two national armies by adding one Portuguese brigade of two line regiments (usually each of two battalions) to each British division, except the 1st Division, and to the 2nd Division only in June 1811, following the horrific losses at Albuera.[148] A battalion of *caçadores*, a powerful light infantry component, was added to most of the Portuguese brigades as they became available during the next two years.

Also in his General Order of 22 February 1810, Wellington put other finishing touches on an organisational structure that would be expanded as additional British troops were subsequently committed to the Iberian contest. Its shape incorporated, as it would throughout the war, the imperatives of customary battle-array that continued to serve it well.

No major general, with the brief exception of Hill in June–August 1809, had yet incumbered (this variant of 'encumber' is used as the verb form of 'incumbent' to indicate the specific nature of the officer's tenure of command) a divisional command, and the appointments of 22 February 1810 did not change this. Major Generals Picton's and Cole's divisional appointments were interim. Though remaining as incumbent brigadiers, they continued at their divisional posts with the difference that they were now 'in orders', eventually becoming incumbent division commanders (presumably no later than their respective appointments to 'local' lieutenant general in September 1811).[149] As a reflection of their anticipated longevity in command, however, two colonels were placed on staff and assigned to interim command of Picton's and Cole's brigades (Mackinnon and Kemmis, respectively) while those generals exercised divisional command. The assignments of Picton and Cole sustained the correlation of seniority of commanders with the numerical precedence of divisions, for Picton, taking the 3rd Division, was senior to Cole, who took command of the 4th. Their brigades were also necessarily the senior brigades of their divisions, and took the right of each division's battle-array. Correlating seniority of rank with the numerical precedence of the divisions formed later would prove more difficult, because assignment was subject to availability of personnel, existing vacancies, and enduring incumbencies.

Yet Wellington sought to shape the leadership of his divisions and brigades through active manipulations of incumbent, interim, and assumptive commands. Forming a new, sixth division on 22 February, Wellington also manipulated numbers to shape his commands. Transferring Robert Craufurd's Light Brigade from the 3rd Division, and attaching two Portuguese *caçador* battalions (which finally joined in April), Wellington formed the 'Light Division'. Although it was probably inescapable that line divisions would be numbered, note that the Light Division was not. This was a naturally available tool for shielding Wellington's desired, but low-ranked selection for its commander from some aspects of the general competition for command by assertion of seniority, for Robert Craufurd was merely a brigadier general – a grade normally too low to incumber a divisional command. In fact, and by intent, it was a large brigade of five battalions, intended to be highly responsive to its commander, yet sufficiently small not to attract the jealous attention of underemployed major generals, or major generals commanding brigades desiring the dignity of a 'division'.[150]

The division's resemblance to a large brigade may have been purposefully enhanced by its unitary command structure: it was the only division with no internal brigading. Thus it was also the only division in which Portuguese and British battalions were integrated within a single command, an integration that would continue even when later brigaded. The army's periodic 'State of the Army' reports focused upon the strengths of British troops, and when Portuguese troops were included, these were usually listed separately. This has sometimes prompted historians to reflect this separation of British and Portuguese units in their own presentation of organisations, leaving an impression, even erroneously asserting, that the Portuguese component of the Light Division was a separate brigade.[151] The Portuguese of the Light Division, however, were *always* an integral and respected part of its organisation and battle-array.

When finally divided into brigades in early August 1810, following Craufurd's misguided combat (against an entire French army corps) on the Coa River, outside the fortress-town of Almeida in July, it was the first time that mere (but capable) lieutenant colonels had appeared in General Orders for appointment to brigade command. So low-ranked were these army staff appointments, that the same General Order conveyed special instructions on allowances for such

appointments. Of particular relevance to battle-array, the General Order specifically divided the riflemen of the 1/95th between the new brigades, assigning four
companies to each – those companies were naturally apportioned by battalion
wings: the *right* wing to Lieutenant Colonel Beckwith's (the senior, or right,)
brigade, the *left* wing to Lieutenant Colonel Barclay's (the junior, or left,) brigade;
the 43rd and 52nd light infantry regiments were likewise posted by seniority, the
senior regiment (43rd) being in the senior brigade (Beckwith's).[152]

Although Wellington had avoided formal numbering of divisional brigades,
perhaps to lessen the inevitable pressures to make assignments based on the
perceived precedence associated with numerical designations, brigade numbers
proved impossible to suppress. It was a widespread usage among the divisional
commanders and their subordinates, down to the rank and file, as attested to by
memoirs and surviving division and brigade reports, to call the senior brigade the
'1st' and the next senior the '2nd' and so on, though the Portuguese brigade
remained simply that for most Britons. (Portugal did have its own customary
numbering system, formalized in August 1813.)[153] These were unofficial but
commonly understood, popular identifiers, appearing even in official reports to
Wellington from general officers.

Directly relevant to battle-array was the equally widespread alternative and
overlapping convention of referring to the senior brigade as the 'right' brigade, to
the second brigade as the 'left' brigade and to the third or junior as the 'centre'
brigade. Whether called the 'first', 'right', or 'senior' brigade, the terms were
effectively synonymous, thereby fusing precedence, place, and seniority. In the
Peninsular army's world of close order drill and combat, the terms were in-
dissolubly linked as normative concepts. And though Wellington assiduously
sidestepped reference, he understood the unshakeable power of this custom, for
the record shows that he exercised exceptional care to avoid unnecessary upset
to the internal precedence of a division's brigades by his command appointments.
He laboured to minimize the alteration of brigade precedence that would occur by
incumbering a junior brigade with a new appointee senior to an elder brigade's
incumbent commander. Nevertheless, changes in relative seniority of brigades did
occur owing to new command assignments, entailing a spatial rearrangement of
the brigades.

Like the alteration in the sequence of a battalion's companies following the
appointment and arrival of a new captain, changes in the sequence of a division's
brigades based on altered precedence, seem likely to have been delayed both until
the physical arrival of the new incumbent commander and until the end, or
sustained suspension, of a campaigning season. Until the new incumbent's arrival,
brigades retained their former precedence, based on the last incumbent
commander. These dynamics played themselves out through the entire war, with
increasing complexity as the size and number of commands of the army grew, and
as simple longevity of existence allowed brigades and divisions to develop collective, corporate identities.

Elements of customary procedure were subject to change with time. During the
eighteenth century, the basis of regimental precedence had evolved from the
relative seniority of their commanders to one based on their relative dates of

formation (in other words, their institutionalized seniority reflected by their regimental number); similarly, the practice of identifying brigades by their commander's name had shifted to identification by the senior regiment's number, and then to a popular numerical or spatial system of identification ('first' or 'right' brigade). Now, with army divisions, the sustained relationship of brigades within some of them engendered an altered basis for precedence separate from, and transcendent of, that bequeathed by centuries of custom. This was almost immediately the case in the Light Division. Its two brigades rapidly acquired, and thereafter retained, their designations as '1st' and '2nd' Brigade[154] and their relationship, like that of older and younger siblings, never changed thereafter, regardless of the seniority of their respective commanders or shifts between the two brigades of the battalions of the 95th or of the *caçadores*. For twenty-nine months, from Colonel Drummond's appointment on 7 February 1811, to command the junior brigade, continuing through Major General Vandeleur's assignment on 30 September 1811, until Major General Skerrett's posting on 2 July 1813, the senior incumbent brigade commander led the 2nd Brigade – but throughout that period, the Brigade remained the '2nd' and took post to the left of the 1st Brigade as the junior brigade. As with so many aspects of the Light Division and its training, this particular development was unique to it, perhaps a harbinger of modern usage in a later age of far more dispersed warfare.

Most of the other infantry divisions experienced some number of alterations in the position of their constituent brigades, over the course of the war, as the result of changing commands. The 1st Division experienced five minor changes of brigade sequence during the war entirely related to the changes in the number of KGL, Line, or Guards brigades it contained; assignments of new commanders resulted in changes to the sequence of brigades in the 2nd Division once in 1810, thrice in 1811 (repercussions of Albuera), and once more in 1813;[155] in the 6th Division were two alterations in 1812; the 7th experienced one in 1813. The 5th Division should have undergone a change in 1810 and its reversal in 1811 (with regard to Generals Hay and Dunlop's assignments), but it is hard to pin down that the first actually occurred, and if it did not, the second was moot. Remarkably, the 4th Division seems to have eluded any changes in brigade precedence throughout the war owing to a consistently judicious series of assignments attentive to the relative seniority of the incumbent brigade commanders. While it is unclear just when Kemmis changed from interim to incumbent command (possibly as early as his promotion to major general in June 1811, but certainly as of Cole's elevation to local lieutenant general), none of the assignments to the junior brigade outranked him.

The 3rd Division seems to have developed a special in-house understanding, undoubtedly shared by Wellington, that retained its British brigades' relative precedence regardless of changes in the relative seniority of their commanders. This stemmed partly from the long period during which Picton had an interim commander acting on his behalf in charge of his nominal brigade. Mackinnon had been assigned as a Colonel on Staff, rose to brigadier general, and then to major general while at the head of Picton's brigade, which took its precedence from Picton's seniority as its incumbent commander. During the whole period that Mackinnon held his post, from February 1810 until his death at Ciudad Rodrigo in January 1812, there does not appear to have been any official order altering the tenure of his command, and so no clearly defined point at which he became the incumbent – an event that would have altered the basis of precedence for the brigade of which he had interim charge. Nevertheless, he seems to have become the incumbent at least by the time Picton received local rank as a lieutenant general (6 September 1811), a rank appropriate to divisional command, thereby relieving Picton of the need to maintain the fiction of being a brigade commander.

By custom, as soon as Mackinnon became the incumbent commander, his brigade would have had to cede precedence to the other British brigade, that commanded by Major General Colville, who was senior to Mackinnon. Colville was also senior to both of Mackinnon's incumbent successors, Major General Kempt (appointed 8 February 1812) and Brigadier General Brisbane (appointed 25 March 1813). Yet, the 1st Brigade remained the '1st' and on the right, and Colville's brigade remained on the left as the '2nd', a spatial relationship which the two brigades maintained from 22 February 1810 to the end of the war. This break with customary precedence based on seniority of commanders seems to have sprung from Wellington's use of Colville as a substitute division commander, available for temporary coverage elsewhere. Colville was absent from his brigade and the division on temporary assignment, for roughly 19 of the 38 months that he held incumbent command of the 2nd Brigade (including all of 1812). Over the course of the nineteen months he was present, Colville's brigade was properly the junior British command during the first 11 months of his duty with the division (before Picton rose to local lieutenant general); in the last two months of his association with the 3rd Division, Colville commanded it. Thus, Colville spent only 6 months of the war with his brigade while senior to the 1st Brigade's commander.

In light of his extended absences during his three year tenure of brigade command, there was little point to asserting his seniority. Besides, Colville developed a great affection for his brigade and was happy to remain with it, whatever its station, if there were no divisional command available to him.

The remaining three infantry divisions were officially formed on 6 October 1810 (the 5th and 6th Divisions) and 5 March 1811 (the 7th). Major General Leith's 5th Division had a slow gestation, initially functioning as an indeterminate 'corps' composed of one British and one, then two, Portuguese brigades before finally taking shape with two British and one Portuguese brigade.[156] The 6th Division began its first 5 months of life similarly with just one British and one Portuguese brigade. The 7th, and most junior, Division had a difficult career and a crisis of identity. The initial desire seems to have been to create a second Light Division; its 'British' brigade, and later a KGL brigade, was composed of light infantry. Yet, this objective was simultaneously contradicted by assigning to it a Portuguese line brigade and numbering the division, which signalled the expectation of it as another division in the line. It never escaped this tension.

The last significant organisational element was the independent infantry brigades, commands that were not incorporated into divisions. These were principally Portuguese, of which there were varying numbers, eventually trending towards two in the field. There were also, though less noticed, several independent British brigades with the field army for shorter periods. Two of them were temporary arrangements. Major General Alten's KGL Light Brigade existed independently from mid-April though June 1811, operating with Hill's command; when its intended exchange with a 2nd Division brigade did not work out, it was assigned to the 7th Division (later transferring, in December 1813, under Colonel Halkett, to the 1st Division). Though Colonel Skerrett's brigade had had a substantial independent history operating around Cadiz and Tarifa, its existence terminated after its march from Cadiz up to the main army, in September–October 1812, with the transfer of its regiments into other brigades. Major General Lord Aylmer's brigade, however, endured as an independent entity from July 1813, to the end of the war, operating most of that time in close association with the 1st Division – it was not, however, a constituent part of it.

These independent brigades, particularly the Portuguese, served as a kind of structural lubricant for the army, allowing for smaller, discrete packets of strength to be shifted to wherever added manpower seemed to be required, or to cover sectors that did not merit an entire division, without having to break up a divisional command. It was common for Wellington to attach them temporarily to divisions to reinforce a particular operation.[157] Thus, though necessarily junior partners to the divisions, the independent brigades took their place in the line of battle as Wellington, or their controlling superior, thought best.

This, then, was the organisational framework of the army that Wellington took with him into the remainder of the war. Though cavalry, by its nature, had less rigid grand tactical bonds, their tactical sequence of troops, squadrons, and regiments iterated the infantry's. These patterns of precedence continued to shape the army's battle-array following principles that had long since merged with its other 'customs of the service', revealing themselves with impressive consistency until the end at Toulouse.

Arraying the Army for Battle: Samples from 1811 and 1814

Without space to survey each battle, two samples will be explored to highlight some further aspects of customary battle-array in action. Albuera (1811) offers a useful example of how customary array may have shaped decision-making. With a passing glance at the smaller, but brutal contest of St Pierre (1813), Toulouse (1814) demonstrates how customary battle-array was applied to the very end of the war.

In May 1811, Wellington's southern corps, temporarily under Marshal Beresford during Lieutenant General Hill's absence in England, fought back French Marshal Soult's attempt to relieve the French garrison at Badajoz. The battle at Albuera was an Allied victory – but only by the slimmest of margins. It was, however the most 'allied' of the battles in the Peninsular army's career. While there can never be accurate numbers for any battle, nominal estimates indicate that the British (including its German allies) and Portuguese troops each numbered roughly 10,000, while Spain appears to have brought the lion's share of approximately 14,000.[158] Its Allied-ness was underscored by a remarkably selfless act on the part of Spanish Captain-General Castaños, who, to facilitate Allied harmony, found a graceful way to accede to Wellington's determination that British troops not fight under Spanish command, but that the allies form a unified command for any battle. Wellington had tried to provide for this by suggesting that command should fall to 'the Officer of the senior rank in the army'.[159]

This solution depended upon Castaños' expected departure from Estremadura to establish headquarters further north, so as to carry out his new added responsibility for Galicia. Castaños, the highest ranking Spanish officer in the area of operations, and senior to Beresford, had diplomatically agreed to let command fall to the general with the largest army. Soult's advance, however, found Castaños still in Estremadura. Castaños going a step further suspended himself from command of his small army, placing his forces under Lieutenant General Blake. By removing himself from command, he cleared the way for Beresford, whose rank as a Portuguese marshal was superior to Blake's as lieutenant general, to direct the battle at Albuera. This self-abnegation explains Beresford's effusive commendation, in his battle report, of Castaños, who commanded nothing, yet having given up his command and his army, had thereafter remained in the field to assist.[160]

The Allies fought on the field foreseen by Wellington, arranged as foreseen in his 23 April memoranda for operations: the Spanish forces were anticipated 'to join upon the right of the army'.[161] This was the natural product of their geographical location with respect to the intended battlefield, the point of view taken by the anonymous author of the *Further Strictures on those Parts of Colonel Napier's History of the Peninsular War*:

> General Blake was stationed on the right, not exactly for the reason assigned by the author, but simply because he came from that flank; and the Marshal did not regret the arrangement, as he considered it the strongest and least likely to be attacked.[162]

Napier had attributed the arrangement to topography:

> The right of the position, which was stronger, and higher, and broader than any other part, was left open for Blake's army, because Beresford, thinking the hill on the Valverde road to be the key of the position, as protecting his only line of retreat, was desirous to secure it with the best troops.[163]

Major General Cole's aide-de-camp, meanwhile, ascribed it to expected safety: 'The Spaniards were placed on the right as being the point least threatened, the English at the centre, the Portuguese on the left, forming a line parallel with the stream.'[164]

While all three reasons were doubtlessly applicable, unmentioned is the simple fact that the battlefield being in Spain, where the British and Portuguese were foreign allies, the host nation had claim to the right in the time-honoured tradition of precedence. This precedence, as previously described, had been manifested in every other prior major Allied battle involving a national army on home territory. Though the choice to place the British 2nd Division in the centre had many merits (even resembling the Anglo-Indian arrangements that centred British troops among the Sepoy units, or the Roman habit of placing their allies or auxiliaries upon the flanks of their legions), it was also the case that the Portuguese thereby occupied the *second* post of honour in precedence to the British, and that must have been a tonic, at a certain level, offsetting undercurrents of mistrust and jealous pride between the two Iberian allies (and also kept them separated, avoiding unnecessary friction). Such are the symbolic issues that can plague international efforts.

Albuera offers a series of illustrative examples of customary battle-array at work (see Fig. 30a–b).[165] Observe that Leslie (29th Foot) listed the 2nd Division's regiments as they stood in line of battle (right to left) within each brigade. An interesting quirk is revealed by the 4th Division's array. Major General Cole's command arrived in the order of battle in which it fought. Kemmis' senior British brigade, delayed on the far side of the Guadiana River, was absent. Normally the remaining British brigade would have taken the right as a matter of precedence, but Myers' junior Fusilier Brigade was on the left. Cole, who could not be sure of what he might encounter at the end of his early morning march to the battlefield, apparently treated the array of the little force, marching from Badajoz, right in front, as a miniature army. In deference to his Spanish allies, Cole allowed de España's brigade to lead the international force's column of march, occupying the post of honour during the movement, while Myers' British brigade occupied the second post of honour, at the rear. As further evidence for this management, the Fusilier Brigade reversed the sequence of its regiments, as was customary for the left flank brigade of an independent force. Thus, the basic array in which Cole would lead his division in battle seems to have been determined by both the military and diplomatic nature of his order of march to reach Albuera[166] (see Fig. 31).[167]

The initial situation of Major General W. Stewart's 2nd Division offers an instructive insight into the power of customary battle-array as an organising principle. Sometime in the late morning, as the initial French feint against the village of Albuera developed, Stewart ordered Colborne's 1st Brigade down the slope from the division's right to support Major General Alten's small but effective KGL Light Brigade (see Fig. 30). It is a seemingly obscure detail, unmentioned in Beresford's report to Wellington, or in D'Urban's 1831 'Report of the Operations of the Right Wing of the Allied Army' and overlooked by Oman in his description of the battle, but noted by Fortescue, who remarked upon Oman's omission.[168] Colborne himself mentions it briefly, as does Leslie (29th) and Major Brooke (2/48th), the latter recording that:

> The fire becoming extremely warm at the village and bridge, Sir William Beresford ordered forward our brigade to support the fatigued battalions of the German Legion, who were gallantly defending those posts. But before we had reached the village the attack there slackened, and the most tremendous fire commenced on the extreme right of our line, at the hill on which Blake's Spaniards were posted. It obliged them to retire, and to take shelter

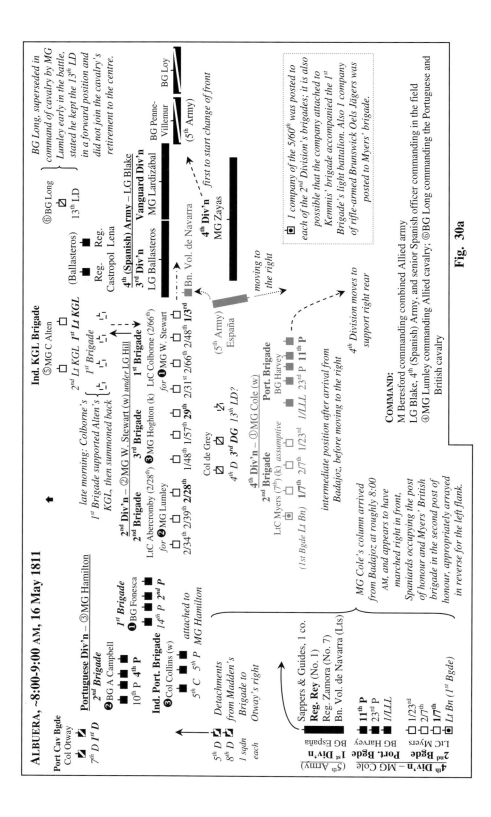

ALBUERA, ~8:00-9:00 AM, 16 May 1811

Ind. KGL Brigade
⑤MG C Alten

BG Long, superseded in command of cavalry by MG Lumley early in the battle, stated he kept the 13th LD in a forward position and did not join the cavalry's retirement to the centre.

©BG Long   13th LD

BG Penne-
Villemur
(5th Army)

BG Loy

4th (Spanish) Army – LG Blake

(Ballasteros)   **Vanguard Div'n**
Reg.   Reg.   MG Lardizábal
Castropol Lena
3rd Div'n
LG Ballasteros   **4th Div'n**
MG Zayas

Bn. Vol. de Navarra   *first to start change of front*

moving to the right

(5th Army)
España

⊡ *1 company of the 5/60th was posted to each of the 2nd Division's brigades; it is also possible that the company attached to Kemmis' brigade accompanied the 1st Brigade; the arrival of rifle-armed Brunswick Oels Jägers was posted to Myers' brigade.*

late morning: Colborne's 1st Brigade supported Alten's KGL, then summoned back

2nd Lt KGL 1st Lt KGL
1st Brigade

1st Brigade

2nd Div'n – ②MG W. Stewart (w) *under LG Hill*

2nd Brigade   **3rd Brigade**   **1st Brigade**
LtC Abercromby (2/28th) ③MG Hoghton (k) LtC Colborne (2/66th) *for* ❶MG W. Stewart
for ❷MG Lumley

2/34th 2/39th **2/28th**   1/48th 1/57th **29th**   2/31st 2/66th 2/48th **1/3rd**

Col de Grey

4th D 3rd DG 13th LD?

4th Div'n – ①MG Cole (w)

2nd Brigade   **Port. Brigade**
LtC Myers (7th) (k) *assumptive*   BG Harvey

(1st Bgde Lt Bn) **1/7th 2/7th 1/23rd** 29th 1/LLL 23rd P **11th P**

intermediate position after arrival from Badajoz, before moving to the right

4th Division moves to support right rear

**4th Division moves to support right rear*

COMMAND:
M Beresford commanding combined Allied army
LG Blake, 4th (Spanish) Army, and senior Spanish officer commanding in the field
④MG Lumley commanding Allied cavalry; ©BG Long commanding the Portuguese and
    British cavalry

Port Cav Bgde
Col Otway

7th D 1st D

5th D 8th D
1 sqdn each

Portuguese Div'n – ③MG Hamilton

2nd Brigade
❷BG A Campbell

10th P 4th P

1st Brigade
❶BG Fonesca

Ind. Port. Brigade   14th P 2nd P
❸Col Collins (w)

*attached to
5th C 5th P MG Hamilton*

*Detachments
from Madden's
Brigade to
Otway's right*

MG Cole's column arrived from Badajoz at roughly 8:00 AM, and appears to have marched right in front, Spaniards occupying the post of honour and Myers' British brigade in the second post of honour, appropriately arrayed in reverse for the left flank.

Sappers & Guides, 1 co.
Reg. Rey (No. 1)
Reg. Zamora (No. 7)
Bn. Vol. de Navarra (Lts)

4th Div'n – MG Cole

(5th Army)   **1st Div'n**   **2nd Bgde**   **Port. Bgde**   **2nd Bgde**
    BG España   BG Harvey   LtC Myers

    11th P   1/23rd
    23rd P   2/7th
    1/LLL   17th
    Lt Bn (1st Bgde)

Fig. 30a

ALBUERA, ~8:00-9:00 AM, 16 May 1811

'The next morning [16 May] our disposition for receiving the enemy was made, being formed in two lines, nearly parallel to the river Albuera, on the ridge of the gradual ascent rising from that river, and covering the roads to Badajoz and Valverde, though your Lordship is aware that the whole face of this country is everywhere passable for all arms. General Blake's corps was on the right in two lines; its left, on the Valverde road, joined the right of Major General the Hon. William Stewart's division, the left of which reached the Badajoz road, where commenced the right of Major General Hamilton's division, which closed the left of the line. General Cole's division, with one brigade of General Hamilton's, formed the second line of the British and Portuguese army.'

~Beresford's report to Wellington.

'In occupying the position, the army was formed as follows:— The Portuguese (in blue) on the left: the English (in red) in the centre—viz., General Houghton's brigade, the 29th, 57th, and 1st battalion of the 48th regiment; General Lumley's, 28th, 39th, and 34th regiments; Colonel Colburn's, the 3rd, the 2nd battalion of the 48th, 66th, and 31st regiments; and the Spaniards (in yellow or other bright colours) formed the right. The whole drawn up as for a grand parade, in full view of the enemy [...]. That part of the 4th division under Sir Lowry Cole, which had just arrived from Badajoz, were posted in second line in our rear.'

~Leslie

Captain-General Castaños, commanding 5th (Spanish) Army (Estremadura), with a rank superior to Beresford's, temporarily resigned command of his troops to LG Blake to facilitate Beresford's temporary assumption of allied command.

From Colborne, Leslie, Brooke, and Beamish's accounts (see text) comes evidence that in the late morning, Colborne's 1st Brigade was ordered to advance to support Alten's KGL in the village of Albuera. He was subsequently recalled when the 2nd Division received orders to move to the right to support the Spanish against the developing main French attack. It is clear from the order of the division's movement that MG W Stewart must have *waited* for Colborne's brigade to return before he put the 2nd Division in motion for the right – an apparent reflection of how important Stewart must have thought it not to change the order of the brigades as he prepared to enter combat.

Available sources do not otherwise clarify the sequence of Hamilton's brigades, but simply state or delineate the division's placement without naming the brigades. However, D'Urban noted in his journal for 15 May, 'Alten held the Village of Albuera and Campbell's Portuguese Brigade was attached to him.' [p. 214] This could support the possibility that Hamilton's division was in reverse order owing to its position on the extreme left of the line of battle, with BG A Campbell's junior brigade on its *right* and, being thus closer to the village, making it the natural choice to support Alten. Such a reversal of brigades would have been entirely consistent with the traditional principles of customary battle-array.

España's later (grayed) movement was mapped by Antonio Burriel (Chief of Staff of Blake's Spanish 4th Army) as moving westward to occupy ground behind Cole's reserve position, having left its light infantry battalion posted toward the village of Albuera. Though there is no indication of the relative chronology, the sequence implied in the maps seems to hint that it may have been after. Burriel's narrative and España's report (both privately translated by Mark S Thompson), however, make clear that it moved well before Cole's redeployment.

Fig. 30b

ALBUERA, 4TH DIVISION, 16 May 1811
Rendezvous with glory: MG Cole advances

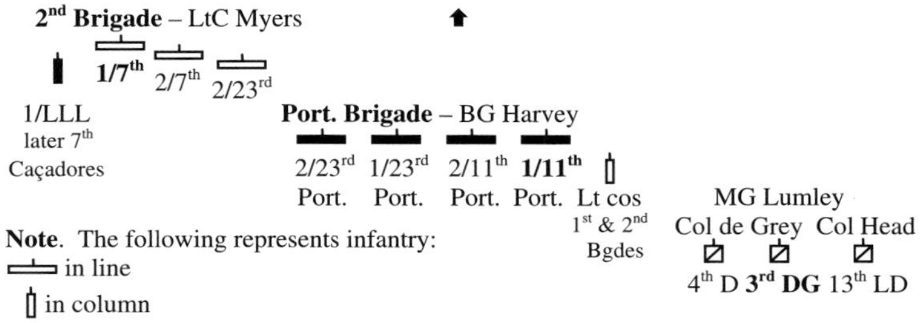

2nd Brigade – LtC Myers

1/7th   2/7th   2/23rd

1/LLL
later 7th
Caçadores

Port. Brigade – BG Harvey

2/23rd 1/23rd 2/11th **1/11th**
Port.   Port.   Port.   Port.

Note. The following represents infantry:

in line

in column

Lt cos
1st & 2nd
Bgdes

MG Lumley
Col de Grey Col Head

4th D **3rd DG** 13th LD

Ordered to move his division from behind the centre 'to the right, and form it at right angles to its original front,' Cole 'deployed his columns into line, with the exception of one, and the light companies of the Fusilier brigade which he kept in column on the right and rear of the Portuguese brigade, which was on the right of his line.' [...]

'Having directed that the flank companies of the division in column of quarter distance, and the brigade of guns should keep on the right of the Portuguese Brigade; that being the extreme right. He moved forward with the Fusilier Brigade, supported by the 7th Cacadores, to reinforce the troops engaged, so as to bring the Brigade up to their right, by a forward and flank movement across the slopes of the heights; and at the same time, he directed the remainder of the division (the Portuguese Brigade, Artillery, and light companies) should follow the movement of the Fusilier Brigade, with as much celerity, as keeping their order in line, and place in echellon with the Fusiliers, would allow of.

'As the whole had to take ground to their left during a quick and forward movement in face of the enemy, the operation was one of some difficulty, and required precision, and constant attention to its execution.

'The Fusiliers advanced rapidly, and approaching the right of the 2nd division just after another charge of the Polish Lancers. The Fusiliers fired on the enemy's Cavalry—closed to their left—and were soon in line, and in action with the 2nd division against the French columns.

'The remainder of the division followed the movement of the Fusiliers, but could not make the same forward progress, and also to keep its order, so as to preserve its echellon to the Fusiliers; but every effort was made, and effectually, to keep the Portuguese line well to the left, to cover the right of the Fusiliers, which at every step became more exposed.

'The cavalry of the allies, had been brought up by General Lumley to the right of the Infantry as it advanced on the plain, having there the support of the guns of the 4th division and the troops in column on that flank.'

~Vere

Cole provided further explicit detail, in 1841: 'In moving forward to the attack, the Fusiliers advanced in echelons of battalions from the left – a manoeuvre always difficult to perform correctly even in a common field day; and as the Portuguese brigade in advancing had two objects to effect, namely, to show front to the enemy's cavalry, and at the same time to preserve its distance from, and cover the right flank of, the Fusilier Brigade, its movement was even more difficult to effect than the former.'

~Cole

'Brig. General Harvey's Portuguese brigade, belonging to General Cole's division, had an opportunity of distinguishing itself when marching in line across the plain, by repulsing, with the utmost steadiness, a charge of the enemy's cavalry.'

~Beresford's report to Wellington

LtC Myers (7th) had assumed command of the 2nd Brigade upon the transfer of its incumbent commander, MG Houston, in January 1811. Maj. T. Pearson (1/23rd) would assume command after his death, holding it until MG Stopford was appointed as the new (incumbent) commanding officer, on 18 June 1811. Meanwhile, BG Harvey assumed command of the division, upon Cole's being wounded, yielding it to BG Kemmis when he arrived the next day.

Fig. 31

in good order under cover of the slope. In consequence of the retreat of the Spaniards our brigade (1st Brigade of the 2nd Division, consisting of the 3rd or Buffs, 31st, 66th, and 2/48th [ )] received orders to mount the hill and dislodge the enemy.[169]

Note Brooke's reference to the brigade by number, a clear reflection of the customary usage of numerical identifiers for brigades.[170]

Fortescue specifically considered the repercussions of the move upon later events:

> According to Beresford's account, he had ordered Stewart to form his division in second line in rear of the Spaniards [. . .]; but it may be doubted whether the Commander-in-Chief allowed time enough for any such movement. We have seen that Stewart received no instructions at all until some time after Soult had developed his flanking attack; and even then it was necessary to recall Colborne's brigade from the neighbourhood of Albuera before the whole could move; all of which incidents must have meant delay. In any case, it is certain that, from what cause or by whose fault soever, Stewart's three brigades came up to the new front in succession, and as fast as they could run in their wet clothing over the soaked and slippery grass.[171]

Something close to over an hour is likely to have passed between the issuance of Beresford's order and the arrival of the head of the 2nd Division at the new position.

The village of Albuera was about a half-mile down-slope from W. Stewart's divisional line.[172] It is not clear just how close to the village Colborne's brigade approached. If the line retrograded 600 yards at the quickstep, the shortest time in which the brigade could have returned to the division and been ready to move again would have been perhaps thirteen minutes under *perfect* conditions (or over fifteen minutes at the common step).[173] They were engaged to some degree around the village and, according to the captain of the KGL battery that supported Colborne's brigade, the French were delivering a lively cannonade at the time.[174] Although Clausewitz had not yet coined his famous dictum regarding the 'friction of war', its effects still applied, and the practical likelihood is that to move 2,000 men in line, under artillery fire and potential threat of attack, perhaps a third of a mile up the gradual slope to retake their place in the division's line, realigned and ready to march, took possibly almost half an hour. Meanwhile, Stewart waited, unwilling to move the division until Colborne had returned. The actual delay is unrecorded and would have depended upon any number of factors. The division still had just over a mile to march southwards to reach its new position. Sherer, in the last regiment (2/34th) of the division's column, remembered:

> We formed in open column of companies at half distance, and moved in rapid double-quick to the scene of action. I remember well, as we moved down in column, shot and shell flew over in quick succession; we sustained little injury from either [. . .] all was hurry and struggle.[175]

To close the columns' intervals to half-distance would have required a couple of minutes' further delay. At the double-quick (120 30-inch paces a minute), the head of Colborne's column might have traversed the distance in a little less than 20 minutes, but probably rather more, in view of slippery ground and the weight each man carried. By this time, the men in his regiments, burdened with some 50lb of equipment, must have been feeling the fatigue. Any tailing-out of the columns would have required some time simply to close up again after so long a move at such a pace. But Stewart, riding at the head with Colborne, gave them no rest. When, upon arrival, Colborne requested permission to form his brigade before advancing up the slope to engage, Stewart declined and after a brief delay, pushed the columns onward into combat, where they were forced to form line under fire.[176] Sherer described the successive arrival of the division:

> The three brigades of the division Stewart marched . . . in double-quick time, led by that General. The first, or right brigade, commanded by Colonel Colborne, was precipitated into action under circumstances most unfavourable: it deployed by corps as it arrived near the enemy, fired, and was in the act of gallantly charging with the bayonet on a heavy column of their infantry, when a body of Polish lancers, having galloped round upon its rear in this most unfortunate moment (for a charge is often a movement of exulting confusion), overthrew it with a great and cruel slaughter. The 31st Regiment, not having deployed, escaped this misfortune; and the third brigade, under General Houghton [sic], and second, under Colonel Abercromby, successfully arriving, re-established the battle, and, with the assistance of the Fusilier Brigade under Sir William Myers, the fortunes of this bloody day were retrieved, and the French driven in every direction from the field.[177]

The 2nd Division arrayed itself on 'that fatal hill' in the same battle order of regiments and brigades as that in which the division had stood earlier in the morning facing the village of Albuera (see Fig. 32).[178]

The survival of the 31st Foot, in Colborne's brigade was owed, in part, to customary array, which fated it to be on the left of the brigade. As Major Brooke noted:

> The 31st Regiment, the left battalion of our brigade, alone escaped: it was still at the foot of the hill in solid column, not having had time to deploy along with the 3rd, 66th, and 48th.[179]

The 3rd Brigade, next to arrive, did so in the wake of the 1st Brigade's destruction:

> The 3rd brigade in that division was the one that was commanded by Major General Hoghton, and was composed of the 29th, 1st Battalion 57th, 1st Battalion 48th. The whole division moved from its ground in open columns of companies, right in front, about a mile, where the line was formed on the leading company.[180]

ALBUERA, 2ND DIVISION, 16 May 1811

Apotheosis of courage: the musketry duel

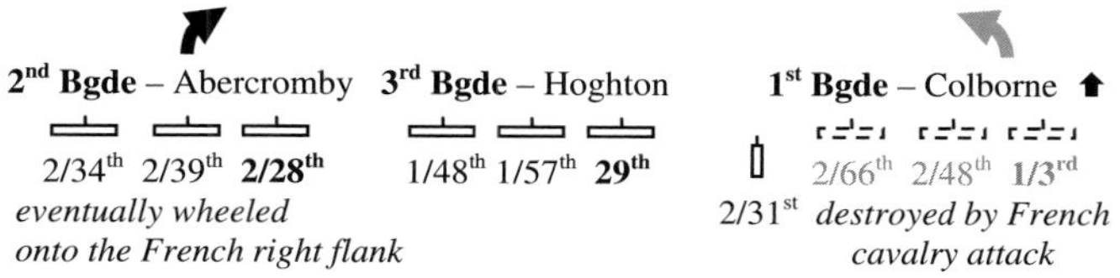

2nd Bgde – Abercromby   **3rd Bgde** – Hoghton   **1st Bgde** – Colborne

2/34th 2/39th **2/28th**   1/48th 1/57th **29th**   2/66th 2/48th **1/3rd**

eventually wheeled   2/31st *destroyed by French*

onto the French right flank   *cavalry attack*

Note. The following represents Infantry…

☐ in line

☐ in column

r╌╌┐ broken

'The right brigade of General Stewart's division, under Lieut. Colonel Colborne, first came into action […]; and, while in the act of charging, a body of Polish lancers (cavalry), which the thickness of the atmosphere and the nature of the ground had concealed (and which was, besides, mistaken by those of the brigade, when discovered, for Spanish cavalry, and therefore not fired upon), turned it; and, being thus attacked unexpectedly in the rear, was unfortunately broken, and suffered immensely. The 31st regiment, being the left one of the brigade, alone escaped this charge, and, under the command of Major L'Estrange, kept its ground until the arrival of the 3d brigade, under Major General Houghton. The conduct of this brigade was most conspicuously gallant; and that of the 2d brigade, under the command of Lieut. Colonel the Hon. A. Abercrombie, was not less so.'

~Beresford's report to Wellington

'There we unflinchingly stood and there we fell, our ranks at some places swept away by sections.'

~An officer of the 29th

'To describe my feelings throughout this wild scene with fidelity, would be impossible : at intervals, a shriek or grown told that men were falling around me ; but it was not always that the tumult of the contest suffered me to catch these sounds. A constant feeling to the centre of the line, and the gradual diminution of our front, more truly bespoke the havock of death. As we moved, though slowly, yet ever a little in advance, our own killed and wounded lay behind us….'

~ Sherer (2/34th)

On the evidence of Ensign Hobhouse (1/57th), it appears that the light companies of at least Hoghton's brigade, but possibly of all the brigades, fought in line of battle with their parent battalions this day:

'…our Colonel, Major, every Captain and 11 subalterns fell; our King's Colours were cut in two; our regimental ones had 17 balls though them, *many* companies were without Officers, and as the light company was next to me, I could not do otherwise than take the command of it which I did, until it was my turn to take up the shattered colours.'

~Hobhouse (1/57th)

Fig. 32

The listing of regiments, here, in their tactical order seems to come naturally from his pen. Reference to forming on the leading company indicates that the 3rd Brigade (as would the 2nd coming up behind) deployed by prolonging the front leftwards (bringing up successive battalions which then likewise prolonged their fronts to the left – see Fig. 9), thereby maintaining the brigade's and regiments' 'natural' order when arrayed in line of battle.

The perceived constraints of battle-array had held Stewart's hand, and the wait for Colborne's brigade to resume its place in line significantly delayed Stewart's response to Beresford's summons, perhaps as much as doubling the time to bring up the 2nd Division. That delay may well have encouraged the choice of a fast, tiring march (which must have winded Stewart's troops) and precipitated his refusal to consider further delay to form Colborne's brigade before mounting to the attack. The outcome was calamitous, fatal for hundreds of Colborne's troops and potentially for Allied victory. If arrival had been earlier and less hurried, Stewart might have made allowance for Colborne to form his brigade in line. Colborne had apparently intended to place a close column on his right flank to secure it[181] – precisely as Cole was effectively to do with the open flanks of his 4th Division's brigades.

Was it mere pedantry to delay the division for Colborne's return? Many factors shape the answer, but this event highlights consideration of some other goals and benefits of battle-array: to preserve order, sustain cohesion, facilitate identification, and speed communication.

Stewart led his division into battle on the right, with regiments and brigades in the same physical sequence as they had stood facing Albuera a mile to the north. His brigades' regiments stood in the same array as they had at Busaco the year before. The sequence of the brigades, however, had changed with the assignment of Major General Lumley (30 September 1810) to the junior brigade of Brigadier General C. Craufurd, following the latter's death. The division's junior brigade had then become its second eldest brigade, for Lumley was senior to Brigadier General R. Stewart, thereby changing the precedence of the division's brigades. The division had had the winter to rehearse their manœuvres with this new sequence, and by May 1811, the changed sequence would have been well integrated into the division's routine. Routine spatial relationship visibly reflected, and was a key tool for, sustaining good order in close order warfare. Maintaining good order facilitated the preservation of good moral and physical cohesion in combat, thereby maximizing battlefield effectiveness.

Amidst the proverbial confusion of a smoke-filled battlefield, saturated with carnage, senses hammered by the roar of musketry and cannon, vision obscured by undulations of ground and other accidents of terrain, identification of units from any distance by the colour of facings, or even their 'colours', was impossible. But knowledge of the customary order in which regiments and brigades stood, and confidence that it was applied, allowed a commander a reasonable chance of determining at a distance, even a great distance, which regiment or brigade was which and where, and permitted extrapolation for those parts of the line of battle obscured by intervening terrain or smoke. Without a key for decoding the battle-field view, a commander had an extremely difficult time evaluating where his forces were, where the enemy's were located, or his next course of action. Without a reasonable sense of where one's forces stood or marched, communication by foot or horse was even slower: not only was the messenger not sure of where to go, the sender would be hard put to determine what message to send if unclear about the correlation of the forces at which he was looking.[182] Warfare, like comedy, feeds on timing.

All of these were reasons for Stewart not to shuffle his brigades on the fly. It was for Stewart to balance speed with order, and in British service, there was little question about which was considered the side upon which to err. In order to achieve victory in close order combat, 'it is necessary to reconcile celerity with order; to prevent hurry, which must always produce confusion, loss of time, unsteadiness, irresolution, inattention to command, &c.' This was the opening admonishment of the *Rules and Regulations*.[183] The highly fluid circumstances of an international force attempting to coordinate an unplanned change of operational front to its flank as quickly as possible created a dynamic that could easily dissolve into chaos even in a peacetime exercise. At Albuera, the combined forces were under threat of imminent attack initially without agreement about where the threat lay. In such circumstances, maintenance of battle order could prove a crucial defence against fatal confusion and disorder, from which there would be no time to recover. Retention of the division's battle-array ensured the greatest opportunity for its commander and his subordinate brigadiers and battalion commanders to be able to determine who was where, what to do, and where to go, in the least time. It was an imperative Stewart shared with every officer, at every level of command, in each army present. The absolute necessity for a battle-array to preserve order as long as possible was universal and unavoidable. Its loss often triggered and reflected the disintegrating morale and command cohesion that was a concomitant of defeat.[184] In the end, Stewart appears to have forgotten the admonishment against disordering hurry.

This is not to argue that battle-array could endure no alteration. It could and did, but the crucial matter was that the relevant parties were aware of and understood the change. Thus could Cole reverse the order of march of his 4th Division's British brigade without difficulty for anyone concerned; he chose, however, not to alter the sequence again once on the battlefield. His light infantry assets – the combined British light battalions on the right, and the 1st Battalion of the Loyal Lusitanian Legion on the left – were another matter. Cole was free to position light infantry as needed, and he chose to use them as reliable bastions for his flanks.

In March and April 1811, the army's successive combats and manœuvres in pursuit of Masséna's retreat from Portugal had demonstrated how flexible the customary battle-array could be when thoughtfully coordinated. Wellington displayed perhaps even greater flexibility in his management of the army's array during the campaign of 1812, notably in the week prior to Salamanca.[185] Customary battle-array continued as a vital management tool throughout Wellington's triumphant 1813 campaign. A glance at the brutal fight at St Pierre, in December 1813, in southern France (Fig. 33a–b),[186] shows customary battle-array still operating, though with ever increasing flexibility, as indeed it did through the remaining battles of the war.

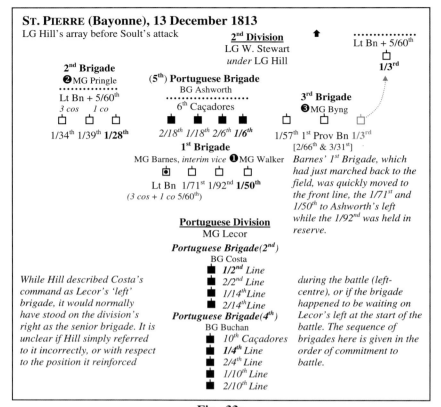

ST. PIERRE (Bayonne), 13 December 1813
LG Hill's array before Soult's attack

2nd Division
LG W. Stewart
under LG Hill

Lt Bn + 5/60th
1/3rd

2nd Brigade
❷MG Pringle
Lt Bn + 5/60th
3 cos   1 co

1/34th 1/39th **1/28th**

(5th) Portuguese Brigade
BG Ashworth
6th Caçadores

2/18th 1/18th 2/6th *1/6th*

3rd Brigade
❸MG Byng

1/57th 1st Prov Bn 1/3rd
[2/66th & 3/31st]

1st Brigade
MG Barnes, *interim vice* ❶MG Walker
Lt Bn 1/71st 1/92nd **1/50th**
(3 cos + 1 co 5/60th)

Barnes' 1st Brigade, which had just marched back to the field, was quickly moved to the front line, the 1/71st and 1/50th to Ashworth's left while the 1/92nd was held in reserve.

Portuguese Division
MG Lecor

Portuguese Brigade(2nd)
BG Costa
1/2nd Line
2/2nd Line
1/14thLine
2/14thLine

While Hill described Costa's command as Lecor's 'left' brigade, it would normally have stood on the division's right as the senior brigade. It is unclear if Hill simply referred to it incorrectly, or with respect to the position it reinforced

Portuguese Brigade(4th)
BG Buchan
10th Caçadores
1/4th Line
2/4th Line
1/10th Line
2/10th Line

during the battle (left-centre), or if the brigade happened to be waiting on Lecor's left at the start of the battle. The sequence of brigades here is given in the order of commitment to battle.

Fig. 33a

On the morning of 10 April 1814, as Wellington took up his post on the knoll of Pujade, his dispositions for his final battle of the Peninsular War were still slowly unfolding across the rain-sodden fields to the north and east of Toulouse. Wellington had orchestrated a succession of feint attacks and preparatory skirmishes to the north of the city to clear the way for coordinated assaults against its eastern defences, along two lines of operation, by four of his eight available divisions.

Although a host of practical military reasons guided his arrangements, the sequence of the Peninsular army's dispositions inescapably reflected, and were guided by, the same principles of customary battle-array that had underpinned the army's order of battle since its first landing in Portugal, in August 1808. Here, in Wellington's last Peninsular battle, the principles manifested themselves in elegant and layered variation. As Marshal General of the Portuguese Army, Generalissimo of Spain, and a British Field Marshal, holding the peerages of Duque de Vitoria (Portugal), Duque de Ciudad Rodrigo (Spain), and Marquis of Wellington, Arthur Wellesley embodied the unified field command of an international army, with issues of protocol to match. His dispositions did not fail to

---

St. Pierre (Bayonne), 13 December 1813

Hill reported to Wellington:

'On the right, Major-Gen. Byng with his Brigade occupied the ridge & village of Vieux Monguerre, Brig. General Ashworth, with his Brigade & two Portuguese guns, was in the centre near the village of St. Pierre, Major-Gen. Pringle was on the left with his Brigade on the ridge of Villefranque, in front of the Village of that name.

'The whole of the Troops in front were immediately under the direction of Lt.-Gen. The Hon. Sir Wm. Stewart. The remainder of the troops were in reserve.

'The point of attack appearing to be the centre, Major-Gen. Barnes with his Brigade, Lt.-Col. Ross's Horse Artillery, & Lt.-Col. Tulloh's Portuguese Artillery (excepting two guns of each) moved to the village of St. Pierre, and on the ridge on which it stands.

'As the attack became more decided against the centre, the whole of Major-Gen. Lecor's Portuguese Division, moved to the support of that point, and Major-Gen. Byng's Brigade (With the exception of the Buffs and light companies) was also drawn from the right to resist the determined efforts of the enemy on our centre. [...]

'[Attention called to the conduct]...of Major-Gen. Lecor for the very seasonable support he gave to the centre of our position, by bringing up his left Brigade (under Major-Genl. Da Costa) at the most critical moment of the struggle, when by a timely & most gallant charge, it decided the fate of the day on that side; and to that of Major-Gen. Byng who assailed that strong height occupied in force by the enemy in front of our right; he ascended the hill first, and himself planted the colours of the 31st regiment on the summit.

'Brigadier-Genl. Buchan gave very effective support in the early part of the day to the left, & subsequently was moved to the support of Major-Gen. Byng's Brigade & contributed much to the success on that side.

'Major-Genl. Pringle was successful in repulsing the enemy's attack on our left.'

The author of A Soldier of the 71st*, explained that prior to the battle:*

'...we received orders to march to our own right to assist a Spanish force, who were engaged with superior numbers. We set off by daylight in the morning of the 13th towards them and were moving on when General Hill sent an aide-de-camp after us, saying, "That is not the direction—follow me". We put to the right about, to the main road towards Bayonne. We soon came to the scene of action....'

Fig. 33b

reflect them internationally, nor did his Anglo-Allied army's arrangement fail to mirror them internally.

Hill, present as Wellington's senior subordinate in British service, occupied the chief operational post of honour on the right with his army corps, as was appropriate to his rank. Internationally, though Portuguese Marshal Beresford was Wellington's senior ranking subordinate, he was, in British service, a lieutenant general junior to Hill, and his corps (the 4th and 6th Divisions) comprising the left, held the second post of honour. The Spanish corps, under Lieutenant General Don Manuel Freyre, had been 'allotted an important and responsible part of the work'[187] in honour of Freyre's desire, 'as a favour to lead the battle'.[188] Yet, although Spain occupied the junior post in the centre, albeit by Spanish request, the right-most infantry of the combined army, on the far flank of Hill's disposition across Garonne, was Major General Morillo's Spanish brigade, perhaps a subtle, symbolic nod to Spanish pride. In Hill's corps, the 2nd Division was on the left, and eventually to the front, of Hill's dispositions, with Major General Lecor's Portuguese in the centre. Grand tactically, the 3rd Division, the senior of the Anglo-Portuguese divisions in the main body east of the river, stood on the right,

Fig. 34a

and the next senior of those divisions, the 4th, was upon the extreme left –
reflecting, once more, a correspondence between the precedence of both
commanders' rank and their divisions' respective seniority, and the customary
posts of honour.

Brigades, too, were posted consistent with customary battle-array. While those
of the 3rd and Light Divisions were arranged with the 1st Brigades on the right
and 2nd Brigades on the left, the 2nd Division's dispositions seemed to have
mimicked the arrangements at St Pierre, the previous December (see Fig. 33).
Major General Barnes' 1st Brigade was, again, in close reserve, though this time
supporting the 3rd Brigade on the left, while the 2nd Brigade stood to the right
(apparently the division had reversed its order in keeping with being the corps' left-
flank command), the Portuguese Brigade in reserve as well.[189]

The brigades of Beresford's column present a last, minor case study. While the
battle was well described by Oman, it is possible to miss the elegance of the grand
tactical arrangement of the pair of divisions composing Beresford's little corps on
the far left, where the greatest bloodletting of the contest occurred.[190] It appears
that Fortescue completely misconstrued Beresford's grand tactical dispositions.
Curiously, both Oman and Fortescue omitted mention of sources for their
conflicting description of arrangements; neither seemed even sufficiently confident
of their assumptions to do anything but leave their best guess to footnotes.[191] While
both historians correctly placed the 4th ahead of the 6th Division, and described
the march as by the flank in three lines, Fortescue placed the Portuguese brigades
to the east, near the Ers River, with all the British brigades to the west, nearer the
French. Such an arrangement makes complete havoc of the usual spatial relationships of the brigades and of each division's likely deployment along the anticipated
lines of operation. Customary battle-array and fragments of direct and circum-
stantial evidence favour Oman's description, which forms the basis of the
schematic presented here.

One important clue for the 4th Division's array comes from Lieutenant Crowe,
3/27th Foot, in W. Anson's 1st Brigade, describing the southward advance of the
columns:

> our division advanced in open column of Brigades over the morass, so soft
> that every general and field officer was compelled to march and have his
> horse led over. Our left Brigade skirted the bank of the River Ers. Our

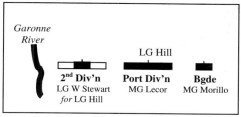

Fig. 34b

Portuguese took the centre of the morass and our Right Brigade proceeded nearer to the heights.[192]

Crowe clearly described the arrangement of the 4th Division's brigades as surmised by Oman, contradicting Fortescue's thesis.

For the 6th Division, there is little doubt about its customary array, for James Anton of the 42nd Highlanders, had described the division's composition as of only five months before:

> It was composed of three brigades – the right, left, and centre. The first, usually termed the Highland brigade, was commanded by Major-general Sir Denis Pack, and consisted of the 42nd (Royal Highlanders), the 79th (Cameron Highlanders), the 91st (Argyle Highlanders), and one company of the 60th (Royal Rifle Corps). The 11th, 32nd, 36th, and 61st Regiments composed the left brigade, under the command of Major-general Sir John Lambert. The centre brigade consisted of three regiments of Portuguese, under the command of Colonel Douglas.[193]

Not only had the array not changed in the interim, but the description correlated with the seniority of the brigade commanders.

At Toulouse, an anonymous soldier of the 42nd noted the moment when Pack's brigade, at the end of its southwards march, finally fronted toward the enemy and the French counter-attack that swept down the slopes of Mount Rave: 'At the time the canal was about 100 yards in rear of us, and the enemy about 300 yards in front . . .'[194] His description of the softness of the ground, which firmed as the British advanced up the heights, combined with an account from Anton of the proximity of water and ditches, strongly implies that Pack's was the brigade of the 6th Division closest to the Ers, again consistent with Oman's arrangement.[195]

Thus, it seems that the disposition adopted by Beresford's corps was, perhaps with some historical irony, a classic French column of attack writ large (Fig. 35). Such a column formed on its centre, with each wing folded back into parallel columns: the right wing leading by the left, the left wing, by the right. One effect was to facilitate rapid outward deployment of the battalion's companies from column, the companies travelling along the hypotenuse to their place in line. Similarly, each of the corps' Anglo-Portuguese divisions constituted a wing: when

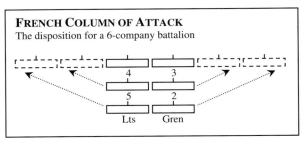

Fig. 35

faced westward toward the French lines, the 6th Division (as the right wing) would be left in front, its brigades queued one behind the other, the junior brigade leading; meanwhile, the 4th Division (the left wing), would be arranged right in front, its senior brigade leading (Fig. 36).[196] Each would be thus in position to extend their brigades to their open, exterior flanks to form line of battle.

To get them to their jump-off position required marching the corps across the main front of the French position, to the right of the line of march, while squeezed against the unfordable Ers River on their immediate left. It was a risky proposition, marching across ground so saturated with the rains that the divisional artillery bogged down and was temporarily left behind. So it was vital that the columns marched prepared both to meet any French counter-attack and to assemble rapidly to mount their own assault upon the far French right flank. In order to do this, the two divisions marched by the left flank in three lines of battle, ready to form line facing the enemy by quarter-wheels of companies to the right, already in their giant column of attack. One may note that the senior of the two divisions occupied the post of honour on the left flank, which was, indeed, the left extremity of the Anglo-Allied army, though it does not appear that the order of brigades had been reversed (the internal order of Major General W. Anson's senior brigade would also have been reversed in that case).

The one anomalous element in the schematized representation is the regimental array of Pack's brigade. The peculiarity of the sequence of regiments also caught Oman's attention. He described the 79th as forming square on Pack's right to fend off cavalry accompanying the French counter-attack made as Beresford's troops moved up the slopes on the southern end of Mt Rave: 'The brigade, as it chanced, was marching left in front, so the 79th was on the right, not the 42nd.'[197] But Oman stumbled on the sequence of customary battle-array. While rightly indicating that the brigade was marching left in front, customary precedence would have placed the 42nd, the senior regiment, at the rear of the column – which would be the right of the line when the regiments of the brigade fronted to their right. The customary position of the 79th would have been at the *head* of the brigade (shown in grey in the schematic), and on the left in line of battle.

Nevertheless, while mis-ascribing the reasons for the 79th's position at the rear of the column, he was correct about its location and its having formed square on the brigade's right. Though unacknowledged, Oman may have drawn upon the

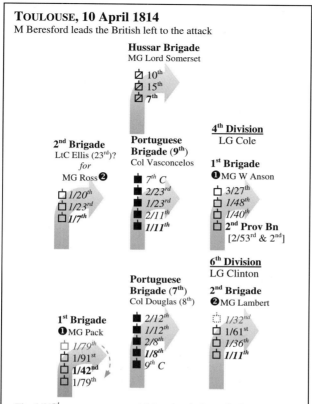

TOULOUSE, 10 April 1814

M Beresford leads the British left to the attack

Hussar Brigade
MG Lord Somerset

☑ 10th
☑ 15th
☑ 7th

4th Division
LG Cole

2nd Brigade
LtC Ellis (23rd)?
for
MG Ross ❷

☐ 1/20th
☐ 1/23rd
☐ 1/7th

Portuguese Brigade (9th)
Col Vasconcelos

■ 7th C
■ 2/23rd
■ 1/23rd
■ 2/11th
■ 1/11th

1st Brigade
❶MG W Anson

☐ 3/27th
☐ 1/48th
☐ 1/40th
☐ **2nd Prov Bn**
[2/53rd & 2nd]

6th Division
LG Clinton

Portuguese Brigade (7th)
Col Douglas (8th)

■ 2/12th
■ 1/12th
■ 2/8th
■ **1/8th**
9th C

2nd Brigade
❷MG Lambert

☐ 1/32nd
☐ 1/61st
☐ 1/36th
☐ **1/11th**

1st Brigade
❶MG Pack

☐ 1/79th
☐ 1/91st
☐ **1/42nd**
☐ 1/79th

The 1/32nd was not present with Lambert's Brigade, but escorting the battering train and pontoons. The 1/79th, in Pack's Brigade, took up a rear-guard post during the march.

Attached: 1 company, 5/60th to Ross's, Lambert's & Pack's Brigades; 1 company of Brunswick Oels Jägers to W. Anson's Brigade.

ॐ ॐ

Beresford's mission was summarized to LtG Freyre:

'The 4th and 6th Divisions 'will proceed in a direction which has been pointed out to Marshal Beresford, until they are far enough advanced to be enabled to act against the right flank of the French position, they are then to ascend the heights and attack the enemy.'

Note that the two divisions advanced by the left flank of three lines of battle disposed so that after the divisions fronted to the right, Beresford's corps was formed on the center, with the 4th Division right in front, the 6th Division left in front, both ready to unfold to their respective open flanks in customary battle array when the time came. While the senior, 4th Division held the post of honour on the left flank, the sequence of the division's brigades does not seem to have been conformably reversed, although while in column of brigades, MG W. Anson's 1st Brigade found itself indeed occupying the post of honour, as it apparently did throughout the day.

Fig. 36

anonymous author of *The Personal Narrative of a Private Soldier in the 42nd Highlanders*, who stated: 'The 79th formed square on the right, as the cavalry had begun to attempt our right flank.'[198]

Fortunately, there appears to be a solution to this mystery. The same soldier-author illustrated Major General Pack's capacity for careful preparations when describing (two pages earlier) Pack's conference with his regimental officers during the dawn halt preceding the final march to the south: 'the general of brigade called all the officers, and told them that he had received orders for the Highland Brigade to attack the enemy's breastworks and redoubts, on the right, saying, at the same time, "The gallant 42nd will lead and attack, and be supported by the 79th and 91st." '[199]

This insight into Pack's anticipatory planning adds credibility to the observation made by Anton (42nd Foot), who recorded an incident that his anonymous colleague did not, providing a clue to the change in the brigade's regimental sequence. When the premature Spanish attack on the French left was repulsed:

> It was apprehended that the enemy would have borne down upon us in the impetuosity of the movement, and we deployed into lines. The 79th regiment was at this time in front of the 42nd, and General Pack, anticipating a charge from the enemy's victorious and elated infantry, after thus scattering the Spaniards, gave orders to the 79th to receive them with a volley, immediately form four deep, face about, and pass through the ranks of the 42nd. The latter received the orders to form four deep, as soon as the former had given its fire; let the line pass through, then form up, give a volley, and charge. This was providing against what might have taken place, but did not, for the enemy was recalled, and the Spaniards were afterwards rallied. We now moved off to our left . . .[200]

Thus, it appears that the 79th was detailed to a rearguard duty that resulted in its becoming the rear regiment on the march, thereby becoming the right when the brigade wheeled up into line of battle.

This resolution to the mystery also serves to illustrate customary battle-array's flexibility, that it could be altered to meet necessity, though it was important that all principal parties be aware of the alteration in order to avoid confusion. These accounts also serve to suggest that Pack's brigade may possibly have trailed the division somewhat (delayed, not least, by having formed line to fend off a French pursuit that did not come), which would have made its later prolongation of the division to the right shorter and quicker, and thereby explain how the highlanders, in the left rear during the march south, were so quickly involved in the combat once the divisions faced toward the enemy on the right and attacked.

The battle at Toulouse concluded the campaigns of Wellington's Peninsular army. The Anglo-Allied army had built a remarkable record of battlefield success across the span of nearly six years. The banners of its triumph were woven of many threads, a number of them drawn by the hand of Wellington, others by those of his subordinates, great and small, and not a few by the courage, confidence, and skills of the multitude of men who filled the ranks or supported their trials. In the weave was a pattern of teamwork, of inter-dependence, without which the parts could not possibly have functioned effectively as a whole. On the battlefield, that pattern was physically manifested in the army's customary battle-array.

Pattern. It is a fundamental method of learning, of knowledge building. It is basic to training troops, at the heart of a coherent fighting doctrine, a tool for the analysis of intelligence about the enemy. Pattern is information organised. An order of battle was the physical corollary to information about the army, arranged in a methodical fashion and available for use. As battle-array, pattern was a template for organising the physical arrangement of troops as well as the basis for the conceptual grasp that commanders at every level could develop about battlefield operations and their relation to them. Battle-array as pattern provided a vital prism through which soldiers could filter and organise infor-mation; pattern as battle-array was a tool by which officers could manipulate troops on the battlefield and allowed those troops to understand and implement those directions coherently. Battle-array was orderliness prepared for action, a primary defence against confusion and chaos in a deafening, smoke-shrouded environment of carnage, a potent weapon in the moral test of opposing wills – memoirs are rich with references to the powerful impressions made by serried ranks, orderly advances, and parade-ground drill amidst battlefield chaos. A coherent pattern of battle-array was an inseparable element of military organisa-tion, reflecting its identity, defining its capabilities, born of and shaping its battlefield doctrines.

The patterning of battle-array had deep roots in history and human psychology. It was born of the fundamental need for identity, both of self and of others. From earliest Western history, the pattern was closely tied to a sense of honour. Customary battle-array incorporated this association of honour and place as a point of organisational reference as an organisation strove for improved efficiency and capability.

The notion of battle-array inherited from ancient Greece and Rome, and cease-lessly revalidated as an integral part of close order warfare ever since, was common coin among Europe's military men, though each country tempered its version through its own cultural filter and experience. France, for instance, enshrined battle-array in its 1791 *Rules and Regulations* based on simple numerical sequencing from the right,[201] and this national pattern manifested itself in various ways in the battle-arrays of Napoleon's campaigns, permitting the Emperor, from his knoll at Austerlitz, in 1805, for instance, to comprehend his army's disposi-tions from a distance, just as Wellington would do from his knoll at Toulouse. The template was an inescapably necessary tool for battlefield management.

It had its corollary at sea, where captains were accustomed to marshalling in a naval line of battle in accordance with a strictly arranged sequence of warships and periodically issued 'Fighting Instructions'. The tactical changes that Lord Nelson vigorously developed at sea which, after bringing a fleet into contact, released each captain into battle to fight it as he best knew how, but in a harmony of action governed by commanders' collective sense of doctrine, mirrored the increased flex-ibility the British army derived by its organisational evolution from a unitary to a divisional structure. Nelsonian naval combat still relied upon battle-array, but far more flexibly than had other maritime practitioners.

The army, too, in varying degrees, applied battle-array flexibly; it was a point of departure, altered to meet changing circumstances as required. Wellington's orders underscored this. But a prudent balance between change and consistency was necessary if chaos and confusion were to be kept at bay. Nonetheless, within the forms of established battle order, regiments and even brigades rotated their order of march when not in proximity to the enemy,[202] and brigades and divisions at the left extremity of the army, in the second post of honour, reversed their internal sequence. While the order of companies in a battalion was tenaciously maintained, brigades had more scope for altering their arrangements, on the fly, if necessary. When divisions materialized as miniature armies in the organisational structure, their place in the army's array became even more flexible with the habit of use.

Appreciation for customary array as a battlefield management tool also permits it to be used as a tool of historical research and analysis. In the same way a commander on a smoky battlefield could identify distant units and commands by their presumed, known sequence, so may a modern historian apply the same template to discerning dispositions for which no contemporary record is available. Awareness of the pattern can help to illuminate changes of position and the spatial relationship between units and commands. While it certainly cannot explain all variations and deviations, battle-array as an analytical tool provides a basis for asking new questions. A brigade that appears not to conform to the customary pattern of regimental disposition prompts various queries. Why not? What circumstances led to the inconsistency? Do they reflect instructions from above, an emergency experienced, or some other exigency?

Oman and Fortescue clearly applied their knowledge of customary battle-array to their historical analyses. Yet, by the early twentieth century, close order warfare had yielded to dispersion in the teeth of weapons of vastly increased lethality. It had also been rendered less important by better communications and better training – training mirroring societal changes that placed increasing value and responsibility on individuals – for individual initiative and capabilities became crucial in dispersed warfare, as Sir John Moore and the advocates of the Shorncliffe light infantry training had understood. While the ancient imperatives of battle order continued to evolve to meet the changing circumstances of warfare, the way in which they had shaped close order warfare was rapidly forgotten, by soldiers and historians alike.

The principles of customary battle-array were so fundamental as to be simply assumed by the soldiers of the Peninsular War, who tended not to discuss them directly, but did reflect the patterns by battlefield application and in their accounts. The record of those patterns is the empirical evidence of the conceptual prism that produced them. Britain's customary battle-array served Wellington and his Peninsular army as an organisational foundation from Roliça to Toulouse, an ancient legacy indispensable to close order warfare upon which Wellington built victory.

NOTES

1 Measurements taken from Wyld, *Atlas*, 'Battle of Toulouse' map, Plan No. 36.

2 Herodotus, quoting Plato's *Gorgias* (484 B.C.), through the poet Pindar, in *The History*, 3.38.

3 Homer, *The Iliad*, Bk 11, lines 1–10. Homer was the very first entry in a list of military works for regimental libraries, as proposed in a letter published in the January 1811 issue of the *Royal Military Chronicle* (p. 212–13), a monthly magazine for British officers.

4 Of the forty-eight named works proposed in the January 1811 edition of the *Royal Military Chronicle* (see preceding note), no fewer than fifteen, nearly one-third, were drawn from the quills of classical Greek and Roman writers or focused on ancient warfare. The contents of the list were not atypical of those made by other contemporaries. Greek and Roman military history was readily and commonly referenced by military writers throughout Europe.

5 Anon., 'A Complete System of Camp Discipline' in *A System of Camp-Discipline*, pp. 7–8.

6 Williamson, *Elements of Military Arrangement*, vol. i, p. 3, fn 1 (pp. 3–4).

7 Adjutant General, *General Regulations* (1804), p. 1. The language of this first sentence remained identical in the 1811/1816 edition (the term 'eldest' here, refers to the date of an officer's commission, of course, not his actual age), but the section's title had changed with the expansion of the regulations, so that duties and matters of 'honour', 'rank', and 'precedence' were separately considered.

8 'Advanced Principles of Military Justice', Judge Advocate General's School, 1–1.

9 War Office, *Articles of War* (1807), Section XV, Article I, 'Rank', pp. 47–8.

10 The subject is well discussed in Fortescue's *British Army*, vols. i–iii, and in his *Four Lectures*, probed in Houlding's *Fit for Service*, explored in Guy's *Œconomy and Discipline*, to name a few sources.

11 The Crown had not always been the exclusive source of commissions; in the seventeenth century a proprietary colonel had the power to commission officers into his regiment, as commanders had commonly had during the English Civil War.

12 If actually serving on a staff appointment, there were additional allowances and pay.

13 See Adjutant General, *General Regulations* (1811): 'Regulations to be observed in the Posting of Officers to Regiments having more than one Battalion . . .', pp. 72–6. While not a matter explicitly addressed in the earlier *General Regulations* (1804), the untimely rotation of officers created a disruption that caused Wellington considerable annoyance (see letter to Liverpool, 14 November 1809, *WD* (new ed.), vol. v, pp. 281–2). By the current method of rotation he lost officers who were 'probably the best of their respective ranks; and they are replaced by others, without experience, who have no knowledge of their men or their duty, or of the orders and regulations of this army, and the whole must be taught to them . . .' The 1811 edition of the *General Regulations* endeavoured to address this issue with more practical guidance, clarifying that the rotation of officers from battalions on 'any *Particular Service*' should not be made 'until the termination of the Campaign or Military Operation on which the Battalion may be engaged, unless they should be previously relieved . . .', while officers present with the battalion should '*succeed, for the time*, to the Vacancies' that occurred on campaign.

14 James, *Military Dictionary* (1810), under 'Brevet'.

15 'Generals in our army are paid only when employed; in which circumstance the land varies from the naval service. It is for this reason that they are allowed to have regiments, and to make such immense profits by the cloathing.' Williamson, *Elements of Military Arrangement* (1791), vol. i, p. 29.

16 James, *Military Dictionary* (1810), under 'Brevet'.

17 'A proper number of General Officers are appointed according to the strength of the army. For this proportion no certain rules are established. When the army is considerable, the following may be considered as an adequate staff, exclusive of the command in chief: a general for the horse, and one for the foot; or a general for each wing of the army: a major-general for every two brigades; and about half that number of lieutenant generals.' Williamson, *Elements of Military Arrangement* (1791), vol. i, p. 26. One can see how command responsibilities for particular ranks would eventually be mapped onto the later organisation by 'army division'.

18 Neave-Hill, 'Rank Titles', *JSAHR*, pp. 96–105; Adjutant General, *General Regulations* (1804), p. 5: 'Officers serving on the staff in the capacity of brigadiers, are to take rank and precedence from their commissions as colonels in the army, not from the dates of their appointments as brigadiers.'

19 An important element of staff were aides-de-camp: 'A general is allowed four aide-du-camps [sic], a lieutenant general two, and a major-general one, to carry their orders.' A footnote states: 'A general may appoint more aid-du-camps [sic]; but pay is allowed only for the number here specified.' Williamson, *Elements of Military Arrangement* (1791), vol. i, p. 28.

20 E.g., Wellington to Col Ross, 1 May 1813, *WD*, vol. x, p. 338 'I shall be very happy to appoint you to the command of a brigade in the army when it shall be in my power. [. . .] If you will refer to the Army List, you will see that there are in this army Brigadier General Brooke, Brigadier General Inglis, and Colonel Fermor, senior to you, without brigades . . .'.

21 For example, see Bland, *Treatise*, pp. 250–53 (1727) and pp. 297–300 (1762):
'The Method of forming the Foot into Brigades, is as follows: The several Battalions are divided, according to Seniority, into four equal Parts or Divisions.
'The first Part is to consist of the eldest Battalions; the second Part of the next eldest; the third Part of those next to the second; and the fourth Part of the youngest Battalions.
'The Battalions being thus divided into four Classes, the first Brigade is composed of the eldest Battalion of each Class; the second Brigade of the Second Battalion of each Class; the third Brigade of the Third Battalion of each; and so on in this manner till the Whole are formed into Brigades; by which Method, there will be a Battalion of every Class in each Brigade, and thereby intermix the old and young Battalions: for as entire Brigades are frequently detached, unless they are mixed in this Manner, One composed of four young Battalions might be commanded on an Affair of Importance, and, for want of Experience, fail of Success; but by intermixing the experienced and inexperienced Battalions together, that Danger is in a great measure avoided; which, in my Opinion, shews the Method not only Right, but Necessary.'

22 Major General Leith, June–July 1810; Major General W. Stewart, August 1810–May 1811; Lieutenant General Tilson-Chowne, April 1812–late 1812; Lieutenant General W. Stewart, March 1813–until the war's end.

23 Fortescue, *British Army*, vol. viii, fn. 1, p. 122 – only a partial listing shown here, excluding other commands and the constituent regiments.

24 Williamson, *Elements of Military Arrangement* (1791), vol. i, p. 1, opening sentence.

25 Jennings, *The Croker Papers*, vol.i, p.537.

26 James, *Military Dictionary* (1810), under 'File'.

27 War Office, *Rules and Regulations* (1803), p. 2.

28 War Office, *Rules and Regulations* (1803), p. iv, first sentence of the Adjutant-General's order of 1 June 1792, requiring its use; for the equivalency of 'platoon' and 'company' see *Rules and Regulations*, Part III, 'Formation of the Company', p. 64; also James, *Military Dictionary* (1810), under 'Platoon'. With large establishments, companies might be divided into two platoons.

29 War Office, *Rules and Regulations*, Part III, p. 67: 'The companies must be equalized in point of numbers, at all times when the battalion is formed for field movement . . .' 'Equalization' was an 'indispensable' part of creating and maintaining regularity of parts, ensuring that each component of a battalion was of as nearly equal numbers and dimension as possible. By shifting men to even the numbers in each subordinate level, it facilitated uniformity of distances of frontage and intervals so that the parts fit together properly in the various evolutions.

30 War Office, *Rules and Regulations* (1803), pp. 33 and 64.

31 War Office, *Rules and Regulations* (1803), p. 63. While three ranks was to be the standard depth, scope was left for two, and this would be the norm in the Peninsula.

32 Derived from: War Office, *Rules and Regulations* (1803), Part III, pp. 64–6. Specific positions in the supernumerary rank conjectured from Dickinson, *Instructions for forming a regiment of infantry* (1798), pp. 5–6, and Langley, *The eighteen manœuvres* (1794), p. [1]. The *Rules and Regulations* did not explicitly provide these details.
Williamson, in his 1791 *Elements of Military Arrangement* (vol. i, pp. 18–19) amplified British manpower practice:
'*Peace Establishment*. The establishment of a company in time of peace consists of a captain, lieutenant, ensign, two serjeants, one drummer, and about 30 rank and file. When they are raised to the number of three serjeants, two drummers, and 50 rank and file, it may be called a medium establishment: but in time of war, they are usually raised by degrees to seventy, and in some regiments to an hundred. When a company consists of 100 rank and file, another lieutenant is always added.

'*War Establishment.* The most convenient war establishment is about 70 rank and file per company, which was that of most of the regiments last war. A battalion then on this establishment would consist of one colonel, one lieutenant colonel, one major (who have their own companies [ed. note: which changed in 1803]), 7 captains, and one captain-lieutenant, 11 lieutenants, 8 ensigns, 30 serjeants, 20 drummers, and 700 rank and file.

'The staff of a regiment are, the chaplain, the surgeon and mate, the quartermaster, the adjutant, and serjeant-major.'

The peacetime establishment is the same as given in the *Rules and Regulations*, and the 'convenient' wartime is generally consistent with Hood's 1804 *Elements of War*, p. 4. Williamson further noted:

'The grenadier and light-infantry companies, instead of a lieutenant and ensign, have each two lieutenants; and in Fusilier regiments, or corps in which the officers and serjeants carry fusils in the room of spontoons and halberds, there are no ensigns, but instead of them an inferior order of lieutenants, who are called second lieutenants, and form a distinct rank between the lieutenants and ensigns . . . There is one regiment, viz. the 7th or English Fuzileers [sic], in which all the subalterns are first lieutenants.'

33 War Office, *Rules and Regulations* (1803), p. 63. The methodology was not defined; in fact, in his original 1787 treatise, *Principles of Military Movement*, Dundas had left this matter to the 'internal regulations of the battalion' (p. 59). However, customary practice seems to have asserted itself. The formula described as that of the Norfolk Militia, in Williamson's *Elements of Military Arrangement* (1791; pp. 78–80), is very similar to that which James identified in his *Military Dictionary* (1810), under 'Size': 'to take the height of men for the purpose of placing them in military array, and of rendering their relative statures more effective. In all regiments, the sizing begins from the flanks to the centre, the tallest men being placed upon the right and left of the several companies in the front rank, and the shortest in the center and rear ranks.' Clearly, corporals and 'intelligent men' were posted regardless of the sizing methodology applied to the rest of the rank and file.

34 War Office, *Rules and Regulations* (1803), p. 33.

35 War Office, *Rules and Regulations* (1803), p. 64. Although unstated, it may be surmised that 'intelligent men' (dependable privates who displayed a solid understanding of drill) were also placed on the 'pivot' flank of sections, and quite possibly on the reverse flank as well, thereby ensuring reliable regulators for the battalion's component parts.

36 Dundas, *Principles* (1787), p. 57.

37 The 'natural' order of a battalion marching in column was to 'lead by the right'. This meant that a column normally expected to form line by wheeling or prolonging its components to the left, making the left flank of each component the pivot and key point for setting intervals vital to the evolutions or for leading files to their correct position.

38 War Office, *Rules and Regulations* (1803), Part III, 'Formation of the Battalion', p. 66. There were always exceptions to any rule, and one such was to be found in the 1st Foot Guards, whose battalions were composed of 8 centre companies, with 2 grenadier and 2 light companies (e.g. see *Royal Military Chronicle*, March 1811, pp. 311–12).

39 Anon., *Perfection of Military Discipline* (1691), p. 63: 'If a Company of Grenadiers belong to the Regiment, it must be drawn up on the right of the Battalion . . .'

40 While not overt in the *Rules and Regulations*, this was made explicit in its 1822 revision (War Office, *Field Exercises and Evolutions of the Army. Field Exercises and Evolutions of the Army*, pp. 135–6).

41 The timing for the alteration of company sequence was perhaps similar to the revision of timing for the rotation of officers between senior and junior battalions when one or both was on active service, which was delayed by the General Regulations (1811) until the end of the campaign or operations.

42 War Office, *Rules and Regulations* (1803), Part IV, paragraph 14.

43 War Office, *Rules and Regulations* (1803); James, *Military Dictionary* (1810).

44 War Office, *General Regulations* (1804), p. 6. The language of the 1811/1816 edition is substantially the same (p. 10), although the regiments of Life Guards and Horse Guards were specifically distinguished; as of March 1813, the Corps of Royal Engineers and the Royal Military Sappers and Miners had a position specified for them between the Royal Artillery and the Foot Guards; the

Royal Veteran Battalions were inserted between the Foot Guards and the Line regiments; the position of regiments within the Militia was fixed by lot, although when British and Irish Militia were serving together, 'the priority of rank is to be considered to belong to the Militia of that part of the United Kingdom, in which the Quarter may be situated.' For further discussion on militia's precedence by lot, see 'Order of Precedence of Militia Regiments', by W.Y. Baldry in *JSAHR*, vol. xv, no. 57, Spring 1936.

45 War Office, from the 'Contents' of *A List of All the Officers of the Army and Royal Marines on Full and Half-Pay: with an Index and Succession of Colonels* (1811).

46 See Bland, *Treatise*, Article XVII, Chapter IV, pp. 250–53 (2nd edition, 1727); the same passage is found under Chapter VII, Article V, on pp. 297–301 (9th edition, 1762).

47 Bland, *Treatise*, p. 251 (1727) and p. 298 (1762).

48 Houlding, *Fit for Service*, pp. 182–4.

49 James, *Military Dictionary* (1810), under 'Post'. James' language had a legacy: identical wording appeared in an anonymous *Military Dictionary* of 1778, and the 'Military Dictionary' of Thomas Simes' *Military Medley* (1768) contained substantially the same wording. It may be worth noting that this same language would still be found in the United States, in Wilhelm's *Military Dictionary and Gazetteer* (p. 448) in 1881.

50 James, *Military Dictionary* (1810), under 'Brigade'; also Simes, *Miiltary Guide*, 1768.

51 Bland, *Treatise*, pp. 251–2 (1727) and pp. 298–9 (1762).

52 War Office, *Rules and Regulations* (1803), Part IV, p. 282. This same hierarchy was a common one, e.g. see Williamson's *Elements of Military Arrangement* (1791), vol. i, p. 12.

53 *Royal Military Chronicle*, June 1811, p. 151.

54 Moore, *Moore*, vol. i, p. 365.

55 Gurwood, *General Orders* (2nd ed.), pp. xviii–xx.

56 Gurwood, *General Orders* (2nd ed.), p. xx. From a regimental officer (Leach, *Rough Sketches*, p.303) comes the corroborating description, pertaining to the winter of 1813: 'In speaking of Sir Rowland Hill's corps, the second division, with some regiments of cavalry and Portuguese brigades attached, are included. Sir Thomas Graham, properly speaking, commanded a corps consisting of the 1st and 5th Divisions; and subsequently other troops were added to his command.'

57 Quoted in Moore Smith, *Life of John Colborne* (n.d.), p. 132.

58 Letter (to John Wilson Croker, whose name is on the mss copy in WP 1/478), 8 August 1815, *WD* (new ed.), vol. xii, p. 590.

59 Stanhope, *Conversations* (5 October 1833), p. 29, giving Wellington's later description of Roliça.

60 Ferguson was actually on the staff of Spencer's force and returning to join it at the anticipated rendezvous (Warre, *Letters*, p. 1).

61 To Hill, 23 June 1808, *WD* (new ed.), vol. iv, p. 14.

62 Castlereagh to Wellesley, 30 June 1808, *WD* (new ed.), vol. iv, p. 20; Wellesley to Hill, 3 July 1808, *WD* (new ed.), vol. iv, p. 21; Warre to father, 8 June, Warre, *Letters*, p. 4.

63 For the 36th, see Geike, *Life of Sir Roderick I. Murchison*, vol. i, p. 25, quoting Murchison's recollections of the events of the war. For the 45th see Leach, *Rough Sketches*, pp. 41 & 49. Hibbert's assertion that the 71st formed part of Fane's brigade is offered without a source and is difficult to credit (*Soldier of the Seventy-First*, pp. 14 and 19). Fane's brigade was the logical choice, as it contained but 14 companies; the addition of the two new under-strength battalions would have brought the brigade's temporary strength to about 2,850, commensurate with the manpower of the other two brigades. Both the 36th and 45th must have been detached shortly after landing, for neither were included in the order of battle of 3 August as a part of Fane's brigade – Wellesley discussed the light brigade in his orders of 3 August only in terms of the 5/60th and 95th Regiments.

64 G.O., 3 Aug. 1808, *WSD*, vol. vi, p. 96 (selected elements given).

65 E.M. Lloyd pointed to precisely this instruction as a noteworthy step in a general shift from deployment in three ranks to two ranks by British troops (*History of Infantry*, p. 217), while Willoughby Verner cited it as having 'marked the definite adoption of a line two-deep in the British army, which hitherto had been usually formed in three ranks'. (Verner, *Rifle Brigade*, vol. i, p. 142.) Yet Wellesley's instruction echoed an old, customary procedure, as articulated in the *Essay on the Art of War* (p. 411), in 1761, in response to a similar debate over the unit depth:

'There are different Opinions, with regard to the Form to be given a Battalion and a Squadron.

The most universal Opinion is to form the Battalion in four or three Ranks, and the Squadron in three or two Ranks; but for the Uniformity and Facility of the Manœuvres, a General ought, at the Beginning of the Campaign, to regulate the Number of Ranks for Action.'

Fortescue points out that the number of ranks early in the eighteenth century was unfixed, and that Marlborough made occasional use of as few as two ranks (*British Army*, vol. i, p. 585), in a period commonly employing six. But then issues of depth had haunted armies and military thinkers since antiquity, and most recently in the heated eighteenth century Continental debates about thin versus deep orders of battle. British use of two ranks had been authorized by Sir Jeffrey Amherst in his 'General Orders for 11 July 1759 in the Americas' (Hawks, *Orderly Book*, pp. 30–31), had been commonly used in the American War of Independence, Lord Moira had ordered the adoption of two ranks in 19 November 1793 (Glazebrook, 'Campaign in Flanders', p. 4), and troops had been ordered to use it in the 1807 Danish Campaign (Gardyne, *Life of a Regiment*, vol. i, p. 129), among other instances. G. A. Steppler notes a collection of correspondence officially sanctioning the use of two ranks in his chapter in Guy, *The Road to Waterloo*, p. 19.

It was appropriate, however, for Wellesley to make this specific statement, in light of the Duke of York's specific clarification of the *Rules and Regulations* issued in the 1804 *General Orders and Observations on the Movement and Field Exercise of the Infantry* : 'the established order for the infantry is in three ranks, which is not to be departed from except in light infantry battalions, or in small or detached corps acting as such, without the especial permission of the Commanding or Reviewing General.' (para. 34, pp. 31–2.)

66 Wellesley, who had been advised from the beginning that the two forces were to be joined (C-in-C to Wellesley, 14 June 1809, *WD* (new ed.), vol. iv, p. 10), had expected to reorganise upon Spencer's arrival (*WD* (new ed.), vol. iv, p. 14). This reorganisation corrects Oman's erroneous placement of the 45th with Fane instead of Craufurd (Oman, *Peninsular War*, vol. i, p. 232 and fn).

67 G.O., 7 Aug. 1808, *WSD*, vol. vi, p. 101 (selected elements given; Nightingall's Brigade originally printed as '2nd', corrected here to '3rd'; assignments of brigade-majors & asst.-commissaries of brigade omitted).

68 A personal element may have played a role in the assignment of three regiments to their respective brigade commanders. Wellesley was aware of a special relationship between Hill and the 9th Foot, quite probably dating to late 1806, when it formed a part of the brigade Hill had commanded in southern England (overlapping with Moore at Shorncliffe), and it had moved with him to Ireland in early 1807 (Wellesley to Hill, 23 June, *WD* (new ed.), vol. iv, p. 14; Teffeteller, *The Surpriser*, pp. 26–7). In the expedition to the Cape of Good Hope, in 1805–6, Ferguson had commanded the 'Highland Brigade', which had included the 71st (*Royal Military Calendar* (1820), vol. ii, pp. 263–4). Bowes, meanwhile, was still the lieutenant colonel of the 6th Foot (Hall, *Biographical Dictionary*, p. 69), lately arriving with it at Gibraltar from duty in Canada, and only recently placed upon Spencer's staff as brigadier general. Such special relationships would be found in future commands in the Peninsular army; for example, Charles Colville's special affection for his brigade in the 3rd Division would underlie his long, but intermittent, association with it.

69 Strength for 5/60th from Rigaud, *Celer et Audax*, p. 32; strength for 95th from Verner, *Rifle Brigade* (n.d.), vol. i, p. 140; their total manpower, when augmenting the number of rank and file given by Horse Guards by the rule-of-thumb of one-eighth (for officers, staff and sergeants), would equal about 1,500. (List from Horse Guards, 20 July 1808, *WD* (new ed.) vol. iv, p.32)

70 The regiments which accompanied Spencer are <u>underlined</u> in the diagram.

71 *WSD*, vol. vi, p. 115. Unfortunately, the *Supplementary Despatches* excised the subsequent portion of this order, leaving the note 'Detail of the order of march' — a lesson to future compilers and historians that one man's minor detail is another's golden key! As the army had camped in the vicinity of Caldas the night before (*WD* (new ed.), vol. iv, p. 96), 'this side of the castle of Obidos' would have meant the assembly occurred to the north and north-east of Obidos.

72 James, *Military Dictionary* (1810), under 'Home Service'.

73 Derived from: Fortescue, *British Army*, vol. vi, 'Roliça', Map No. 4; Foy, *Atlas* for his *Histoire*, 'Roliça' map; Verner, *Rifle Brigade*, vol. i, 'Obidos & Roliça', Map VII.

74 Butler, *Wellington's Operations*, vol. i, p. 56.

75 Fortescue, *British Army*, vol. vi, 'Roliça', Map No. 4; Verner, *Rifle Brigade*, vol. i, 'Obidos & Roliça', Map VII.

76 'Memorandum for the Quartermaster-General', n.d. (probably 16 June 1812), *WSD*, vol. xiv, pp. 70–1.

77 Derived from: 'Memorandum for the Quartermaster-General', n.d. [probably 16 June 1812], *WSD*, vol. xiv, pp. 70–1.

78 Wellesley to Gordon, 18 August 1808, *WD* (new ed.), vol. iv, p. 102.

79 Derived from: Eliot, *Treatise*, pp. 204–9 & 'Vimeiera' map; Fortescue, *British Army*, vol. vi, p. 223; Oman, *Peninsular War*, vol. i, p. 248–59; Verner, *Rifle Brigade*, vol. i, p.156 & 'Vimeiro' map; *WD* (new ed.), vol. iv, to Castlereagh, 21 Aug. 1808, pp. 108–12; to Duke of York, 22 Aug. 1808, pp. 113–14; *WSD*, vol. vi, G.O., 20 Aug. 1808, p. 120; G.O., 21 Aug. 1808, pp.121; vol. xvii, M.G.O., 18 Aug. 1808, p. 294–5; Wyld, *Memoir*, p. 3, quoting Anstruther's 'Journal' & *Atlas*, Plan No. 3: 'Vimeiro.'

80 Derived from same sources as Fig. 12, plus: Hibbert, *Seventy-First*, p. 17–18; Landmann, *Recollections*, p. 239; Lawrence (40th), *Sgt. William Lawrence*, p. 44–5; Leslie (29th), *Military Journal*, p. 50–1; Warre (Ferguson's adc), *Letters*, p. 18 & 21–22; Wood (82nd), *Subaltern Officer*, p. 54.

81 M.G.O., 18 Aug. 1808, *WSD*, vol. xiii, p. 294; Rigaud, *Celer et Audax*, pp. 34 & 40.

82 This order seems to have been overlooked by Fortescue, who attributed this innovative distribution to what was, in fact, Wellesley's resumption of the arrangement in May 1809 (Fortescue, *British Army* , vol. vii, pp. 149–50). Wellesley had extended the distribution still further immediately after the Battle of Vimeiro. In his congratulatory General Order on the *same* day of the battle, he had instructed that: 'one rifle company of the 60th will be transferred immediately from the 6th to the 7th brigade, and another from the 6th to the 8th brigade.' (G.O., 21 Aug. 1808, *WSD*, vol. vi, p. 121.)

83 Derived from: Blakeney, *A Boy in the Peninsular War*, pp. 109–10, 114–15; Fortescue, *British Army*, vol. vi, pp. 378–9, 382–8 & 'Coruña' map No. 6; Gardyne, *Life of a Regiment*, vol. i, p. 160; Hibbert, *Coruña*, pp. 141 & ill. 38, 'Battle of Coruña' map p. 166; Londonderry, *Narrative*, p. 228 & 'Coruna' map; Moore, *Moore*, p. 339 & 'Coruna' map after p. 354; Oman, *Peninsular War*, vol. i, p. 584, 590–1; Verner, *Rifle Brigade*, vol. i, pp. 201–6, 208–11 & 'Coruña' map; 'Returns of the Troops in Portugal and Spain', 1808–9, *WSD*, vol. xiii, p. 323–6; Wyld, *Memoir*, pp. 5–6 & *Atlas*, Plan No. 4, 'Coruña' map.

84 See Chapter 2, 'The Origin of Wellington's Peninsular Army', pp. 66–7.

85 Bateson, *Mind and Nature*, p. 52.

86 Most curiously, Lieutenant Colonel Bingham (53rd), in A Campbell's brigade, could write home in April, after Cradock's reorganisation and before Wellesley's arrival, of being in the same 'division' with the Guards and Hill's Brigade. Yet, each brigade was in a different line of Cradock's array, though they were in the same wing in Wellesley's later array of 8 May. While Bingham's use of 'division' here was surely in the older sense of 'a portion', it seems likely that some internal alterations were already afoot before Wellesley's arrival. (McGuffie, 'The Bingham Manuscripts', *Army Quarterly*, p. 125.)

87 From Dickson, *Manuscripts* (1987), vol. i, p. 29–30. Corroborative and additional sources: Beamish, *King's German Legion*, vol. i, p. 189; Londonderry, *Narrative*, pp. 256–8 & 'State of the Forces . . .', 6 May 1809, Appendix No. I; Maxwell, 'The British Campaign of 1809' (Fitzclarence), *Peninsular Sketches*, vol. i, pp. 82–3; Atkinson's essay in Oman, *Wellington's Army*, pp. 342–4; Stothert, *Narrative*, pp. 31–4; Wyld, *Memoir*, fn. 1, pp. 11–12; G.O., Coimbra, 4 May 1809, *General Orders*, pp. 9–11, & in *WSD*, vol. vi, pp. 250–1. One curious anomaly shared across the sources is the switch in the order of the 87th and 88th Regiments in the 3rd Brigade.

88 Ron McGuigan's research notes. The 1st Guards Brigade, meanwhile, was destined for the Scheldt with the ill-fated Walcheren expedition, accompanied by the flank companies of the 3rd Guards Brigade (Fortescue, *British Army*, vol. vii, p. 57).

89 See Beamish, *King's German Legion*, vol. i, p. 84, for January 1805 & p. 91, for April and May 1806.

90 Beamish, *King's German Legion*, vol. i, pp. 140–1.

91 For example, see Londonderry, *Narrative*, 'State' in Appendix No. I.

92 Curiously, Oman provided the new order of battle (*Peninsular War*, vol. ii, fn. p. 320), but though the cavalry and Guards preceded the rest, the line brigades were presented in no particular order and without indication of their brigade numbers. Moreover, the regiments were listed administra-

tively (in numerical order, followed by light infantry, followed by foreign infantry). Oman then commented broadly about Wellesley's new army: 'The army was not yet distributed into regular divisions, but the beginnings of the later divisional arrangement were indicated by telling of the brigades of Richard Stewart and Murray to serve together under Edward Paget (who commanded Moore's reserve division with such splendid credit to himself during the Coruña retreat), while those of H. Campbell, A. Campbell, and Sontag were to take their orders from Sherbrooke, and those of Hill and Cameron to move under charge of the former brigadier. The cavalry was under General Cotton, with Payne as brigadier . . .' (vol. ii, p. 320) – something is confounded here, for Lieutenant General Payne outranked Cotton and commanded the cavalry, while 'Fane' was a brigade commander. Oman presented the KGL as a single brigade under Murray, with no mention of the German brigadier generals. Fortescue (*British Army*, vol. vii, p. 150) did give the KGL in two brigades, under Langwerth (1st & 2nd Bns) and Low (5th and 7th Bns).

93 Selected portion from G.O., 4 May 1809, *General Orders*, pp. 10–11 (also in *WSD*, vol. vi, pp. 251).

94 *WD* (new ed.), vol. iv, p. 263.

95 *WD* (new ed.), vol. iv: to Castlereagh, 24 Apr. 1809, p. 270; and an indirect reference in Wellesley's letter to Captain Dench, 4 May 1809, p. 300; and to Admiral Berkeley, 7 May 1809, p. 307.

96 Reide, *Treatise*, p. 288.

97 For example, Williamson, *Elements of Military Arrangement* (1791), vol. i, p. 17; when describing the flank companies, Williamson noted: 'In time of peace, these flank companies always remain with their regiments; but upon service are generally formed into separate battalions, and are employed upon the most arduous and important enterprises.'

98 To W. Stewart, 27 Mar. 1810, *WD* (new ed.), vol. v, p. 398.

99 Beamish, *King's German Legion*, vol. i, fn. p. 189.

100 Verner, *Rifle Brigade*, vol. ii, pp. 5–15.

101 G.O., Coimbra, 6 May 1809, p. 18; see Fortescue's discussion, *British Army*, vii, pp. 151–2.

102 Hawker, *Journal*, p. 45. May 6 is the date given by the editor in Dickson, *Manuscripts* (1987), vol. i, p. 18; (Fitzclarence) 'The British Campaign of 1809', in Maxwell, *Peninsular Sketches*, vol. i, pp. 84–5; Eliot, *Treatise*, p. 224; to Beresford, 6 May 1809, *WD* (new ed.), vol. iv, p. 303 (wherein Wellesley expressed his lack of satisfaction with the 'bad figure' cut by Portuguese troops); Londonderry, however, indicated the review as on 5 May in *Narrative*, p. 265.

103 Selected portion from G.O., 8 May 1809, *General Orders*, p. 24 (also *WSD*, vol. vi, p. 257–8).

104 G.O. & A.G.O., 8 May 1808, *General Orders*, pp. 24–5.

105 Simes, *Military Medley* (1768), p. 114.

106 G.O., 9 May 1809, *General Orders*, pp. 25–6.

107 To Castlereagh, 12 May 1809, *WD* (new ed.), vol. iv, p. 322.

108 To Castlereagh, 17 June 1809, *WD* (new ed.), vol. iv, p. 435. In 1810, Wellington again alluded to the size of his command, when lamenting that he had no significant influence over the promotion of those serving under his command in the field, observing: 'I [. . .] command the largest British army that has been employed against the enemy for many years, and [. . .] have upon my hands certainly the most extensive and difficult concern that was ever imposed upon any British officer . . .' (to Torrens, 4 Aug. 1810, *WD* (new ed.), vol. vi, p. 326).

109 Selected portion from G.O., 18 Jun. 1809, *General Orders*, pp. 70–1 (also *WSD*, vol. vi, pp. 288–89).

110 To Cotton, 24 June 1809, *WSD*, vol. vi, pp. 294–5; clearly, Wellesley had been considering Hill's nomination *prior* to Tilson's assignment to take Hill's brigade.

111 For example, see (Fitzclarence) 'The British Campaign of 1809', Maxwell, *Peninsular Sketches*, vol. i, pp. 106–7.

112 As Wellington wrote to one disappointed, but unnamed Colonel (10 May 1813, *WD*, vol. x, vol. 369–70): 'As, however, you feel mortified upon your reassuming the command of your regiment, from the command of a brigade, of which your regiment forms a part, I trust that you will now see the propriety of my determination not to remove officers from the command of their regiments to the temporary command of brigades of which their regiments do not form a part; as it is probable that your feelings would have been mortified to a greater degree if you had now been obliged to return to command of your regiment from a brigade of the line.'

113 Stothert, *A Narrative*, p. 77.

114 *Rules and Regulations* (1803), p. 282.
115 For example, James, *Military Dictionary*, under 'Castrametation': 'the art of measuring or tracing out the form of a camp on the ground'; but the security of the 'camp consists in the facility and convenience of drawing out their troops at the head of their encampment; for which reason, whatever particular order of battle is regarded as the best disposition for fighting, it follows of course, that we should encamp in such a manner as to assemble and parade our troops in that order and disposition as soon as possible.'
116 Polybius, *Histories*, 6.24.
117 Furse, *Marching*, p. 297; Furse's example of the 'Battle-array of a Division' (p. 298) placed the 1st Brigade to the right of the 2nd Brigade.
118 Bland, *Treatise*, pp. 250 (1727) & p. 297 (1762). Advice to treat the camp as a potential battlefield was still current in the Peninsular War, as can be seen from the article in the February 1811 edition of the *Royal Military Chronicle*, p. 309.
119 Williamson, *Elements of Military Arrangement*, vol. i, p. 1, and reiterated vol. ii, p. 5. In the second volume, Bland's formulae for forming and encamping an army and its brigades were recapitulated, guided by the principle that 'the flanks being in an army, as well as in a brigade and battalion, the posts of honour. The same order is observed in drawing up the battalions or squadrons that compose a brigade . . .' (vol. ii, pp. 4–5).
120 Hawker, *Journal*, p. 89.
121 Derived from: G.O., 21 July 1809, *General Orders*, pp. 110–11 (also *WSD*, vol. vi, p. 319).
122 Bland, *Treatise*, p. 252 (1727) & pp. 299–300 (1762).
123 At Vimeiro, the Portuguese contingent had not been in the line of battle, but to the rear, and their subsequent movement to the left rear with C. Craufurd did not bring them into the fight.
124 Wyld, *Memoir*, p. 15.
125 Derived also from: Wyld, *Memoir*, fn. 1, p. 16.
126 In an interesting, possibly intentional correlation, the 3rd Division was formed by the two brigades that Wellesley had selected for independent service during the Oporto campaign – perhaps signalling the degree of Wellesley's confidence in them for the kind of work an advance guard performed.
127 Derived from Londonderry, *Narrative*, pp.329–31.
128 Napier, *Peninsular War* (5 vols., 1862), vol. ii (Bk. vii, Chap. vi), p. 151.
129 First quotation: Wellesley to Castlereagh, 29 July, 1809, *WD* (new ed.),vol. iv, p. 533. Second quotation: 'Memorandum upon the Battle of Talavera', n.d., *WD* (new ed.), vol. iv, p. 539.
130 Fortescue, *British Army*, vol. vii, p. 222.
131 Fortescue, *British Army*, vol. vii, p. 225. Fortescue, however, went on to describe a line of battle with Mackenzie between Campbell and Sherbrooke, but failed to note a source for this. Fortescue also placed the blame upon Sherbrooke's shoulders for a division arrangement that was 'very nearly disastrous'.
132 To Castlereagh, 29 July 1809, *WD* (new ed.), vol. iv, p. 535.
133 Derived from: Leith Hay (29th), *Narrative*, pp. 101 & 103; Sidney, *Lord Hill*, pp. 111–12; Leslie (29th), *Military Journal*, p. 141.
134 Sidney, *Lord Hill*, Hill's 'memorandum' of 1827, p. 111–12; Leslie, *Military Journal*, p. 140; Leith Hay, *Narrative*, pp. 103–4.
135 Derived from: Beamish, *King's German Legion*, vol. i, pp. 207–12 & 'Talavera' map following p. 218 and vol. ii, correspondence on pp. xxiii–xxvii; Butler, *Wellington's Operations*, vol. i, pp. 196–8 & 205–9; Eliot, *Treatise*, 'Talavera' map; Fortescue, *British Army*, vol. vii, pp. 224–230 & 'Talavera, 27 July', Maps, vol. vii, No. 9; Hall, *Biographical Dictionary;* Hawker (14th LD), *Journal* (1810), 'Talavera' map; Leslie (29th), *Military Journal*, pp. 140–50; Londonderry, *Narrative*, pp. 331–8 & 'Talavera' map and Appendix Nos. IV–V, IX; Maxwell, *Peninsular Sketches*, (Fitzclarence) '*The British Campaign of 1809*', vol. i, p. 107; Napier, *Peninsular War* (5 vols., 1862), vol. ii, p. 151 (Bk 8, Ch 6) & 'Talavera' map after p. 150; Oman, *Peninsular War*, vol. ii, p. 510 & 'Talavera' map following p. 551; Atkinson's essay in Oman, *Wellington's Army*, pp. 344–6; Sidney, *Lord Hill*, pp. 108–12; Wood, *The Subaltern Officer*, pp. 87–8; to Castlereagh, 29 July 1809, *WD* (new ed.), vol. iv, pp. 532–7; 'Memorandum upon the Battle of Talavera', n.d.,

WD (new ed.), vol. iv, pp. 539–40; Wyld, *Atlas*, 'Talavera de la Reyna' map, Plan No. 5. Quotation from: Wellesley to Castlereagh, 29 July, *WD* (new ed.), vol. iv, p. 533–4.

136 Fortescue, *British Army*, vol. vii, p. 230; also Oman, *Peninsular War*, vol. ii, p. 511.

137 Beamish, *King's German Legion*, vol. i, p. 207. This error was noted by Fortescue (*British Army*, vol. vii, p. 225).

138 Von Berger's letter, 3 December 1834, quoted in Beamish, *King's German Legion*, vol. ii, p. xxiv. This information presumably confirmed Oman in his description (*Peninsular War*, vol. iii, pp. 510–11), justifying him in the face of Fortescue's later claim that the 5th Battalion held the left (*British Army*, vol. vii, fn p. 232).

139 To Castlereagh, 29 July, *WD* (new ed.), vol. iv, p. 534. For the perspective that chance or Donkin's own judgement guided him, see Rigaud, *Celer et Audax*, p. 95 (Donkin's brigade had 5 companies of the 5/60th Foot); also Napier, quoted in Fortescue, *British Army*, vol. vii, p. 230; Fortescue placed Donkin initially in the position that the KGL had not yet arrived to fill (p. 229).

140 Fortescue, *British Army*, vol. vii, p. 235; Leslie, *Military Journal*, p. 147.

141 Leslie, *Military Journal*, p. 144; see also Leith Hay, *Narrative*, p. 106.

142 Leslie, *Military Journal*, p. 150.

143 Oman, *Peninsular War*, vol. ii, p. 519. An arrangement of Hill's division with which Fortescue concurred (*British Army*, vol. vii, p. 235), even though he had previously asserted (p. 230) that Tilson was initially on R. Stewart's left.

144 Fortescue, *British Army*, vol. vii, fn p. 235, citing Leith Hay, *Narrative*, p. 140. It is worth clarifying Fortescue's own use of language here. Fortescue was referring to the division posted on the left extremity of an army's battle line; by 'left brigade', he meant the brigade standing on the left of a division's line of battle when it has reversed the order of its brigades to place its senior (or 'right') brigade on its left flank, in the second post of honour.

145 Derived from: Londonderry, *Narrative*, Appendix, 'Talavera' map; Hawker, *Journal*, 'Talavera' map.

146 This description includes the Hanoverians of the KGL, electoral subjects of the same prince who was also the British monarch, and who were viewed very much as compatriots by British contemporaries into whose army they continued to be ever more integrated.

147 To his brother James, in Page, *Intelligence Officer*, p. 126.

148 Within each brigade, the senior Portuguese regiment normally stood on the right, and within each regiment, the 1st battalion stood on the right of the 2nd battalion.

149 There is no record in the *General Orders*, Wellington's *Dispatches*, or the *Supplementary Despatches*, of orders altering the terms of their command, but it is quite clear that they had acquired the status of incumbents no later than their respective appointments to local lieutenant general, the grade of command considered normal for the charge of an army division.

150 In reply to one of Craufurd's requests for leave, Wellington noted to Craufurd (9 Dec 1810, *WD (new ed.)*, vol. vii, p. 40): 'Adverting to the number of General Officers senior to you in the army, it has not been an easy task to keep you in your command; and, if you should go, I fear that I should not be able to appoint you to it again, or to one that would be so agreeable to you, or in which you could be so useful.'

151 For example, see Fortescue, *British Army*, vol. viii, fn 1, pp. 154–5, and the Portuguese battalions were left out of the division in part I, 'British Troops', of Appendix I (pp. 627–31) and simply mentioned as 'attached' in Part II – while Oman did exactly the same in *Peninsular War*, vol. v, pp. 395–9; Oman, *Peninsular War*, vol. iv, p. 620, Appendix IX, listed the two brigades for British units with the Portuguese *caçador* battalions grouped separately, implying a third brigade, and repeated this format again in vol. vi, p. 732, Appendix VIII. In a similar fashion, Captain Butler listed the Portuguese *caçador* battalions of the division in the same way the Portuguese brigades of other divisions were listed, separately, implying a separate organisational status, in *Wellington's Operations*, vol. i, p. 298; he actually described the battalions as forming a separate 'brigade' early in 1811 (vol. ii, p. 433), integrated the *caçadores* in his organisation for later in the year (vol. ii, p. 489), only again to distinguish the battalions as a separate 'brigade' of the division a few months later (vol. ii, p. 552)!

152 G.O. 4 Aug., War Office, *General Orders*, 1810, pp. 124–5.

153 For example, Ward, 'Portuguese Infantry Brigades', *JSAHR*, pp. 110–11.

154 For example, Leach, *Rough Sketches*, p. 143–4 (1810); Simmons, *Rifle Man*, p. 89 (1810); Moore Smith, *Life of John Colborne*, pp. 186 & 190 (1813); Hennell, *A Gentleman Volunteer*, pp. 88–9 & 153 (1813); Surtees, *Twenty-Five Years*, pp. 199, 241 (1813), & 278 (1814).

155 The following survey of the evolving relative precedence of brigades within the 2nd Division offers an example of the way in which changing brigade seniority shifted a brigade's station in the divisional line of battle.

1809. Hill's brigade, which by 23 June had become Major General Tilson's, was the eldest brigade, and took the right, while Brigadier R. Stewart's brigade, being the junior, took the left, and in this array, the division fought at Talavera. On 4 September, the brigade of Brigadier General C. Craufurd was added to the division; being the most junior brigadier, his brigade took the centre position. In this array, the division fought at Busaco, though Craufurd had died 25 September, leaving Lieutenant Colonel Wilson (2/39th) to assume command. R. Stewart was also ill at the time of the battle, and Lieutenant Colonel Inglis (1/57th) assumed command, while Lieutenant Colonel Colborne (2/66th) was the assumptive commander for W. Stewart, who commanded the division 'under Hill'. Thus, at Busaco, none of the incumbent commanders was at the helm of their respective brigades, but the brigades still stood in battle-array based upon their incumbent commanders' relative seniority.

1810. On 30 September, Major General Lumley's appointment to C. Craufurd's former junior brigade made it the second eldest, and it exchanged places with R. Stewart's brigade, shifting from the centre to the left of the division's line of battle, while W. Stewart's 1st Brigade (under Colborne's assumptive command) remained on the right. In this battle-array, it would fight at Albuera (Fig. 30).

1811. On 6 June, after Albuera, Lumley's brigade, containing the consolidation of all the surviving British regiments still with the division, became the senior brigade (taking the right), while Major General Howard's newly formed brigade became the junior British brigade (taking the left), and Ashworth's newly assigned Portuguese brigade took the centre. With the arrival of replacements for a number of the regiments in the consolidated 1st Brigade (still senior, despite Lumley's August departure for England), a new brigade was rebuilt on 7 August (temporarily under Lieutenant Colonel W. Stewart [1/3rd], the senior officer present) as a third and necessarily the most junior British brigade (taking the right centre position). On 9 October, Colonel Wilson, the senior officer in the 1st Brigade who had assumed charge on Lumley's departure, was appointed to command of the brigade, changing its precedence to the most junior, becoming the 3rd British Brigade; this moved from the right flank to the right-centre position, exchanging places with Major General Howard, senior of the brigadiers, and his brigade. Meanwhile, the former most junior (reconstituted) British brigade, under the orders of Colonel Byng since 21 September, became the second eldest, and took the left flank.

1813. By this time, Major General Walker had command of Howard's former brigade, sustaining its seniority as 1st Brigade, while Major General Pringle's assignment to Wilson's former brigade, on or about 23 July, made the formerly junior British brigade senior to the brigade of the recently promoted (4 June) Major General Byng. It is not quite clear just when this alteration would have been implemented in the divisional array, for the Battle of the Pyrenees erupted on 25 July; however, the new array, with Pringle on the left and Byng in the right centre, appears to have been implemented by the time of the Nivelle (10 November), and was reflected at St. Pierre (13 December 1813; see Fig. 33).

156 When Captain Gomm (9th Foot), in Leith's original British brigade, wrote home in July 1810, noting the brigade's composition, it was apparently natural for him to list the regiments in battle order (as the regiments stood, left to right), rather than simply numerically: 'The brigade formed of the 9th, 2nd battalion 38th, and 3rd Royals [1st Foot] marched from Lisbon about three weeks ago to Leyria . . .'   Carr-Gomm, *Letters and Journals*, p. 161. Similar examples abound among British memoirs.

157 For instance, Pack's Portuguese brigade was attached to Craufurd's Light Division during the period immediately preceding the battle at Busaco (1810); Ashworth's Portuguese were temporarily attached to Picton's division at Fuentes de Oñoro (1811); at Vitoria (1813), Pack's Portuguese operated with Oswald's 5th Division, while Bradford's Portuguese operated with Graham's 1st Division.

158 Calculations based on the numbers provided in Appendix 5 of Thompson, *Fatal Hill*, pp. 189–191, which agree closely with Oman's numbers in Appendix XV, *Peninsular War*, vol. iv, pp. 631–3. There was (and remains) significant debate about the actual numbers available and present at the battle.

159 'Memorandum' to Beresford & 'Memorandum To the Officers in Command of Corps in Estremadura', 23 Apr. 1811, *WD* (new ed.), vol. vii, pp. 492 & 496; the second, the memorandum sent to the Spanish commanders, amended the reference to seniority to read 'highest military rank', possibly to forestall a claim by Blake that his rank as Captain-General, or even his position as a Regent, entitled him to precedence. Curiously, Napier's discussion of these preparations omitted Wellington's discussion of who would command (*Peninsular War* (5 vols., 1862), vol. iii (Bk XII, Chap. V), p. 77); it was yet another issue later between the historian and Beresford (Anon., *Further Strictures*, pp. 79–80; Beresford, *Refutation*, pp. 105–6), and still a source of some confusion even after the war.

160 *WD* (new ed.), vol. vii: to Spencer, 16 April, p. 473; to Liverpool (public & private), 22 May 1811, pp. 593 & 594–5; Beresford's report to Wellington, 18 May 1811, p. 592.

161 *WD* (new ed.), vol. vii, memorandum to Beresford, 23 Apr. 1811, p. 492 & memorandum 'To the Officers in Command of Corps in Estremadura', 23 Apr. 1811, p. 496. Years later, talking of the battle, Wellington said simply: '[Blake] claimed the post of honour and lost it.' (Jennings, *Croker Papers*, vol.i, p. 352.)

162 Anon., *Further Strictures*, p. 115.

163 Napier, *Peninsular War* (5 vols., 1862), vol. iii (Bk XII, Chap. VI), p. 94.

164 Cole & Gwynn, *Memoirs*, p. 71.

165 Derived from: 'D'Urban's Report of the Operations . . .', Anon., *Further Strictures*, pp. 24–7, 51–5 & 'Albuera' map at back; Beamish, *King's German Legion*, vol. i, pp. 333–7, 385–6; Bueno, *Uniformes Militares Españoles*, pp. 12, 54, 72; D'Urban, *Journal* (1930), pp. 214–15; Fortescue, *British Army*, vol. viii, pp. 184–192, 207–8 & 'Albuera' map No. 5; McGuffie, *Peninsular Cavalry General*, pp. 106–7; Oman, *Peninsular War*, vol. iv, pp. 371–98 & Appendix XV, pp. 631–3 & map after p. 385; Leslie, *Military Journal*, pp. 218–21 (as in 'The Twenty-Ninth at Albuera', Maxwell, *Peninsular Sketches*, vol. ii, pp. 322–3); Moore Smith, *Life of John Colborne* (n.d), pp. 158–62; Oman, *Peninsular War*, vol. iv, pp. 366, 370–93, 631–3 & maps of 'Albuera No. 1', after p. 385, & of 'Albuera No. 2', after p. 395; Atkinson's essay in Oman, *Wellington's Army*, pp. 351–5; Thompson, *Fatal Hill*, pp. 107–10, 116 & map in Fig. 5.3, p. 110; Vere, *Marches, Movements, and Operations*, p. 10; Worley, *Atlas*, (Burriel's) 'Albuera' maps, pp. 136–9; Beresford to Wellington, 18 May 1811, *WD* (new ed.), vol. vii, pp. 588–93; Beresford's report to Wellington, 18 May 1811, *WD* (new ed.), vol, vii, p. 589; Wyld, *Atlas*, 'Albuera', Plan No. 20. First quotation: Beresford's report to Wellington, 18 May 1811, *WD* (new ed.), vol. vii, p. 589. Second Quotation: Leslie (29th), *Military Journal*, pp. 218–19.

166 A minor oddity that seemed to puzzle Fortescue and Oman was the presence with Cole of the three light companies from Kemmis' brigade. Whatever the reason that had brought them to the left bank of the Guadiana, it was hardly surprising that they would be together, for they were the ad hoc light battalion of the brigade and would normally have operated together; what is more, it may be that the rifle company from the 5/60th, attached to Kemmis' brigade, was also present with the light battalion, their normal home when the battalion was operating – but there is no extant proof for this. Both historians, however, seem to have missed the presence of a company of the Brunswick-Oels Jägers posted to Myers' brigade since the previous November (G.O., Pero Negro, 12 Nov 1810, *General Orders*, p. 205; Atkinson's essay in Oman, *Wellington's Army*, pp. 349, 351, 355).

167 Derived from: Cole & Gwynn, *Memoirs*, pp. 70–78; Beamish, *King's German Legion*, vol. i, 'Albuera' map after p. 342; Major Roverea's journal, quoted in Cole & Gwynn, *Memoirs*, p. 73; Fortescue, *British Army*, vol. viii, pp. 204–5; McGuffie, *Peninsular Cavalry General*, 'Sketch . . . of . . . Albuera', endpiece; Napier, *Peninsular War* (5 vols., 1862), vol. iii (Bk. XII, Chap. VI) p. 99; Oman, *Peninsular War*, vol. iv, pp. 389–92; Thompson, *Fatal Hill*, pp. 132–140 & Fig. 6.7 on p. 137; Vere, *Marches, Movements, and Operations*, p. 11–16; Beresford to Wellington, 18 May 1811, *WD* (new ed.), vol. vii, p. 590.

168 Fortescue, *British Army*, vol. viii, fn. 2 p. 191. First quotation: Vere, *Marches, Movements, and*

Operations, pp. 12 & 13–14. Second quotation: Cole, quoted in Thompson, *Fatal Hill*, p. 135. Third quotation: Beresford's report to Wellington, 18 May 1811, *WD* (new ed.), vol. vii, p. 590.

169 Quoted in Fletcher, *Voices*, p. 115. See also Moore Smith, *Life of John Colborne* (n.d.), letter of 18 May 1811, p. 160; Leslie, *Military Journal*, p. 219; Beamish, *King's German Legion*, vol. i, p. 336.

170 Brooke's list of the regiments began in numerical order, with the 2/48th perhaps overlooked and added at the end, for Brooke gave the regiments in their actual tactical order shortly afterward in the same narrative.

171 Fortescue, *British Army*, vol. viii, p. 196.

172 As measured on the map in Wyld, *Atlas*, for 'Albuera', Plan. No. 20; Leslie (29th) estimated the distance to the rivulet of Albuera at 600 yards from the division's position (*Military Journal*, p. 218).

173 With over 2,000 men in line of battle, the brigade's front was about 680 yards long. Allowing: 2 minutes for a courier to transmit Stewart's orders, at the gallop, to Colborne; 2 minutes for Colborne to issue his own, to counter-march the colours and directing sergeants, pass the supernumeraries to the front of the line, for company commanders and covering sergeants to exchange places, and about-face the brigade; 7 minutes to retrograde the line 600 yards at quick-time (108 30-inch paces per minute); another 2 minutes to face front, return the colours, directing sergeants, supernumeraries, company commanders and covering sergeants to their proper posts, and to realign the brigade, the *shortest* possible time for Colborne's brigade to return to its post in the division, with perfect execution, would seem to have been about 13 minutes. The pace at common-time was 75 per minute, taking 9½ minutes to cover the 600 yards.

174 Letter from Captain Cleeves, 20 May 1811, reproduced in Beamish, *King's German Legion*, vol. i, p. 385.

175 Sherer, *Recollections*, p. 159.

176 Colborne to Yonge, 18 May 1811, in Moore Smith, *Life of John Colborne*, p. 160; Thompson, *Fatal Hill*, p. 123.

177 Sherer, *Recollections*, p. 155.

178 Derived from: D'Urban's 'Report of the Operations . . . ,' in Anon., *Further Strictures*, pp. 31–33; Fortescue, *British Army*, vol. viii, pp.196–201; Oman, *Peninsular War*, vol. iv, pp. 382–7; Sherer, *Recollections*, pp. 154–61; Thompson, *Fatal Hill*, pp. 122–131 & Figs. 6.6, 6.7 on pp. 124, 136; 'The "Die Hards" at Albuera', *The Times*, 25 Feb 1915, p. 6, col. A; Beresford to Wellington, 18 May 1811, *WD* (new ed.), vol. vii, pp. 589–90. First quotation: Beresford's report to Wellington, 18 May 1811, *WD* (new ed.), vol. vii, pp. 589–90. Second quotation: An officer of the 29th, quoted in *Fatal Hill*, p.130. Third quotation: Sherer, *Recollections*, p. 161.

179 Quoted in Fletcher, *Voices*, p. 116.

180 The account was by Sir William Inglis, colonel of the 57th Foot, published in June 1832, in the United Service Gazette and was quoted by Beresford in his *Refutation*, pp. 212–13.

181 Noted without further reference in Thompson, *Fatal Hill*, p. 123.

182 In a related example of how familiarity with customary battle-array could serve memory of a past event, consider Beresford's refutation of one of Napier's points, during their bitter pamphlet war, based on a claim made by a major of the 29th about the arrangement and motion of Hoghton's brigade: 'At the time of which he speaks, the 57th were in line in rear of the Spaniards; and I rather think the first battalion, 48th, to its left. [. . .] the 29th [. . .] was the right regiment of Hoghton's brigade.' (Beresford, *Refutation*, p. 201.) Beresford could depend upon his recollections bolstered by the certainty given him by the habitual use of customary principles of array.

183 *Rules and Regulations* (1803), pp. iii–iv.

184 Consider Williamson's 1791 description (*Elements of Military Arrangement*, vol. i, pp. 1–3) of the relationship between discipline and order, and its disintegration:

'When troops are said to be routed, nothing more is meant, than that they are put into confusion; or that order, subordination, and obedience to command, are fled: in which case every man consults his own personal safety, at the instigation of the predominant passion, fear, or the desire of self-preservation. Now those troops that are the best disciplined will retain the longest that order and obedience: therefore, the best disciplined troops are with most difficulty put into confusion; or, in other words, are the least liable to be conquered.'

185 For a consideration of the application of the principles of customary battle-array at the Battle of Salamanca, see Muir, 'Observations', *First Empire*, pp. 8–18.

186 Derived from: Fortescue, *British Army*, vol. ix, pp. 465–6 & 'St. Pierre' map, No. 12; Gardyne, *Life of a Regiment*, vol. i, pp. 317–26; Hibbert, *Seventy-First*, p. 97; 'Hill to Wellington', 16 Dec. 1813, in Leslie, *Dickson Manuscripts* (1987), vol. v, pp. 1145–6; L'Estrange, *Recollections*, pp. 144–7; Oman, *Peninsular War*, vol. vii, pp. 265–66 & 'St. Pierre' map pp. 274–5; Atkinson's essay in Oman, *Wellington's Army*, pp. 366, 368, & 370–1; 'to Bathurst', 14 Dec. 1813, *WD* (new ed.), vol. xi, pp. 369–70.

187 Oman, *Peninsular War*, vol. vii, p. 469.

188 Napier, *Peninsular War* (5 vols., 1862), vol. v (Bk XXIV, Chap V) p. 190.

189 Derived from: Oman, *Peninsular War*, vol. vii, pp. 472–3.

190 Oman, *Peninsular War*, vol. vii, p. 475: the professor's footnote offering the sequence of each division's brigades omitted any observation at all upon their unusual order with respect to one another. Napier implies the same arrangements as those offered by Fortescue, namely with the Portuguese brigades forming the third line or eastern-most column, see *Peninsular War*, (5 vols., 1862), vol. v, (Bk XXIV, Chap V) p. 193.

191 Oman, *Peninsular War*, vol. vii, p. 475; Fortescue, *British Army*, vol. x, fn 1 p. 82.

192 Memoirs of Lieutenant Charles Crowe, 10 April, as published in Cassidy, *Marching with Wellington*, p. 109. Cole's report to Beresford, 11 Apr 1811, *WSD*, vol. viii, p. 741, corroborates that Ross' brigade was the 'left brigade' of the 4th Division.

193 Anton, *Retrospect*, p. 84.

194 Anon., *Personal Narrative*, p. 245.

195 Anon., *Personal Narrative*, pp. 246–7; Anton, *Retrospect*, pp. 126–7.

196 Derived from: Anon. (42nd), *Personal Narrative*, pp. 243–54; Anton (42nd), *Retrospective*, pp. 125–41; Cassidy (3/27th), *Marching with Wellington*, pp. 109–13; Cooper (7th), *Rough Notes*, pp. 116–18; Lawrence (40th), *Autobiography*, pp.180–1; Oman, *Peninsular War*, vol. vii, pp. 469–70, 475–6, 478–82; Atkinson's essay in Oman, *Wellington's Army*, pp. 371–3; Ross-Lewin (32nd), *With the 32nd*, pp. 234–5; to Bathurst, 12 Apr. 1814, *WD* (new ed.), vol. xi, pp. 633–5; Cole to Beresford, 11 Apr 1814, *WSD*, vol viii, p. 741; 'Instructions for Lt-Gen. Freyre', 10 April 1814, in Wyld, *Memoir*, p. 186.

197 Oman, *Peninsular War*, vol. vii, fn 2 p. 480.

198 P. 246.

199 Anon., *Personal Narrative*, p. 244.

200 Anton, *Retrospect*, p. 126. Forming four deep in this context would appear to relate to doubling companies, filing one sub-division or section of the company behind another, for a passage of lines.

201 See its Section (*Titre*) I. The United States would later laminate the French version of the principles onto a similar precedence that had evolved with respect to the ranking of militia and provincial forces during earlier wars fought under or against Britain.

202 Cooper, *Rough Notes*, p. 144; Green, *Vicissitudes*, p. 64: writing in July 1811, 'In order to give each the advantage in turn, the right of the regiment, brigade, or division, went first one day, and the left the next, unless it was at a time we were near the enemy, and in expectation of an engagement: we then went according to circumstances.' The incumbent brigadier of the left brigade was Major General Ross, who had been severely wounded (in the jaw) at Orthez, on 27 February. Although Ross would shortly receive an appointment to command a division destined for the war in America, it does not appear that he had yet recovered sufficiently to lead his brigade, and was not present at Toulouse. This left the brigade's senior officer to assume command – this appears likely to have been Lieutenant Colonel Ellis, 23rd Royal Welsh Fusiliers.

Chapter Five

Wellington's Generals in Portugal, Spain and France 1809–1814

RON MCGUIGAN

'The system whereby generals in the British Army were created militated against the supply of capable commanders but, with more than 600 officers of the rank of major general or above on the Army List, it might have been supposed that enough able men could be found to supply an army . . .'[1]

Everyone is aware of the military prowess of Sir Arthur Wellesley, 1st Duke of Wellington. The histories of his campaigns are both well documented and studied. Yet, even one such as the Duke of Wellington cannot do all things himself and must rely upon subordinates to implement plans and carry out orders. Many of Wellington's subordinates are also well known; men such as Rowland Hill, Robert Craufurd, Thomas Picton and William Beresford. Yet so many others are now lost to history. That they not be forgotten is why they are presented here.

This article is a brief overview of Wellington's generals and is neither a concise biography nor a critical assessment of them; as such, it is restricted to those generals who served in either the British or the Portuguese service. I have not recorded those of the Spanish Army, even of British officers in Spanish service, although Wellington was the Commander-in-Chief from approximately 1812 to 1814.

For those who wish to pursue the topic of Wellington's Generals, I recommend the following works: Glover's *Wellington as Military Commander* and *Wellington's Army in the Peninsula 1808–1814*, Oman's *Wellington's Army 1808–1814*, and Reid's *Wellington's Army in the Peninsula 1809–14*. For casualties, see Hall's *The Biographical Dictionary*. Short biographical sketches on many of Wellington's generals see either *Dictionary of National Biography* and its Supplement, or the new reprinted series, *Oxford Dictionary of National Biography*.

I have referred to Wellington as such throughout this article, although he was only Sir Arthur Wellesley in April 1809 until raised to the peerage as Lord Wellington in August 1809. The spelling of the officers' names are, for the most part, those used in the army lists of the period, which spelling sometimes changed from edition to edition. Officers are listed by army seniority and their ranks shown are those held at the time they served in the formation indicated and are not necessarily their highest rank in the peninsula.

Officer's Rank

For general officers, there were only the three substantive ranks of major general, lieutenant general and general in the British army of the time. The rank of field marshal was rarely granted outside the Royal Family and then usually only to generals of old age and long standing. The last field marshals appointed outside the Royal Family, there were only seven, date from 1796 and these were all officers who had seen service as general officers in the Seven Years War which had ended some thirty plus years before. The appointment of Wellington as a Field Marshal in 1813 broke all precedent, and although the Commander-in-Chief had reservations about its effect on seniority within the army, Wellington was promoted at the express wish of the Prince Regent.

Depending upon its size, an army or large force would more often than not be commanded by a senior lieutenant general. It was the usual practice in the British Army by 1805 for a division to be commanded by a lieutenant general and a brigade by a major general, although circumstances would see a major general assigned to command a division and either a brigadier general or a colonel on the staff assigned to a brigade command. Army corps were not then a regular part of the army organization, but were later formed in the Peninsula as required to assist with controlling the divisions of the army there. Brigadier general or brigadier (both terms were used interchangeably) was a rank usually associated with an appointment and was not a substantive rank of itself. The rank was an intermediate one between that of colonel and major general. It was most often conferred when a colonel was placed upon the staff of an army to command a brigade or department and when in command of a station or district. In practice, the command of a brigade usually carried the description of brigadier. Thus an officer commanding a brigade would often be referred to as its brigadier regardless of his actual rank in the army; be it either lieutenant colonel, colonel or major general. A regimental colonelcy was usually awarded to a general officer as a reward for military service. This colonel never directly commanded the regiment in the field.

There were two methods of determining an officer's rank. One was substantive rank in the regiment and the other was rank in the army. Substantive rank (rank for which you receive pay and could not be reduced to lower rank except by court martial) in the regiment was usually the same as rank in the army (i.e. a captain promoted on 1 January 1810 in the regiment would be a captain in the army on 1 January 1810). An officer's position (i.e. regimental seniority) in the regiment was determined by the date on which he was either promoted in the regiment or exchanged to the regiment (it was called an exchange if an officer traded places with another officer from outside the regiment). Promotion within the regiment was usually by strict regimental seniority, especially for vacancies caused by casualties of war. Rank in the army was determined by the date an officer was promoted in the army. Thus an officer could be a captain senior in the army to all other captains, but be the junior captain in his regiment if he exchanged into it, as he would go to the bottom of the list of captains in the regiment. Rank in the army could also be affected by the other method of determining rank: brevet rank. Brevet rank was higher permanent army rank without any regimental pay or responsibility. Officers of the rank of captain, major and lieutenant colonel were eligible to be awarded superior brevet rank in the army. Brevet rank did give an officer a chance for promotion, through the patronage of the Commander-in-Chief of the British Army, to substantive regimental rank in another unit. An officer could only exchange to another regiment in his substantive rank and not in his brevet rank.

Awarding a brevet was a way of rewarding meritorious officers and of progressive promotion in the army. As an example, an officer might be a captain in his regiment, but, also be a brevet lieutenant colonel in the army; as such, he could succeed to the temporary command of his brigade if he was the senior in army rank present, even though other lieutenant colonels in the brigade were present and held this substantive rank in their regiment. This was due to the fact that the seniority of brevet army rank counted for command purposes where more than one army unit was involved.

Promotions in the army were given in what was called a general brevet. This was simply the progressive promotion of all officers to a higher rank, in the army, who had been appointed in their current rank between certain dates. Promotion to a general officer was in the army and not in the regiment, so brevet rank counted for progressive promotion through brevets of major, lieutenant colonel and colonel to major general and so on. The date an officer reached lieutenant colonel's rank settled the order in which he was promoted to brevet colonel and then through the ranks of a general officer. It did not matter how an officer achieved the rank of lieutenant colonel, by seniority or by purchase within the regiment (i.e. substantive rank) or by brevet rank in the army (either by progressive promotion or for meritorious service). The only difference would be if a lieutenant colonel was appointed an aide-de-camp to the King or Prince Regent in which case he would be promoted a brevet colonel in the army irrespective of his seniority date as a lieutenant colonel and he would then leap ahead of all the lieutenant colonels who were not promoted brevet colonel at that time. He would take the precedence of his rank from the date of his appointment and promotion. The Duke of York, British Army Commander-in-Chief, never awarded the brevet of colonel for meritorious service; it was only granted in general brevets.[2]

Such an officer progressively promoted went on half-pay (i.e. not regimentally employed) in most cases and did so based upon his last substantive regimental rank before he reached the rank of a general officer. 'Progressive promotion' promoted officers regardless of whether they ever went on active service or not. Until 1814, general officers were not paid except when they were placed upon the staff; so it did not matter how many generals were created or progressively promoted as there was no requirement to employ all of them.

Officers could be temporarily promoted to what was called 'local rank'. This was simply a grant of a higher army rank while serving in a particular location. If the officer left this location, he would revert to his substantive rank. When he returned to the location, he would resume the local rank. Local rank was granted to ensure that an officer held rank and received pay and allowances commensurate with his command (e.g. a major general commanding a division would be granted the local rank of lieutenant general), was equal or higher in rank to his

Allied counterparts (e.g. a lieutenant general commanding an army would be granted the local rank of general), or to add prestige to a particular appointment. There was no restriction to receiving more than one promotion to 'on the staff' or to 'local rank' and some officers became a colonel on the staff, brigadier general and then local major general in the Peninsula while ranking as only lieutenant colonels and brevet colonels in the army.

There was also 'temporary army rank'. Temporary army rank was usually granted to officers of the foreign regiments in British service. While holding temporary rank, they were the junior of their rank with those officers appointed on the same date; but, they were still considered the senior in army rank to officers who held permanent army rank being appointed on a subsequent date and below them in the army list. They were progressively promoted in their turn during the awards of general brevets. When the officer ceased to serve he lost his rank in the army. By 1812 there were few of these officers left as they were either no longer serving with the army or their rank had been converted to permanent army rank. Those affected in the peninsular army were the officers serving with the King's German Legion and the Duke of Brunswick-Oels's corps. The officers of the King's German Legion were placed upon the permanent strength of the British army in 1812 in recognition of the Legion's services.

The rank structure in the Foot Guards regiments was different from that of the line regiments. Officers had what was called 'Dual Rank'. In essence, all regimental lieutenants were also substantive captains and all regimental captains were also substantive lieutenant colonels in the army. Thus an officer could be a lieutenant in the Guards, a substantive captain and a brevet major in the army or a captain in the Guards and a substantive lieutenant colonel and brevet colonel in the army. If a captain of the Guards exchanged to a line regiment, he would automatically be a substantive regimental lieutenant colonel in his new regiment and conversely, if a substantive regimental lieutenant colonel of a line regiment exchanged into the Guards, he would become the junior captain in the regiment. The Guards also claimed the exclusive right to be commanded only by a Guards officer when organized as a brigade. Therefore, although a Guards officer would be appointed to the command of a line brigade, a line officer was never appointed to the command of a Foot Guards brigade during this period.

At this time officers of the Royal Engineers and Royal Artillery (together called the Ordnance Corps) were rarely given command over the line regiments. The engineers and artillery were each considered as a single separate organization, the artillery as one regiment of multiple battalions and the engineers as a corps. Promotion was within the organization, similar to an infantry regiment, and so brevet rank did not affect decisions about who commanded their constituent units. Thus, for example, two or more artillery units would be commanded by the senior regimental officer, regardless of whether another officer held higher brevet rank in the army. It should be noted that the officers in the Ordnance Corps could be promoted to substantive colonel's rank unlike for the infantry and cavalry. The equivalent rank in the Ordnance Corps for regimental colonel was colonel-commandant. This rank would be conferred on a general officer of the Ordnance Corps similar to the infantry or cavalry.

Wellington and his Generals

Wellington was a lieutenant general in the army and had been granted the local rank of general in Spain and Portugal in 1811. He was almost the junior lieutenant general in the British army in 1809 and therefore only officers junior to him could be sent out to serve in his army. Many of his divisional generals also received higher local army rank to command divisions in the Peninsula. Army seniority was jealously guarded in the British army of the time. Once an officer reached the rank of lieutenant colonel he could not be required to serve under a junior officer even if the junior officer held higher local rank. The Commander-in-Chief noted:

> According, however, to the general received opinions of the service, no officer in the British Army, after the rank of Lieutenant Colonel, is ever expected to serve under an officer junior to himself, even though he may possess a superior local commission.
>
> At least the Commander-in-chief knows of no instance of the kind, while there are many precedents for the admitted refusal of officers to act under the supersession of such local commissions.[3]

It was rare indeed for an officer to agree to serve under his junior in the service.

When temporary vacancies occurred in the divisional commands, Wellington would allow the senior brigade commander, in the division, to succeed to the command. However, if the absence was to be extensive, Wellington would sometimes appoint the senior major general only commanding a brigade from his army as a whole to take the temporary command. He also used an alternate method, though, to place some junior officers in temporary command of divisions when their seniors were only commanding brigades in other divisions. As temporary absences in divisional commands were commonly allowed to be filled by the senior brigade commander in the division, Wellington would simply assign a senior officer to a brigade in that division knowing that this officer would succeed to the temporary command by virtue of his seniority over the other brigade commanders. The permanent command was thereby held open for the absent incumbent. Thus Pakenham in 1812 was assigned to command Colville's brigade in the 3rd Division and as both Picton and Colville were absent, Pakenham took command of the division as the current senior brigade commander in the division.

Early in the war, Wellington made the decision to allow generals who left on leave of absence to resume their former commands when they returned.[4] This was to cause him problems later in the war as generals would request extended periods of leave safe in the knowledge that they could return to their commands at any time.[5] This left Wellington with both a constant turnover in commanders and a problem that he had difficulty dealing with. He wrote to the Military Secretary of the Commander-in-Chief to request of him to make it clear to newly appointed generals to his army that they should expect no leave:

> I shall be very much obliged to you, however if you will tell any General Officer who may come out in future, to settle all his business before he comes out, for that he will get no leave to go home.[6]

However, this did not prevent them from requesting it and Wellington usually granted the leave, although he did make the officers either appear before a medical board, if the request was health-related, or certify that the leave was of such a nature as to be paramount above all other considerations. In the end, Wellington regretted that early decision.

Wellington did specify his feelings regarding the type of general officers needed in the Peninsular Army after having conducted four campaigns in the peninsula:

> What we want in them is health, goodwill, and abilities to perform the duties of their situation. I am sorry to say that the perpetual changes which we are making, owing to the infirmities, or the wounds, or the disinclination of the General Officers to serve in this country, are by no means favourable to the discipline and success of the army; and do not augment the ease of my situation.[7]

On many occasions, the temporary command of brigades fell to the senior regimental commander within the brigade. Wellington followed a simple principle when these occurred. He allowed the command to be held by the senior officer in the brigade, even if this meant that other more senior regimental commanders in other brigades remained in command of only their own regiment:

> It has been the practice of this army not to move officers from the command of their regiments to command brigades, until it is quite certain, that by the arrival of other officers with the army, they would not be obliged to return to the command of their regiments; and it is very desirable not to depart from this practice.[8]

At this time, general officers sent out by the Horse Guards (as the Commander-in-Chief's headquarters was known due to its location at the Horse Guards Parade in London) were asked if they would accept an appointment on the staff of the army. While they would receive notification for service, they could decline the service. For example, Lord William Bentinck was placed upon the staff of Wellington's army in April 1809. He declined to serve in the Peninsula at that time. He was later appointed to be the commander-in-chief in Sicily and commanded the troops on the east coast of Spain for a time in 1813. In September 1813, Lord William Bentinck wrote to Wellington asking to be allowed to transfer to the staff of the army in Spain if he should resign his command in the Mediterranean.[9]

Early in the war, Wellington requested certain officers be sent out to take commands in his army. They included William Dyott, James Leith, Thomas Picton, Robert Meade, William Houston and Miles Nightingall.[10] Of this list, only Dyott and Meade were not placed upon his staff. Dyott had declined an appointment due to family commitments. Later, Wellington was informed that Robert Macfarlane and William Clinton were offered divisional commands in his army. They both declined as they preferred to serve with the force in Sicily under Lord William Bentinck.[11] In 1811, when Wellington was made a local general, this allowed the government the opportunity to offer the chief cavalry command to

Henry Lord Paget, as he now held a rank junior to Wellington, but only in the army serving in the Peninsula. Lord Paget declined the offer of command as this would have meant that he had to waive his seniority in the army overall as he was still the senior in permanent army rank to Wellington.[12]

The number of general officers and colonels serving with the army fluctuated greatly during the war. In the early years, it was hard to get generals to serve in the Peninsula, perhaps because many did not believe that the war would end successfully for the British and their Allies. As it became clear into 1811 that the British would not evacuate Portugal, this attitude changed and he received more generals and applications from generals to be placed upon the staff of his army than he could possibly employ. At the start of the campaign in April 1809, Wellington had seventeen generals and colonels on his staff. As his army expanded during the first two years of the war and the war hung in the balance, for 1809 he had seven new generals and for 1810 he received thirteen more, many of whom were just to replace those generals who had either died or permanently left the peninsula. Wellington complained in July 1810 that he had three brigades without even a colonel to command them and no spare generals either to use for any special service or to command the reinforcements due to arrive for his army.[13]

Several of these officers arrived months after being appointed to the army or put in general orders. For example, William Anson, when he arrived, was in orders to command a brigade from 9 April 1812; yet, he had been appointed to the army to date from November 1811. By early 1813, Wellington was writing that he had more generals than he could employ with his army.[14] For the last three years and four months of the war, he had fifteen appointed to his army in 1811, with fourteen appointed for 1812, another eleven for 1813, and three more for 1814 appointed to his staff, again with a number of those to replace officers who had either died or permanently left the peninsula. Yet, his army had not significantly grown, its increase was mostly in cavalry brigades, since the formation of the 7th Division in 1811. All during this time he was also appointing some of the senior colonels from within his army to brigade commands. At the height of its strength, not counting the Ordnance Corps, the Military Departments and the Portuguese army, Wellington's field army required a total of forty general officers (and/or colonels) to command its formations.

If Wellington wished to be relieved of any general officers, they could only be ordered home on the written recall orders of the Horse Guards. He could not, on his own, relieve them of a command. He did, however on some occasions, request that certain generals be recalled home when they proved, although able, to be unsatisfactory in performing their duties. Yet, he was always reluctant to request the recall of generals who proved unable to perform satisfactorily through no fault of their own. He felt that as they were doing their best, they should not be publicly recalled unless they could be provided for on the staff of the army at home or elsewhere.[15]

In certain cases, generals were sent out in command of formations to reinforce the army without consulting Wellington or with regard to how this might upset the organization of the army as a whole: 'I have nothing to do with the choice of

General Officers sent here or with their numbers, or the army with which they are to serve and when they do come, I must employ them as I am ordered.'[16]

Wellington also had a number of officers placed upon the staff of his army or whom he had to place upon the staff, as they were the senior of their rank in the Peninsula to officers already placed upon the staff. He never assigned them to a combat command. They included John Saunders (later recalled), Alexander Goldie (departed on account of his health), William Brooke (assigned to serve at Lisbon) and William Hutchinson (appointed to the staff at Malta).

Later in the war, Wellington was to remark that he required no more generals to be sent out as they replaced useful officers from within his army whom he wished to assign to commands. It would take time to train and familiarize these new generals to peninsular conditions and the ways of how the army operated: 'I hope I shall have no more new Generals; they really do us but little good, and they take the places of officers who would be of use. Then they are all desirous of returning to England.'[17]

At least until 1813, his wishes were largely ignored. By then, Wellington could become more selective as his victories gave him greater prestige within the British army as a whole. By August 1813, he could write regarding a proposed appointment to any vacant divisional command of a high-ranking officer, who had never served in the Peninsula, 'and if such a one should open, it will be but fair to attend to the claims of those officers high among the Major Generals, who have long commanded brigades in the army.'[18]

The general brevet of 4 June 1813 created many major generals amongst the colonels with his army, so many that Wellington was given discretionary orders to retain on the staff or send home any of the newly promoted generals he wished, with those colonels already placed upon his staff as brigadier generals to be retained. Wellington placed newly promoted John Skerrett, Denis Pack, Lord Edward Somerset, Robert Ross and John Lambert on the staff of his army to command brigades. He retained newly promoted Matthew Lord Aylmer as the Deputy Adjutant General. Wellington did not appoint upon the staff any of newly promoted Thomas Fermor, Granby Calcraft, Michael Head or Charles Griffiths.[19] The Horse Guards placed Griffiths upon the staff at Gibraltar and later placed Calcraft upon the staff in Scotland.

The Second-in-Command

Both questions of whether Wellington required a second-in-command for his army and who should it be, remained a topic of discussion until 1813. Wellington had some strong views on the subject:

> As far as I am concerned, I certainly should prefer that no officer should be sent out. There are few officers who understand the situation of the officer second in command of these armies. Unless he should be posted to command a division of cavalry or infantry, and perform that duty, he really has, on ordinary circumstances, nothing to do; and at the same time that his opinion relieves me but little from responsibility and that after all I must act according to my own judgement in case of a difference of opinion: there are

but few officers who should be sent from England as second in command, who would not come here with opinions formed . . . and with very extravagant pretensions. To this add, that when necessary to detach a body of troops in any situation, but few would be satisfied to remain with the detachment, unless indeed it should consist of nearly the whole army.[20]

Nevertheless, the Home Government decided that one was required to be available to take the chief command should Wellington become incapacitated by the chances of war and so designated certain officers for the task. This general officer would then become both the commander of the British army in the Peninsula and the commander of the Allied army. To compound the problem was the position of Sir William Beresford in the British and Allied army. Wellington was the Marshal General of the Portuguese army and commanded the Allied army in that rank. Beresford was the Marshal of the Portuguese army and commanded it as such. Wellington always maintained that Beresford should succeed him in command as the officer with the highest Allied rank.[21] This caused problems as Beresford was not the senior British general in the Peninsula and before 1813 was a major general and held only local rank as lieutenant general in the British service. The decision finally came down from the Commander-in-Chief of the British army that Beresford was not to be considered the second-in-command of the Allied army.[22] He would only temporarily have the chief command, should anything befall Wellington for a lengthy period of time, until an officer designated by the Home Government arrived to take over the command from him. Wellington countered with the opinion that this officer would have to be appointed the Marshal General of the Portuguese army should anything fatal befall him. The Portuguese Regency would have to be consulted.[23] It should be noted that other than the general officer designated to succeed Wellington in command, no general officer senior to Beresford was later placed on the staff of the army in the Peninsula.

In April 1809, John Sherbrooke formally held the position of Wellington's second-in-command; one he had held under Lieutenant General Sir John Cradock, the previous Commander-in-Chief in Portugal. Sherbrooke had been a major in the 33rd Regiment of Foot when Wellington had been the lieutenant colonel of the regiment. In late 1809, Sherbrooke's health began to fail and it was necessary to find a replacement for him for 1810. Wellington recommended several general officers senior enough to avoid controversy. They were Thomas Graham, Hildebrand Oakes and Sir George Prevost, Bt. They were all senior in army rank to William Payne, commanding the cavalry, the next senior officer in the Peninsula. If the government would decide to recall Payne, to thus allow others junior in army rank to him to be appointed, then Wellington suggested Lord William Bentinck, Edward Paget and Brent Spencer.[24] The Government decided to appoint Graham as the designated second-in-command;[25] but by the time Graham was to replace Sherbrooke in 1810, he had been appointed to command in Cadiz and was considered too important to be removed from there at the present time. Oakes and Colin Campbell (suggested by the Government) could not be sent out as they were holding important commands elsewhere, Oakes in Malta and Campbell at Gibraltar, and Prevost, with a command in British North America, could not arrive for at least three months. It was then decided to send out Brent Spencer as third in line of command in the peninsula. Spencer was appointed to the army to act as second-in-command in Portugal. Graham was to only be called to command in the peninsula should Wellington be incapacitated or worse. Lord William Bentinck had declined due to his position in the army in the peninsula in relation to Graham's position as designated second-in-command; that is, he did not want to serve as third in command. Paget's health would not allow him to go out.[26] Spencer had previously acted as second-in-command to Wellington during the Vimeiro Campaign of 1808.

This situation continued until mid-1811 when, as the threat to Cadiz lessened, Graham was called to the army as second-in-command. Spencer went home as he now felt that he had been superseded. Graham's health failed in 1812 and he left the peninsula. In the fall of 1812, Edward Paget came out to serve as a lieutenant general. It was understood that as Thomas Graham was to return, Paget, as the next senior British officer with the army there, would temporarily become the second-in-command although not officially designated as such.[27] Unfortunately he was captured shortly thereafter and no one served in the position until Graham's return in 1813.

Graham's health again failing later in 1813, John Hope was the unanimous choice to be sent out to take his place. Hope could now join the peninsular army because Wellington's promotion to Field Marshal, in June 1813, made Hope his junior in the army. Before this, Hope had been Wellington's senior in the army as a lieutenant general. At this point, it was decided to dispense with a designated second-in-command altogether and Hope, who concurred,[28] went out as a division commander. However, it was understood that as the senior British officer with the army there, he would succeed to the command should anything happen to Wellington.[29] Another officer considered at the time was the Duke of Richmond, the former Lord Lieutenant of Ireland and a general officer in the army who had petitioned the government to serve in the Peninsula. As with John Hope, he had been Wellington's senior in army rank until the promotion to field marshal. Although the government would have been prepared to send him out as a division commander now, both his high seniority making him the next in line to command after Wellington and his lack of actual combat experience were against his appointment and the government finally declined to offer him a staff position in deference to John Hope, also Lord Richmond's junior in army rank.[30]

During the campaigns of 1813 and 1814, Wellington formed two temporary army corps to assist with controlling his widely dispersed divisions, one commanded by Graham and then Graham's successor, John Hope, and one by himself; although, he used Beresford to command this corps at different times. Hill continued to command his corps, formed in 1809, throughout.

For their services at the war's end, Thomas Graham was created Baron Lynedoch and William Beresford was created Baron Beresford and later created Viscount Beresford. Wellington's comment on Beresford, 'I am quite certain that he is the only person capable of conducting a large concern.'[31]

The Adjutant General and the Quartermaster-General

Charles Stewart served as the Adjutant General for most of the period 1809–1812 with several extended absences. When he was absent, Edward Pakenham, as the deputy, acted for him. Pakenham wanted active commands himself and frequently was assigned to the command of infantry brigades or divisions. He was finally replaced in 1812 as the Deputy Adjutant General by Matthew Aylmer, 5th Baron Aylmer. When available, John Waters acted for these officers whenever they were absent. When Stewart was appointed to a diplomatic position on the Continent in 1813, Edward Pakenham was officially appointed the Adjutant General and Lord Aylmer remained as the Deputy Adjutant General, although Lord Aylmer too was given command of an independent brigade late in the war.

George Murray filled the position of Quartermaster-General for 1809–1812. In 1812, James Willoughby Gordon was appointed to serve, as Murray was removed to a position on the Home Staff. Gordon's health broke down and he left by the end of the year. Murray then returned in 1813 and served until the end of the war. Whenever Murray was absent for short periods William Howe de Lancey, as the Deputy Quartermaster-General acted in his place.

Wellington described Murray as, 'most fit to be at the head of the Quartermaster-General's department with an army in the field'[32] and Pakenham, Wellington's brother-in-law, as one who, 'may not be the brightest genius, but . . . he is one of the best we have.'[33]

Officers of the Military Departments were: Major Generals Sir Charles Stewart, Sir George Murray, Sir Edward Pakenham, Colonel James Willoughby Gordon, Major General Matthew Aylmer, 5th Baron Aylmer, Colonel William Howe de Lancey and Brevet Lieutenant Colonel John Waters (served as Lieutenant Colonel in Portuguese Service).

The Royal Artillery

Only two of the officers who commanded the Royal Artillery with Wellington's army ranked higher than regimental lieutenant colonel. They were regimental colonels when appointed and had both been granted the rank of brigadier general and one had been granted that of local major general. After both Edward Howorth and then later William Borthwick his replacement departed, Hoylet Framingham took the command for a period and then it was held by William Robe. Wellington was pleased enough with Robe who had ably served with him in the Vimeiro Campaign of 1808. He had hoped that Robe, who had been wounded in the fall of 1812, would return once his wound healed. Wellington wanted to keep the command open for Robe (who never did return) and decided to choose his own commander in the meantime and so wrote to the Master General of the Ordnance that he was satisfied with George Fisher and requested that no other senior officer be sent out to supersede him.[34] However, Fisher did not, in fact, prove satisfactory in the chief command and so Wellington determined to replace him in May of 1813.[35] The officer he selected to command his artillery with the field army was Alexander Dickson, only a regimental captain and brevet lieutenant colonel, but a substantive lieutenant colonel in the Portuguese service. He was appointed to command in his Portuguese rank as he was also junior in regimental rank to a number of other Royal Artillery officers serving with the army. The senior officer of the Royal Artillery then in the Peninsula, Charles Waller, was required to remain at Lisbon.[36] Waller took exception to being left in Lisbon and eventually resigned his staff appointment and left in August 1813. Dickson served in command of Wellington's artillery until the war's end.

Officers commanding the Royal Artillery were Major Generals Edward Howorth and William Borthwick, Lieutenant Colonels Hoylet Framingham, William Robe, George Fisher, Charles Waller and Brevet Lieutenant Colonel Alexander Dickson (served as Lieutenant Colonel in Portuguese Service).

The Royal Engineers

The highest ranking engineer officer serving with Wellington's army in 1809 was a brevet major in the army. This was Richard Fletcher, who was only a regimental captain; although, he had been granted the local rank of lieutenant colonel in the Peninsula. He commanded the engineers until his death in 1813. Fletcher remained behind to repair Badajoz in April 1812 and then went on leave. This placed John Fox Burgoyne, a regimental captain and brevet lieutenant colonel, temporarily in command with the field army till April 1813 when Fletcher returned. After Fletcher's death, Howard Elphinstone succeeded in command. Wellington had wanted Burgoyne to remain in command of the Royal Engineers with the field army, but with two officers present in the Peninsula senior to Burgoyne in the Corps of Engineers, he could not do so; although, Burgoyne was senior to both by virtue of his brevet army rank which, of course, did not apply within the corps.[37]

Officers commanding the Royal Engineers were: Lieutenant Colonels Sir Richard Fletcher Bt., Howard Elphinstone and Brevet Lieutenant Colonel John Fox Burgoyne.

The Army Organization of April and May 1809

When Wellington took over the command of the army in Portugal in late April 1809, it consisted of three cavalry brigades, one Guards Brigade, seven line brigades and two brigades of the King's German Legion. It had no higher command structure. Wellington had every intention of organizing his army into permanent divisions; however, not all the lieutenant generals had arrived and so in early May, Wellington temporarily organized his army into wings under Sherbrooke and Paget, the cavalry under Payne and the King's German Legion under Murray. Later in May, Wellington reorganized his infantry into three temporary divisions under Sherbrooke, Paget and Hill. After Paget was wounded at Oporto, Murray succeeded to his command.

Officers who served, on the staff, in May were: Major Generals John Sherbrooke, William Payne, Edward Paget, Stapleton Cotton, Rowland Hill, John Murray, James Erskine, John Randoll Mackenzie and Christopher Tilson (later changed his name to Chowne), Colonels John Sontag, Alexander Campbell, Henry Campbell, Richard Stewart, Charles Stewart, George de Drieberg, Ernest Baron Langwerth, Alan Cameron, Henry Fane, Edward Howorth and George Murray.

Charles Colville   Henry Clinton   William Beresford

George Murray   James Leith   Lowry Cole

Rowland Hill   John Hope   Richard Fletcher

Duke of Wellington

Thomas Picton

Thomas Graham

Stapleton Cotton

The Permanent Divisions – June 1809 to April 1814

When Wellington formed his army into permanent divisions, by a general order of 18 June 1809, he had only two local lieutenant generals present to assign to command divisions, one (John Sherbrooke) was the designated second-in-command and the other (William Payne) was to command the cavalry. Lord William Bentinck was employed elsewhere, as he declined to serve in the Peninsula, Edward Paget was recovering from his wound and Brent Spencer's health was in question. Therefore Wellington temporarily assigned the senior brigade commanders to take charge of the divisions until the arrival of senior officers.

Stapleton Cotton and Rowland Hill were the senior major generals in the Peninsula and were also senior to William Beresford; therefore, Wellington requested that these two officers be granted local rank of lieutenant general.[38] Thereafter, most of his divisional commanders were local lieutenant generals until the general brevets of 1 January 1812 and 4 June 1813 promoted them to substantive lieutenant generals in the army.

At this time, both Beresford's local rank of British lieutenant general and his rank of marshal in the Portuguese service were causing problems.[39] John Murray and Christopher Tilson felt aggrieved by Beresford's rank. Murray was just senior to Beresford (eleven places above in the army list) and although it was soon decided the local rank did not affect him, he resigned his staff appointment and left the army lest he be commanded by Beresford in his rank of Marshal.[40] Had Murray remained, Wellington would have both assigned him to command a division and applied for local lieutenant general's rank for him as well.[41] Later when he applied to be reinstated with the main army, Wellington used the excuse of no vacancy to turn down his application.[42] Tilson was junior to Beresford (thirty-five places below in the army list) and although he was not affected by the local rank issue, he too declined to serve if it meant serving with Beresford and the Portuguese army. Wellington immediately granted his request, 'I only hope that General [Tilson] will not be placed upon the staff of the army anywhere else.'[43] Tilson later withdrew his resignation: 'in which he has, in my opinion, sufficiently retracted his erroneous military notion . . .'[44] and was reappointed to a brigade command.

At its height, Wellington's army consisted of two cavalry divisions, nine infantry divisions (eight British and one Portuguese) and several independent infantry brigades.

The Cavalry Division
When Wellington was reappointed to the command in Portugal in 1809, William Payne was sent out to command his cavalry. When it was decided that Brent Spencer, to whom Payne was senior in the army, would act as the second-in-command, Payne left the Peninsula in June 1810. It was felt that as Payne had only ever commanded in the cavalry, he did not have the experience to command an army of all arms. 'The ground of the preference of Sir Brent Spencer to yourself to fill the situation of Sir John Sherbrooke in this army during the absence of General Graham appears to have been that your service has been generally confined to the cavalry . . .'[45] Stapleton Cotton had been the senior cavalry general in the Peninsula prior to Payne's arrival. He served as the second-in-command of the cavalry from November 1809 until April 1810, when he was appointed to the command of the 1st Infantry Division. When Payne left in June 1810, Cotton took over the chief command of the cavalry and held it until the war's end. During his absences, the cavalry was temporarily commanded, at different times, by William Erskine, John Slade and George Baron Bock.

At first Wellington organized the cavalry as one division under Payne. When Wellington detached a force under Hill in 1810, he assigned cavalry to it. First commanded by Henry Fane and then when he left on sick leave in late 1810, by

Robert Long in March 1811. In May 1811, Long was temporarily replaced by William Lumley, from the 2nd Infantry Division, the official reason being that Long, then only a brigadier general on the staff, was not senior enough in rank to command the Allied cavalry when Beresford's force was joined by the Spanish army. In May 1811, William Erskine requested and was appointed to this command at first only until Fane should return to take up the command again. Due to poor health, Fane did not return for a number of years. However in mid-1812, after Cotton had been wounded, the Government inquired if Wellington would like Fane to rejoin if his health would allow him. While Wellington wished for Fane to come out, there was then no vacancy for him as Erskine, his senior officer, had now been permanently appointed to his former command.[46]

When Erskine joined Hill's corps in June, 1811 Wellington then decided to formalize this separation of the cavalry into two cavalry divisions. The 1st Division under Cotton with the main army and the 2nd Division under Erskine with Hill's detached corps. Cotton, as senior officer, was to also regulate all the cavalry issuing orders to the 2nd Division through its commanding officer. This separation of the cavalry lasted until April 1813 when all the cavalry brigades were again consolidated into one division under Cotton's command upon his return to the peninsula. In late 1811, when Erskine went on leave, Long again commanded the cavalry under Hill. At the end of 1812, it was proposed that Charles Stewart, the Adjutant General then on leave of absence, return to the army in command of a cavalry brigade and perhaps even a division of cavalry. Wellington was against the idea due to the defects in sight and hearing that Stewart suffered from and the proposal was dropped.[47] Henry Fane was again chosen to command the cavalry detached with Hill's corps in late 1813. He commanded the equivalent of a small division made up of two brigades in 1814.[48] Fane was well liked by Wellington and when at the end of 1812, Wellington requested certain cavalry generals be recalled in the new year, he did not wish for any replacements, except for Fane, to be sent out.[49]

There was a shortage of good cavalry generals at different times. The Duke of York had written Wellington in 1811, ' [of] the extreme difficulty of finding a sufficient number of General officers of talent and experience to command cavalry in the field . . .'[50]

Wellington observed later in the war: 'I do not see that the service would derive much advantage from sending to England any one of the three General Officers [John Slade, Victor Baron Alten or Robert Long] . . . in order that [Sir Granby Calcraft] may command a brigade.'[51]

During the course of the war, a total of nine British cavalry brigades were formed. They did not all serve at the same time, as one was broken up in 1812 and others continued to arrive in 1811, 1812 and 1813. Wellington also had the use of the Portuguese cavalry brigades, whose numbers and availability fluctuated during the war.

At the war's end, for his services, Stapleton Cotton was created Baron Combermere (later becoming Viscount Combermere). Wellington's comment on Cotton, 'I do not know where we should find an officer who would command our cavalry in this country half so well as he does.'[52]

Officers who served in the cavalry, on the staff, were: Major General William Payne, Lieutenant General Sir Stapleton Cotton Bt., Major Generals James Erskine, Sir William Erskine Bt., John Slade, George Baron Bock, Victor Baron Alten, Henry Fane, George Anson, John Le Marchant, John Vandeleur, Robert Long, George de Grey, Terence O'Loghlin, Francis Rebow, William Ponsonby and Lord Edward Somerset, Colonels Colquhoun Grant, Richard Vivian and Frederick de Arentschildt.

Portuguese cavalry commanders included: Brigadiers Manuel de Lusignano, 2nd Conde de Sampaio, Daniel Seddon, George Madden and Benjamin D'Urban, Colonels Christovão da Costa de Atiade Teive, Loftus Otway, John Campbell and Francisco de Mendonça, 7th Visconde de Barbacena.

The 1st Division

The 1st Division was always to be commanded by either the designated second-in-command or the senior lieutenant general with Wellington's army. When that particular officer went home, his replacement was automatically assigned to command the division. When the division was formed in June 1809, John Sherbrooke held the command until the spring of 1810. He was followed by Stapleton Cotton who was appointed, as the next to senior officer then in the Peninsula (Payne of the cavalry was the senior), to the command of the division and held it until June 1810, when Brent Spencer arrived and took command. In the spring of 1811, Spencer commanded a temporary corps and then the army for a time, when Wellington went to Estremadura. During this time, Miles Nightingall had the temporary command of the division as the senior brigade commander. From the summer of 1811 to the summer of 1812, Thomas Graham was in command and when he went home unwell in July, Henry Campbell had temporary command. On 11 October 1812, Edward Paget arrived and took command, but, he was captured shortly after his arrival 16/17 November 1812. William Stewart having arrived to join the army shortly before this, had been assigned to the division as an assistant to Paget and he continued to hold the command until at his own request he was transferred in March 1813 to the 2nd Division. Kenneth Howard then had the command until May 1813 when Graham returned. Graham held the command until late 1813, when his health again failed and John Hope arrived to replace him. Hope held the command until he was captured 14 April 1814. However due to the nature of the campaign for 1813, the second-in-command was going to command a temporary corps, Wellington decided to assign a general officer to assist the permanent commander. Kenneth Howard, the senior brigade commander in the division was relieved of command of his brigade and officiated in command of the 1st Division under both Graham and Hope. In early 1811, William Erskine was removed from his brigade to command the advance guard of the army, then to the temporary command of the 5th Division and finally to command the 2nd Cavalry Division.

The 1st Division was originally composed of a Guards brigade, two King's German Legion brigades and a line brigade. The number of four brigades remained almost constant throughout the many transfers and amalgamations of the brigades serving with the division at different times. The division never had a

Portuguese brigade assigned to it. At the end of the war, the division had three brigades (two of Guards and one of the King's German Legion; although, in action, the KGL Brigade was sometimes split into two brigades, one of line battalions and one of light battalions) with Lord Aylmer's independent brigade operating closely with it.

Comments attributed to Wellington on Sherbrooke, 'a very good officer, but the most passionate man I think I ever knew' and on Spencer, 'was exceedingly puzzle-headed but very formal . . .'[53] Wellington's comments on Edward Paget: 'I have a great regard for, and entertain a very high opinion of . . .'[54] and on John Hope: 'I am quite certain that he is the ablest man in the army.'[55] At the war's end, for his services, John Hope was created Baron Niddry. He later succeeded as 4th Earl of Hopetoun.

Officers who served in the 1st Division, on the staff, were: Lieutenant Generals Sir John Hope, Sir Thomas Graham, Major General Sir John Sherbrooke, Lieutenant Generals Sir Edward Paget, Sir Brent Spencer, Major Generals Stapleton Cotton, William Erskine, William Stewart, Miles Nightingall, Henry Campbell, Colonel Ernest Baron Langwerth, Major Generals Sigismund Baron Low, Alan Cameron, Kenneth Howard, Henry de Hinüber, Edward Stopford, Colonel Edward Pakenham, Major General William Wheatley, Colonels Thomas Fermor, James Stirling and Colin Halkett.

The 2nd Division

The 2nd Division is closely identified with Rowland Hill. Hill and Wellington had a history of serving together on occasion since 1805. Hill took the temporary command of the division as the senior brigade commander at its formation in June 1809, was appointed shortly thereafter to the permanent command, and never relinquished command of the division during the course of the war. The division was unique in that it was composed of three British brigades, two brigades when it was formed with a third added in September 1809. The 2nd Division always had the Portuguese Division attached and so it did not receive its own Portuguese brigade until 1811. The division was however directly commanded from the summer of 1810 onwards by a general assigned to superintend under Hill. This was done to allow Hill to command a small detached corps of which the 2nd Division always formed a part. The officers who commanded under Hill were James Leith in July 1810 (in orders, but may never have taken the command as he took command of Leith's corps instead), William Stewart in 1810, 1811, 1813, 1814 and Christopher Chowne for a period in 1812 (Chowne was the former Christopher Tilson). When Stewart was absent in 1811, Kenneth Howard had the temporary command under Hill until Chowne arrived. Stewart, then commanding the 1st Division, at his own request in 1813 was reassigned to serve under Hill's command as Wellington could not trust him to command on his own, 'It is likewise necessary that General [Stewart] should be under the particular charge of somebody . . . With the utmost zeal, and good intentions and abilities, he cannot obey an order.'[56]

Hill had the temporary command of the army in December 1812 and January 1813 when Wellington was absent having gone to Cadiz. In late 1813, apparently Hill was one of several generals considered for the chief command on the east coast of Spain in succession to William Clinton. Wellington requested that Hill remain with his army and not take that command.[57] In April 1811, Wellington had proposed to assign Charles Baron Alten's brigade from the 7th Division to the division in exchange for Hoghton's brigade. This was never implemented. William Lumley was removed from his brigade and temporarily assigned to command Beresford's cavalry in May 1811. In the spring of 1813, John Oswald was going to be appointed to a brigade if he was superseded in the command of the 5th Division. He never joined. George Walker commanded the division for a month in the summer of 1813, after Stewart was wounded, and was later removed from his brigade and appointed to the temporary command of the 7th Division in late 1813. When later another senior officer, Charles Colville, was chosen to command the 7th Division, Walker requested to return to his old brigade in the 2nd Division. This would displace Edward Barnes who was to be appointed to Colville's old brigade in the 3rd Division.[58] In the event Colville was appointed to the 5th Division temporarily and Walker temporarily kept the 7th Division. When Walker was wounded and left in February 1814, these arrangements became unnecessary and Barnes retained the brigade in the 2nd Division. John Byng was highly regarded by Hill and when, at one point, he might lose his brigade to a senior officer, Hill wrote to Wellington to ensure that Byng would remain with the division. Wellington made other arrangements and Byng stayed with the 2nd Division. Hill temporarily commanded the army for a short period in the spring of 1814 when Wellington was called away on government business.

Hill's detached corps was usually composed of his 2nd Division, the Portuguese Division and either a few British and Portuguese cavalry brigades or the 2nd Cavalry Division (and later with a Spanish division attached). When Hill was absent in late 1810 to mid-1811, his corps had been commanded for a short time by William Stewart and when Stewart felt himself unequal to the task, then William Beresford until Hill's return to duty.[59]

At the war's end, for his services, Rowland Hill was created Baron Hill and he later became Viscount Hill. Wellington trusted Hill in an independent command, 'and I am convinced that whatever you decide upon will be right.'[60] Wellington's comment, 'The best of Hill is I always know where to find him.'[61]

Officers who served in the 2nd Division, on the staff, were: Lieutenant General Sir Rowland Hill, Major Generals James Leith, Christopher Tilson, Lieutenant General Sir William Stewart, Major Generals William Lumley, Richard Stewart, Daniel Hoghton, Kenneth Howard, Colonel James Catlin Craufurd, Major Generals George Walker, William Pringle, Edward Barnes, John Byng, Colonels George Wilson and Robert O'Callaghan.

Portuguese brigade commanders included: Brigadier Charles Ashworth and Colonel Henry Hardinge.

The 3rd Division

The 3rd Division is always associated with Thomas Picton. However at its formation in June 1809 of two British brigades, it was temporarily commanded by John Randoll Mackenzie as the senior brigade commander. He being killed at Talavera in 1809, the division came under the command of Robert Craufurd whose Light Brigade was added to the division. In February 1810, Thomas Picton arrived and being senior to Craufurd was assigned to the command. The division was now reorganized with the formation that was to become the standard in Wellington's army, that of two British brigades and a Portuguese brigade. The division's brigades went through a number of amalgamations and transfers during its early years. Craufurd's Light Brigade was removed and renamed the Light Division. Picton was appointed as a brigade commander and temporary commander of the division until a senior officer should arrive. Picton retained the command until the end of the war, except for absences. During these periods, either Edward Pakenham, Charles Colville or Manley Power acted in command. After the casualties at Badajoz, Lieutenant Colonel Alexander Wallace was in temporary command of the division for a short time. Picton specifically requested that Pakenham temporarily replace him in command in 1812 when Picton went on leave. Wellington liked Colville and chose him on several occasions to command – albeit temporarily – other divisions during the absence of their permanent commander. In late 1811, Colville was given temporary command of the 4th Division and in the summer of 1813, he was given temporary command of the 6th Division. When Picton left to go home in October 1813, Colville was given the command of the division. In late 1813, Picton was also considered for the chief command on the east coast of Spain in succession to William Clinton. Picton declined as he preferred to return to command his 3rd Division.[62] When Picton returned in December, he was reappointed to the 3rd Division. Wellington would have left Colville in command had Picton not returned. As Colville had been promised a divisional command by Wellington, it was decided to give him command of the 7th Division and Edward Barnes was to be appointed to Colville's old brigade in the 3rd Division. Due to other circumstances, Colville was appointed to the permanent command of the 5th Division in 1814 and Barnes was never appointed to the 3rd Division.

Comment attributed to Wellington on Picton: 'I found him a rough, foul-mouthed devil as ever lived, but he always behaved extremely well; no man could do better the different services I assigned to him.'[63]

Officers who served in the 3rd Division, on the staff, were: Major General John Randoll Mackenzie, Lieutenant General Sir Thomas Picton, Major General Stafford Lightburne, Colonel Robert Craufurd, Major General Charles Colville, Colonel Rufane Donkin, Major Generals James Kempt, Edward Pakenham, Henry Mackinnon, Thomas Brisbane and Colonel John Keane.

Portuguese brigade commanders included: Brigadiers Luiz Palmeirim, José Champalimaud, Major General Manley Power and Colonel Charles Sutton.

The 4th Division

The 4th Division is always associated with Galbraith Lowry Cole. However at its formation in June 1809, it was temporarily commanded by Alexander Campbell as the senior brigade commander. Originally of two British brigades, with a third British brigade temporarily added for two months in early 1810, it was reorganized at the end of February 1810 with the formation that was to become the standard in Wellington's army, that of two British brigades and a Portuguese brigade. The division's brigades went through a number of amalgamations and transfers during its early years. Campbell going home in the summer of 1809, the division had no permanent commander until the arrival of Cole in the fall of 1809. Cole was appointed as a brigade commander and temporary commander of the division until a senior officer should arrive. Cole retained the command until the end of the war, except for absences. During these periods the division was usually commanded by the senior brigade commander present, James Kemmis or William Anson. Charles Colville from the 3rd Division though was chosen to command it in late 1811 through early 1812. Warren Peacocke was removed from his brigade in 1809 to assume the position of Commandant of Lisbon, which he retained for the remainder of the war. In 1810, Alexander Campbell and his brigade were removed to form the 6th Division. In early 1811, William Houston was removed from his brigade to command the newly formed 7th Division. Edward Pakenham was removed from his Fusilier Brigade to the temporary command of the 3rd Division, and then the 6th Division, after which he was appointed the Adjutant General in the peninsula.

Lowry Cole: '[if] lacking the ability for an independent command . . . was a popular and competent divisional commander.'[64] Cole had once courted Lady Catherine Pakenham, who later became Wellington's wife, but this does not appear to have affected either their working or their personal relationship.

Officers who served in the 4th Division, on the staff, were: Lieutenant General Sir Galbraith Lowry Cole, Major Generals Stafford Lightburne, William Houston, Alexander Campbell, Barnard Bowes, George Anson, William Anson, Colonel Warren Peacocke, Major General James Kemmis, Colonel Edward Pakenham, Major Generals Edward Stopford, John Skerrett and Robert Ross.

Portuguese brigade commanders included: Brigadiers Thomas McMahon, William Harvey, Thomas Stubbs and Colonel José de Vasconcelos e Sá.

The 5th Division

The 5th Division was originally formed in July 1810 as a supporting force for Hill's detached corps. It was commanded by James Leith and was referred to as Leith's corps. The first mention of a 5th Division, in the general orders, was dated 6 October 1810. Before then it consisted of one British brigade, two Portuguese line brigades and a Portuguese militia brigade with George Madden's Portuguese cavalry brigade attached. In October, it was reorganized with the formation that was the standard in Wellington's army, that of two British brigades and a Portuguese brigade. During Leith's absence in 1811, William Erskine was appointed, in orders, to the command, but only held it briefly (about 10 days) between commanding the advance guard in early 1811 and then commanding Hill's cavalry in June 1811. In late 1811, Wellington thought of appointing William Clinton to the command if he joined the army, but he went to Sicily instead and then Leith returned later in 1811. Leith was absent for periods in 1812 and 1813.

Wellington always kept a divisional command open for Leith's return. The division was then commanded by a succession of temporary commanders. Richard Hulse, from the 6th Division was in temporary command in the summer of 1812.

John Oswald, newly arrived in late 1812, was assigned directly to the command until Leith should return. Oswald left on leave in November 1813. In December Colville was in command of the 5th Division and in January 1814, he was permanently appointed as Leith accepted a staff appointment elsewhere.[65] Other temporary commanders were the senior brigade commanders in the division including James Dunlop, Andrew Hay, George Walker, William Pringle and Frederick Robinson who was commanding at the war's end. James Dunlop left near the end of 1811. He had served with Wellington in India years before and Wellington felt that his absence was a loss and expressed the hope that Dunlop would return (but he never did).[66] Charles Colville took over command of the temporary corps, blockading Bayonne, after John Hope's capture in April 1814.

Officers who served in the 5th Division, on the staff, were: Lieutenant General Sir James Leith, Major Generals William Erskine, James Dunlop, Charles Colville, John Oswald, Andrew Hay, George Walker, Richard Hulse, William Pringle, Frederick Robinson and Edward Barnes.

Portuguese brigade commanders included: Brigadiers William Spry, Frederick Baron Eben and Colonel Luiz de Rego Barréto.

The 6th Division

The 6th Division was formed on 6 October 1810 of one British brigade, transferred from the 4th Division, and one Portuguese brigade. It was first commanded by Alexander Campbell, who had lost the command of the 4th Division to a senior officer. In March 1811, it received its second British brigade and then it conformed to the standard organization of peninsular divisions. When Campbell left in 1811, Robert Burne temporarily succeeded to the command. Wellington had wanted, at first, to appoint Robert Macfarlane to this division and when he chose to go to Sicily, then perhaps William Clinton, but he too went to Sicily instead. Wellington then appointed Henry Clinton, William's brother, to the command which he held until the end of the war. During Clinton's absences, either Edward Pakenham, Denis Pack, Charles Colville or George Madden held temporary command. Richard Hulse was removed from his brigade and placed in temporary command of the 5th Division in 1812. There were some transfers and amalgamations of brigades.

Officers who served in the 6th Division, on the staff, were: Major Generals Sir Henry Clinton, Sir Alexander Campbell Kt., Barnard Bowes, Robert Burne, Richard Hulse, Denis Pack, John Lambert and Colonels James Stirling and Samuel Hinde.

Portuguese brigade commanders included: Major General George Madden, Brigadiers Frederick Baron Eben, Luiz de Castro Conde de Rezende and Colonel James Douglas.

The 7th Division

The 7th Division was formed, in general orders, on 5 March 1811 with the organization that was the standard in Wellington's army, that of two British brigades and a Portuguese brigade. It was the last infantry division formed in the Peninsular army. At first it had only one British brigade as its second brigade of the King's

German Legion under Charles Baron Alten was serving independently under Beresford's command. In April 1811, Wellington had thought to assign Alten's brigade to the 2nd Division in exchange for Hoghton's brigade of that division. This was never implemented and Alten's brigade joined the 7th Division after the Battle of Albuera, summer of 1811. Its other British brigade was Robert Long's, but Long himself may never have actually joined the division as he was appointed to command the cavalry of Hill's corps in early March 1811. William Houston was its first commander. Houston left due to health problems in late 1811. William Clinton was then Wellington's choice to command this division, but, he chose to go to Sicily instead. Wellington then expressed a hope that James Dunlop, a brigade commander in the 5th Division would return to the Peninsula and he would then appoint him to the command of the 7th Division if Houston did not return.[67] Dunlop never rejoined. Houston, later in 1813, reapplied for a command, but, Wellington turned him down as there was then no vacancy.[68] Permanent commanders included John Hope (not to be confused with his relative and name-sake, the commander of the 1st Division), and George Ramsay, 9th Earl of Dalhousie who held it until the end of the war.

In late 1813, Lord Dalhousie was another officer whose name was suggested to take the command on the east coast of Spain in succession to William Clinton. Nothing appears to have come of the suggestion.[69] When Lord Dalhousie went on leave, George Walker from the 2nd Division was temporarily appointed to the command in late 1813. In December, Charles Colville, from the 3rd Division was going to supersede Walker in command once Picton returned to take over the 3rd Division. However, another arrangement was made and Walker continued in command. Henry Fane was offered the temporary command of the division, in early 1814, until Lord Dalhousie's return. If he declined, then John Oswald would be offered the appointment.[70] However, Oswald had gone on leave near the end of 1813 and never did return. Fane chose to remain with the cavalry of Hill's corps. George Walker then retained the command until Lord Dalhousie's return. Other temporary commanders came from the senior brigade commanders, John Sontag, Charles Baron Alten, John de Bernewitz and Carlos Frederico Lecor. John Sontag was appointed to a brigade from his previous command of Torres Vedras, where in 1810 Wellington had specifically appointed him to the command. In early 1814, the Provisional Militia Brigade was attached to the division. Lord Dalhousie exercised the temporary command of the army after the armistice in 1814, when the more senior officers departed, and he supervised its breakup.

Officers who served in the 7th Division, on the staff, were: Lieutenant General Sir George Ramsay, 9th Earl of Dalhousie, Major Generals William Houston, John Sontag, Charles Baron Alten, John Hope, Colonel Robert Long, Major Generals John de Bernewitz, Edward Barnes and William Inglis.

Portuguese brigade commanders included: Brigadier Francis Coleman, Major General Carlos Frederico Lecor, Brigadier Luiz Palmeirim, Colonels Richard Collins and John Doyle.

The Light Division

Wellington is supposed to have stated that, 'The Light, 3rd and 4th Divisions were the *élite* of my army, but the Light had this peculiar perfection. No matter what was the arduous service they were employed on . . . I still found a *division*.'[71]

The Light Division was formed in February 1810 under the command of Robert Craufurd. The division was really only the Light Brigade, removed from the 3rd Division, with Portuguese regiments now attached. Wellington could not organize it as a standard Peninsular division formation. This was because Craufurd was a junior colonel at the time and any attempt to expand his command to divisional strength would lay it open to claims for command by senior officers serving with the army who were only commanding brigades. It was only in August 1810, the so-called division was now split into two small brigades. This remained its formation until the end of the war.

Wellington very much wished to retain Craufurd in the command:

Since you have joined the army, I have always wished that you should command our outposts . . . and I was in hopes that I had made up for you a corps which would answer tolerably well of which I could give you the command without interfering with the claims of others.[72]

Adverting to the number of General Officers senior to you in the army, it has not been an easy task to keep you in your command . . .[73]

There was correspondence on this subject as Craufurd wished for a more extensive command:

Your feeling respecting your command is exactly what it ought to be . . . As long as I can make up a division of the proper strength for service, with your brigade, and Portuguese troops and cavalry, nobody would have had reason to complain; but a Lieutenant General, and the senior Major General of the army, recently arrived, are without commands, and it would not answer to throw more English troops into your division, leaving them unemployed.[74]

I should be happy to make your division stronger, and I have had in contemplation various modes of effecting that object; but you must see the difficulty which is created by the arrival of General Officers, of rank superior to yours.[75]

The truth is, that if I should make you as strong as I wish, there will be other claimants for the command of the division; and I think it much better to keep a Portuguese brigade in reserve and unattached, to be attached to you when it is necessary to reinforce you, than to place one permanently under your command which would give claims to others.[76]

As Wellington added a regiment and part of regiments to the division over the next year, it appears that Craufurd let the matter drop.

With Craufurd's death in early 1812, Wellington was not certain whom he should choose to replace him. He thought of assigning either Charles Baron Alten or Henry Clinton.[77] The command was finally assigned to Alten, an experienced light infantry commander in the King's German Legion, who would retain it until the end of the war. During Craufurd's absence, after his death and Alten's absence as well, the division was commanded temporarily at different periods by William Erskine and its senior brigade commanders, including John Vandeleur and James Kempt. In the summer of 1811, Edward Pakenham was selected to take the temporary command of a brigade, but, Craufurd suggested another officer instead.[78] Because, early in the war the division was in reality only a large brigade split in two, its brigade commanders were regimental lieutenant colonels and in fact the division was on a number of occasions temporarily commanded by either George Drummond or Lieutenant Colonel Andrew Barnard.

'It is a measure of Wellington's confidence in Craufurd that he put him in charge of the Light Division and kept him there at a time when nine senior officers were only commanding brigades.'[79] Wellington's comment on Alten, 'who is by far the best of the Hanoverian officers, and his opinion most consulted and respected . . .'[80]

Officers who served in the Light Division, on the staff, were: Major Generals Charles Baron Alten, Robert Craufurd, John Vandeleur, James Kempt, John Skerrett, Colonels George Drummond, James Wynch, and Lieutenant Colonels Thomas Sydney Beckwith and Robert Barclay.

The Portuguese Division

The Portuguese division was formally organized on 5 March 1810 when John Hamilton took the command. Hamilton also served as the Inspector General of Portuguese Infantry. It consisted of two Portuguese brigades. It had a third Portuguese brigade temporarily operating with it for the Albuera Campaign, 1811. It always served with the 2nd Division in a small corps under Rowland Hill. John Hamilton went on sick leave in 1813. It was then successively commanded by Conde de Amarante, temporarily by Archibald Campbell, John Hamilton again and Carlos Frederico Lecor to the end of the war. Wellington had wanted to organize it in the standard formation of his Peninsular divisions, but, the heavy casualties suffered at Albuera in 1811 prevented this and it remained a purely Portuguese division for the remainder of the war.[81]

Officers who served in the Portuguese Division, on the staff, included: Lieutenant Generals Francisco da Silveira Pinto da Fonseca Teixeira Conde de Amarante, Sir John Hamilton Kt., Brigadier Agostinho Luiz da Fonseca, Major General Carlos Frederico Lecor, Brigadiers Antonio Hippolyto Costa, Joâo Lobo Brandáo de Almeida, Archibald Campbell, Manley Power and John Buchan.

The Independent Infantry Brigades

There were four independent brigades which served with Wellington's army during the war. One British, formed in mid-1813, was commanded by Major General Matthew Aylmer, 5th Baron Aylmer and served with the 1st Division. The other British Brigade, formed in early 1814 and commanded by Major General Henry Bayly, was made up of three provisional militia regiments drawn from volunteers of the British militia. See Chapter 6 – Filling the Ranks. It was to be used for garrison duties in France and served with the 7th Division.

The Portuguese infantry brigades had all been independent at the start of the war. In early 1810, Wellington began to assign them to his infantry divisions and continued this practice as he organized new divisions. By the time the last infantry division was formed in 1811, only two Portuguese brigades were left independent. These Portuguese independent brigade commanders included: Brigadiers William Campbell, Charles Millar, Denis Pack, John Wilson, Thomas McMahon, Major General Thomas Bradford and Brigadier Archibald Campbell.

The Portuguese army also made up several temporary brigades including some from the garrisons of the fortresses. They served with the field army as required and were then either broken up or returned to garrison duties. They were commanded by officers such as Major Generals Manoel Bacellar, José Lopes de Sousa, Brigadiers Antonio da Victoria, Robert Wilson, Richard Blunt, Robert McLeroth, Manley Power, Colonels William Cox, Richard Collins and John Buchan.

When the war was being fought in Portugal, Wellington could call upon the militia of the country. They would be embodied in divisions under such officers as Colonel Carlos Frederico Lecor, Brigadiers Charles Millar, Nicholas Trant and John Wilson.

Wellington's Other Generals

During the war, Wellington's responsibilities were expanded beyond just his peninsular army. He was made responsible for Cadiz and later Cartagena.[82] As the threat to Cadiz diminished during the war, many of the officers assigned to the Cadiz garrison applied for and received staff appointments to Wellington's field army. The officers on the east coast of Spain were from the garrison of Sicily and originally only came under Wellington's command when they landed in Spain. In March 1814, Wellington was informed that Lord William Bentinck and a portion of his force in Sicily and the force on the east coast of Spain were to both be at his disposal and strengthen his main army.[83] It was left to Lord William Bentinck to decide if he would, personally, join Wellington's army or remain in Sicily. However, Wellington was also left to decide if Bentinck's force should join him if he could arrange to transport it quickly by sea. Wellington did not, in fact, order Bentinck's force to join him as it had already landed in Italy. Wellington did order the break up of the army on the east coast of Spain, ordering two brigades to join his army and requesting William Clinton to join and take command of a division.[84] Clinton delayed implementing this order as the French had not evacuated all of Catalonia and this force did not join Wellington's army until after the war had ended.

Officers assigned on the staff or who served included: at Cadiz: Lieutenant General Thomas Graham, Major Generals Ronald Ferguson, William Stewart, Moore Disney, Colonels John Sontag, Daniel Hoghton, Barnard Bowes, William Dilkes, Major General George Cooke, Colonels George Walker, Kenneth Mackenzie, William Wheatley and John Skerrett. At Cartagena: Major General

Andrew Ross and Colonel John Lambert. On the east coast of Spain: Lieutenant Generals John Murray, Frederick Maitland, Major General James Campbell, Lieutenant General William Clinton, Major Generals John MacKenzie, Augustus Honstedt, Adolphus Baron Barsse, Rufane Donkin and Haviland Smith.

Conclusion

These officers represented some of the best that Great Britain had available to command its forces. Wellington paid them several compliments. One was in a letter to Earl Bathurst in 1815, where he complained of the treatment he was receiving from the Horse Guards because at the time he thought that he was not being allowed to have the general officers who had served with him during the Peninsular War.[85]

The officers never forgot their service and the Duke of Wellington summed it up nicely when he wrote in 1815:

> I wish I could bring every thing together as I had it when I took leave of the army at Bordeaux . . . It is a symptom of the old spirit we had amongst us, than which we cannot have a better.[86]

NOTES

1   *Wellington as Military Commander*, p. 194.
2   Quoted in *Wellington's Army*, p. 80.
3   *WSD* vol. vii, Memorandum of the Duke of York, 26 December 1812, p. 516.
4   *WD* (enlarged ed.) vol. iv, to Major General Erskine, 29 April 1811, p. 778.
5   *WD* (enlarged ed.) vol. iv, to Robert Craufurd, 28 January 1811, p. 558.
6   *WD* (new ed.) vol. vii, to Lieutnant Colonel Torrens, 28 January 1811, p. 204.
7   *WD* (new ed.) vol. ix, to Lieutnant Colonel Torrens, 13 September 1812, p. 427.
8   *WD* (new ed.) vol. x, to Colonel Ross, 20th Regiment, 1 May 1813, p. 338.
9   *WSD* vol. viii, Lord Bentinck to Wellington, 1 September 1813, p. 219.
10   *WD* (new ed.) vol. v, to Earl of Liverpool, 21 December 1809, p. 385.
11   *WD* (new ed.) vol. viii, to Major General W. Clinton, 5 December 1811, p. 439.
12   *WSD* vol. vii, Earl of Liverpool to Wellington, 8 August 1811, p. 196.
13   *WD* (new ed.) vol. vi, to Earl of Liverpool, 14 July 1810, p. 270.
14   *WD* (new ed.) vol. x, to Major General Houston, 23 March 1813, p. 224.
15   *Wellington as Military Commander*, pp. 195–196.
16   *WD* (new ed.) vol. x, to Major General Vandeleur, 26 April 1813, p. 330.
17   *WSD* vol. vii, to Colonel Torrens, 2 December 1812, p. 486.
18   *WD* (new ed.) vol. x, to Lieutenant General Sir T. Graham, 5 August 1813, pp. 601–603.
19   *WSD* vol. vii, Colonel Torrens to Wellington, 3 June 1813, pp. 626–627.
20   *WD* (new ed.) vol. ix, to Earl of Liverpool, 3 June 1812, pp. 206–207.
21   *WD* (new ed.) vol. ix, to Marshal Beresford, 2 December 1812, p. 591.
22   *WSD* vol. vii, Earl Bathurst to Wellington, 6 January 1813, pp. 514–515.
23   *WD* (new ed.) vol. xi, to Earl Bathurst, 18 October 1813, p. 208.
24   *WD* (new ed.) vol. v, to Earl of Liverpool, 21 December 1809, pp. 384–385.
25   *WSD* vol. vi, Earl of Liverpool to Wellington, 9 January 1810, p. 468.
26   *WSD* vol. vi, Earl of Liverpool to Wellington, 4 May 1810, pp. 520–521.
27   *WSD* vol. vii, Earl of Liverpool to Wellington, 6 August 1812, p. 374.
28   *WSD* vol. viii, Colonel Torrens to Wellington, 21 September 1813, pp. 263–264.
29   *WD* (new ed.) vol. xi, to Colonel Torrens, 18 October 1813, p. 204.
30   *WSD* vol. viii, Earl Bathurst to Wellington, 9 September 1813, p. 246.
31   *WSD* vol. vii, to Earl Bathurst, 2 December 1812, p. 484.

32 *WSD* vol. vii, to Colonel Torrens, 2 December 1812, p. 485.
33 *WD* (new ed.) vol. ix, to Colonel Torrens, 7 September 1812, pp. 398–399.
34 *WD* (new ed.) vol. x, to the Earl of Mulgrave, 27 January 1813, p. 45.
35 *WD* (new ed.) vol. x, to 'blank' (but to George Fisher), 6 May 1813, p. 359.
36 Quoted in *History of the Royal Regiment of Artillery*, p. 346.
37 *Life and Letters of Sir John Burgoyne*, vol. 1, p. 282. The officers were Elphinstone and Lieutenant Colonel Henry Goldfinch.
38 *WD* (new ed.) vol. iv, to Viscount Castlereagh, 26 June 1809, pp. 466–467.
39 *WD* (new ed.) vol. iv, to J. Villiers, 19 May 1809, p. 346.
40 *WD* (new ed.) vol. iv, to J. Villiers, 30 May 1809, p. 370.
41 *WD* (new ed.) vol. iv, to Viscount Castlereagh, 26 June 1809, p. 467.
42 *WD* (new ed.) vol. ix, to Colonel Torrens, 7 September 1812, p. 399, and to John Murray, 7 September 1812, p. 399.
43 *WD* (new ed.) vol. iv, to Viscount Castlereagh, 16 June 1809, pp. 428–429.
44 *WD* (new ed.) vol. iv, to Viscount Castlereagh, 23 June 1809, p. 462.
45 *WD* (new ed.) vol. vi, to Lieutenant General Payne, 28 May 1810, pp. 153–154.
46 *WSD* vol. vii, to Earl Bathurst, 7 September 1812, p. 414.
47 *WSD* vol. vii, to Earl Bathurst, 14 February 1813, p. 548.
48 Appendix II, *Wellington's Army 1808–1814*, pp. 372–373.
49 *WSD* vol. vii, to Colonel Torrens, 2 December 1812, p. 485.
50 *WSD* vol. vii, Duke of York to Wellington, 31 May 1811, p. 166.
51 *WD* (new ed.) vol. x, to Lieutenant General Sir Stapleton Cotton, 7 April 1813, pp. 267–269.
52 *WD* (new ed.) vol. ix, to Earl Bathurst, 24 July 1812, pp. 308–309.
53 Quoted in *Wellington as Military Commander*, p. 203.
54 *WD* (new ed.) vol. ix, to Earl Bathurst, 9 July 1812, p. 278.
55 *WD* (new ed.) vol. xi, to Earl Bathurst, 23 September 1813, p. 143.
56 *WSD* vol. vii, to Colonel Torrens, 6 December 1812, p. 494.
57 Quoted in *The Surpriser*, p. 162.
58 *WSD* vol. xiv, Adjutant General to Major General Walker and Major General Barnes, 12 February 1814, p. 384.
59 *WD* (new ed.) vol. vii, to Major General W. Stewart, 29 December 1810, p. 82.
60 *WD* (new ed.) vol. vi, to Lieutenant General Hill, 17 May 1810, p. 124.
61 Quoted in *The Life of John Colborne*, p. 140.
62 *WD* (new ed.) vol. xi, to Major General William Clinton, 25 December 1813, p. 397.
63 Quoted in *The Peninsular War*, p. 353.
64 *Wellington's Generals*, p. 23.
65 *WSD* vol. xiv, Adjutant General to Major General Walker and Major General Colville, 17 December 1813, pp. 334–335.
66 *WD* (new ed.) vol. viii, to Lieutenant Colonel Torrens, 16 October 1811, pp. 345–346.
67 *WD* (new ed.) vol. viii, to Lieutenant Colonel Torrens, 16 October 1811, p. 346.
68 *WD* (new ed.) vol. x, to Major General Houston, 23 March 1813, p. 224.
69 *WSD* vol. viii, Earl Bathurst to Earl of Liverpool, 19 October 1813, p. 316.
70 *WSD* vol. xiv, Adjutant General to Major General Fane, 21 January 1814, p. 366.
71 Quoted in *Wellington as Military Commander*, p. 201.
72 *WD* (new ed.) vol. vi, to Robert Craufurd, 9 April 1810, p. 28.
73 *WD* (new ed.) vol. vii, to Robert Craufurd, 9 December 1810, p. 39.
74 *WD* (new ed.) vol. vi, to Robert Craufurd, 15 April 1810, p. 37.
75 *WD* (new ed.) vol. vi, to Robert Craufurd, 23 October 1810, p. 531.
76 *WD* (new ed.) vol. vi, to Robert Craufurd, November 1810, p. 614.
77 *WD* (new ed.) vol. viii, to Lt Colonel Torrens, 28 January 1812, p. 570.
78 *WD* (new ed.) vol. viii, to Robert Craufurd, 21 July 1811, p.130. The officer selected was Lieutenant Colonel Andrew Barnard.
79 *Wellington as Military Commander*, p. 201.
80 *WD* (new ed.) vol. x, to Earl Bathurst, 20 April 1813, p. 307.
81 *WD* (enlarged ed.) vol. v, to Marshal Beresford, 17 July 1811, p. 162.

82 *Life of Thomas Graham Lord Lynedoch*, p. 302.
83 *WSD* vol. viii, Earl Bathurst to Wellington, 10 March 1814, p. 635.
84 *WD* (new ed.) vol. xi, to Lieutenant General W. Clinton, 4 March 1814, pp. 544–546.
85 *WSD* vol. x, to Earl Bathurst, 4 May 1815, p. 219.
86 *WD* (new ed.) vol. xii, to Lieutenant General Sir G. L. Cole, 2 June 1815, pp. 435–436.

Chapter Six

Filling the Ranks: How Wellington Kept His Units up to Strength

ROBERT BURNHAM

Wellington was faced with a chronic shortage of men throughout the Peninsular War. Although he was successful in raising and integrating Portuguese units into his army, Wellington fought a constant battle with his own government not only to give him additional British units, but also to provide replacements for existing units. Throughout much of the war, Wellington did not receive the support that a winning general should have received when it came to manpower. In 1809, the British government sent an expedition to Holland to capture or destroy the French fleet at Antwerp. This force consisted of over 39,000 men[1] while Wellington's force at this time had only 23,000 British troops.[2] The number of British troops in his army expanded slowly reaching 34,000 in November 1810, to about 38,000 at the end of 1811. By April 1812, Wellington was only able to field about 38,000 British troops due to the high casualties he took during the sieges of Ciudad Rodrigo and Badajoz in early 1812.[3] The year 1812 also saw Great Britain go to war with the United States and even fewer units became available for deployment to the Peninsula. Although 20,000 additional troops were sent to the Peninsula in 1812, they were not ready for the field until August. In 1813, only three cavalry regiments, one artillery battery, and an infantry battalion reinforced the British army in the Peninsula. This infantry battalion however, was considered so unfit for active service, it was sent to Gibraltar to free a more seasoned battalion for the field. This problem was not just unique to Wellington's army. By 1813, the whole army was feeling the shortage. The regulars were authorized by Parliament to have strength of 347,734 yet on 25 January 1813, they had a strength of only 255,826, a shortfall of 26 per cent.[4] The following year, things were no better. By late 1813, Wellington had written that of the sixty-four British infantry battalions assigned to his army, fourteen had fewer than 450 rank and file fit for duty, while another eighteen had fewer than 350 rank and file![5]

It was not just a matter of sending out new units to reinforce Wellington. The British army was deployed throughout the world and the government had to replace the casualties not only in Wellington's army, but also in units worldwide. The British had no conscription and relied upon volunteers to fill the ranks of its regiments. In 1811, the British army serving overseas had 22,000 casualties. While this is small compared to the casualties of the French, Russians, or Austrians in 1805, 1807, or 1809, it placed an incredible strain on the British military system.

In 1811, the British army only recruited 26,000 men to replace the 22,000 casualties, plus to serve as replacements for those soldiers who were not fit for active service or to bring units up to strength in all regiments on active duty, not just those serving in Spain and Portugal.[6]

Wellington's battalions were chronically understrength and at times he took radical steps to field a fighting force. Although much has already been published on how he integrated the Portuguese army in his army, little has been written on the methods he used to keep the rest of his force up to strength. Wellington's methods included retaining previously formed battalions of detachments, allowing Spaniards to enlist in British regiments, combining under strength regiments into provisional battalions, permitting militia battalions to serve with the army, and even at one point accepting an offer from the Russians to provide troops. None of these proposals were popular and were usually reluctantly implemented. Occasionally they put him at direct odds with the wishes of his superiors in Great Britain. Yet Wellington was willing to do whatever it took to keep up the strength of his army.

The British Battalions of Detachment in 1809

In mid-January 1809, the situation of the British army in the Iberian Peninsula was grim. Moore's army had been forced to evacuate Coruña after a disastrous retreat and to return to England. In Portugal there remained fewer than 14,000 men under General Cradock. French forces were threatening from several directions. For many the only option was to evacuate Cradock's troops and to cut the British losses. Yet those orders never came. Instead Cradock began to organize the remaining troops for the defence of Portugal.

Within Portugal there were about 3,000 officers and men from all three arms, whose regiments were evacuated at Coruña. Some of these men were on detached duty when their regiments marched off to fight the French, while others were in hospitals, too sick to undertake the rigours of a winter campaign. Many of them had been with Moore's army, but had either become separated during the horrendous retreat to Coruña or had been captured by the French and escaped. Many had managed to make it to Oporto, where a brigade of British forces still held out. General Alan Cameron, the brigade commander, sent the following message to General Cradock on 16 January:

> I have collected several detachments of recovered men belonging to sir J. Moore's army, whom I found scattered in all directions, without necessaries, and some of them committing every possible excess that could render the name of a British soldier odious to the nation.[7]

On 16 January 1809, the same date that General Cameron wrote his scathing message, the 1st Battalion of Detachments was formed. By early February the 2nd Battalion had also come into existence. On 6 February, the muster-rolls[8] for the two battalions were:

1st Battalion of Detachments: 6 February 1809

Unit	Field Officers	Captains	Subalterns	Staff	NCOs & Men
3rd Foot	1	0	0	0	0
20th Foot	0	1	1	0	47
28th Foot	0	1	6	1	120
32nd Foot	0	0	0	1	0
38th Foot	1	3	2	0	59
42nd Highlanders	0	0	2	1	23
2/43rd Light	0	1	2	1	119
50th Foot	0	0	0	1	0
52nd Light	0	1	3	2	123
79th Highlanders	0	0	4	1	64
91st Highlanders	0	1	2	1	164
92nd Highlanders	0	1	2	2	74
95th Rifles	0	0	0	0	35
Totals	2	9	24	11	58 NCOs 770 Men

2nd Battalion of Detachments: 6 February 1809

Unit	Field Officers	Captains	Subalterns	Staff	NCOs & Men
2nd Foot	0	1	3	0	96
4th Foot	0	0	3	2	78
5th Foot	1	0	2	1	93
6th Foot	1	0	0	0	38
32nd Foot	0	1	8	1	74
36th Foot	0	0	5	1	75
42nd Highlanders	0	0	0	1	0
50th Foot	0	1	1	1	75
71st Highlanders	0	0	3	0	107
82nd Foot	0	1	7	1	96
Totals	2	4	32	8	732

Men continued to be assigned to the battalions until late summer 1809. These men were described as 'escaped from the French' or 'from the frontiers'. The 1st Battalion had men join from the 14th, 35th, 59th, 76th, and 81st Regiments, while the 2nd Battalion picked up soldiers from the 1st, 9th, 23rd, 26th, 59th, and the Staff Corps![9]

By the beginning of May, the 1st Battalion was commanded by Lieutenant Colonel William H. Bunbury of the 3rd Foot. Its exact organization is unknown, however the 2/43rd Light Infantry, the 52nd Light Infantry, the 92nd Highlanders, and the 95th Rifles formed separate companies.[10] The riflemen from the 95th Rifles were formed into the 1st Rifle Company that consisted of seven sergeants, three corporals and forty-two other ranks. It had no officers from the 95th Rifles assigned to it and it was commanded by Lieutenant Thomas Munro of the 42nd

Highlanders.[11] Lieutenant Colonel Edward Copson of the 5th Foot commanded the 2nd Battalion, and it too had enough men from different regiments to form them into separate companies. The soldiers from the 82nd Foot were in a company commanded by Captain Carew.[12]

The Douro Campaign

On 22 April 1809, Sir Arthur Wellesley (the future Duke of Wellington) arrived in Lisbon with an additional 8,300 men to bring the British forces there to almost 29,000 men. He decided to attack the French forces under Marshal Soult who had captured Oporto in late March. The 1st Battalion of Detachments was brigaded with the 29th Foot and the 1/16th Portuguese Infantry under the command of General Richard Stewart, while the 2nd Battalion of Detachments was brigaded with the 97th Foot and the 2/16th Portuguese Infantry under General John Sontag. In early May, he began moving the army northward. The 1st Battalion of Detachments was blooded for the first time on 10 and 11 May near the village of Grijo:

> The infantry of the advance guard consisted of the Rifle Company of the 1st Battalion of Detachments, the Companies of the 43rd and 52nd Light Infantry and the Light Company of the 29th Foot, the whole under the command of Major Way of the 29th. [Stapleton] Cotton with the British Cavalry came in touch with the French at dawn on the 10th, but [General] Francheschi had some infantry with him and Stewart's Brigade was delayed and did not come for some time; Francheschi thereupon fell back and joined [General] Mermet at Grijo. On the 11th Wellesley ordered [General] Rowland] Hill to endeavour to outflank Mermet's position on the east whilst he with Paget's division advanced. In the afternoon the Light Companies of the 1st Battalion of Detachments attacked Mermet but met with a stiff resistance and lost not a few. Wellesley now ordered the King's German Legion to turn the French left and the 16th Portuguese to turn their right and with the rest of Stewart's Brigade renewed the attack on the wooded heights in the centre above the village of Grijo. Mermet thereupon withdrew . . .[13]

Marshal Soult, realizing the danger his forces were in, ordered the French forces to evacuate Oporto via Tras-os-Montes. He instructed all boats were to be brought from the south bank of the Douro and decided to hold Oporto until all of his outlying forces could begin their movement. On 12 May, the British forces were stopped at the Douro, having no way to cross. A search of the south bank of the river was made and three barges were found. General Hill was able to send most of his brigade across the river and capture the large seminary on the north bank, before the French responded. As the French rearguard began its attack against the British, they left the river unguarded. The Portuguese civilians responded immediately by launching all the boats on the north to help the British. General Stewart's brigade was ferried over and caught the French counter-attack in the flank. This attack was the final blow to the French and what had begun as an orderly retreat became a rout. According to Sergeant Daniel Nicol: 'in the fighting the battalion had lost sixty men; and when they had got to quarters Sir Arthur [Wellesley] addressed them and expressed how thankful he was to them for the way in which they had crossed the river, and enabled the other regiments to follow so easily.'[14]

Nicol's figures are probably close to the mark. Verner states that in the soldiers from the 43rd Light Infantry Regiment had ten killed and wounded, while the 52nd Light Infantry had 'one officer and six men wounded and four missing . . .'[15]

Wellington was pleased with the campaign and although he did not single out the Battalions of Detachments by name, he did mention several of the companies in a General Order dated 12 May 1809:

> The Commander of the Forces congratulates the troops upon the success which has attended their operations for the last four days, upon which they have traversed above 80 miles of a most difficult country, in which they have carried some formidable positions, have beaten the enemy repeatedly, and have ended by forcing the passage of the Douro, and defending the position they had so boldly taken up, with numbers far inferior to those with which they were attacked. In course of this short expedition the Commander of the Forces has had repeated opportunities of witnessing and applauding the gallantry of the officers and the troops, the activity and conduct of the 95th, and of the Light Infantry of the 29th the 43rd and 52nd.[16]

Daniel Nicol went on to write that in late May, the battalion had begun to move again 'over the bridge of boats across the broad and rapid Douro and bade adieu to Oporto forever, with its churches, convents, and port wine. To the last the British troops paid more devotion than to the first.' On 4 June they celebrated the King's birthday with each man receiving a pint of wine and a chance to bathe in the Mondego River.

The Talavera Campaign

In June, Wellington received permission to conduct operations in Spain with the Spanish Army. On 27 June, the British forces left Abrantes to link with the Spanish Army under the command of General Cuesta. Once there, the combined forces would attack Marshal Victor, who was operating near Talavera. The march to central Spain was a rigorous one for the battalions. Lieutenant Wood of the 82nd Regiment, who was assigned to the 2nd Battalion of Detachments, left a vivid description:

> in Portugal we had experienced the most distressing cold and wet weather; it was now as suddenly as intensely hot, and we had very little except the olive trees, which we were prohibited from cutting, to screen us from the scorching rays of a sun almost vertical. This being an open corn country, we were the whole day exposed to its beams, and the ground was so exceedingly warm, that it produced the greatest number of insects I ever saw. We were infested and annoyed, beyond measure, by the scorpions and centipedes crawling over us, and the mosquitoes stinging us in such a manner, that I have

frequently seen officers and men with their eyes so swollen that they could not see out of them for some hours . . . our advance continued, and the weather retained its sultry heat. Many a weary step, over many a dreary league, we dragged through the dusty way; sometimes not seeing a house for days together, sometimes without a drop of water to wet the parched and swollen tongue of the way-dropped soldier – for there were many who sunk under the oppression of this excessive heat. We had frequently no fuel, not even a shrub that would serve as a picquet for the baggage-horse; and occasionally no forage was to be had for these poor animals after their hard day's labour, in which case they had to move till they came to a more verdant spot. However, as our commissariat had hitherto procured us plentiful, and we received our rations very regularly, we were enabled to continue our exertions till we arrived at Talavera de la Reyna.[17]

Wellington chose to fight the French forces under Marshal Victor, just north of the city of Talavera. The Tagus River and the city itself secured the right flank of the position. North of the city, the position was fairly flat for about 2 kilometres. There the Cerro de Medellin rose out of the earth. This massive ridgeline towers 200 feet above the plains. The slopes on all sides are steep, but steepest on the eastern side – the side that faced the French. North of the Cerro de Medellin was another broad plain. To the east, separating the two armies was the La Portina creek, which was a shallow trickle of stagnant water in a 10-metre deep gully.

On 27 July Stewart's brigade was in the second line on the south-west side of the Cerro de Medellin. In front of them were Tilson's, Donkin's, and Low's brigades. Tilson's Brigade formed the right of the British line and was charged with holding the ridgeline – the key to the whole British position. Marshal Victor ordered General Ruffin to seize the position and at 9 p.m. the attack began. The French 9th *Légère* Regiment crossed La Portina and caught Low's Germans by surprise and swept to the summit of the Medellin. General Hill, the British division commander, rode forward to see what all the noise was about, and was nearly captured. A volley from the French killed his brigade-major and wounded his horse. General Hill galloped down to Stewart's brigade and it was 'formed in column of companies at quarter distance. The 48th and the battalion of detachments met with formidable resistance, and were driven back at this critical moment.'[18] Daniel Nicol wrote of the confused fighting that occurred that night:

At this time our brigade got a biscuit each man served out, when a cry was heard, 'The hill! the hill!' General Stewart called out for the detachments to make for the top of the hill, for he was certain that no regiment could be there so soon as we. Off we ran in the dark, and very dark it was; but the French got on top of the hill before us, and some of them ran through the battalion, calling out, 'Espanioles, Espanioles,' and others calling 'Allemands.'

Our officer cried out 'Don't fire on the Spaniards.' I and many others jumped to the side to let them pass down the hill, where they were either killed or taken prisoners in our rear. I saw those on the top of the hill by the flashes of their pieces; then we knew who they were; but I and many more of our company were actually in rear of the French for a few moments, and did not know it until they seized some of our men by the collar and were dragging them away prisoners. This opened our eyes, and bayonets and the butts of our firelocks were used with great dexterity – a dreadful mêlée.[19]

However the French were too many and the 1st Battalion of Detachments were being forced down the hill, when the two other regiments in the brigade (29th and 48th Regiments) arrived. According to one eyewitness in the 1st Battalion of Detachments 'the 29th by a most splendid charge, drove back the enemy in confusion, and established themselves on the summit.'[20] An officer in the 29th blamed the 1st Battalion's poor leadership and as the 29th swept through them to attack the French, he stated they 'seemed much vexed; we could hear them bravely calling out, "There is nobody to command us. Only tell us what to do and we're ready to do it!"'[21] The 29th Regiment restored the line by forcing the French off the Cerro de Medellin. According to Daniel Nicol:

Order was restored, and a deathlike silence reigned among us. The French kindled great fires in rear of their lines. I had a sound sleep for a short time . . . When daylight appeared each army gazed on the other and viewed the operations of last night. Round the top of the hill many a redcoat lay dead; about 30 yards on the other side the red and blue lay mixed, and a few yards farther, and down in the valley below, they were all blue.[22]

The next day brought little relief for the 1st Battalion of Detachments. At 5 a.m. they were still posted on the Cerro de Medellin, when the massed French guns began pounding their position. Wellington immediately ordered Stewart's brigade to withdraw behind the ridgeline and to lie down. Soon another French attack began and General Hill ordered the brigade up to the ridge to meet the attack. The 1st Battalion was in the centre of the line. The French columns closed quickly, forcing the French gunners to shift their fire to the left – directly onto the 1st Battalion. The carnage in the battalion was fierce. The French attack was beaten off and the brigade did not see much action until late afternoon when the French skirmishers came forward to harass the British line. Once again Daniel Nicol provides an unforgettable picture of the fight:

General Stewart's brigade was ordered to advance to the top of the hollow, when all the others were ordered to lie close to the ground, as the French had taken up a position with their heads above the rise, and were doing much mischief. We sustained a heavy fire from the enemy's guns on the other side of the hill; they were making lanes through us, and their musketry attacked us on our flanks. We cleared the enemy from our front and right, but they maintained the heights on the other side; and as we were lower than they, they punished us severely . . . Captain MacPherson of the 35th Regiment, who commanded our company this day, was down and my right file was taken off by a cannon-shot. William Bowie and John Shewan were killed on my left, and Adam Much lay in the rear wounded.[23]

There Nicol was wounded:

About four o'clock I was struck by a musket ball, which grazed my left knee and passed through my right leg about 2 inches below the cap of the knee. I finished my loading and fired my last shot at the man who wounded me, for I could plainly see him on a height a few yards to my front. I think I should have known him if he had come in my way afterwards. I called out to Sergeant John Gordon that I was wounded; he was the only non-commissioned officer belonging to the regiment I saw at his post. I made along the side of the hill as well as I could, using my firelock as a crutch.[24]

This attack ended the 1st Battalion's involvement. In the two days of the fight, they suffered over 250 casualties, over 200 of them on the second day. Total casualties were: one officer and forty men killed; nine officers and 206 men wounded; two officers and sixteen men missing. Officer casualties included Major Ross, the battalion's senior major, and Lieutenant George Brown of the 43rd Regiment, who would go on to command the Light Division in the Crimean War. Oman states that one of the officers was not captured but 'turned up at Oropesa next morning, nominally sick.'[25]

The 2nd Battalion of Detachments was part of General James Kemmis' brigade (1/40th Foot, 97th Foot, and the 2nd Battalion of Detachments), which was on the far right of the British line. The 2nd Battalion was on the right of the brigade and was thus on the extreme right of the whole British Army. On their right were the Spanish. The battalion saw little action during the battle and lost seven men killed, thirteen wounded, and one missing. On the night of 28 July, Lieutenant Wood and twenty men were sent down to the La Portina to gather any wounded (both British and French) and protect the wounded French from the Spanish:

I had only gone about 100 yards, when one of my men, who were scattered for the purpose, called out for me to go to him, and told me that a Spaniard, whom he pointed out, was about to shoot a Frenchman, badly wounded; who was crying most piteously. 'Mon Dieu! Mon Dieu!' I waited to see what were really the Spaniard's intentions: he deliberately loaded his piece, and was going to present it at this unfortunate creature, when I arrested his arm, and sent him away; but on looking behind me, I observed him creeping through the vineyard to return and accomplish the diabolical and cowardly act of killing a fallen enemy in cool blood! On seeing this I ordered my men to take the wounded man and remove him from the spot where he was, to some shady olive trees, with which this plain was planted; and there I formed a kind of depot for these poor suffering wretches, with a guard to protect them till the carts came to take them away.[26]

The Disbandment

Despite their gallant service at Talavera, the battle was the beginning of the end for the Battalions of Detachments. On 29 July, the day after the battle, the Light Brigade arrived after making a forced march of 42 miles in twenty-six hours. The men who belonged to the Rifle Company of the 1st Battalion of Detachments immediately joined their fellow riflemen in the 1st Battalion 95th Rifles, while the officers and soldiers of the 43rd and 52nd Light Infantry joined their regiments— although this was not made official until a General Order on 14 September 1809 sent them and the soldiers from the 5th, 42nd, and 28th Regiments to battalions from their regiments serving in the Peninsula.

On 21 September, the battalions began marching to Lisbon. Upon arriving there, those soldiers who did not have a regiment serving in the Peninsula, were sent home. The battalions were not officially disbanded until they reached England. The 2nd Battalion landed at Gosport and marched to Salisbury, where the officers were invited to dinner with the Mayor. There the battalion was disbanded and according to Lieutenant Wood:

> each detachment proceeding to join its respective regiment. I marched with mine to Lewes, in Sussex; and on our arrival we certainly cut a very ludicrous appearance, from our ragged state, but were received with a hearty welcome by our long-lost comrades . . .[27]

An Assessment

The effectiveness of the two battalions of detachments was perceived differently even at the same headquarters. In a General Order written in Badajoz on 22 September 1809, Sir Arthur Wellesley, the future Duke of Wellington, wrote:

> The Commander of the Forces cannot avoid to express his regret upon losing the services of the two battalions of detachments, which are about to join their corps in England . . . He requests Lieutenant Colonel Banbury [*sic*], Lieutenant Colonel Copson and the Officers attached to these battalions, to accept his acknowledgement for the attention they have given to them.

Charles Stewart, Wellington's Adjutant General, had a different opinion of their worth, when he wrote on 15 June 1809 to Robert Stewart, Lord Castlereagh (later 2nd Marquess of Londonderry) the Secretary for War:

> I wish these detachment battalions were replaced. I am sure they are the cause of great disorder – no *esprit de corps* for their interior economy among them, though they will all fight. They are careless of all else, and the officers do not look to their temporary field officers and superiors under whom they are placed, as in an established regiment. I see much of their indiscipline.[28]

It should be noted that Wellington in his general order also mentioned that he had to remind them of proper conduct and when they returned to their parent units, the men were to ensure they behaved properly.

Several factors affected their discipline and combat readiness:

1. The battalions were composed mostly of the men who were previously wounded or too sick to campaign or men who became separated from their parent units during the horrendous retreat to Coruña. In the latter case they were stragglers. Stragglers as a group tended to be poorly disciplined or in poor health – a combination that would affect any unit. The two campaigns took a heavy toll on the battalions and the last return for the two battalions showed the 1st Battalion of Detachments had 496 men listed as being 'sick' and only 359 present for duty. The 2nd Battalion was marginally better with 388 'sick' and 514 effectives. On a side note, many of those wounded at Talavera, were left in a makeshift hospital at Talavera and were captured by the French, including Daniel Nicol.

2. The heart of the British Army was the regiment. This system was based on tradition and pride. Yet the Battalions of Detachments had none of these. Although men from the same regiment were grouped in the same company, if their numbers were too small, their company was formed with men from other regiments.

3. The company officers were not necessarily from the soldier's own regiment. In many cases, while the soldiers served under a subaltern from their regiment, the company commanders were not. During the Douro Campaign in the spring of 1809, the 1st Company of the 1st Battalion was composed of men from the 95th Rifles. The company commander was Lieutenant Thomas Monro of the 42nd Regiment. Daniel Nicol of the 92nd Gordon Highlanders was a bit more fortunate. The men in his company during the Douro Campaign were all from his regiment and consisted of 'Captain Logie, Lieutenant Cattanach, Lieutenant Durie, Surgeon Beattie, eight sergeants, a piper, and seventy-six rank and file.'[29] Yet at Talavera Captain MacPherson of the 35th Foot commanded his company.

4. Although the battalions received their share of rations and ammunition, replacement of uniform items and other essentials was a regimental function. The soldiers' regiments were back home and they often went wanting. Lieutenant Wood, wrote that by the end of the Talavera Campaign, he was still wearing the same clothes he left England with two years previously. When he returned to England in 1809 he and his soldiers were 'in a most motley and tattered condition. Our coats were patched over with different coloured cloth, for which purpose we had even cut off our skirts. My own coat was mended with the breeches of a dead Frenchman, which I found on the field . . .'[30]

Spanish Recruits in the British Army 1812–13

'I never saw better, more orderly, perfectly sober soldiers in my life, and as vedettes, the old German Hussar did not exceed them.'
– Sir Harry Smith, 95th Rifles>

One of the little-known episodes of the Peninsular War was the active recruitment of Spanish men into the British army in 1812 and 1813. For years the British looked with disdain at their Spanish counterparts and for most officers, it was unthinkable to have them in their regiments. As late as 1811, Wellington was opposed to the idea. This negative attitude carried over into the twentieth century and neither Sir Charles Oman, in his definitive work on the Peninsular War, nor John Fortescue, in his massive study of the British army, mentions their recruitment. But enlisted they were; and in some cases, almost 35 per cent of the unit's recruits in 1812 were Spanish. By most accounts they served honourably.

The first question that must be asked is given the widespread scorn for the fighting abilities of the Spanish by the British officer corps, what were the circumstances that would drive them to recruit them into their regiments? It was a matter of numbers. The regiments relied upon fresh recruits or volunteers from the militia to fill their ranks. By 1812, the attrition of men from combat, fatigue, disease, and accidents was greater than the number of replacements being received. To put it simply, Wellington's army could not replace the men it was losing.

The situation in the first four months of 1812 placed a great strain on the system. Although Wellington gained two notable victories at the sieges of Ciudad Rodrigo and Badajoz, it was at a horrendous cost. During the two sieges, the British lost almost 4,000 of their own men not including Portuguese casualties. This was over 10 per cent of Wellington's British soldiers before he fought a battle against the main French armies. Some of the best units in the army took tremendous losses and there were no replacements in sight. The Light Division and the 'Fighting' 3rd Division, were particularly hard hit. The 1/88 Regiment (the Connaught Rangers) lost 25 per cent of their men and fourteen of twenty-four officers in the two sieges. The 1/95 Rifles were in worse shape. Their strength at the beginning of 1812 was about 700 officers and men. By the time Badajoz was captured the 1/95th had sixteen officers and 198 soldiers killed or wounded; a staggering 30 per cent casualties![31]

These figures of course, only account for combat casualties. If 1812 was going to be anything like 1811, Wellington had to be worried! The previous year had seen many troops either as casualties or unfit for service. The autumn of 1811, the British army had almost 17,000 troops or 45 per cent of the British troops in hospitals![32]

A DEAL IS STRUCK

Wellington realized that he would have to find troops elsewhere. When the idea of incorporating Spaniards into British regiments was first proposed in 1811, he was adamantly opposed, but by mid-1812 he had no choice. According to William Napier, an agreement was reached that in exchange for 'a grant of one million of money, with arms and clothing for one hundred thousand men, in return for which five thousand Spanish were to be enlisted for the British ranks.' On 18 May 1812, Wellington sent the following letter to all of his divisional commanders:

The Spanish Government having been pleased to allow a limited number of natives of Spain to serve His Majesty in the British regiments composing this army, I have to request that you will authorize the regiments named in the margin to enlist and bear on their strength 100 Spanish volunteers, on the following conditions:

First; the men must not be under 5 feet 6 inches high, strongly made, and not under nineteen years of age, nor older than twenty-seven.

Secondly; they are to be attested according to the following form by the commanding officer of the regiment to serve during the present war; but in case the regiment into which they shall enlist should be ordered from the Peninsula the Spanish volunteers are to be discharged, and each of them is to receive one month's full pay to carry him to his home.

Form of Attestation:

I, A.B. do make oath that I will serve His Majesty the King of Great Britain and Ireland, in the – battalion of the – regiment of foot, during the existing war in the Peninsula, if His Majesty should so long require my services, and provided that the – battalion of the – regiment shall continue in the Peninsula during that period.

Thirdly; they are to be allowed to attend Divine service according to the tenets of the Roman Catholic religion, in the same manner as British soldiers, His Majesty's subjects are.

Fourthly, they are to be fed, and clothed, and paid in the same manner as the other soldiers; and they are to be posted to companies indiscriminately, as any other recruits would be.

Fifthly; they are to receive pay from the date of their attestation, but no bounty. The captain of the company to which any of these volunteers shall be posted, will be allowed eight dollars for each to supply him with necessaries, from which must be purchased a knapsack, two pair of shoes, and two shirts. The officer commanding the company must be accountable to the volunteer for the residue of the sum after purchasing these articles in the same manner, as for his pay. The shoes may be received at the usual rate from the commissariat.

In communicating this arrangement to the several regiments, I request you to point out to the commanding officers of regiments how desirable it is that these volunteers should be treated with the utmost kindness and indulgence, and brought by degrees to the system of discipline of the army.[33]

It is unclear from this letter which regiments were authorized to enlist the Spaniards, since the units noted in the margins were not mentioned in the published *Dispatches*. However in a letter to his brother, Sir Henry Wellesley, dated 27 May 1812, he states:

the Government of Spain having signified to Mariscal de Campo Don Miguel Alava their consent that His Catholic Majesty's subjects, to the number of 5,000 might be permitted to enlist into His Majesty's army serving in the Peninsula, I enclose the copy of a circular letter I have written to the General Officers commanding divisions to permit the regiments in their several divisions to enlist His Catholic Majesty's subjects, and specifying the terms on which the enlistment is to be made.

You will observe that this letter provides for enlisting 4,100 men, which is all that I have thought it proper at present to allow of; and I have not allowed the foreign regiments in the British service to enlist any Spaniards.[34]

From these numbers it appears that Wellington authorized every British line regiment serving in his army to recruit up to 100 Spaniards. At this time, a British regiment serving on active duty usually only consisted of one battalion. There were 41 line battalions in the eight divisions of his army. Unfortunately he does not state why he forbade the foreign regiments (King's German Legion, the Brunswick-Oels, and the Chasseurs Britanniques) to recruit them.

THE RECRUITING PARTIES ARE SENT OUT

It is difficult to determine how Wellington's letter to his division commanders was received by the regiments, for few of the officers and men who left memoirs, diaries, and letters, mention the Spanish recruits or served in a recruiting party. William Surtees, of the 2nd Battalion 95th Rifles, reported that:

> I was sent in company with another officer into the mountains of Gata, not far from the city of Placentia. We were not successful, for although we obtained the names of some who promised they would follow us to La Encina, none made their appearance.[35]

William Napier, of the 43rd Regiment, who was initially optimistic about the recruitment, wrote in a letter to his wife on 3 June 1812:

> This plan of enlisting the Spaniards I think fails, at least hereabouts; the young men already have been swept away, and the people who do offer are very few and for the most part unfit. It becomes a very painful business; if we refuse them, their answer is that they must go and die, for that they had but strength sufficient to carry them to us, many not having eaten for several days before: their appearance fully justifies their words. We are too nice in our choice, and we want men taller than they grow in the country; for my part, I would take women sooner than none, as I think the time is too short to admit of being fastidious.[36]

Edward Costello, of the 1st Battalion 95th Rifles, was a bit more successful:

> Our regiments, by constant collision with the French, were getting exceedingly thinned, and recruits from England came but very slowly, until we found it necessary at last to incorporate some of the Spaniards; for this purpose several non-commissioned officers and men were sent into the adjacent villages recruiting. In the course of a short time, and to our surprise, we were joined by a sufficient number of Spaniards to give ten or twelve men to each company in the battalion. But the mystery was soon unravelled, and by the recruits themselves, who on joining gave us to understand, by a significant twist of the neck, and a 'Carajo' (much like the breaking of one), that they had but three alternatives to choose from, to enter either the

British, or Don Julian's service, or be hanged! The despotic sway of Sanchez, and his threat in the bargain, so disjointed their inclination for the Guerrillas that they hastily fled their native 'woods' and 'threshold' for fear of really finding themselves noosed up to them and gladly joined the British regiments.[37]

By early July 1812, Wellington was ready to admit defeat in the project and wrote to the Duke of York's military secretary, Colonel Henry Torrens, on 7 July:

> The fact is, that I adopted it because any other that was preferred might be adopted in lieu of it; and I suspected what has turned out to be the case, that we should get but few or no recruits. We have not got enough in the whole army to form one company; and I am sorry to add that some have deserted.[38]

Wellington may have been premature in his pessimism. George Hennell, of the 43rd Regiment, wrote home on 19 September 1812, that his regiment had twelve Spaniards.[39] By the end of the year the 95th Rifles had recruited forty-six Spaniards into its 1st Battalion, none into its 2nd Battalion (William Surtees' unit), and nine into the 3rd Battalion. The Spanish recruits for the 1st Battalion comprised 34 per cent of all replacements for the battalion in 1812! Things went better in 1813 for the Rifles.

Willoughby Verner, in his *History of the Rifle Brigade* reported that when the campaign began in May, 1813 the Regiment had '134 recruits joined (mostly Spaniards).' Edward Costello reported that by 1814, sixteen Spaniards had served in his company, but only five had survived the war.[40]

THEIR PERFORMANCE AS SOLDIERS

Very few eyewitness reports survive describing the performance of these Spanish soldiers. It must have been fairly good, since many were promoted to corporal. Sir Harry Smith, 1st Battalion 95th Rifles, gave them the following glowing praise:

> We had also ten men a Company in our British Regiments, Spaniards, many of them the most daring of sharpshooters in our corps, who nobly regained the distinction attached to the name of Spanish infantry of Charles V's time. I never saw better, more orderly, perfectly sober soldiers in my life, and as vedettes the old German Hussar did not exceed them.[41]

Sergeant Edward Costello, 1st Battalion 95th Rifles, left the following description of one of the Spaniards in his company:

> we had several Spaniards in our regiment. These men were generally brave; but one in particular, named Blanco, was one of the most skilful and daring skirmishers we had in the battalion. His great courage, however, was sullied by a love of cruelty towards the French, whom he detested, and never named but with the most ferocious expressions. In every affair we had since the

advance from Portugal he was always in the front; and the only wonder is how he managed to escape the enemy's shot, but his singular activity and intelligence frequently saved him. His hatred to the French was, I believe, occasioned by his father and brother, who were peasants, having been murdered by a French foraging party. On this day he gave many awful proofs of this feeling by mercilessly stabbing and mangling the wounded French he came up to. In this massacre he was however, stopped by a veteran of our regiment, who, although suffering from a severe wound in the face, was so exasperated at the Spaniard's cruelty, that he knocked him down with a blow from the butt of his rifle. It was only by force we could prevent the Spaniard from stabbing him on the spot.[42]

THE SPANIARDS ARE DISCHARGED

One of their conditions of service was that once the war in the Peninsula was over, all Spanish soldiers serving within British regiments would be discharged and not be required to serve elsewhere. There is some question on whether this occurred in late 1813 when the Allied forces moved into France, or in 1814 after peace was declared and the British army departed for the British Isles or other locations. Whatever the date, the Spaniards were released and in at least the 95th Rifles, their parting was not a happy one for either side. Once again Sergeant Costello records what happened:

> In a few days [31 May 1814] we received an order to proceed to Bordeaux, to embark for England. The delightful emotions of pleasure this generally induced throughout our men, after all their hardships and sufferings, may be better imagined than described. The second day's march we stopped at a village [Bazas, 11 June], the name of which I forget, where we had to part from our allies, the Spanish and Portuguese. Much, and even deep feelings of regret, were particularly felt by the men of our battalion on parting from the Spaniards, who had been for so long a period incorporated in our ranks. They had been distinguished for their gallantry, and although sixteen had been drafted into our company, but five had survived to bid us farewell. Poor fellows, they had grown attached to the battalion, and express much grief on leaving! Even Blanco, the sanguinary Blanco, actually shed tears.[43]

So closed a little-known story of the Napoleonic Wars. The number of Spaniards who served in the British Army in the Peninsula will probably never be known. William Napier, in his *History of the War in the Peninsula* states that no more than 300 served and these primarily in the Light Division. All evidence supports his claim. Those who served, were noted by their British counterparts for their steadiness, courage, and devotion to duty. Not bad traits in any soldier!

The Provisional Battalions

'One soldier who has served one or two campaigns will render more service than two recently sent from England.'[44]

The normal practice for the British army in the Peninsula was to send home those regiments that could not maintain their strength with drafts from home to recruit and bring them up to strength. If a regiment had only one battalion serving in country, when it fell below strength, it would be replaced in country by a battalion from the same regiment from home. Wellington disliked this system for it often took experienced and campaign hardened soldiers away and replaced them with callow troops that could not withstand the rigours of active campaigning. If a regiment had two battalions serving in the theatre and they were under strength, those soldiers who were still fit for duty would be transferred from the 2nd Battalion to the 1st Battalion to bring it up to strength. The officers and non-commissioned officers of the 2nd Battalion would then return to the British Isles to recruit. Although this was better than replacing weak battalions with fully manned units from home, Wellington was opposed to this practice because it too deprived him of many seasoned campaigners. He understood the need to send home officers and NCOs to recruit, but rather than letting whole units return to Great Britain, he preferred to send home only small cadres, keeping those who were not needed for recruiting, in country.

If Wellington had followed past practices, in June 1811 he would have sent the remnants of the 3rd, 29th, 2/31st, 57th, and 2/66th Regiments back to England to recruit up to strength. These regiments took heavy casualties the month before at Albuera and were severely under strength. Instead he took the radical step of forming them into an ad hoc unit called the 1st Provisional Battalion. It was to be commanded by Lieutenant Colonel John Colborne of the 2/66th Regiment. Each regiment was to organize those soldiers fit for duty into two companies and turn them over to Colonel Colborne for duty in the 1st Provisional Battalion. Colonel Colborne was responsible for ensuring the appropriate number of officers and non-commissioned officers were assigned to each company; and that he had a regimental staff to support him. Those officers and NCOs who were in excess of the needs of the provisional battalion, with those soldiers who were unfit for duty, were ordered to Elvas, where they would begin reforming and re-equipping their regiments. The regimental colours were also sent to Elvas, and were left in charge of the senior regimental officer there. The 1st Provisional Battalion was assigned to Major General Lumley's brigade in the 2nd Division.[45] Lieutenant Colonel Colborne, however, did not command for long. On 11 July 1811, he exchanged into the 1/52nd Foot.

The units in the 1st Provisional Battalion served together until 7 August 1811, when the 1/3rd Foot and the 1/57th received enough replacements to become separate battalions again. The three remaining battalions (29th, 2/31st, and 2/66th) had enough troops return from the hospitals for the 29th and 2/66th to form three companies, while the 2/31st was formed into four companies.[46] The light company was from the 2/31st Foot.[47] The 1st Provisional Battalion was brigaded with the

1/3rd Foot and the 1/57th Foot in a new brigade that would be commanded by Colonel Inglis of the 57th Regiment. (Colonel Inglis was severely wounded at Albuera and did not take command of a brigade until well into 1813.) This brigade remained in the 2nd Division and Colonel Byng took command of it on 21 September 1811.[48] On 3 October 1811, the companies from the 29th Foot were ordered back to Great Britain to recruit.[49] Lieutenant Colonel Alexander Leith, the senior officer in the 31st Regiment, would command the battalion until it returned to England in 1814.

In late 1812, Wellington decided to form three more provisional battalions from six severely under strength battalions – the 2nd, 2/24th, 2/30th, 2/44th, 2/53rd, and the 2/58th. These battalions were chosen, not only because of how few men they had, but because they had few men available as replacements. In November 1812, the 2/30th had 552 men in the Peninsula, of which 214 were fit for duty, while 338 were listed as sick. The 2/44th had 149 effective and 250 sick out of 399 total men. Neither regiment had many troops in their home depot available for deployment. The 2/44th had none, while the 2/30th had only 16 men. Each of the battalions had to provide four companies to the new provisional battalions. These companies had to be of equal strength and would contain all able-bodied privates remaining with the regiment, plus the respective company officers and NCOs. The officers and NCOs of the remaining six companies would return to Great Britain to recruit up to strength. The commanding officers and their staffs from the 2/24th, 2/30th, and the 2/53rd Regiments would remain to command the new battalions.

The 2nd Provisional Battalion consisted of the eight companies of the 2nd and the 2/53rd Regiment and was commanded by Lieutenant Colonel George R. Bingham of the 53rd Regiment, who had been severely wounded at Salamanca. He was not happy about not being allowed to return to Great Britain and stated so in a letter to his mother on 12 December 1812:

> Since I last wrote Lord Wellington has decided on a measure which I am sorry to say puts my return to England out of the question. So we must look forward to peace or some other equally fortunate event to restore me to my home, which at all times and under all circumstances I cannot help looking forward to as the end of my labours. The measure alluded to is this; he has ordered all the effective men in this country of the 2nd and 53rd Regiments to be drafted into four companies of each corps; the remaining six companies of each, comprising only officers and non-commissioned officers to return to England; these eight effective companies to be formed into a battalion, and removed into the 4th Division. To be again under the command of Cole is some qualification for the disappointment I feel at having my return delayed; from which delay I see no advantage likely to arise to myself. Lieutenant colonels rise by gradation, and those people of that rank who are enjoying themselves at home, get rank equally with those who are fagging here. As for the rewards, they go no further than Lord Wellington. The end of our labour will be making him a duke; but as to any reward, that is quite out of the question.[50]

The eight companies from the 2/24th and the 2/58th Regiments formed the 3rd Provisional Battalion. Lieutenant Colonel William Kelly of the 24th Regiment commanded it.[51] The 4th Provisional Regiment had the eight companies of the 2/30th and the 2/44th Regiments and was commanded by Lieutenant Colonel Alexander Hamilton of the 30th Regiment.[52]

The 2nd Provisional Battalion was assigned to Anson's brigade of the 4th Division, while the 3rd Provisional Battalion went to Barnes' brigade in the 7th Division. The 4th Provisional Battalion became part of Walker's brigade in the 5th Division.[53] The 4th Provisional Battalion was the weakest of the four battalions. On 26 April 1813 it had only 403 rank and file assigned. The 2/59th Foot was assigned to Walker's brigade and on 10 May 1813, the two regiments of the 4th Provisional Battalion were ordered home.[54]

Wellington's decision was not well received by his superiors in Great Britain. On 13 January 1813, His Royal Highness, the Duke of York, wrote to him expressing his concerns. He felt the forming of the provisional battalions was not good for the army on the whole. He did however, stop short of ordering Wellington to send the battalions home. He had made his wishes on the matter known and being the Commander-in-Chief of the Army, had reasonable expectations that Wellington would comply with them. Instead Wellington refused to budge and stated that if His Royal Highness wanted these troops to come home, he would have to give him an order to do so. Otherwise, they were staying put. Wellington believed that his decision was correct for his army and that the army 'in America, the Mediterranean, or at home, are not my concern, and cannot, nor ought not, to enter into my consideration in any case; and when anything is left to my discretion, that discretion must be guided by my view of what is best for the services here.'[55]

In the same letter, Wellington laid out his justification for keeping the troops. It would be the same justification he would use over the next two years to ignore higher headquarters on the matter:

> I am of opinion, from long experience, that it is better for the service here to have one soldier or officer, whether of cavalry or infantry, who has served one or two campaigns, than it is to have two or even three who have not. Not only the new soldiers can perform no service, but by filling the hospital they are a burthen to us. For this reason, I am so unwilling to part with the men whom I have formed into the provisional regiments; and I never will part with them as long as it is left to my discretion.[56]

In September 1813, Wellington considered forming a 5th provisional battalion by combining the 51st and 68th Regiments. Both units had taken heavy casualties among the enlisted men, yet the regiments had a full quota of officers. He was concerned because of the reduced numbers of men, the regimental officers were beginning to take abnormally high casualties. In one recent action the 51st Regiment had 12 officers either killed or wounded, while the number of enlisted casualties were less than 100. He also considered sending them home. In the end, he kept them with the army as separate regiments.[57]

The matter of the provisional battalions was still not resolved. The Duke of York wanted the battalions sent home. Rather than depriving Wellington of the veterans, he gave permission for Wellington to ask for volunteers from the provisional battalions to be disbanded to serve in a regiment of Wellington's choosing.[58] Wellington apparently ignored this suggestion. Not only did he refuse to send the battalions back to England, he wrote to Earl Bathurst requesting that he approach the Duke of York about setting up a new system for replacements in the army. Wellington proposed that whenever a regiment, that did not have a sister battalion in the British Isles, fall below 350 enlisted soldiers fit for duty, that they be formed into four companies, while the officers and NCOs of the other six companies be sent home to recruit. The four companies would be formed into a provisional battalion with the companies from another under strength regiment until the six companies returned with the replacements. Nothing ever came of this proposal however.[59] Earl Bathurst refused to submit his proposal to the Duke of York until he had more information on the affected battalions. He also reminded Wellington that he still had the Duke of York's permission to place volunteers from the provisional battalions into other battalions.[60]

In January 1814, the Duke of York wrote to Wellington asking for information on the strength of his different infantry battalions. Once again he suggested that Wellington disband the provisional battalions, allowing the soldiers in those battalions to volunteer into a regiment of Wellington's choosing. Those who did not volunteer would be returned to their home depots. The Duke of York did give Wellington a way out, when he wrote 'you will, at all events, be pleased to break up the provisional battalions which they form, whenever you can do it without inconvenience to your present operations . . .'[61] This was all Wellington needed. Until the war was over three months later, there would never be a convenient time for him to disband the provisional battalions!

Wellington knew that he would need hardened veterans to beat the French. He recognized the value of his provisional battalions and did everything possible to keep the men with his army. On 11 August 1813, Wellington wrote to Earl Bathurst 'I assure you that some of the best battalions of the army are the provisional battalions. I have lately seen two of them engaged, viz., that formed of the 2nd Battalions of the 24th and 58th regiments; and that formed of the Queen's and 2nd battalion 53rd regiments; it is impossible for any troops to behave better.'[62] There was no way he would ever voluntarily send those troops back to Great Britain. He repeatedly ignored the wishes of not only his superiors on the matter, but also those of the Duke of York. Nothing short of a direct order would have got him to disband the provisional battalions. His obstinacy paid off. He was never ordered to send them home and they were with him when the war ended in April 1814.

The Russians

In February 1813, Wellington received at his headquarters in Freneda, Portugal, Mr. C.A. Mackenzie, who conveyed a message to him from Vice-Admiral Alexis Greig, the son of a Scottish *émigré* serving in the Russian Navy. Greig, who was part of the Russian diplomatic mission conducting negotiations with the Ottoman Porte, had a personal message from the Tsar for Wellington. The Tsar was offering

Russian troops for service under Wellington, as long as the British paid their expenses. Wellington was a bit surprised by the offer, considering the extent of Russian casualties from the previous year. He felt that they could be better used under their own commanders in central Europe. Mackenzie assured Wellington the Tsar believed that he had more troops than he could effectively employ there.

Because of the political ramifications, Wellington did not feel he could accept the offer without the approval of the British government. On 14 February he wrote to Earl Bathurst that he would like to have 15,000 Russian troops under his command and:

> There can be no doubt that this number of troops (of Russians particularly) would have the most decisive effect on the next campaign. Even if 1000 or 2000 only were sent, it would show the power of the Russian empire; the inclination of the Emperor towards the cause of the nations of the Peninsula; and the measure would have the best effects, as well on the enemy and his few partisans in these countries, as on all the good patriots.[63]

Wellington placed some conditions on his willingness to accept the Russian troops:

1. That he would be accepted into the Russian Army as a general officer, senior to the Russian general who would actually command the troops.

2. All Russian troops would be placed under his command.

3. The Russian commander would send directly to him 'all reports, &c. regarding them and their operations.'[64]

4. That the Spanish and Portuguese governments be willing to accept the troops.[65]

The proposed Russian forces would come from the army of Admiral Tchichagoff, which was deployed along the Danube.[66] Not surprisingly, the Portuguese government accepted the Russian offer enthusiastically by 21 February.[67] However, the Spanish Cortes was reluctant to accept more foreign troops on their soil.[68]

On 4 March 1813, Mackenzie wrote to Wellington again. The Russian Ambassador had told him that the Tsar had withdrawn his offer of providing troops from Admiral Tchichagoff's army, because:

> owing to the extraordinary circumstances which led to the recall and future employment of that army, the prior intentions of His Imperial Majesty the Emperor of Russia have been entirely altered, and it is supposed that the exertions of the Russian government in the north of Europe will fully provide for all the disposable forces.[69]

Although the realities of the war in Central Europe prevented the deployment of Russian troops to the Peninsula, even if they were sent, they probably would have had little impact on the situation there in 1813. The troops would then have to be mobilized and transported to the Peninsula, where they would be integrated into the Allied army. If the war had continued for several more years, these troops might have seen service; however, events were proceeding at a rapid pace and Napoleon abdicated in April 1814.

The Militia

On 4 November 1813, a bill was introduced into Parliament to permit militia regiments to volunteer to serve in the war in Europe. The government hoped to raise 30,000 recruits and to be able to send whole regiments. Their expectations were not met, with fewer than 8,000 men volunteering from the militia.[70] This lack of enthusiasm among the men forced them to put together three provisional militia battalions. The 1st Provisional Militia Battalion with a strength of 970 men was commanded by the Lieutenant Colonel Commandant Richard Grenville 2nd Marquis of Buckingham and Lieutenant Colonel William Young as his second-in-command. Both Buckingham and Young came from the Buckinghamshire Militia. The battalion's majors were two regular army captains promoted to permanent majors and the officers drawn from Buckinghamshire, 1st & 2nd Royal Surrey, Cambridgeshire, Northamptonshire and Worcestershire Militia.[71]

Buckingham was described by one contemporary as being 'enormously fat, and not unlike the pictures which are represented of Falstaff.'[72] He was the nephew of Lord Grenville, Pitt's Foreign Secretary and Prime Minister from 1806–7 and a close friend of Lord Wellesley. His father, the 1st Marquis of Buckingham, was the Lord Lieutenant of Ireland when Arthur Wellesley was appointed one of his aides-de-camp.

Lieutenant Colonel Edward Bayley commanded the 925 men of the 2nd Provisional Militia Battalion and Lieutenant Colonel William F. Hulse was his second-in-command. Bayley was from the West Middlesex Militia while Hulse was from Leicestershire's. Like the 1st Battalion, the two battalion majors were regular army captains promoted to permanent major. The officers were mostly from the West Middlesex, Leicestershire, Wiltshire, Sussex and East Suffolk Militias.[73]

The 3rd Provisional Militia Battalion had 881 men[74] and was commanded by Colonel Watkin Wynne – who was 'an active politician and member of the Cabinet George Canning thought him the "worst man of business" he had ever come across.'[75] His second-in-command was Lieutenant Colonel John Berington. Wynne was with the Denbighshire Militia, while Berington was from the Herefordshire Militia. One of the battalion majors was a regular army captain promoted to permanent major, while the other was a militia major from the 2nd West York Militia. The officers were primarily drawn from the 2nd West York, Derbyshire, Westmorland, Herefordshire and Denbighshire Militias.[76]

The appointments to lieutenant colonel for all the commanders and their seconds-in-command were temporary ranks in the army, dated 22 January 1814. When the idea was first proposed to Wellington in September,[77] he was not too enthusiastic about it. Although he welcomed the opportunity for fresh troops, Wellington felt that it would be better to draft the volunteers into existing line regiments to bring them up to strength. Furthermore, he argued that it was far more expensive to bring the militia regiments on active duty than it would be to incorporate the soldiers into existing regiments. He also predicted, correctly, that they would not make it to the army before March or April.[78]

Wellington saw the proposal as an attempt to force him to return the veteran provisional battalions back to Great Britain and replace them with untrained militia battalions, of which he had a low opinion. In a letter to Earl Bathurst on 24 September 1813, he wrote candidly about the militia:

> I found that, however, to be so entirely divested of interior economy, and real discipline and subordination, that, however well the soldiers may be disciplined, as far as regards their exercise and movements, I should very much doubt that a large militia army would be very useful in the field for more than a momentary exertion. My notion of them is, that the officers have all the faults of those of the line to an aggravated degree, and some peculiarly their own.[79]

By the end of January the three militia battalions were to have been recruited up to strength. Things apparently did not go smoothly. Colonel Torrens, the military secretary to the Commander-in-Chief, wrote to Wellington that:

> I hope that when the three provisional battalions of militia now forming reach you, they will fight well; but at present they are more troublesome than the whole army put together.[80]

By early March, the battalions were ready and despite Wellington's objections, they were placed in the same brigade, under the command of Lord Buckingham. They boarded their transports on 10 and 11 March, and arrived in Bordeaux on 12 April, the day after the city received word that Napoleon had capitulated. Wellington appeared to accept the inevitable and wrote Buckingham a welcoming letter on 27 April: 'I have long waited for the arrival of the brigade of troops to which you belong . . .'[81]

An officer in the 1st Guards left us the following description of their service:

> they arrived 'a day after the fair', for the treaty of peace had been signed by the Allied sovereigns; so as the King of France with forty thousand men, 'Marched up a hill, and then marched down again . . .'.

Before they re-embarked for their native land, however, they took good care to impress upon the inhabitants of Bordeaux their value as soldiers, by parading their battalions with all the pomp and circumstance of war, both in the morning and at noon. Those for whose benefit this spectacle was intended never failed attending these military parades; not with the idea of gaining any hints as to evolutions, &c., but to gaze on the commanding officers, whom they denominated, 'Les boeufs-gras anglais'. The militia regiments appeared but a sorry sight in comparison with British veterans who had marched through Portugal and Spain, fighting a hundred battles, and afterwards remained some time at Bordeaux, where they gained the respect of the inhabitants by their orderly conduct and manly bearing. Unfortunately, too, our militiamen did not conduct themselves in a becoming manner; for, delighted at the cheapness of the wine and brandy, and happening to be officered by men incapable of looking after them properly, when off duty they were constantly tipsy, and getting into all sorts of scrapes and broils with the inhabitants; so much so, that their conduct was reported to the Commander-in-Chief, who ordered them home without delay.'[82]

The Militia Brigade departed France on 6 June 1814 and arrived back in Great Britain on 16 June. Fortunately for the British army, Wellington was able to keep his Provisional Battalions to the end of the war even after the militia was sent out. The arrival of the militia brigade appeared to have little or no impact on the war, other than providing amusement for the veterans who observed them.

Conclusion

Above all else, Wellington was a pragmatist and knew that he had to have trained, seasoned troops to defeat the French. When possible he tried to uphold the regimental system. However, by 1812 the needs of his army outweighed the regimental traditions. Although he usually acquiesced with the wishes of the Horse Guards, Wellington opposed any measures that impacted on the strength of his army. It appears that he took the approach that it was easier to gain forgiveness than permission when it came to fulfilling his manpower requirements. He was known to use the lengthy time it took to correspond with the British government to provide them with a *fait accompli* when their instructions conflicted with his needs. As demonstrated with the provisional battalions, he outright refused to take suggestions to return them home, while stating numerous times, he would only send them back if he was ordered to do so. Wellington was able to do this because he always won. His solutions to his manpower problems – whether forming provisional units, enlisting foreigners into British regiments, etc. – were often unpopular and put him at odds with his superiors in the Horse Guards. However they were effective. The British army that invaded France in late 1813 was filled with tough veterans who knew both how to fight and how to win.

NOTES

1 Fortescue, John, *A History of the British Army*, London, MacMillan & Co., 1920, vol. vii, p. 56.
2 Oman, Charles, *A History of the Peninsular War*, New York, AMS Press, 1980, vol. ii, p. 642.
3 Ibid, vol. iii, pp. 647 and 649, vol. v, p. 598.
4 Fortescue, John, *The County Lieutenancies and the Army 1803–1814*, London, MacMillan, 1909, p. 269.
5 Memorandum in Wellington's handwriting printed with letter from Duke of York to Wellington, dated 10 January 1814, *Supplementary Despatches, Correspondance, and Memorandum of Field Marshal Arthur Duke of Wellington*, London, John Murray, 1861, vol. viii, pp. 495–98.
6 *County Lieutenancies*, p. 292.
7 Napier, William, *History of the war in the Peninsula and in the south of France from A.D. 1807 to A.D. 1814*, vol. ii, London, Constable, 1995, p. 492.
8 Haythornthwaite, Philip J., 'The Battalions of Detachments in 1809' *Empires, Eagles, and Lions*, #69, 15 January 1983, p. 6.

9   Ibid, p. 6.
10 Gibbs, Peter and David Watkins (Editors), *Spanish Adventures*, Bridgnorth, First Empire, 1995, p. 16.
11 Verner, Willoughby, *The History and Campaigns of the Rifle Brigade: 1800–1813*, London, Buckland and Brown, 1995, vol. ii, p. 52.
12 Morley, Stephen, *Memoirs of a Sergeant of the 5th Regiment of Foot, containing an Account of His Service, in Hanover, South America, and the Peninsula*, Cambridge, Ken Trotman, 1999, p. 87.
13 Verner, vol. ii, p. 53.
14 Gibbs, Peter and David Watkins (Editors), 'Daniel Nicol's with the First Battalion of Detachments', *Spanish Adventures*, Bridgnorth, First Empire Publishing, 1996, pp. 16–17.
15 Verner, vol. ii, p. 55.
16 General Orders, dated 12 May 1809.
17 Wood, George, *The Subaltern Officer*, Cambridge, Ken Trotman, 1986, pp. 84–6.
18 Hay, Andrew Leith, *A Narrative of the Peninsular War*, London, John Hearse, 1850, p. 104.
19 Gibbs, p. 20.
20 Hamilton, Anthony, *Hamilton's Campaign with Moore and Wellington during the Peninsular War*, Staplehurst, Spellmount, 1998, p. 74.
21 Leslie, 'Journal of the Peninsular War of Colonel Leslie of Balquain' quoted in Oman, Charles, *A History of the Peninsular War*, New York, AMS Press, 1980, vol. ii, p. 518.
22 Gibbs, p. 21.
23 Ibid, p. 22.
24 Ibid, p. 22.
25 Oman, vol. ii, p. 649.
26 Wood, pp. 89–90.
27 Wood, p. 113.
28 Fortescue, vol. viii, p. 234.
29 Gibbs, p. 16.
30 Wood, p. 112.
31 Oman, vol. v, pp. 588, 594–95.
32 Wellington to Henry Wellesley dated 8 November 1811 in *Wellington's Dispatches* (New Edition), London, John Murray, 1838, vol. viii, p. 384.
33 Ibid, vol. ix, pp. 155–56.
34 Ibid, vol. ix, p. 179.
35 Surtees, William, *Twenty-Five Years in the Rifle Brigade*, London, Greenhill Books, 1996, p. 156.
36 Bruce, H.A., *Life of General Sir William Napier*, vol. i, London, John Murray, 1864, pp. 96–7.
37 Costello, Edward, *The Peninsular and Waterloo Campaigns*, Hamden, Archon Books, 1968, p. 117.
38 *WD* (New Edition) vol. ix, pp. 273–74.
39 Glover, Michael (Editor), *A Gentleman Volunteer: The Letters of George Hennell from the Peninsular War, 1812–13*, London, Heinemann, 1979, p. 50.
40 Costello, p. 149.
41 Smith, G.C. Moore (Editor), *The Autobiography of Sir Harry Smith: 1787–1819*, London, John Murray, 1910, p. 185.
42 Costello, pp. 125–6.
43 Ibid, p. 149.
44 Letter from Wellington to Earl Bathurst, dated 27 January 1813, *WD* (New Edition) vol. x, p. 51.
45 General Orders, dated 6 June 1811.
46 General Orders, dated 7 August 1811.
47 L'Estrange, George B., *Recollections of Sir George B. L'Estrange*, London, Sapson, Low, Marston, Low, & Searle, no date, pp. 160–61.
48 General Orders, 21 September 1811.
49 General Orders, 3 October 1811.
50 Glover, Gareth, *Wellington's Lieutenants Napoleon's Gaoler: the Peninsula Letters & St Helena Diaries of Sir George Ridout Bingham*, Barnsley, Pen and Sword, 2005, pp. 168–169.
51 Hall, John A., *A History of the Peninsular War: the Biographical Dictionary of British Officers Killed and Wounded, 1808–1814*, vol. viii, London, Greenhill Books, 1998, pp. 56 and 322.

52 General Orders, 6 December 1812.
53 Ibid.
54 Oman, Charles, *Wellington's Army, 1809–1814*, London, Greenhill Books, 1993, p. 369.
55 Letter from Wellington to Colonel Torrens, dated 2 February 1813, *WD* (New Edition) vol. x, p. 77.
56 Ibid, p. 77.
57 Letter from Wellington to Earl Bathurst, dated 3 September 1813, *WD* (New Edition) vol. xi, p. 77.
58 Letter from Earl Bathurst to Wellington, dated 10 September 1813, *WSD* vol. viii, p. 247.
59 *WD* (New Edition) vol. xi, p. 180.
60 Letter from Earl Bathurst to Wellington, dated 27 October 1813, *WSD* vol. viii, p. 323.
61 Letter from Duke of York to Wellington, dated 10 January 1814, *WSD* vol. viii, pp. 495–498.
62 *WD* (New Edition) vol. x, p. 629.
63 *WD* (New Edition) vol. x, p. 118.
64 Ibid. p. 119.
65 Ibid. p. 120.
66 Letter from Mackenzie to Wellington, dated 4 March 1813, *WSD* vol. viii, pp. 564–65.
67 Letter from Charles Stuart to Wellington, dated 21 February 1813 in *WSD*, vol. vii, p. 558.
68 Letter from Henry Wellesley to Wellington, dated 5 March 1813 in *WSD* vol. vii, pp. 570–3.
69 *WSD*, vol. vii, pp. 564–65.
70 Letter from Colonel Torrens to Wellington, dated 5 January 1814, *WSD* vol. viii, p. 82.
71 Davis, John, *Historical Records of the Second Royal Surrey, or Eleventh Regiment of Militia, with Introductory Chapters*, London, Marcus Ward & Co., London, 1877, pp. 188–200.
72 Hibbert, Christopher, *Captain Gronow: His Reminiscences of Regency and Victorian Life: 1810–60*, London, Kyle Cathie Limited, 1991, p. 69.
73 Davis, pp. 188–200.
74 *County Lieutenancies*, p. 280.
75 Hibbert, p. 69.
76 Davis, pp. 188–200.
77 Letter from Earl Bathurst to Wellington, dated 11 Sept 1813, *WSD* vol. viii, p. 249.
78 Letter from Wellington to Earl Bathurst, dated 24 September 1813, *WD*, vol. xi p. 140.
79 Ibid, p. 140.
80 Letter dated 26 January 1814, *WSD* vol. viii, p. 544.
81 Letter from Wellington to Lord Buckingham, dated 27 April 1814, *WSD* vol. viii.
82 Hibbert, pp. 69–70.

Chapter Seven

British Bridging Operations in the Peninsula

ROBERT BURNHAM

Several great rivers mark the Iberian Peninsula: the Tagus, the Ebro, the Duero (in Spain) or the Douro (in Portugal), the Guadiana, and Guadalquivir. These rivers cross the length of both countries and create serious obstacles for an army. They are old rivers and run in channels that are well below their banks. In some cases they flow through steep, rocky canyons, while in others they meander through the wide plains. During the rainy season in the winter and spring, they are fast moving, dangerous rivers. During the dry summers, they could dry up to the size of a gentle stream. In the Napoleonic Era, bridges were few – along the Tagus River in Spain there were only four – and the loss of one could have a major impact on the movements of an army. The destruction of bridges became a common occurrence and the army that could build, maintain, and protect bridges, would have a distinct advantage over its enemy.

During the Peninsular War, nowhere was this truer than with Wellington's army. The British built many bridges that allowed Wellington to move his troops much quicker than the French commanders. Some were built for tactical reasons and quickly dismantled, while others were used at the strategic level – vital to keeping open lines of communication. Yet until late in the war, Wellington had no pontoon train! Instead he relied on a small corps of British officers to build the bridges when he needed them. These officers displayed a talent for building bridges, overcoming numerous obstacles – including harsh terrain, raging rivers, bad weather, lack of bridging material, and even the enemy – to repair, construct, and maintain bridges that were vital to Wellington's plans. Their ability to design and build bridges quickly, using a variety of material and methods, was often revolutionary and bordered on pure genius. In one case when no bridging material was available when the army needed to cross the Douro River, between Tordesillas and Toro, the engineers used:

> the spring waggons of the army. The bottom of the river was hard and even; the average depth from 3 to 4 feet. The waggons were placed longitudinally at distances suited to the lengths of the planks that had been collected for flooring, which were laid from waggon to waggon, the tail and front boards being taken out.[1]

On another occasion, Colonel William De Lancey of Waterloo fame, built a similar bridge using local ox carts. They were laid end-to-end, with the shaft of one resting on the bed of the other.[2]

Quite often the officers would be tasked to repair an existing bridge that had been heavily damaged by one army or the other. Occasionally the tasks would be seemingly impossible. When repairing a major bridge across the Agueda River near Ciudad Rodrigo, they had to cover a gap that was of over 100 feet wide. This breach was a major problem because it was too large to bridge using timber found in the area. Most trees were less than 60 feet long. They solved the problem with typical ingenuity. Six spars were used to span the gap. Three were placed on each side of the river and frames were built with platforms on each end. Two rollers, one larger in diameter than the other, were placed under the beams and the platforms were weighed down with heavy stones and sandbags. The two frames were rolled forward until they met in the centre, where they tied together. The two platforms were then planked over and the problem was solved.[3]

These officers kept detailed notes on what they did and discussed their ideas among themselves. What they learned from doing, they passed back to England so it could be taught at the Royal Staff College. The students at the College studied their methods and were well prepared when they went on active service in the Peninsula. Some of their memoranda still exist – for example the following was written by a member of the Royal Staff Corps on methods used during the Peninsular War to build pontoons from locally acquired materials:

> In countries where timber is plenty, a pontoon or ferry boat may quickly be made thus. Fell seven trees of about 16 inches diameter and cut off 18 feet length from each. Lay five of these on any level spot, parallel to each other, at 3 feet asunder, and reduce their upper surfaces to a level. Plank them throughout. If nails are not at hand, trundles or tree-nails (wooden pins) will answer. If planks cannot be had, ready-made, set sawyers to cut up the first trees that can be felled. If tow or oakum are not to be found, rushes, or even moss, with tallow and beeswax, will answer for immediate use. As soon as the platform is caulked, turn it over, and bolt down the two remaining trees over the ends of those forming the platform. Plank the sides and ends of the vessel, taking care the bottom planks overlay the sides; otherwise the nails would be driven into the ends of the planks forming the bottom, on two sides of the vessel, and would not hold. The flat thus formed would be about 18 feet square, and about 34 inches deep.[4]

Considerations for Placing a Bridge

To comprehend their accomplishments, one must have a basic understanding of the complexity of combat bridge-building. A general could not just tell his engineers that he wanted a bridge to be built at a certain place and by a certain time. There were too many factors that had to be considered when choosing a site for building a bridge. Ignoring these factors could result in failure at a critical time in an operation.[5] First, and foremost was the enemy. Bridge construction, no matter how carefully planned, was time-consuming and dangerous. Building it under enemy fire made a difficult task almost impossible! Friendly forces needed to control both sides of the river. Ideally the bridges would be built where the enemy was not.

The others factors were topographical, but were as important as the location of the enemy:

1.   The approach to and from the bridging site was as critical as the actual bridge. Were there good roads on both sides of the river? Would these roads support heavy vehicles, such as artillery pieces? Would they stand up to the passage of thousands of troops and horses or would they quickly deteriorate into quagmires if it rains?

2.   How high were the riverbanks? If they were too high, waggons and other vehicles would have difficulty getting down and then back up. If they were too low, a rise in the depth of the water could flood the approaches to the bridge. What were the conditions of the riverbanks? Would they be strong enough to support the passage of the troops? If the soil was too boggy or sandy, an approach ramp might have to be built, costing time, labour, and material. If a pontoon bridge was being used, was there a spot to anchor the bridge to the banks?

3.   What was the width of the river? The wider the river, the more material would be needed. But narrow rivers are often swifter and thus created a different set of problems.

      What was the current of the river? If it was too fast, pontoons would have trouble staying anchored in place. Additionally, although all rivers carried debris, such as tree trunks, wood, and animal carcasses, a fast running river would cause greater danger, due to the momentum and speed of the debris, and the shorter response time of the bridging team to get it safely out of the way.

4.   What was the rise and fall of the river water? Was it affected by tides? Heavy rains could cause the river to rise significantly. If the bridge was fixed in place, this could cause the roadway to be flooded or the bridge to be washed out or swept away. (This was a common problem.) Additionally, a drop in the water could affect the ramps from the banks to the bridge itself.

5.   Another key element was the river bottom. Was it too deep for the bridge pilings? Was the bottom stable enough to support the piles or would shifting sands cause problems? Would it hold an anchor?

6.   The final factor, which was key, was the availability of building materials. During the Peninsular War, most combat bridges were made of locally procured materials. Even late in the war, when pontoons were available, additional material for building roadways and ramps and maintaining the bridge after it was built, was always needed. Yet the ability or inability to procure these materials was often the difference between success and failure.

Logistical and Materials Problems

The Iberian Peninsula presented some unique challenges to bridge-builders, chief among them was the lack of proper building materials. Compared to Central Europe, Spain and Portugal were sparsely populated, and except for the cities, lacked the facilities for the manufacture of the hardware and miscellaneous items necessary for the construction and maintenance of the bridges. All armies had to bring their own equipment and forge or be prepared to improvise with whatever was available.

General Jean Baptiste Eblé, who saved the *Grande Armée* by building the bridge across the Berezina during the 1812 Russian Campaign, in a comment to one of Marshal Masséna's aides-de-camp about the availability of bridging material in Portugal in 1810, stated that he 'lack everything – materials, workers, tools, money, and resources of every kind.' The aide went on to note the city had been stripped so bare by the British that there was no coal, usable wood, rope and other essentials such as tar and oakum. The French improvised where they could, making their own axes and anchors out of axles, but they could do little.[6]

The chief item that was usually lacking, however, was a ready supply of lumber. Wood was in such short supply, that often firewood was not available to the soldiers to cook their meals.[7] The few trees that were available were often inadequate for the bridging task. The lack of wood was just not a problem for the French. During the Peninsular War, the British rarely had a regular supply of lumber and usually stripped the surrounding countryside of any pieces of wood. Time and again they built bridges using whatever material they could find! It was not uncommon for the bed of the bridge to be made from shutters, doors, old cabinets, and ceiling joists. In one case, the British demolished an inn and used all the wood in it for their bridge!

The lack of proper building material could have disastrous results. In April 1811, during the opening stages of the first British Siege of Badajoz, a trestle bridge was built across the Guadiana River. 'The trestle-bridge (made only 7 feet in height because trees to supply timber of larger dimensions could not be found near the spot) was put down . . . During the night the water rose 3 feet and passed over the planking of the bridge . . . On the 4th, the river continued to rise and the bridge having become perfectly useless . . .'[8] In the end, the British were forced to used rafts to ferry their men across the river. This delay was one of the factors that eventually forced the British to lift the siege.

The Royal Staff Corps

Until late in the war, Wellington's army had no pontoon train. Instead he relied on a little-known unit called the Royal Staff Corps. Its concept originated during the Duke of York's expedition to the Low Countries in 1794. His Royal Highness requested several companies of engineers to go with his expedition. This request was unheard-of and the Master-General of Ordnance was unable to comply with it. This infuriated the Duke and he was 'determined to establish a corps competent to discharge the duties usually devolving upon the Royal Engineers, which should be absolutely at the disposal of the Horse Guards . . .'[9] When deployed, the Royal Staff Corps would be under the direct control of the army's commander.[10]

Each company was commanded by either a major or a captain and had three subalterns and about 50 enlisted soldiers.[11] According to Philip Haythornthwaite: 'Each company had a sergeant major and quartermaster sergeant, and the rank of "sergeant-overseer" also existed; the privates were divided into 1st, 2nd, and 3rd classes, the 1st class intended to act as sergeants in charge of unskilled labourers, the 2nd class as corporals . . .'[12]

The Royal Staff Corps was with the Peninsular army from its inception. In 1808, a company was with Brent Spencer's Corps in Gibraltar, while two others were attached to Moore's Expedition to Spain. Wellington took two companies with him into central Spain in 1809 during the Talavera Campaign. By January 1813 there were five companies, commanded by Lieutenant Colonel Robert Dundas, assigned to Wellington's army. The Royal Staff Corps had several missions. Its primary one was to build and repair bridges. RSC officers were tasked also to help map the theatre operations and by 1810, most of central Portugal had been mapped to the scale of 4 miles to the inch. Other tasks included building temporary fortifications and running the army's post office. In short, anything the Quartermaster General needed doing. Two areas the RSC were not involved in, were sieges and the destruction of bridges. These were the responsibilities of the Royal Engineers, who belonged to a separate corps and were under the Master-General of Ordnance's direction.

This blurring of roles between the Royal Staff Corps and the Royal Engineers caused some resentment and rivalry between the two organizations. Sir John Burgoyne, a Royal Engineer, made the following observations in his diary about a senior Royal Staff Corps officer, on 26 October 1812:

> At Cabezon on the Pisuerga. During my absence, Lord Wellington wanted to have the bridge at this place mined, and no officer of the Royal Engineers being present, Colonel Sturgeon, of the Staff Corps, offered to do it, and gave him a memorandum of the means and time required, mentioning thirty-six hours for the latter, which struck his Lordship as extraordinary, and on my appearance he gave me the paper, and said he did not think we used to be so long; to which I replied, 'Certainly not,' and by his orders, went about it, and had it ready in four or five hours. After it was commenced according to my directions, Sturgeon met me and said that I, 'had better go and see what they were about, for they seemed to be proceeding oddly.' I found his idea was to work into the *side* of the bridge through the masonry, which would have been quite impracticable.[13]

This rivalry went even so far as the Royal Engineers taking credit for the construction of what was the greatest bridging feat of the Peninsular War, if not the Napoleonic Wars: the bridge of boats across the Adour in 1814. Major General John Jones, in his *Journal of the Sieges Carried on by the Army under the Duke of Wellington in Spain* stated that Lieutenant Colonel Howard Elphinstone supervised the preparation and construction of the bridge, while Major Alexander Tod, Royal Staff Corps, was only in charge of constructing and fixing the cables to the river bank.[14] In reality, it was quite different. William Napier, in his *History of the War in the Peninsula*, wrote 'The plan of the bridge and boom were the conception of colonel Sturgeon and major Tod, but the execution was confided entirely to the latter . . .'[15] Sir Charles Oman also confirmed this.[16]

An examination of the records will show that the Royal Staff Corps built or repaired the majority of bridges that were used by Wellington's army. This is not to denigrate the efforts of the Royal Engineers during the War. Their numbers were small – about 30 officers and another 35 enlisted soldiers during much of the war. [17] Most of their efforts were directed at building fortifications, such as the Lines of Torres Vedras, or conducting sieges.

The Bridges

The following are some of the bridges built by Wellington's Peninsular army. Although none of them are as famous as the pontoon bridge at Aspern–Essling in 1809 or the bridge across the Berezina in 1812, many of them are mentioned in the surviving memoirs, letters, and diaries of the British soldiers who crossed them.

BRIDGING THE TIETAR: 16–17 JULY 1809

In late spring, 1809 Wellington took the offensive and marched on central Spain from his bases in Portugal. The plan called for the joining of Wellington's Anglo-Allied army with General Cuesta's Spanish army of Estremadura. Together they would march to liberate Madrid. Marshal Victor, with the French I Corps, was also in central Spain, resting and resupplying his troops in the fertile farmlands around Plascenia. Victor was forced to withdraw to Talavera, when King Joseph ordered one of his three divisions and a large part of his cavalry be sent to reinforce General Sébastiani's IV Corps.

By mid-July, Wellington was at Plascenia and still had not had the opportunity to combine his forces with the Spanish. Wellington received word that Marshal Victor had got his troops back from the IV Corps and was beginning to threaten the Spanish army.

On 16 July, Wellington ordered Captain Tod (RSC) to take two companies of the Royal Staff Corps and 500 men[18] to build a bridge across the Tietar River near Baragona. The bridge had to be in place by the morning of the 18th.

Captain Tod chose the same site to build the bridge as the French used the previous month. The French bridge consisted of 15 pontoons, which they burned when they retreated in late June.[19] The Tietar River was fordable in several places, however a bridge would facilitate communications. The river was about 70 feet wide at the site, however the approach to it was over soft sand, which would require bridging if artillery and waggons were to be able to use it.

Captain Tod had no pontoons to build the bridge and would have to use local material. On the morning of 17 July, he and his troops 'could find no other materials with which to effect this, than the timber of a large inn and its outhouses, about a mile and a half distant and some pine trees that grew in a neighbouring wood. The building was therefore immediately unroofed, and timber of the following descriptions and dimensions procured, from its demolition. Six beams of dry fir, each about 20 feet long and 2 feet square; 3 or 400 rafters about 10 feet long, and 4 by 6 inches; 6 large doors and 20 running feet of manger.'[20]

The six large beams and the manger's planks were used to make a raft. Nails were in short supply so holes were bored into the end of each beam and a rope connected them. This raft could hold a load of about 13,500 pounds – between 60 and 70 men. The raft was placed in the deepest part of the river. The raft was attached to a sheer line that was tied to a tree on the far bank and to a stake on the near bank.[21]

Once the roof had been dismantled, Lieutenant John Westmacott, RSC, took

500 men to a small pine grove 3 miles away. There the soldiers cut down 20 pine trees 25–30 feet long. These would be used to make the piles that would be driven into the loose sand at the approach of the crossing site. Men standing on home-made stools and using crudely manufactured mallets pounded seven pairs of piles into the sand. A crosspiece of wood was placed horizontally on the top of each pair to form a trestle. Bearers were then run from the bank, across the caps, to the raft, on to the other riverbank. The bearers were secured to the caps and the raft, by long ribbons. Ribbons were thin strips of wood cut from the pine trees that were flexible enough to wrap around the bearers and caps and to tie in a knot!

Once the bearers were in place, the doors, rafters, and mangers from the inn were used to make the flooring of the bridge. This wood was too thick for the men to nail down, so once again they used ribbons to secure the planks in place.

On the morning of 18 July, the British army began crossing the bridge that Captain Tod and his men had built in 24 hours! The bridge was only meant to be a temporary one, so Lieutenant William Staveley, RSC, was left there to dismantle it, once the army had passed.[22]

BRIDGING THE ALVA AT PONTE DE MURCELLA: 18–19 MARCH 1811

In early 1811, the French army under Marshal Masséna began its slow retreat from Portugal back to Spain. Marshal Ney conducted a brilliant rearguard action for much of the retreat. A major communications point along this route was the bridge over the Alva River at Ponte de Murcella. The British had destroyed this bridge during the previous year. Marshal Masséna ordered General Drouet to protect the point and to build a bridge for Marshal Ney's troops to cross. On 16 March, Colonel Pelet, an aide-de-camp to Masséna reported that the bridge would not be repaired for two more days. The army was halted and defensive positions were prepared on both sides of the river. All the sapper companies of the French army worked on the bridge and were able to complete it by five o'clock.[23]

Marshal Ney's VI Corps remained on the left bank of the river, to cover the retreat of the main body of the army. On the morning of 18 March, the British Light Division caught up to him and he ordered his troops to cross the river. Once his troops were safely across, the French bridge was destroyed. Ney remained until that afternoon, buying time for the rest of the army. He finally pulled out when he received word that he was in danger of being outflanked.

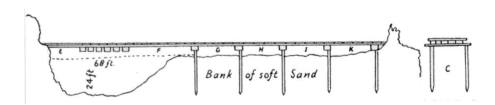

The Bridge Across the Tietar. *By Ensign Charles Scott, RSC*

The Alva was a fast moving, wide river that fed off the snows of the Serra da Estrella. In the vicinity of Ponte de Murcella, its width was about 100 feet, while the depth was too deep to allow for the use of pilings, as the British used on the Tietar River. Late on the evening of 18 March, the Royal Staff Corps was given orders to build a bridge across the Alva, so that the Light Division could continue to pursue Marshal Ney's retreating VI Corps. According to Lieutenant Charles Scott, Royal Staff Corps:[24]

> Timber of a sufficient length could not be got there and a bridge was made, as follows, at some distance above [Ponte de Murcella]. The stream was too rapid and the water too deep to admit of anything being fixed in the river. The left bank [the side the British occupied] was rocky and nearly level with the water.
>
> A working party of 200 men was immediately sent into the village to collect all kinds of dry timber to make a raft. A sufficient quantity being collected it was formed on the Bank at A. While the timber was collecting two Ringbolts were let into the rocks at D and C and six pine trees of about 60 ft long were felled and brought to the spot by the marauders, who accompanied the Army and who were seized on and compelled to perform the service. The Raft being ready one of these trees was laid on it and well secured by spikes and cords; a hole was bored in the other end of the tree and it was secured by a heel rope to the ringbolt at D. Bearers were laid under the raft, while it was constructing, to launch it, which was done and a strong party held on the rope EF easing it down the stream to G, the place proposed for the bridge. The rope was then secured to the ringbolt at C, and two additional turns were taken round the tree and through the bolt to secure it against the force of the current. A firm footing being thus secured in the middle of the river, a second tree was prepared by boring a hole in its end; it was then slipped along the first beam and secured by a heel rope to it at G. A large cask was procured from the village and well lashed under the other

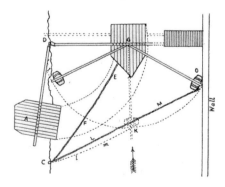

The Bridge at Ponte de Murcella.
By Ensign Charles Scott

end of it; the tree and cask were then launched into the stream and shoved out by poles and boat-hooks from I to K when being caught by the stream, it was gently and carefully eased down by the rope LM in the situation O against the wall. About 30 men were then sent along across this tree and by the help of a small tackle, fixt to a post on the wharf, hoisted the Cask and end of the tree on the wall.

   Two other trees were immediately laid parallel to the others and the whole planked over with doors, chests and such other articles as had been collected during the time the work was going on.[25]

The construction of the bridge took all night and most of the next day. Although the Light Division was able to cross it on the morning of 19 March, it was not until the following day could cavalry cross.[26] To the modern reader, the bridge appears to be a feat of military ingenuity, yet it was unremarkable to those who crossed it. One diarist only noted that it was built overnight, but then required another 24 hours of work before cavalry could use it![27]

THE BRIDGES OVER THE COA: MAY 1811

By early 1811, Marshal Masséna's Army of Portugal had been forced out of most of Portugal by Wellington. Masséna decided to make a stand along the Coa River, which flowed parallel to the Spanish border. In late March, Masséna ordered the bridges along the Coa River destroyed, including the ones at Pinhel and Almeida.[28] On 31 March, Masséna sent a letter to Marshal Berthier stating that the bridges over the River Coa were being destroyed.[29] Wellington wrote to Beresford on 6 April that 'They have destroyed all of the bridges over the Coa, except for that at Sabugal . . .' Wellington crossed the Coa at Sabugal and defeated Masséna on 3 April. The French pulled back to Ciudad Rodrigo, about 60 kilometres to the east but left a garrison in the Portuguese border fortress of Almeida.

   The Coa is a fast-moving river that spills over rocks near the bridge. The bridge was built in 1745 and was made of cut stone. It is approximately 100 yards long, 4 yards wide, and 70 feet high. Despite a French garrison still in Almeida, which was about 3 kilometres from the bridge, Wellington ordered that the bridge be repaired.

   Once again, Lieutenant Charles Scott writes:

Notches were made in the masonry by men lowered down on a scaffold for that purpose. Two frames were then made. When completed the cills were laid on the notches A B and the frames put together in an upright position as represented by the dotted lines AF BE. Tackles were then applied to both sides of each frame at the extremities E and F. The other end of the tackles being fixed to the bolts let into the masonry about 30 feet back of the fracture. 50 men were then put on each of the tackle-falls and the frames were lowered down to H. Gangboards . . . were then shoved out and men sent out on them to put in key bolts which were previously prepared. A ridge pole was then laid on from which to the sides the timber we had was sufficient to reach. The braces 1, 2, 3 were afterwards put on to secure it.[30]

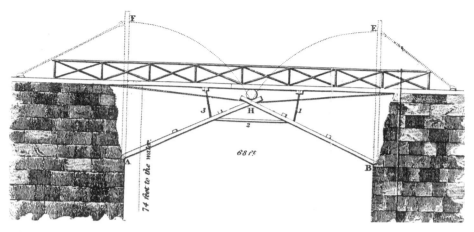

The Bridge across the Coa at Almeida. *By Major General Howard Douglas*

Unfortunately the officer does not record how long it took to build the bridge nor when it was replaced with a more substantial structure.

In early May, Marshal Masséna advanced to relieve his beleaguered garrison in Almeida. Wellington chose to stand and fight at Fuentes d'Oñoro, with his back to the Coa River, which was less than 4 miles away. In a belated move, after days of fighting, on 6 May Wellington ordered Captain Tod and two companies of the Royal Staff Corps, to build two bridges in the vicinity of Pinhel, should the British be defeated and have to retreat.

Lieutenant Scott continues the story:

On their arrival at the spot it was found impracticable to repair the stone bridge, from the shattered state of the remaining part of the piers, and almost total want of materials within any reasonable distance. Six poplars and some large elms that grew on the bank about 2 miles upwards, were all that could be procured. These were immediately felled and with very great difficulty floated down the river to two places that had been fixed on, to attempt making temporary bridges. Both these places were where the river narrowed, forming rapids so deep and strong that no hold could be got of the bottom. Each of these places was from 60 to 70 feet wide, but as both Bridges were made similar, I shall only describe one.

The farthest side of the river could not be got at by any means in our power, it being then a considerable flood. The profile of the bank next us was the line from A to B in solid granite rock. It was immediately altered to C D by cutting a notch at D about 8 feet long horizontally, one foot high, and about the same depth and raising the space to C with dry masonry, coped by a beam of Timber on the extreme edge. Meanwhile a road was made along the face of the rock.

Two trees were then placed sideways with their large ends inserted in the notch above-mentioned and by the help of levers and iron bars were levered into position overhanging the stream. The ends still continuing to be secured in the notch.

Handspikes were then lashed on these trees at certain distances to enable men to go out on their extremities and push across to the opposite bank two light poles, represented by the dotted lines H I, across which poles some men were sent and having thus reached the opposite bank, the rest of the work was soon completed.[31]

Once the men were on the far bank of the river, it too was prepared in a similar fashion. Notches were cut for the placing of the trees that would serve as the rest of the bed of the bridge and masonry was used to build the foundation.

Once again, there is no record of how long these bridges were in place.

THE BRIDGE AT VILLA VELHA: 1811

The Tagus River in Portugal effectively splits the southern part of the kingdom from the central and northern sections. Oman describes the river as 'broad, absolutely bridgeless, and fickle in the extreme in its alternations of high and low water.' [32] From the Spanish border south-west to the Atlantic Ocean, the river passed through steep gorges and narrow valleys and averaged about 200 metres in depth.[33] It was much the same for about 150 miles until further west, when it widened to 500–600 yards: eventually, in the vicinity of Lisbon, it would widen to almost 1½ miles.

In 1809, across this 200-mile obstacle were only two bridges! The first was the

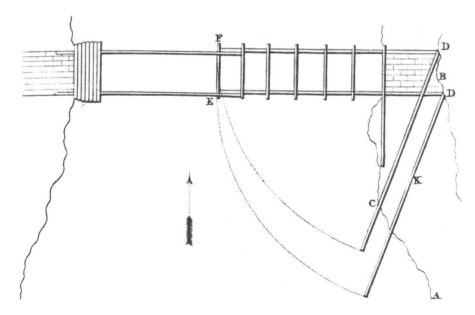

Building the Bridge Across the Coa at Pinhel. *By Major General Howard Douglas*

The Bridge across the Coa at Pinhel. *By Major General Howard Douglas*

old Roman bridge at Alcantara, Spain. The second was a pontoon bridge at Abrantes, about 100 miles east of Lisbon. The bridge at Alcantara was rendered useless for all traffic, when Portuguese forces under Colonel Mayne destroyed one of its arches on 14 May 1809, to prevent French forces under Marshal Victor from seizing it.

After the unsuccessful Talavera Campaign in the summer of 1809, Wellington's Army retreated to the Portuguese border. Wellington had to divide his forces to cover the major invasion routes into Portugal – the northern route via Ciudad Rodrigo and the southern route via Badajoz. Wellington's problem was the Tagus River, which ran between the two routes. Wellington had to split his army into two wings and had no way of communicating between the two forces except by going south-east to Abrantes, crossing the bridge there and then moving along the other bank of the river. The lack of bridges across the Tagus prevented him from rapidly reinforcing either wing of his army should one be threatened.

Wellington recognized the importance of a bridge at Villa Velha, which was 30 miles north of Abrantes. A bridge there would save his troops 4–5 days of marching. In early 1810, Wellington ordered the bridge built.

Villa Velha was not an easy place to get to. Alexander Dickson, Wellington's Chief of Artillery, left a vivid description of it in 1810:

> A league further is the bridge of Villa Velha the descent to which is long, very steep, and with bad road. The banks of the river are here excessively high and steep, but the road passes down a hollow which takes off from its abruptness.[34]

Dickson reported in July, 1810 that the bridge was 'a very strong and commodious bridge of boats.' [35] In early November 1810 the bridge was burned to prevent it from being captured by the French. By late winter 1811, the French had been expelled from most of Portugal and the bridge at Villa Velha was rebuilt.

Lieutenant John Westmacott, RSC, who help build the bridge across the Tietar, was given the mission of building the bridge. Limited building material was available, so he used two large country boats to form a flying bridge. These were lashed together and large timbers were secured from gunnel to gunnel of the two boats. Across these timbers was laid wood flooring. A rail was placed around the sides to prevent any animals from panicking and jumping into the water. A ramp was built on each bank to ease the loading and unloading of wheeled vehicles onto the boat. Upstream of the crossing site, an anchor was dropped. A heavy rope was attached to the anchor and then lifted out of the water by placing it on the masts of two small boats. The other end of the rope was attached to a large hoop on the end of the boat. This prevented the bridge from floating downstream. Another rope was stretched between the riverbanks. The bridge was manned 24 hours a day by twelve sailors, who would use this rope to pull the bridge across the river.[36]

Ensign John Mills, of the Coldstream Guards, wrote of the problem of its design. His company stayed the night before the crossing, in a village about 1 mile from Villa Velha. The next morning, they 'marched at two o'clock to Villa Velha. From thence about half a mile to the banks of the Tagus. We were delayed here some time, as there were but two boats joined to pass an army of 30,000 men. Got over about eleven.' [37] It took his company nine hours to travel less than 2 miles.

A more permanent bridge, using 12 boats was eventually built. In April 1812, a French excursion near the bridge gave Wellington some concern. On 10 April, he ordered Major John Burgoyne there with the instructions:

'If on his arrival at Villa Velha, he shall find the enemy at Castello Branco, he is to have the bridge taken up at Villa Velha, and all the materials put into the boats, and the boats must be sent about a league down the stream, and left there on the left bank, in a place to which the enemy cannot get at them, ready to be drawn up and replaced as a bridge as soon as the troops will arrive at Villa Velha to cross the Tagus. The bridge is not to be taken up till the enemy arrives at Castello Branco.'[38]

Burgoyne writes that upon arrival at the bridge at 9 a.m. on 12 April, he:

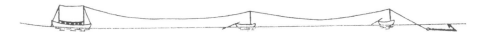

The Flying Bridge at Villa Velha as Viewed from the Left Bank. *By Ensign Charles Scott, RSC*

A Contemporary View of the Bridge of Boats at Villa Velha. *By Colonel Alexander Dickson*

Found the Portuguese captain of Engineers in charge of the bridge, in great distress, having received an order from Marshal Beresford to remove the bridge when the enemy should arrive, that is, in his immediate presence. Knowing how impossible this would be, from the nature of the business, and the few experienced people he had, he determined on preparing to burn it, as the only resource, in the presence of the enemy, for the French had entered Castello Branco yesterday about 7000 strong at 4 p.m . . . On my arrival, however, I had it immediately withdrawn, and the boats removed down to just below the bold narrow pass of the river within the mountains to a sandy bay, about 2 miles below the site of the bridge. This operation took an hour and a half, the boats being twelve in number. The cables were thrown into the river, except those which would reach the left bank . . .

14th April: Received a note from General Alten that the enemy had retired yesterday morning at daybreak from Castello Branco . . . Immediately order the bridge to be re-established. Rode down to where the boats are situated under Monte do Duque . . . Found there already two or three hundred peasants and the Portuguese engineer, at work getting the boats up. He assures me the bridge will be ready early tomorrow morning. A sufficient number of the cables thrown into the river are recovered for immediate use, and the rest will be gained when there is more leisure.[39]

The bridge at Villa Velha remained in place when the British left Portugal in 1813 for their final campaign that would take them to the frontiers of France.

THE BRIDGE ACROSS THE AGUEDA
In the fall of 1811, Major Sturgeon of the Royal Staff Corps was tasked to build a bridge across the Agueda River, in support of future operations around Ciudad

Rodrigo. The ford at Marialva was chosen for the site. The Agueda was 396 feet wide at the ford and the British considered it a major obstacle. Wellington wrote that:

It is difficult for an army to pass this river at any time; but the only road by which it is practicable for an army to pass to the eastward, when the rains have filled the rivers, is by the bridge of Ciudad Rodrigo; and the torrent of water in the Agueda during the rains is of that description, that it is impossible to overcome this obstacle.[40]

The Agueda was considered unusable for pontoons, so a decision was made to make a trestle bridge. Wellington keeping in mind the dangers of the winter floodwaters, intended to only have it in place when it was needed and to store it when it was not.[41] The problem Major Sturgeon had to overcome was devising a means to secure the trestles to prevent them from being swept away. To do so, the trestles:

were made to contain between their legs a considerable weight of well-packed stones, secured by strong planks, in narrow, pointed cases, to increase as little as possible the breadth or section of the trestles, and their resistance to the current. Sloping piles were set below each trestle, and braced to its head, to support it better against the action of the stream; and to strong piles driven into the bottom of the river, directly above the several trestles, these were fastened by chains, which lying at the bottom, formed secure horizontal holdings.[42]

To secure the trestles a pile would be placed 18 feet upriver of each trestle:

a chain being passed round each pile was secured to the framework, so as to prevent the whole from floating away in the event of the river rising over the top of the bridge, which was 12 feet higher than the usual surface of the water.[43]

The bridge needed considerable material and Major Sturgeon did not receive the support he required from the Portuguese governor of Almeida. On 21 October 1811, Wellington was forced to write a letter to the governor requesting that he provide the materials that Major Sturgeon needed. In particular:

I request that you will let him have from the old carriages, &c., any axletrees or other iron which he may want, brass boxes from wheels, &c., which he may require; likewise the use of the grinding stones and smith's forges in Almeida, and a certain quantity of timber for the construction of a pile engine, and a trustle.[44]

When work began in earnest: 'The ram was worked by hand-ropes . . . Attached to the fall . . . The pile engine was provided with a tackle fastened at its head, by

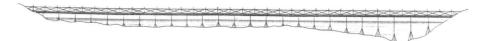

Cross-Section of the Bridge across the Agueda. *By Major General Howard Douglas*

which to sling the pile, and set it in its place.'[45] But the amount of material needed was staggering:

30 trestles
500 14 foot long planks
160 beams: 18 feet x 5 inches x 10 inches
30 piles
1 pile driving machine on wheels
180 fathom of strong chain
3,000 6-inch spikes
6,000 2-inch nails
hawsers, tackles, and small stores[46]

On 18 November, a General Order was issued to the 3rd, 4th, 5th, and 6th Divisions. Each division was tasked to provide artificers to support Major Sturgeon. The numbers each division had to provide were:

Division	Carpenters	Sawyers	Wheelers	Blacksmiths
3rd	20	10	1	4
4th	20	10	2	4
5th	20	10	6	4
6th	22	10	1	4
Total	82	40	10	16

The 148 artificers, who were actually infantrymen who had the requested skills, were to march by 27 November, with each division providing a 'steady Non-commissioned Officer' to provide supervision.[47]

The bridge was finished by the end of the year, however its maintenance required Major Sturgeon to keep his carts until 12 January, just four days before the city fell.[48] The bridge was so well built that it survived the siege with no serious problems. It was removed the day after Ciudad Rodrigo was captured and stored in Almeida under the care of Lieutenant Henry Dumaresq.[49]

THE BRIDGE AT ALCANTARA: EUROPE'S FIRST SUSPENSION BRIDGE

In 1812, Wellington planned to go on the offensive and move into central Spain against French Marshal Marmont. To do this he first had to capture the great fortress of Ciudad Rodrigo, which was along the main route of march he intended to advance. Additionally, he had to secure southern Portugal from a possible invasion by French Marshal Soult. This he would do by capturing the fortress city of Badajoz. Ciudad Rodrigo fell to the Allies in January, while Badajoz was stormed and taken in April. The capture of them permitted Wellington to move forward with the next phase of his campaign.

The British army was capable of beating either Marshal Marmont's Army of Portugal or Marshal Soult's Army of the South. However, Wellington knew that he could not beat them together. He had to ensure that he could fight Marmont before he could unite with Soult. A major obstacle was between the two French armies: the Tagus River. This river was wide and flowed east–west, effectively bisecting Spain. There were few bridges across the Tagus. From east to west, these bridges were at Toledo, Talavera, Arzobispo, Almaraz, and Alcantara. The bridges at Toledo, Talavera, and Arzobispo were under French control, however the Spanish destroyed the bridge at Almaraz on 14 March 1809 to prevent its use by the French, while the Portuguese, under Colonel Mayne, destroyed the bridge at Alcantara on 14 May 1809. Rather than trying to repair the King Charles Bridge at Almaraz, the French built a pontoon bridge.

Wellington saw that if he could destroy the pontoon bridge at Almaraz, any French force moving between the Army of Portugal in the north and the Army of the South would have to go via Toledo, an extra 450 miles. In late April 1812, Wellington ordered General Hill to make a raid on Almaraz and destroy the bridge. In a lightning stroke, Hill caught the French by surprise and was able to destroy the bridge on 18 May.

Wellington realized that destroying the bridge at Almaraz was only a partial solution to his problems. He also needed the ability to shift his own troops rapidly from the south to the north or vice versa. On 25 April 1812, Wellington ordered Lieutenant Colonel Henry Sturgeon of the Royal Staff Corps to repair the damage done to the bridge Alcantara. By repairing the bridge at Alcantara Wellington would shorten the distance between the two main staging areas for his troops (Ciudad Rodrigo and Badajoz) to about 150 miles.

The old Roman bridge, known as the Trajan Bridge (named for the Roman Emperor at the time it was built), was 626 feet long, 26 feet wide, and was 190 feet above the water.[50] It had six arches, which ranging from the left bank, had spans of 45 feet, 75 feet, 104 feet, 104 feet, 75 feet, and 75 feet![51] Here the Tagus river passes through a narrow gorge and was swift flowing. It was deep (typical depth was 37 feet) and during the flood season it had been known to rise to 180 feet![52]

The task given to Lieutenant Colonel Sturgeon was monumental. The 2nd arch from the right bank had been blown up, which created a 75-foot gap in the bridge. Creating a pontoon bridge was impossible due to the high riverbanks. The scarcity of large trees, made the bridging of the 75-foot gap impossible. So Sturgeon decided to create a suspension bridge. A large net would be laid across the gap and a roadway would be built upon it.

Lieutenant Colonel Sturgeon was able to obtain the following material:

4 Beams of Poplar, each 30 feet long by 12 inches by 8 inches
8 Beams of Poplar, each 20 feet long by 6 inches square
48 Joists each 12 feet long by 3 inches by 5 inches[53]

120 Joists each 12 feet long by 1½ inches by 5 inches
100 ½-inch screw bolts each 10 inches long
100 1½-inch planks, each 12 feet long, 1 foot wide
50 2-inch planks, each 12 feet long, 1 foot wide
10 Triple Blocks; sheaves 12 inches in diameter; brass cogged and iron pinned
10 Double Blocks; sheaves 12 inches in diameter; brass cogged and iron pinned
10 Double Blocks; sheaves 6 inches in diameter for working tacks and guy
10 Single Blocks; sheaves 6 inches in diameter for working tacks and guy
450 fathoms (900 yards) 6½-inch Rope for great mat and bridge bearers
200 fathoms (400 yards) 4½-inch Rope for falls for bridge tackles
200 fathoms (400 yards) 2½-inch Rope for working tackles and guys
100 fathoms (200 yards) 4½-inch Rope for straps round the beams
1000 fathoms (2,000 yards) 3 and 4 yard, spun yarn
140 yards strong tarred canvas
5 cwt (500 pounds) bar iron for cramps and bolts
200 pounds of lead
Two Pontoon Carriages
4 Crabs or small capstans
30 Common Carriages
6 Galera Carriages (a light cart pulled by 4 mules)

Additional material included 'Tar, rosin, grease, marling spikes, fids, old canvas for parcelling, salvages, straps, tail tackles, twine needles, a portable forge, blacksmiths', masons' and carpenters' tools, drill hammers, scrapers, and needles.'[54]

Sturgeon set up operations at the cavernous Pontoon House in the Portuguese fortress city of Elvas. There he placed two of the 30 foot long beams on 4 foot high stools 90 feet apart. He secured the beams in place with braces and trestles to keep the distance constant. Eighteen lengths of the 6½-inch rope were placed one foot apart on the beams and then stretched between them using the capstan and the tackles to ensure that a uniform strain was placed on each so that they were the same length. These ropes were then lashed together to form a giant net. The eight 20 foot beams were notched and then seared with an iron axle rod to prevent the ropes from chafing. The beams were then placed approximately 10 feet apart in the net with the ropes going in the notches. The beams were then secured to the net with the 4 yards of spun yarn.

The next step was to create chains of sleepers from one end beam to the other. Starting at one end, two short joists (12 feet by 3 inches by 5 inches) were laid. At one end, another joist (12 feet by 1½ inches by 5 inches) was laid. The two thicker

The Bridge Hanging from the Wall of the Pontoon House. *By Ensign Charles Scott*

joists were joined to the end of the thinner joist, using a ½-inch screw bolt that was 10 inches long. This was similar in design to a chain. At the other end of the thinner joist, two thicker joists were connected, which then had a thinner joist bolted to their end. This was continued until the 'chain' reached the other end beam. These chains were then secured to the end beams. The joints of the 'chain' rested on the beams that were laid every 10 feet across the 6½-inch ropes. The exact number of chains laid is unknown, however, it was probably ten. The chains were then lashed to the ends of the bridge.

The flooring of the bridge was made using planks that were 12 feet long and 12 inches wide and 1½ inches thick. Holes half an inch in diameter were bored in both ends of these planks and they were lashed to the 'chains' that ran the length of the net.

When this was completed, the bridge was removed from the wall and rolled into a bundle! This bundle was placed on two pontoon carriages, which were pulled by six oxen each. An additional eight large four oxen carts and seventeen two oxen light carts were used to move the rest of the material to Alcantara. Total weight of the bridge, based on the materials listed above was estimated at 18,000 pounds.[55]

While Lieutenant Colonel Sturgeon was making the bridge, Lieutenant Samuel Perry, Royal Staff Corps, was at Alcantara preparing the site. The edges of the gap were smoothed to prevent any chafing of the ropes and channels to hold the end beams were cut in the masonry. A 30-foot poplar beam was laid in the channel on each side of the gap. Unfortunately there is no record on how they secured the beams into the channels.[56] Attached to these end beams were five tackles (pulleys). Two heavy hawsers were also laid to assist in the hauling of the bridge across the gap. These ropes were used to pull the great bridge across the gap. To prevent the bridge from swaying too much, tackles were hung from two cross-beams and ropes were secured to ringbolts placed in the masonry of the arch of the bridge.[57] Once the bridge was in place, a ramp, using the 2-inch planks, were built on both ends of the bridge.

Along both sides of the bridge was a four-foot high railing made of wood and rope. These railings were covered with a tarpaulin that blocked the vision of the horses and oxen, and thus prevented a possible panic![58] The bridge was strong and could hold wheeled vehicles. Capstans were placed at either end to tighten the ropes when heavy vehicles passed over it. In the event that the French might approach, the whole bridge could be disconnected on one side and rolled up. There

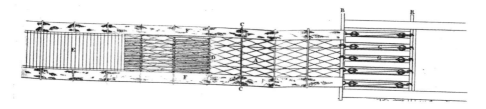

The Flooring of the Bridge at Alcantara. *By Major General Howard Douglas*

Cross-Section of the Suspension Bridge at Alcantara. *By Major General Howard Douglas*

is some confusion on how long it would take to do this. The Royal Staff College stated that it could be taken up in an hour and it would take only a matter of a few hours to have it back in place. [59] However, Wellington did not believe this. On 11 June 1812, he stated in a letter to Lieutenant General Hill, the commander of the 2nd Division, that:

> We have repaired this bridge by a piece of machinery which can be taken up and laid down at pleasure, but it will require two days' notice to lay it down, and as much time to take it up. I enclose the copy of the instructions which I have given regarding this bridge, and you will only send notice if you want to use it. If you should find it necessary on any account to retire into Portugal, you will in that case send orders to Lieutenant Pery [*sic*] at Alcantara, to lodge his bridge, &c., at Marva?; and his bullocks, people, &c., had better continue their march by Castello de Vide, Niza, &c., to Abrantes. [60]

Designing and building the bridge took about 3 weeks! Lieutenant Perry was left in charge of maintaining the bridge and it was still in use until 1860, when it was dismantled after the arch was repaired. [61]

Few eyewitnesses left their impressions on what it was like to cross the bridge. Colonel Alexander Dickson crossed it with his brigade of howitzers on 11 June and was in Salamanca 9 days later. [62] Unfortunately he left no record other than a brief diary entry of the crossing. His observations on the bridge and what it took to entice animals to cross it would have made interesting reading! Captain William Webber, a Royal Artillery officer, wrote the following on 13 February 1813:

> it answers every purpose and only requires the attendance of a man to prevent people or animals from meeting in the middle, as the action would become irregular and perhaps disengage some of the tackle. [63]

This irregular action may be a bit more dangerous than Webber lets on. The journal for the regimental mess of the 1st (Royal) Dragoons reports that the bridge 'swayed so horribly, and bullocks often took fright and came to grief. Horses hated

A Contemporary View of the Bridge at Alcantara as Seen from the Left Bank. *By Major General Howard Douglas*

it . . . the regimental paymaster, hated it so much that, whenever he had to go down to the base to draw money for the regiment, he would ride miles out of his way merely to avoid it.' [64] It must have been quite a sight to see a team of slow-moving oxen crossing on a swaying bridge 190 feet in the air!

Lieutenant Colonel Sturgeon also designed and built a similar structure in late 1812, for the King Charles Bridge at Almaraz. This bridge had to span a gap of 143 feet!

THE BRIDGE OF BOATS: CROSSING THE ADOUR, FEBRUARY 1814

In early 1814, the Anglo-Allied army was in southern France, poised to strike against the French army commanded by Marshal Soult. The marshal had thrown 15,000 troops into the fortified city of Bayonne, which was located on the Adour River. Wellington decided to force the French Army eastward, away from the city. Once Soult was too far away to come to the assistance of the garrison, the Anglo-Allied left wing, under the command of Lieutenant General John Hope would attack Bayonne.

Bayonne sat astride the Adour River, with strong Vauban style fortifications on the south side of the river. British engineers estimated that these walls alone would be capable of withstanding a siege of 25 to 30 days. Additionally, Marshal Soult had built field fortifications 500–600 yards in front of the main walls.

Connecting the fortifications on the left bank with the city was a wooden bridge that would permit the garrison to be reinforced quickly. On the right bank, the city was protected by a small square citadel, which sat on a height that dominated both the city and bridge. Wellington believed that if he could keep the French pinned on the southern bank, he would have little problem taking the city from the north bank. The question was how to get Hope's corps across the Adour River?

Bridging the Adour River would be no easy task. It had few of the factors that make a good crossing site. Its width averaged 500 yards wide and during the late winter, numerous mountain streams that fed it made the current extremely strong. Furthermore, it was a tidal river and the spring tides could change the height of the water by over 14 feet on any given day. Strong winds blowing from the coast also created turbulence that would easily swamp the British pontoons. At the mouth of the river was a large sandbar that would have to be navigated by any vessel trying to move upstream.[65] Along a long stretch of the river, walls that were 14 feet thick and towering 14 feet above the water lined the banks on both sides of the river. The wall on the left bank (which the British controlled) was level with the land behind it; however on the right bank, the land behind the wall was 12 feet lower than the top of the wall and at high tide was under 7 feet of water![66]

Clearly Wellington had given much thought to this crossing. On 23 January he rode to the mouth of the river, with a small cavalry escort and several of his staff. There they spent only a few minutes examining the area, and then returned to Saint Jean de Luz.[67] He took Captain John Burgoyne of the Royal Engineers with him. About ten days later, Wellington and the commander of the British naval forces in the area, Admiral Charles Penrose,[68] made another reconnaissance of the river.[69] Wellington, being ever cautious, took steps to ensure he did not provide the French with a clue to his intentions. Both men rode together along the river without any aides, to see how formidable an obstacle it would be.[70] It became apparent to Wellington the Adour would be a major problem for his pontoon-bridging train – it might be able to build a bridge across the river, but would not be capable of keeping it operational.[71]

Captain Browne, a staff officer in Wellington's headquarters, claims that Wellington and Penrose, after their recon of the river decided the only feasible way across it was to use boats instead of pontoons.[72] Wellington's Judge Advocate, Francis Larpent, reported that Colonel Sturgeon, who built so many bridges for the Duke, told him that Wellington never consulted him and 'he shall do all he can to execute what he is ordered, and be quiet.'[73]

In early February, the British began looking for material to build the bridge. The builders estimated that they would need 25–30 boats to build the bridge, but that they would also lose one-third of the boats while making the dangerous crossing of the sandbar at the mouth of the Adour River.[74] The task of finding suitable boats was assigned to Lieutenant John Debenham of the Royal Navy, 'a very old officer and the senior officer on this station.'[75] Old he may have been, however Debenham was able to secure 48 coastal trading boats, called *chasse-marées*, by scouring the local fishing ports of Saint Jean de Luz, Passages, and Socoa. These boats, owned and crewed by both Spaniards and Frenchmen:

varied very considerably in their dimensions, 5 or 6 being of the length of 53 feet and upwards of 15 feet 4 inches in breadth, and their decks being 3 feet 10 inches above the water; whilst the smallest measured only 40 feet long, by 10 feet 2 inches in breadth, and floated with their decks only 2 feet 6 inches above the water.[76]

The boats did not come cheap. Their total cost for each day was £123, 8 shillings, and 6 pence plus daily rations for the 200 crew.[77]

At the same time the area was searched for suitable material for the beams that would support the bridge between the boats. The masts and spars of a shipwreck provided some of the necessary wood, while others were secured in Saint Jean de Luz. It was not long before they realized that this would not be enough and an alternate would have to be used. Lieutenant Colonel Sturgeon proposed that he build a bridge similar to the one at Alcantara, using ropes instead of wood. Wellington gave permission to proceed with the design; Sturgeon would do the planning, while Major Tod, who was involved in building many of the other bridges over the past 5 years, would do the actual building.[78] Thirteen-inch cables would be substituted for the beams and 16 cables were either bought locally or provided by Admiral Penrose. These cables were 13 inches in circumference and had a diameter of about 4 inches. They usually were found in 100-yard lengths and when dry, weighed about 2,200 pounds. Anchor cables were usually double that length. Either way the cables would have to be spliced together to get the required length.[79]

The exact date the idea for the bridge was conceived is unknown. There is evidence the engineers had begun stockpiling material for it for several months. However, according to Colonel John Jones, author of *Journal of the Sieges Carried on by the Army under the Duke of Wellington in Spain*, it was only on 7 February that Wellington ordered his senior engineer, Lieutenant Colonel Elphinstone, to begin planning and preparing to cross the Adour. On the same day, in a letter to Rear Admiral Penrose, Wellington lays out his concept for the bridge:

> I propose that our bridge should be constructed of vessels from 15 to 30 tons burthen, two-masted, and each well ballasted, and provided with anchors and cables to be anchored by head and stern, of which I have ordered the Commissary General to provide forty . . . I propose to lay cables across these vessels from bank to bank, which we have reason to believe is an extent of 400 yards; and on the cables we shall tie the planks . . .[80]

Within a few days of receiving Wellington's instructions, the engineers made their own reconnaissance of the river. A site chosen for the crossing was at a bend in the river, 4 kilometres downstream of Bayonne, about 500 metres downstream from the village of Le Boucau, and about 2.5 kilometres upstream of where the river flowed into the Bay of Biscay. The river narrowed at this point and was about 250 metres wide. Due to the bend in the river, the crossing site was not in view of the French defenders in Bayonne.[81]

The plan called for the anchoring of the boats 30 feet apart, with two anchors each, one fore and one aft. On each boat, the gunnels would be removed and a

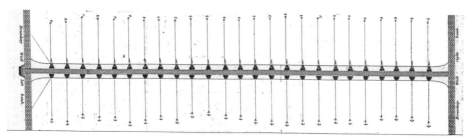

The Plan. *By Colonel John T. Jones RE*

wooden sleeper (beams) would be nailed in the centre of the boat. These beams had 5 notches cut into them, each 2 feet apart. The 13-inch cables would be laid from bank to bank and lay in the notches in the sleepers on each boat, to keep them apart.

On the right bank of the river, each cable would be secured to an 18-pounder cannon, which would be dropped off the dike and buried in the marsh.[82] On the left bank of the river, a frame 32 feet long and 14 feet wide would be laid. Within this frame, six more sleepers would be laid, parallel to the cables. In the space between these sleepers, double blocks and gin tackles[83] would be connected to each cable. Capstans placed on the landside of the platform would be used to keep the cables taut and to allow them to let out or bring in slack, to compensate for the 14-foot tide. The frame would be placed in a hole 3 feet below the top of the left bank. Over this frame a platform would be built. On the end furthest from the river, sixty tons of sandbags would be placed. Flooring would cover the cables and the sandbags to allow the approach to be level with the riverbank.[84]

To prevent the cables from chaffing on the stone dikes 'green bullocks' hides were to be laid under them on the right bank; and a piece of timber, with scores cut in it, corresponding with the grooved sleepers spike fore and aft on the decks of the boats, was to be laid on the top of the wall of the left bank.[85] A 12-foot wide roadway, made of planks 3 inches thick and 12 inches wide would then be secured to the cables using rope.

One of Wellington's concerns was the possible reaction of the French once they learned about the bridge. A common counter-bridge tactic was to float large items or fireships down the river to ram and break the bridge. To prevent this from

Cross-Section of the Pulley System Used to Keep the Cables Taut. *By Colonel John T. Jones RE*

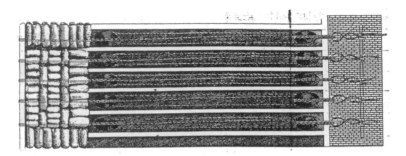

A Top View of the Pulley System. *By Colonel John T. Jones RE*

happening, Wellington in his 7 February letter to Admiral Penrose laid out his thoughts on the matter:

> I should propose, then, that your gun boats and other craft should enter, and that they should anchor above the spot intended for the bridge, in order to cover its formation . . . As soon as the gun vessels and craft have anchored, I should propose that they should form a boom across the river . . . The mode in which I should propose that this boom should be formed is of spars, of from 50 to 60 feet long, attached to each other by chains, if they can be got; if not, by cable, leaving an interval between each spar of about 10 feet. We calculate the breadth of the river above where we shall place the bridge at about 520 yards, and we ought properly to have about 600 yards of boom anchored by six anchors; that is to say, thirty lengths of boom, and chain or rope. We will endeavour to make here ten lengths of the boom; and I shall be very much obliged to you if you will have the other twenty lengths made at Passages . . . For the anchors of the boom, six small cables or hawsers will be required, which I shall be obliged to you if you get out of the transports.[86]

Admiral Penrose took the responsibility for building the boom and large numbers of sailors would be used. Wellington's plan for the boom was modified. Instead of one boom, two booms would be built and placed at least 24 feet apart. Larger masts than the ones suggested by Wellington were chosen – these ranging from 50 to 100 feet long and 1 or 2 feet diameter. Each mast was:

> to be anchored separately and independently by the centre, those of the front line having their anchors up the stream, and those of the second line down the stream, to resist the flood tide. The masts of each line were to be anchored at 20 feet apart, and their extremities connected with each other by means of strong chains, lying slack about 2 feet under the water. The centre of the masts of the second line were to be placed opposite the intervals in the first line [to cover the gap], their extremities being similarly connected by slack chains; and the two lines being also united by slack chains, so as to give the

boom the necessary elasticity throughout, to resist the shock of any body sent to break it. Further, two 13-inch cables were to be stretched as tight as possible along the line of masts, and each end of the mast to be securely lashed to them.[87]

The small village of Socoa, next to St Jean de Luz, was the assembly point for the *chasse-marées*, the booms, and the massive amount of material needed for building the bridge:

> Capstans were constructed, cables spliced, and chain adapted to the boom; all timber, anchors, &c., that could be procured from the neighbouring ports, or from the fleet, were appropriated to these objects . . . six 4-oared jolly-boats were purchased from transports, and fitted on the ordinary pontoon carriages to accompany the march of the troops, and to be used whilst fixing the bridges.[88]

Although material was scarce at times, Wellington would accept no excuses for delays. If there was a problem, he found solutions – some that made his subordinates unhappy. When his chief engineer, Lieutenant Colonel Elphinstone, reported there were not enough boards for the flooring of the bridge and they would have to delay the operation, Wellington responded:

> 'No,' says he, 'there are all your platforms of your batteries which have been sent out, in case of a siege. Cut them all up.' 'Then when we proceed with the siege, what is to be done!' quoth Elphinstone. 'Oh, work your guns in the sand until you can make new ones out of the pinewood near Bayonne.' So all the English battering platforms have been cut up accordingly.[89]

On 19 February, Elphinstone informed Wellington that they had completed their preparations and were ready to go. Transportation of the boom was given to the Royal Navy and would be placed on two transport ships (the brig sloops *Lyra* and *Woodlark*, each with 12 guns) and the brig, *Martial*. The bridge itself was a different story. On each of the 48 *chasse-marées* the following material was placed:

48 planks measuring 3 inches thick and 12 feet long and one foot wide with holes drilled
   in the ends for the flooring of the bridge
1 wooden beam 10-inch by 10-inch by 12 feet long with five notches cut into it
2 handsaws
2 axes
2 skeins (240 yards) of Hambro line[90] for lashing the planks to the cables[91]

On the sturdiest boats, which would be placed in the centre of the bridge, the 13-inch cables were coiled in such a way that they could be played out in both directions simultaneously.

    Each boat had a yellow number painted on its bow and the 48 boats were divided into five divisions.[92] The two right divisions were under the direction of two Royal Engineers: Lieutenant Henry J. Savage, who commanded the boats closest to the left bank, and Lieutenant George J. West, who led the boats on his left. Captain William H. Slade of the Royal Engineers, with Lieutenant George V. Tinling, RE and Lieutenant Alexander W. Wallace, Royal Sappers and Artificers Corps, to assist him, would command the centre. All three of these officers would ride in *chasse-marée* number 38 – a mistake that would cause problems later. Lieutenant Alexander W. Robe's division was to the left of the centre, while Lieutenant Charles Rivers' division would be closest to the right bank. (Both Robe and Rivers were Royal Engineers.) On each boat would be two sailors to assist with the anchoring and two soldiers from the Royal Sappers and Artificers Corps. The sappers' job would be to cut the sideboards out of the boats once they were in position and spike the notch sleeper beam in place. They would then run the 13-inch cables across the notched sleeper and pass it on to the next boat. The cables would be spliced together after they were laid. Once the cables were in place, they would then secure the planks on to the cables to make the roadway.

Two other engineer officers would go on the boats. Lieutenant William Reid would ride with Rivers' division (the one closest to the right bank) and would supervise the securing of the cables to the 18-pounder cannon and dropping them into the marsh. These cannon were French guns captured when the British drove the French out of their defensive lines along the Nivelle in November. Lieutenant Samuel C. Melhuish would go with Lieutenant Savage's division and secure the cables on the left bank.

In order for the crossing to be successful, the right bank of the river had to be in British hands before the bridge could be built. Troops from the 2nd Guards Brigade of the 1st Division would be ferried across the river on pontoons to secure the far bank. Once it was secured the *chasse-marées* would then enter the river and the building would begin.

THE OPERATION BEGINS

Wellington's plan called for the bridge to be built on 24 February. To accomplish this, the various forces had to be in place beforehand. On 20 February, the pontoon bridge company that would ferry the troops across the Adour was at Fuentarabia, a small town along the Spanish border, about 25 miles from the crossing site. The plan originally called for this company to position itself in the rear of the foremost British units in the vicinity of the crossing site. However, an unknown staff officer informed Wellington that there would be no trouble moving the pontoons to the Adour in one night, if they were left in Bidart, a small village about 10 miles from the Adour. Wellington accepted this advice and six of the pontoons were ordered forward on the 20th, while the other 6 would move forward on the 21st. This would have unforeseen consequences for the operation, because the staff officer's information was wrong. It did not take into account the difficulty of moving the heavy pontoons along the sandy roads of the area.

On the 22 February the flotilla of *chasse-marées*, under the command of Captain Dowell O'Reilly, of the Royal Navy, put to sea. The passage from Socoa to the mouth of the Adour was expected to take 16–18 hours and the boats should be ready to enter the river by noon on the 23rd.

The troops that would secure the far bank of the Adour and invest Bayonne from the north, were under the command of Lieutenant General Sir John Hope. This corps had about 22,000 troops and consisted of Major General Kenneth Howard's 1st and Major General Charles Colville's 5th British Divisions, Major General Lord Aylmer's Independent British Brigade, Brigadier General Archibald Campbell's and Major General Thomas Bradford's Independent Portuguese Brigades, España's Spanish Division, and Major General John Vandeleur's Light Cavalry Brigade. The 1st Division, accompanied by a brigade of heavy artillery and a Royal Horse Artillery Rocket Troop, moved towards the river at 1 a.m. on the 23rd, a few hours after the flotilla left. The left column of the force, dragging four jolly boats and four 18-pounder artillery pieces, began to move cross-country through the pinewoods that covered the land just south of the river:

> within a short distance of Anglet, the whole turned off to the left by a cross-road towards the coast, observing the strictest silence, to avoid exciting the attention of the enemy, along the skirts of whose outposts the division was then marching. The night was so dark that it was impossible to discern any object beyond a few paces' distance; the crossroad along which the troops advanced was very narrow and muddy, with deep ditches at the sides. One of the eighteen-pounders, owing to the extreme obscurity, was drawn too near the edge, and by its enormous weight broke down the roadside, and sank into the deep muddy ditch, dragging the near horses after it. This occurrence delayed the march for some time, and it was not without the greatest exertions that the gun was drawn up out of the mud, and the march continued.[93]

Operational security was key to the success of the operation – sound and light discipline was strictly enforced. An officer in the Light Company of the 1st Battalion 3rd Foot Guards wrote:

> Alexander and myself were smoking our cigars and laughing and talking, when an officer of rank rode up, evidently much out of temper, and expressed great anger at finding us, as he said, 'making so much noise,' where silence was of so much consequence; 'and actually smoking!' exclaimed he. Our cigars were, of course, instantly thrown away, and Colonel Alexander made no reply. He merely pointed to the guns, which were marching with flambeaux at the horses' heads; and the rumbling that the said guns made enough to have aroused the 'seven sleepers'.[94]

The column, led by Lieutenant Colonel Sturgeon, Royal Staff Corps, Lieutenant Colonel Burgoyne of the Royal Engineers, and Lieutenant Colonel Augustus Frazer of the Royal Horse Artillery, arrived shortly before dawn on the bank of the river. The three officers examined it for the best place to launch the pontoons. While there, a French sentry on the far bank challenged them. Sturgeon ordered the troops to withdraw behind the sand dunes, until the pontoons arrived.[95] There they waited for the pontoons that were supposed to have little trouble moving. Three hours later, six of the twelve pontoons arrived and these only by taking horses from the artillery and teaming 20 horses to each carriage.[96] These too, however, got stuck in the sand about 500 yards from the water and even when thirty horses were attached to the carriages, they could not be moved.[97]

The right column, consisting of the 1st Guards Brigade, 1st Division plus the heavy artillery and a rocket troop, had the mission of preventing the French gunboats from moving downriver to stop the crossing. As the 1st Guards Brigade moved towards the river from the woods, they came under fire from the French corvette, *Sappho*, and some gunboats that were anchored across the river near the village of Le Boucaut. Williamson's 18-pounders and the RHA Rocket troop were brought up and a brisk artillery duel began. To the amazement of the watching troops:

> the rockets went skipping about the river like mad things, and dancing quadrilles in every direction but the right one. Some of them came back to ourselves, but happily without doing any mischief. The only one that took effect – and this seemed quite an accident – stuck in the bow of one of the boats, and sank her. The French soldiers, at that period wholly unaccustomed to this arm, were so frightened, that they jumped overboard with all their accoutrements and were drowned. The practice from our battery was not good at first, from the want of platforms; but this was soon rectified, and the corvette got a most handsome pummelling, and was glad at last to sheer off with the loss of her captain, and more than half her crew killed and wounded. One of our shots cut her flagstaff in two, and the tricolour was seen floating down the stream . . . Captain M—n, of the artillery, was walking about that evening a most ridiculous figure. A shot had shaved off the skirts of his coat, and being a rather Dutch-built, he looked just like a fat cock-pheasant, whose tail had been shot away by a bungling sportsman.[98]

A soldier named Lehmann, of the 1st King's German Legion Light Battalion saw the flag in the water. He stripped off his accoutrements and dove into the river, swimming furiously for the flag. The French sailors fired at him, but luck was with him and he returned to the bank unharmed:

> This exploit was rewarded by a liberal subscription from the officers who witnessed it, and Lehmann, a social spirit, employed the donation in treating the men of his company to a bottle of Lafitte each.[99]

At 11 a.m. the flow of the Adour had gone slack and the river was relatively calm. General Hope gave the order to begin the crossing. The sand was too deep for the pontoon carriages to move through, so the six jolly boats were removed from the carriages and the guardsmen carried them to the river on their shoulders. The French picquet on the far bank:

seemed at a loss what to do, and the moment our first boats were carried to the water's edge on men's shoulders, fairly ran off without firing a single shot, the advanced sentry's piece having missed fire.[100]

Thirty-six men from the Light Company of the 1st Battalion 3rd Foot Guards crossed over in the six boats and secured a hawser that stretched between the two banks. At the same time the six pontoons were removed from their carriages and each was carried on the shoulders of twenty-six guardsmen down to the water. There the pontoons were converted into two rafts, each made of three pontoons and capable of carrying about fifty men. The work was completed by noon. Word was received that the rest of the pontoons would be up shortly and the ferrying operation ceased until 2 p.m. Only the two light companies of the 3rd Guards had made it across.

This proved to be a mistake. By the time the crossing began again, the tide had turned and was running fast about 7 knots. This caused great difficulty in moving the rafts between the banks and by 5.30 p.m. about 500 men, under the command of the 2nd Guards Brigade Commander, Major General Edward Stopford, had crossed. One raft was stuck in the middle of the river until the slack tide at 6 p.m. The British force on the right bank now consisted of four companies from the 3rd Foot Guards; two light companies, one from the 3rd Foot Guards and one from the Coldstream Guards; and two rifle companies from the 5th Battalion 60th Regiment.

The French in Bayonne were not sitting idle. Around 5.30 p.m., about 1,000 French infantry, a mixed force of partial battalions from the 5th *Légère* and the 62nd *Ligne* Regiments, was seen approaching in three columns the British on the right bank. General Stopford prepared his forces to receive the enemy. On the last raft to make it over, General Hope sent two RHA Rocket teams under the command of Captain Henry Lane.[101] The rocketmen could not bring their horses and had to carry the rockets by themselves: 'each with one rocket ready in his hand, and three on his back in a case, with three poles on his shoulder . . .' [102] The 18-pounders on the left bank were placed in a position to hit the columns in the flank.

Lieutenant Colonel Willoughby Cotton deployed the light infantry into a skirmish screen, but it was forced back by the advancing French column. The skirmish was enough to cause the French numerous casualties. By the time they reached the British line, they fled at the first volley.[103] The retreating French were harassed by the British light infantry and by the rockets which caused considerable panic. An officer in the Light Infantry Company of the 3rd Foot Guards who was in the skirmish line, leaves us with an additional impression of the rocket fire:

as soon as the French came close enough, the rockets were fired, and most fortunately, at the first discharge, three went smack into the very centre of them. Instantly the drums ceased, and the large column burst and fled in irretrievable confusion. The ground was very favourable for light troops, and they were followed for a considerable distance, and suffered severely. Our loss was only five men killed and wounded.[104]

Things quieted down and the troops on the far bank:

> bivouacked during the night nearly on the same positions they had held
> during the day. Strong picquets were placed in observation of the intrenched
> camp [on the outskirts of Bayonne], Colonel Maitland's brigade [still on the
> left bank] retiring for the night into the wood; where, by felling trees and
> kindling large fires, the soldiers endeavoured to protect themselves against
> the piercing cold. It was a most brilliant moonlight night, and its stillness was
> uninterrupted, except by the murmur of the waves of the sea breaking on the
> sandy beach.[105]

Later in the evening six more pontoons arrived. Rather than taking the time to
build rafts, the pontoons were launched and twelve men were loaded on each.
Three hundred men who could row were detailed to the crossing. Shifts were set
up and rum from the commissary was found to fortify them – a half ration of rum
was given to each soldier right before he went on shift and when he came off.
Despite the tide, they found that except when it was flowing out, they could cross
over four hours in every six hour tide.[106]

Through the night, the rest of the Stopford's 2nd Guards Brigade was ferried
across. The next morning, the rest of the 1st Division began to cross. First came
Lieutenant Colonel Louis Baron Bussche's KGL Light Brigade, followed by the
Major General Henry de Hinüber's KGL Infantry Brigade, which was still
crossing at 3:00 in the afternoon. An officer in the KGL 5th Line Battalion,
observed of the passing: 'If the men do not sit still the boat begins to rock and the
motion increases of itself until the whole are in imminent Danger.' [107]

By dusk, the 1st Guards Brigade had crossed and as the 'last men of Colonel
Stuart's battalion were ferried over; the tide had now turned, and was running out
at such an amazing rate, that it was not without hard rowing that the last boat was
prevented from being drifted out to sea.' [108] The whole of the 1st Division, 'about
6000 strong were over, with thirty cavalry and two guns with their horses; the guns
were conveyed over on the raft, and the cavalry horses were swum over.' [109] The
rest of the artillery, supply trains, and officers' baggage would have to wait. Once
again it was a cold night with clear skies and a heavy frost, forcing the soldiers to
dig into the sand for warmth.[110]

THE FLOTILLA

The flotilla carrying the bridge set sail early on the evening of the 22nd. It immediately ran into problems with the weather. The wind refused to cooperate,
blowing strong in a southerly direction. On the 23rd, the flotilla was off the mouth
of the river, however the wind had dropped to a light breeze that changed direction often. Finally, on the 24th it changed again, this time blowing directly
landward, but causing heavy surf.

The mouth of the Adour River was a dangerous place.

> The wind had become more favourable, but the surf increased in a pro-
> portionate degree, rolling heavy waves over the bar of sand already

mentioned. This bar of sand, extending from the right bank of the river nearly across its mouth, renders the entrance to the harbour particularly dangerous whenever the wind is high; and, as it changes its positions with the change of wind and tide, it requires at different seasons of the year, a totally different pilotage. Towards the close of the evening the sky became overcast with heavy clouds, the wind rose, and threatened a violent storm; the whole extent of coast exhibited a tremendous and uninterrupted line of surf, and the heavy waves rolling over the bar were awfully grand.[111]

About 8 a.m., Admiral Penrose, who had transferred his flag to the survey ketch, *Gleaner*, ordered the flotilla to go in. The hired pilots, who knew of the dangers, refused to try it. Lieutenant Debenham, the Royal Navy's Agent of Transport, who had assembled the *chasse-marées*, was the first to attempt to cross the bar. Despite being considered very old by one Royal Engineer officer, he bravely went forward in a six-oar cutter. He made it to the bar, but because of mistiming the surf, he ended up beaching the boat. He and the crew quickly jumped out and hauled the boat into the calmer waters of the river.[112] Captain O'Reilly, the captain of the flotilla, leading by example, was the next to make the attempt. With him, was Captain Peter Faddy of the Royal Artillery. Captain O'Reilly's luck ran out and his boat hit the bar and tipped over. O'Reilly was stunned by a blow to his back, but survived. Five of his crew, however, drowned. Once he recovered, he and the rest of his crew also dragged their boat into the river.[113] The third boat, commanded by Lieutenant George Cheynee of the *Woodlark*, successfully navigated the passage.

The tide was falling quickly and the combination of the heavy surf and the outward flowing tide would make it too difficult to pass over the bar or through the channel. Compounding the problem, if the boat made it across the bar it would still have to fight the falling tide to get upriver. Much to the exasperation of the infantry on shore, Admiral Penrose ordered the operation to halt until the tide changed again,[114] a wait of almost six hours!

Admiral Penrose realized, too late for the first boats, that to find the channel the boats needed something to guide on – something that would show the safe passage into the river. In peacetime the main channel was normally marked by large pole on the left bank, called the *Balise Occidentale*. Behind it on the same bank, on a high hill about a mile and a half inland, was another marker, the *Balise Orientale*. Seamen used these to find the channel. The French commandant of Bayonne, however, had the *Balise Occidentale* removed to prevent any enemy vessels from using it as a marker. Admiral Penrose sent ashore a pilot who was familiar with the river, to set up a halberd with a handkerchief as flag on the line that the boats were to steer.[115]

Around 2 p.m., an hour after low tide, sufficient water was flowing back into the Adour to make the crossing of the bar possible. Admiral Penrose ordered the next wave of boats in. The first two boats to go in immediately ran into problems. The first was from the sloop, *Lyra*. It too wrecked on the bar, killing Mr Bloye, the *Lyra*'s master mate, and all of the crew. The second boat was from the brig, *Martial*. Captain George Elliot, the brig's captain, went in with it, and he, the ship's surgeon, and the crew drowned when the boat capsized in the surf. The surgeon initially survived the capsizing and was picked up by the third boat, which was from one of the transports and had been converted into a gunboat. But this boat also ran aground and the shock knocked the 24-pounder gun loose and it crushed the hapless surgeon.[116]

No other crews would attempt the crossing. To encourage the crews, Admiral Penrose offered 50 gold Guineas to the crew of the first *chasse-marée* to enter the river. This worked. A *chasse-marée* 'ventured thro' the surf & after almost disappearing, & when every one thought she was gone to the bottom, she rose again, & entered the river. Her Crew had tied themselves to the Masts, & were not washed away. Her entrance into the river was greeted with three cheers by the Troops . . .' [117] This success inspired the other boats and soon others were trying their luck. Three boats and their crews from the transports were lost crossing the bar. According to one eyewitness:

> a Spanish *chasse-marée* had nearly struggled through the surf, when an enormous wave was seen gradually nearing the vessel; and, just before it reached it, raising its curling ridge high above the deck, with one fatal sweep bore it down to the bottom. A moment after, parts of the shattered vessel rose to the surface, and exhibited the wretched mariners clinging to its fragments; some were drifted till they actually got footing on the shore, and, as it was flood tide, hopes were entertained of saving them, by means of ropes thrown to them; but another tremendous wave rolling majestically on to the beach, in a moment bore them away for ever.[118]

The original flotilla consisted of one sloop, two brigs, five gunboats, and forty-eight *chasse-marées*. Thirty-four of the *chasse-marées* made it safely across the bar, one was destroyed on it, and another was wrecked on the shore. The two sloops carrying the boom made it across, however the *Martial* ran ashore. Four of the gunboats made it through, however the fifth (the one that picked up the surgeon of the *Martial*) was dashed to pieces on the shore. Between 30 and 40 men were killed in the crossing.[119]

Twelve of the *chasse-marées* did not attempt the crossing and returned to St Jean de Luz. Admiral Penrose wrote in his official dispatch on the 25th 'that so many *chasse-marées* ventured the experiment, I attribute to there having been one or more sappers placed in each of them, and a captain and eight lieutenants of engineers commanding them in divisions.' [120] In a letter to Lord Bathurst, Wellington praised the naval officers stating it 'was effected with a degree of gallantry and skill seldom equalled.'[121]

As the *chasse-marées* and the brigs entered the calmer waters of the river, they were directed into their proper position. The four gunboats, under the command of Lieutenant Cheshire, moved up beyond Le Boucaut, to provide protection for the bridge. Each boat carried an 18-pounder gun and had ten Royal Artillerymen to man it. Although Lieutenant Cheshire commanded the gunboats, the actual guns were under the command of Captain Faddy of the Royal Artillery.[122] Lieutenant Douglas led the brigs carrying the boom upriver, while Lieutenant

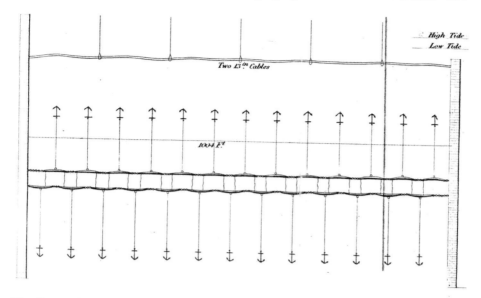

The Boom Protecting the Bridge of Boats on the Adour river. *By Major General Howard Douglas*

Collins, of the frigate *Porcupine*, directed the *chasse-marées*, which would form the bridge, into place.

Once the two sloops carrying the boom were in place, they began laying the boom. It was supervised and built by the navy. The booms were laid parallel to each other about 20–25 feet apart. Each mast or spar was anchored at its centre, with the outer boom having its anchor laid upstream, while the boom closest to the bridge had its anchor laid downstream. The masts in each line were placed 20 feet apart and secured to each other by chains, end to end. The second boom was placed so that its masts covered the gaps in the first boom. To further strengthen the boom, a 13-inch cable was stretched from bank to bank, made taut, and then lashed to the ends of each mast. The booms were supposed to be 24 feet apart, and were connected to each other by 35–40 foot long chains. These chains were supposed to hang 12 feet under the surface of the water, where it was hoped that they would take up the shock should the first boom be rammed.[123] Napier, who interviewed Major Tod (the officer responsible for building the bridge), described it the best:

> The boom, moored with anchors above and below, was a double line of masts connected with chains and cables, so as to form a succession of squares, in the design that if a vessel broke through the outside, it should by the shock turn round in the square and become entangled with the floating wrecks of the line through which it had broken.[124]

The boom took almost 2 days to build, and was in place by noon on 26

February. The navy would continue to maintain the boom until the war was over.

Unfortunately for the bridge-builders, *chasse-marée* number 38 was not among the boats that made it across the bar. Number 38 was one of the largest boats and was supposed to occupy the centre of the bridge. It not only carried Captain Slade and Lieutenants Tinling and Wallace, but also three of the 13-inch cables that were to support the roadway. The crew of *chasse-marée* number 26, which carried two more of the cables, also refused to cross the bar and returned to St Jean de Luz.[125]

As the *chasse-marées* crossed the bar, they were directed to a site about a half-mile upriver, opposite of two houses called Areachon. Here the river narrowed to about 270 yards wide. Lieutenant Collins directed them into position. A large staff was placed on the left bank and as each boat passed, it would drop its anchor. Each boat had two anchors and placed one off the bow and the other off the stern. The planners felt the strength of the tide would be too powerful for conventional anchors, so where possible, artillery pieces taken from the captured French fortifications on the Nivelle, were used instead. Twenty-six of the boats were anchored 40 feet apart (measured from mast to mast). Once all the boats were lined up, they were secured with lines fore and aft to the boats on either side of them.

As soon as a boat was anchored, the two sappers aboard began removing the top gunnel on each side of the boat. Once all the boats were in place, the heavy 13-inch cables were played out from the centre boats to the banks. When the 100 yard long cables were paid out, another cable was spliced to each end. As the boats in Lieutenant Rivers' division came in, the six boats that were carrying the 18-pounders were sent to the right bank. In addition to the cannon, each boat also carried the necessary tackle and hoists for lifting the gun. Lieutenant Reid, the engineer officer in charge on the left bank, directed the hoisting of the 18-pounder cannon, each weighing over 2,000 pounds, from the decks of the *chasse-marées*. When a 13-inch cable was passed to the right bank, it was tied to one of the cannon, which was then lowered into the marshy ground on the other side of the wall. Green bullock hides were placed between the cables and the wall, to prevent chafing from breaking the cables.

On the left bank, Lieutenant Melhuish was not so fortunate. Things went wrong from the very beginning. Aboard *chasse-marée* number 38 (one of the boats that did not cross the bar), was the commissary officer, who had the sandbags and other engineer stores that would be used to build the platform. The capstans and blocks had been placed on six different boats, so he could begin to assemble the machinery that would keep the cables taut. Although the engineers worked through that night, little headway was made by first light on the 25th.[126]

Lieutenant General Hope could not wait for the bridge to be completed. He had to get the rest of his infantry, artillery, and cavalry across. The indefatigable Lieutenant Debenham, the transport agent who procured the *chasse-marées* and the first officer to cross the bar successfully, took charge of the last six pontoons to arrive and constructed two more rafts. Each raft consisted of three pontoons that were secured with baulks and floored with chesses (i.e. the floorboards of a pontoon bridge). These rafts were strong enough to carry four artillery pieces or sixteen horses. The crossings did not go smoothly. On one crossing, one of the rafts sunk close to the shore, but they were able to retrieve it. Through trial and error, they discovered that no weight could be placed over the centre pontoon. The guns or horses had to be placed along the outer edges to prevent the raft bowing in the middle and having the pontoons fill with water. The raft secured to a hawser had been rowed to the opposite side of the river. Once the raft was loaded, the crew cast off from the bank and let the flow of the river swing them to the other bank. The crew hauled on the rope, to lessen the arch of swing, so they could land at their chosen spot. Each round trip took about an hour to complete.[127]

On the 25th, Campbell's and Bradford's Portuguese Brigades, Bull's Royal Horse Artillery troop, and two squadrons of Vandeleur's light dragoons crossed. Lieutenant General Hope also crossed that day and set up his headquarters in Le Boucaut. As his brigades arrived on the right bank, he moved them east towards Bayonne to begin the investment of the city from the north.

By noon on the 26th, about 40 hours after the boats crossed the bar at the entrance to the river, the engineers had completed the bridge. Over 800 planks had been laid to form the roadway. But despite the detailed planning and the Herculean efforts of the engineers, they were too late. Most of the force had already been ferried across and had moved on. Once the bridge was complete, the rest of the cavalry, artillery, the officers' baggage, and España's Spanish division crossed.

Eight 18-pounders also crossed and a battery was constructed upriver of the boom. Another battery, with eight 18-pounders, was built opposite it on the left bank. These 16 guns were to fire on any ships or boats the French might send downriver in an attempt to break the bridge. Upriver of the boom were the four gunboats under the command of Lieutenant Cheshire. In case a fireship or a large, floating object, such as the mill that broke the French bridge over the Danube in 1809, made it past the gunboats, the batteries, and the two booms, several rowboats were stationed between the booms and the bridge. These were manned 24 hours a day and were equipped with fire grapples, to allow the crews to catch the object and either drag it ashore or anchor it before it reached the bridge. Four *chasse-marées* were kept in reserve in case the bridge was damaged and a boat had to be replaced. The French never tried to break the bridge, however.[128]

Once built, the bridge required constant attention. Major Tod, of the Royal Staff Corps, was placed in charge of maintaining it. In the beginning, the need to get troops across was the primary concern. The cables were constantly wet and stretched so much the planking between the boats was only a few inches above the waterline. When the wind blew and the swells on the water picked up, waves would lap over the boards. It was not uncommon for the waves to be so high that it would cause the bridge to rock dangerously and all traffic would have to be halted

The Bridge of Boats across the Adour. *By Major General Howard Douglas*

until they subsided. The gun tackles on the left bank were constantly being tightened to prevent this, however this problem was never fully solved until hostilities ceased. Once peace was declared, the two booms were dismantled. Large pine trees from the local forest were cut and used to replace the cables, providing a relatively stable platform. This allowed the removal of six of the *chasse-marées* from the bridge.

Peace brought other problems for Major Tod and his men. The bridge blocked all commercial navigation on the river. A system was devised to open the bridge when a ship needed to pass through. The crew maintaining the bridge became so adept at doing this, they could open a gap and close it in a few minutes. An approaching vessel was required to anchor until the gap was opened and permission was given to proceed. At least one collision occurred when:

> owing to the clumsiness of some French sailors, in not dropping an anchor in sufficient time, a brig drifted with the current, which was now running rapidly out, against the centre of the bridge; and, by the impetus with which it struck it, three *chasse-marées* were driven out of their proper positions, the spars and planking of the bridge all displaced, and the French vessel completely entangled by its bowsprit and shrouds in the rigging of the *chasse-marées*. The French sailors seemed to despair of being able to remedy the mischief, and were alarmed at the consequences of their carelessness; many were their exclamations, but they never once attempted to repair the damage. Not so the English sailors and Staff Corps, who were employed on the bridge; these under the indefatigable activity and prompt ingenuity of Major Tod, soon carried anchors high up the river, warped off the French brig, brought up the bridge-vessels again into line, and in less than two hours restored the whole to its former perfection.[129]

The bridge was finally dismantled on 12 May 1814.

The Pontoon Train

> *'I shall have sad work with this bridge throughout the campaign, and yet we can do nothing without it.'*
> – WELLINGTON 11 MAY 1813

By early 1811, Wellington realized that he needed a pontoon train with his army. On 31 March, he wrote to the Earl of Liverpool requesting a bridging train, consisting of 80 pontoons and carriages, with the necessary ropes and tools, be sent to him. In a remarkable lack of foresight in the same letter, he states: 'I do not think it necessary to require horses for it, and I propose to move it by bullocks.' On 18 April, he wrote once again to the Earl of Liverpool, when he realized the British army had no troops trained to build pontoon bridges. This time he requested that when the pontoons were sent to him, that master pontooneers be sent with them. His plan was to use these warrant officers to train locally hired Portuguese to build the bridges.

On 29 June 1811, 24 pontoons arrived in Lisbon. Over the next two years, Wellington was able to obtain more pontoons – using a combination of Spanish, Portuguese, and captured French pontoons – to expand his train and as replacements for those that were lost or unserviceable. In 1813, the train was huge and consisted of forty-eight waggons:

38 Carriages, with pontoon complete
1 Carriage with baulks, 6 chesses, etc. of a pontoon condemned
3 Carriages with spare wheels
2 Carriages with spare baulks and chesses
1 Carriage with spare rope
1 Carriage with a small boat
1 Carriage with camp equipment
4 waggons for small stores
2 Forge waggons
The number of animals to move it were:
520 Oxen
283 Draught horses
28 Riding horse[130]

These were a combination of heavy and light pontoons. A heavy pontoon was 21 feet 1 inch long on its top, 16 feet 8 inches long on the bottom, 4 feet 10 inches wide, and 2 feet 3 inches deep. The pontoon was an open top, rectangular shaped box with straight sides and a 45-degree angle in both the bow and the stern. It had a wooden frame that was covered with two layers of tin. The pontoon weighed about 1,060 pounds, the carriage over 1,400 pounds, and the equipment and planking another 1,400 pounds. Total weight of the heavy pontoon and all of its equipment was over 3,800 pounds,[131] a light pontoon weighed about 750 pounds. Its carriage weighed about 1,200 pounds, and its planking and equipment approximately 900 pounds. Total weight for the light pontoon, its carriage, and equipment was about 2,850 pounds.[132]

According to the 1801 edition of the *Pocket Gunner*, each pontoon carried the following equipment:

4 baulks each 22 feet 8 inches x 12 inches x 4 inches
1 gang-board 22 feet x 12 inches x 2¼ inches
6 chesses each 11 feet 6 inches x 2 feet 4 inches x 1½ inches
2 oars
1 anchor
1 grappling hook
1 setter
4 iron bolts with keys
2 mounting bars
4 binding sticks
4 spring lines
4 fauxes
1 cable
1 sheer line

1 boat-hook
1 maul
1 pump
1 windlass
4 picquet stakes
1 small pump[133]

The pontoons had a serious design flaw. Instead of being an enclosed box, the top of the pontoon was opened. In a fast-moving river or one with heavy swells, they tended to fill with water and were in danger of sinking. A pontoon bridge was built across the Guadiana River to support the British siege of Badajoz in 1811. A heavy rain caused the river to rise and swamp and sink one of the pontoons. The bridge was swept away and its loss caused much hardship for the besiegers. A year later, the British pontoon bridge over the Tagus River at Almaraz had to be removed from the river several times because the rough water was threatening to swamp the pontoons. This problem was never solved during the Peninsular War. At the crossing of the Garonne in 1814, heavy rains caused the river to rise swamping several of the pontoons and forcing the bridge to be lifted until the river had subsided.[134]

These pontoons were carried on a modified six-pounder artillery carriage that could not stand up to the rough roads of the Iberian Peninsula. The main problem appeared to be with the wheels. They were too large to carry the pontoons safely. In early January 1813, Wellington's Artillery Commander, Colonel Dickson (who had been ordered by Wellington to oversee the pontoon equipment), decided to cut them down and rebuild them. Yet there were problems with this as he explained on 25 January 1813:

> It was my intention to have cut the wheels to draw them together, but they had not all shrunk, and if they had been cut now, they would have required it again in a very short time as soon as they became exposed to the weather, and the seldomer this operation is done the better. The Master artificers that I consulted said it would be a prejudice to the wheels to touch them now, and I am sorry to say that they added that the wheels are of an indifferent description being contract made, and after running a short time will be in frequent want of repair. I am more particular in mentioning this, that your Lordship may keep in view the necessity that after the first considerable march the Pontoons make, they should halt at some convenient place, for the purpose of cutting and putting the wheels to rights, to ensure their going through any service in view.[135]

Lieutenant Colonel Frazer, the commander of Wellington's horse artillery, noted in May 1813, that 'they travel badly, break down, and in short do all that is not wished.' Frazer was forced to send all his spare wheels to the pontoon train to keep them moving.[136] One artillery officer, who was forced to provide horses to move the train, wrote in a letter to his stepfather:

> The Pontoon (all things included) travels 40 cwt, and on a six Pr. Carriage the play or swing of the Pontoon on the carriage when it comes over stony

or other uneven ground, is so very great, that nothing but the slow steady pull of the ox prevents it either from upsetting or breaking something. Yesterday (the first day of the horses drawing them) our accidents between Louzaa (about 2 leagues on this side of Castello Branco) & Pedrogão (being four leagues, of which two were hilly & very rough) we upset two Pontoons, snapped two pintails [the pin, or hook, at the rear of the axletree bed of a limber, to which the gun trail or waggon perch is secured when limbered up] & broke two axletree arms.[137]

The situation was so bad, that Wellington wrote to Lord Bathurst on 11 May 1813:

We have been sadly delayed by the bridge, without which it is obvious we can do nothing. The equipment is quite new, and has marched only from Abrantes; but there has already been much breakage, and I understand that the carriages are shamefully bad. The truth is, that English tradesmen, particularly contractors, are become so dishonest, that no reliance can be placed on any work, particularly in iron, done by contract.

The carriages were only part of the problem. Wellington planned to use oxen to move the train. A minimum of 3 teams of oxen was required to move each pontoon. This meant the pontoon train required at least 150 oxen. Oxen of course were not the fastest animals and the pontoon train could only average 10 miles a day on the bad roads in the Iberian Peninsula. Mules were also tried, with six mules pulling each pontoon. In early May 1813, before the start of the campaign that would see the British in France by the end of the year, Wellington ordered the pontoon train be equipped with horses. The Royal Artillery Drivers, under the command of Second Lieutenant Alexander Mathieson, were detached from Captain Cairnes' nine-pounder artillery brigade and with those of the 18-pounder brigade in the artillery reserve at Covilhã. The commanders were told the horses, the forage mules, and the necessary harnesses for the animals had to be sent to the pontoon train. A total of 264 horses were soon transferred.

Neither Captain Cairnes nor Captain Thompson of the 18-pounder brigade were too happy with having to give up their horses. In place of his trained horses that were acclimatized to the area, Captain Cairnes received a draft of horses coming up from Lisbon. He wrote to his stepfather, Major General William Cuppage, Royal Artillery, that the situation 'has mortified & vexed me beyond all possible expression . . .' Captain Thompson, who instead of receiving replacement horses, had to make do with the oxen from the pontoon train, wrote a letter of protest to Colonel Dickson, Wellington's Chief of Artillery. In it, he asked to be removed from the command and to be allowed to rejoin Captain Lawson's artillery brigade, that was attached to the 5th Division, because 'I find my dignity and consequence as an Officer so much lessened in the eyes of all . . .'[138]

The horse also proved to be unsatisfactory and when the pontoon train had reached France in late autumn, oxen were pulling it once again. But the campaign had taken a terrible toll on the oxen of the pontoon train as well as the pontoons themselves. By the time Wellington's army reached France, in late 1813 the pontoon train had only 34 functional pontoons.[139] In early February 1814, Lieutenant Colonel Elphinstone reported to Wellington that over five hundred oxen had died in the past nine months![140] Once again the artillery was tasked to provide the horses from one of their batteries and from those used to haul the reserve artillery ammunition, so that the 34 pontoons could move.[141]

Compounding all of these problems was a shortage of trained officers and men who would build the pontoon bridges.

The British Army had no school to teach the soldiers how to build pontoon bridges. On 25 December 1811, the first commander of the pontoon train was appointed – Lieutenant Robert Piper, of the Royal Engineers. Also assigned to the train was Mr Packenham, who has been described as a bridgemaster, a foreman of bridges, and a master of pontooneers in a variety of sources. He was most likely Lieutenant Piper's second-in-command, and did operate independently with several of the pontoons, when the situation demanded it. In 1813, the commander of the pontoon train was Captain Richard Boteler, RE.[142]

It took 356 men to man it (five officers, eight civilians, 343 enlisted men) and they were a mixture of British and Portuguese troops:

From the Engineer Department
2 Engineer Officers
1 Superintendent
1 Master Artificer (Civil)
7 Civil Artificers
10 Royal Sappers and Miners
From the Portuguese Navy
1 Lieutenant
2 Ensigns
4 Boatswains
60 Seamen
Other Personnel
1 Deputy Assistant Commissary General
2 Clerks
3 Conductors
2 Conductors (2nd Class)
250 Drivers[143]

The Portuguese sailors were to receive 16 *vinteens* of pay a day and the same rations as the British soldiers. On 18 January 1813, seven Ordnance Civil Engineers – 2 wheelers, 2 smiths, 2 tinmen, and 1 carpenter – were furnished to the pontoon train from the siege-train by Colonel Dickson.[144] In January 1814, Captain Frederick English, a 24 year-old Royal Engineer who had not been in the Peninsula since the evacuation at Coruña in 1809, took command.

Although the pontoon train was used during the campaigns of 1812 and 1813, it was mostly laid to assist in keeping lines of communications open. It performed adequately in this role. However, in 1814, the train was deployed in support of combat operations along the Garonne River. There, in full view of the army, the bridge-builders would face spectacular failure due to a combination of poor planning, faulty equipment, and horrendous weather. During it, a third of the Anglo-Allied army would be isolated on the far bank of an impassable river – exposed to potential destruction for several days while the pontoon bridge was out of action.

In late March 1814, the pontoon train was tasked with bridging the Garonne River in support of the Army's assault on Toulouse. The crossing was to take place at Portet on the night of 27 March. Heavy rains had turned the roads into a quagmire and movement was very slow. Francis Larpent, the army's judge advocate general left a vivid description of these roads:

> Yesterday was entirely rainy, and our road was, I might almost say, as bad as any we have ever passed with artillery, and that is saying much. The troops were splashed up to their caps, and hundreds were walking barefoot in the clay up to the calves of their legs for about 5 miles . . . To give you a notion of it I may mention that Lord Wellington's barouche was three hours fast in it at one place; one hind wheel up to the axle, the other in the air . . . I left them endeavouring to move it by means of four artillery horses, in addition to his own six mules, in vain; six oxen in addition got it clear at last.[145]

The train did not arrive at the site until 2200 hours. The initial plan was to have a covering force rowed across the river in pontoons, while preparations were made for laying the bridge. Lieutenant Peter Wright, an officer assigned to the train was to oversee the crossing of the covering force, while Captain English would direct operations from the near bank.[146]

The heavy rains that made the approach so difficult had caused the river to rise and to flow fast. Things began to go wrong from the very beginning:

> The whole of this plan was very shortly knocked on the head; English first sent his jolly boat with the sheer line; whether from mismanagement or the rapidity of the current, the boat went down the river and it was about an hour before it could be brought up again. They then tried the thing again, and with the same success. It was then thought wise to go higher up the river and at last they fastened it to the other bank. Unfortunately the rope instead of swimming down the river stuck so fast at the bottom, that it was a full hour before they could get it loose, and it then immediately stuck again in the same kind of way. When it first got fast at the bottom I tried to persuade English to place two or three pontoons under it, some distance apart, in order that the rope might be floated; however they were afraid that the pontoons might be lost in so rapid a current. At last after sticking at it for two or three hours or more they tried this plan and succeeded in stretching the sheer line across after five hours of hard labour.[147]

But their problems had just begun! They used the sheer line to measure the width of the river and discovered that the river was 159 yards wide – 26 yards too wide for their bridge. Something they should have known if a proper reconnaissance had been conducted prior to their arrival. An officer of the 52nd Foot, recorded that 'Wellington was furious. I never saw him in such a rage, and no wonder; for this unpardonable mistake was the cause of many days delay.'[148]

On 31 March, another attempt was made to lay a bridge. The plan was to lay the bridge at Rocques, which was on the opposite bank. Once the bridge was built, Hill's corps would cross and seize the bridge across the Ariege River at Antagabele. Captain English and his pontoon train arrived at the site on time and began constructing it at dusk. Once again there were a series of mishaps: 'from the rapidity of the current, the clumsiness of the workmen and from the two or three accidents, the bridge was not complete until daylight.' [149] Compounding English's problems was the condition of the river bottom – it consisted of loose, shifting gravel, which provided no purchase for the anchors. The bridge had to be kept in place with the sheer lines that were tied to trees on the banks.

Although the bridge held, the British luck did not. Once General Hill was across, his forces discovered the heavy rains had flooded the countryside and the road system would not support the movement of his troops and their guns. On 1 April, Wellington ordered Hill back across the river and the bridge was removed. The marching and countermarching exhausted the troops, who were at a loss for why they had to go back – especially after it took so long to build in the first place.[150]

A third attempt was ordered. This time a thorough reconnaissance was made to ensure the problems with the first two crossings were not repeated. The French were alert to any possible crossing and had cavalry patrols all along the river. Lieutenant Wright found a suitable spot about 3 miles upstream of the town of Grenade. The site was at a bend in the river and was dominated by the heights on the British side. Although the site looked good, Wright needed to measure it to ensure it was not too wide. When he approached the bank, a French soldier on the opposite bank engaged him in a lengthy conversation and would not leave. Wright finally 'pretended that the calls of nature were imperative. The Frenchman, out of decency, withdrew. The engineer popped out his sextant, took the angle, &c., and was off.'[151]

After the previous two failures, Wellington had to see for himself the proposed site. He covered his cocked hat with an oilskin and rode to the river with only two others. There he struck up a conversation with the French picquet,[152] while he dismounted, walked down to the river and checked it out. Lieutenant Wright suggested to Wellington that it would be better to make the crossing during daylight hours to minimize the problems encountered in the first two crossings.

Construction began at 5 a.m. on 4 April. Wright's estimate of the width of the river was correct and 4 hours later a 125-yard bridge was laid. The crossing site was not perfect due to the high bank on the British side, which made getting to the bridge difficult. Additionally, they had the same problems with a shifting riverbed that prevented the anchors from holding. The sheer lines were fastened to trees on the nearside, however there were none on the far bank. Based on a suggestion from Wellington, the anchors were buried on the shore, to secure the lines on the right bank.[153]

Hill's corps began crossing, while the regimental bands played *The British Grenadiers* and *The Downfall of Paris*. Vivian's Cavalry Brigade and Gardiner's

Royal Horse Artillery troop followed the 4th Division. To prevent vibrations that could cause the bridge to collapse, the infantry crossed three abreast; the cavalry in single file, while the horse artillery was unlimbered and the horses led across separately. The guns and limbers were then pulled across by hand. When the guns reached the far bank, the local peasants who were observing the activities, helped to drag them up the bank. By early afternoon, heavy rains began to fall and the river began to rise. The speed of the current was placing so much stress on the bridge; it began to have a large bow in it.[154]

Captain English's luck was about to fail once again:

> English thought it best to take up everything except the pontoons which were well secured by sheer lines and anchors. The bad weather now appeared to have set in and on the 5th, the river still continuing to swell, English took away four or five pontoons from the centre. The sheer lines immediately fell in the water and one pontoon was sunk by the weight of the sheer line. Lord Wellington, who was on the spot, ordered the whole to be taken up.[155]

It turns out that although the pontoon was swamped, it did not sink. Instead it floated away down the river. Lieutenant Reid, who helped build the bridge of boats across the Adour six weeks earlier, galloped downstream to the town of Verdan. There he:

> offered a reward of *cent francs*, or five pounds, to any inhabitants who would get boats and stop the pontoon and bring it ashore. The deserter was thus secured, and today brought back in triumph by a party of soldiers.[156]

The heavy rain continued through the night and by the morning of 5 April had risen about 2 feet. The conditions of the roads worsened and horses sunk up to their knees in the mud and clay. Hill's corps was trapped on the far side of the river and had the French shown any initiative, could have been destroyed by the French. The river fell over 3 feet the night of the 5th, however more rains caused it to rise again that night. The rain finally let up and on the 7th the bridge was rebuilt.[157]

The crisis had passed. Communications had been re-established with the isolated II Corps. The British moved on to Toulouse, where they defeated Marshal Soult on 10 April in the next to last battle of the Peninsular War.

Wellington appears to have learned from his experiences in the Peninsula. During the Waterloo Campaign, he had two pontoon companies (5th Company, 2nd Battalion and the 2nd Company, 4th Battalion) and a hawser bridge assigned to his army.

Colonel Sturgeon, the brains behind many of the bridges, did not survive the war. He was killed by French skirmishers on 19 March 1814 at Vic-de-Bigorre. Major Tod survived the war, but was placed on half-pay after Waterloo.

Wellington's operations benefited enormously from the ingenuity and skill of the officers of the Royal Staff Corps, who made it possible for the army to cross rivers securely and promptly, even though, for most of the war, they lacked proper bridging equipment and had to make do with materials they found to hand. This had the advantage that Wellington was not tied to a slow-moving pontoon train and was able to advance rapidly when the opportunity arose, both in 1809 against Victor and in 1811 in pursuit of Masséna.

Elsewhere, the construction of the bridge at Villa Velha and the repair of that at Alcantara greatly improved his strategic communications and helped to create conditions for his advance into Spain in 1812. The Staff Corps officers exemplify the benefits of the reforms and growing professionalism of the army brought about by the long years of war and the Duke of York's reforms. In the Peninsula they had the opportunity to turn their training to practical account, and, by overcoming real and unforeseeable difficulties, to become more expert in their field. They played a crucial, if often overlooked, part in ensuring the efficiency of Wellington's army in the Peninsula.

NOTES

1   Douglas, Howard, *An Essay on the Principles and Construction of Military Bridges and the Passage of Rivers in Military Operations*, 2nd edition, London, Thomas and William Boone, 1832, pp. 300–301.
2   Ibid, p. 301.
3   Ibid, p. 394.
4   Ibid, pp. 113–14.
5   The inability of the French engineers to keep the bridge across the Danube river operational, almost resulted in the destruction of the French Army at Aspern–Essling in May 1809.
6   Horward, Donald D., *The French Campaign in Portugal 1810–1811, An Account by Jean Jacques Pelet*, Minneapolis, University of Minnesota Press, 1973, pp. 251–52.
7   A common practice among both the French and British armies was to use doors, shutters, and roofs as a ready source of firewood. The situation was so prevalent that Wellington had to issue orders to his soldiers forbidding this practice.
8   Jones, John, *Journal of the Sieges Carried on by the Army under the Duke of Wellington in Spain*, 2nd Edition, vol. 1, London, T. Egerton, 1826, p. 4.
9   Garwood, F.S., 'The Royal Staff Corps, 1800–1837' *Royal Engineer Journal*, vol. 57, 1943, p. 81.
10 Ward, S.G.P., *Wellington's Headquarters, A Study in the Administrative Problems in the Peninsula 1809–1814*, Oxford, Oxford University Press, 1957, pp. 28–29.
11 Garwood, p. 82.
12 Haythornthwaite, Philip, *Wellington's Specialist Troops*, London, Osprey, 1988, p. 34.
13 Burgoyne, John, *Life and Correspondence of Field Marshal Sir John Burgoyne*, London, Richard Bentley, 1893, p. 242.
14 Jones, vol. 2, p. 110.
15 Napier, William F., *History of the War in the Peninsula and in the South of France*, vol. 6, London, Constable, 1993, p. 541.
16 Oman, however, muddies the water when he implies that both Sturgeon and Tod were engineers. He also misspells Tod's name, Oman, Charles, *A History of the Peninsular War*, vol. 7, New York, AMS, 1980, p. 338.
17 'The number of trained officers of engineers with the Peninsular Army was very small – not much over thirty, but of rank and file to serve under them there were practically none. Of the corps called the Royal Military Artificers . . . there were only thirty-four attached to the army in 1810, and it was far on in 1811 before their numbers reached a hundred,' Oman, Charles, *Wellington's Army, 1809–1814*, London, Greenhill Books, 1993, pp. 281–82.
18 Unfortunately what unit the 500 men were from is not known.
19 Napier, vol. III, pp. 357–366.
20 Douglas, pp. 230–31, Garwood states it was 200 feet of mangers that were used, p. 83.
21 Douglas, pp. 231–32.
22 Garwood, pp. 83–84.

23 Horward, p. 474.
24 Garwood, p. 82. Scott did not actually observe the operations. At the time he was a cadet at the Royal Military College at Hythe. After he had been there a year, according to F.S. Garwood, 'he commenced filling a notebook with the subjects in which a young officer of the Royal Staff Corps was instructed. He was a neat writer and an excellent draughtsman. This small book contains detailed descriptions of every expedient used in crossing rivers employed by military engineers in the operations in the Spanish Peninsula, it was compiled while the war was still in progress.' It is highly likely that Scott copied the descriptions verbatim from memoranda written by the officers who built the bridges. In 1816, Colonel Douglas wrote a book on bridging operations and often used the exact words that Scott used in his descriptions, Douglas's book was the standard work on the subject and was reprinted in 1832 and 1856.
25 Ibid, pp. 86–87.
26 Simmons, George, *A British Rifle Man*, London, Greenhill, 1986, p. 149.
27 Tomkinson, William, *The Diary of a Cavalry Officer*, London, Frederick Muller, 1971, pp. 86–87.
28 The Almeida Bridge was the site of a fierce action between the British Light Division and units of Marshal Ney's VI Corps on 24 July 1810. The British commander, General Robert Craufurd, disobeying Wellington's orders, kept his division deployed on the far side of the bridge and was caught by surprise. With only one bridge to cross the river, the Light Division had to make a fighting withdrawal in the face of overwhelming odds. Craufurd came close to losing his division, due to his poor judgement.
29 The letter, with others, in French is in the appendix to *Wellington's Dispatches*, (New Edition), London, John Murray, 1838, Volume IV.
30 Garwood, pp. 87–88.
31 Garwood, pp. 88–89.
32 Oman, vol. 3, p. 156.
33 Horward, p. 300.
34 Dickson, Alexander, *The Dickson Manuscripts*, vol. 2, Cambridge, Ken Trotman, 1987, p. 239.
35 Ibid, p. 239.
36 Garwood, p. 85.
37 Mills, John, *For King and Country, The Letters and Diaries of John Mills Coldstream Guards, 1811–1814*, Staplehurst, Spellmount, 1995, p. 42.
38 Burgoyne, p. 181.
39 Burgoyne, pp. 182–83.
40 *WD* (New Edition), vol. VIII, p. 378.
41 Ibid, p. 406.
42 Douglas, pp. 358–59.
43 Garwood, p. 90.
44 *WD* (New Edition), vol. VIII, pp. 345–46.
45 Douglas, pp. 375–76.
46 Ibid, p. 359, Garwood, p. 90.
47 *General Orders Spain and Portugal 1 January–31 December 1811*, vol. III, London, T. Egerton, 1812, p. 249.
48 Dickson, vol. 4, p. 563.
49 Garwood, p. 90. Lieutenant Dumaresq was not a member of the Royal Staff Corps or the Royal Engineers. He was of the 9th Regiment of Foot and was serving as a volunteer with the engineers. The British Army in the Peninsula had a chronic shortage of engineers and often had infantry officers serving as engineer assistants.
50 These dimensions are about 190 metres long, 60 metres high, and 8 metres wide.
51 Garwood, p. 91.
52 Dickson, p. 216.
53 According to *Webster's New World Dictionary*, a joist is 'any of the parallel planks or beams that hold up the planks of a floor or the laths of a celling.'
54 Douglas, p. 315.
55 Douglas, pp. 318–19.
56 Garwood, pp. 91–92.

57 Douglas, p. 358.
58 Ibid, p. 358.
59 *WD* (New Edition), vol. 9, p. 233.
60 Ibid, vol. 9, p. 233.
61 Garwood, pp. 91–92.
62 Douglas, p. 359.
63 Webber, William, *With the Guns in the Peninsula, The Peninsular War Journal of Captain William Webber, Royal Artillery*, London, Greenhill Books, 1991, p. 136.
64 Clark-Kennedy, A.E., *Attack the Colour, The Royal Dragoons in the Peninsula and at Waterloo*, London, Research Publishing, 1975, p. 69.
65 Jones, vol. 2, pp. 102–03.
66 Garwood, p. 94.
67 Sabine, Edward, *Letters of Colonel Sir Augustus Simon Frazer, Commanding the Royal Horse Artillery in the Army under the Duke of Wellington*, Uckfield, Naval & Military Press, 2001, p. 292.
68 Sir Charles Vinicombe Penrose (1759–1830) was a Commodore at Gibraltar from 1810–1813. On 4 December 1813, he was promoted to Rear Admiral and assigned to command a squadron of small craft on the north coast of Spain and France co-operating with the army.
69 The exact date of when this reconnaissance took place is unknown. Rear Admiral Penrose did not arrive in country until around January 25 or 26. It was most likely around 1 February. Larpent, George (editor), *The Private Journal of F.S. Larpent*, vol. 3, London, Richard Bentley, 1853, page 272.
70 Buckley, Roger N. (editor), *The Napoleonic War Journal of Captain Thomas Henry Browne, 1807–1816*, London, Army Records Society, 1987, p. 259.
71 Wellington's prior experience with the pontoons showed that they were unreliable even under the best of conditions. He could not afford to risk the whole operation on such a weak resource.
72 Buckley, p. 259.
73 Larpent, vol. 2, p. 299.
74 Jones, vol. 2, p. 108.
75 Duke of Wellington (editor), *Supplementary Despatches, Correspondance, and Memoranda of Field Marshal Arthur Duke of Wellington*, London, John Murray, 1861, p. 595.
76 Jones, vol. 2, p. 103.
77 Ibid, p. 103.
78 Napier, vol. 6, p. 541.
79 According to Jones, it was not until *after* 7 February did they start looking for materials and found they would have to use cables instead. Yet in a letter on 7 February to Admiral Penrose, Wellington specifically asks for the cables.
80 *WD* (New Edition), vol. 11, p. 505.
81 Jones, vol. 2, pp. 101–02.
82 These were captured French guns, mostly likely 16-pounder siege artillery pieces. The French did not produce an 18-pounder gun, however their 16-pounder was similar in size and calibre to the British 18-pounder gun. The British primary sources all refer to the guns as 18-pounders, so for the sake of consistency, I will refer to them as 18-pounders also.
83 A gin tackle is a termed derived from the now obsolete German word *Gientalje*, and most commonly refers to the system of ropes and pulleys used to move naval guns of the period.
84 Ibid, pp. 105–06.
85 Ibid, p. 106.
86 *WD* (New Edition), vol. 11, p. 506.
87 Jones, vol. 2, p. 106–07.
88 Ibid, pp. 107–08.
89 Larpent, vol. 2, p. 306.
90 'Hambro' line is three-strand flax or hemp cord, polished and tarred for heavy servings or lacing up canvas.
91 Ibid, p. 108, Garwood, p. 93.
92 Burgoyne, p. 292.

93 Batty, Robert, *Campaign of the Left Wing of the Allied Army, in the Western Pyrenees and South of France, in the Years 1813–14*, London, Ken Trotman, 1983, pp. 115–116.
94 Anonymous, 'Reminiscences of Bayonne' published in William Maxwell's *Peninsular Sketches, by Actors on the Scene*, vol. 2, Cambridge, Ken Trotman, 1998, p. 164.
95 Sabine, p. 414.
96 Thompson, W.F.K. (editor), *An Ensign in the Peninsular War, The Letters of John Aichison*, London, Michael Joseph, 1981, p. 301.
97 Larpent, vol. 2I, p. 9.
98 Anonymous in Maxwell, pp. 165–66.
99 Lehmann was discharged from the KGL in 1814, 'but on the 17th of June 1815, just after the first light battalion had arrived in the position of Waterloo, Lehmann made his appearance and offered his services as a volunteer in the company to which he formerly belonged! They were accepted, but the gallant soldier shared the fate of many a brave man in the fierce contest of the following day, and fell . . .' Beamish, North Ludlow, *History of the King's German Legion*, vol. 2 London, Buckland and Brown, 1993, p. 278.
100 Sabine, p. 415.
101 Sabine, p. 415.
102 Larpent, p. 9.
103 Thompson, p. 301.
104 Anonymous in Maxwell, p. 167.
105 Batty, pp. 121–22.
106 Burgoyne, p. 294.
107 Hibbert, Christopher, *The Wheatley Diary, A Journal and Sketchbook Kept during the Peninsular War and the Waterloo Campaign*, London, Longmans, Green and Co., 1964, p. 40.
108 Batty, pp. 124–25.
109 Burgoyne, p. 295.
110 Aitchison, p. 302.
111 Batty, p. 122.
112 Burgoyne, p. 294.
113 Batty, p. 123.
114 High tide was at 7.11 a.m. Low tide was at 1.12 p.m.
115 Batty, p. 123.
116 Buckley, p. 263, Sabine, p. 417.
117 Buckley, p. 263.
118 Batty, pp. 123–24.
119 Burgoyne, p. 294.
120 Jones, vol. II, pp. 117–18.
121 *WD* (New Edition), vol. 11, p. 538.
122 Sabine, p. 417.
123 Garwood, pp. 94–95.
124 Napier, p. 542.
125 Garwood, p. 95.
126 Garwood, p. 95.
127 Burgoyne, p. 295.
128 Jones, vol. II, p. 118.
129 Batty, p. 172.
130 'Description of the Pontoon Train in the Peninsula', *Royal Engineer Journal*, Issue III, 2 January 1870, p. 14.
131 Douglas, p. 33.
132 Dickson, vol. 5, p. 830.
133 *The Little Bombardier and Pocket Gunner*, London, T. Egerton, 1801, pp. 176–77.
134 Douglas, pp. 62 and 70.
135 Dickson, vol. 5, pp. 830–31.
136 Sabine, pp. 104–05.

137 Captain Robert M. Cairnes to Major General William Cuppage, Royal Artillery, May 12 1813, in Dickson, vol. 5, p. 882.
138 Dickson, vol. 5, pp. 878–85.
139 On 18 May 1813, Wellington wrote Lord Bathurst requesting that 20 new pontoons with carriages and 18 carriages capable of carrying large pontoons be shipped to Coruña.
140 Larpent, vol. 2, p. 291.
141 Sabine, p. 402.
142 Hough, Henry, 'The Journal of Second Lieutenant Henry Hough, Royal Artillery, 1812–13', *Journal of the Royal United Service Institution*, #444 vol. LXI, 1916, page 42.
143 'Description of the Pontoon Train in the Peninsula', *Royal Engineer Journal*, Issue III, 2 January 1870, p. 14.
144 Jones, vol. 1, pp. 229, 371, 372, & 374, Dickson vol. 4, p. 642, Dickson vol. 5, p. 830.
145 Larpent, vol. 3, pp. 88–89.
146 Hancock, p. 167.
147 Letter from Lieutenant Peter Wright to Lieutenant Colonel John Burgoyne dated 28 March 1814, quoted in Hancock, pp. 168–69.
148 Napier, p. 211.
149 Letter from Lieutenant Peter Wright to Lieutenant Colonel John Burgoyne dated 13 April 1814, quoted in Hancock, p. 169.
150 Bell, George, *Soldier's Glory, Being 'Rough Notes of an Old Soldier'*, Tunbridge Wells, Spellmount, 1991, p. 131.
151 Larpent, vol. 3, pp. 120–21.
152 Ibid, p. 121, Hancock, p. 169.
153 Douglas, pp. 60–61.
154 Sabine, p. 453.
155 Letter from Lieutenant Peter Wright to Lieutenant Colonel John Burgoyne dated 13 April 1814, quoted in Hancock, p. 169.
156 Larpent, vol. 3, p. 119.
157 Sabine, pp. 454–55.

Appendix

British Memoirs of the Napoleonic Wars

ROBERT BURNHAM

In 1913, Sir Charles Oman, noted author of *A History of the Peninsular War* wrote a book that chronicled many aspects of the British Army under Lord Wellington. This book, *Wellington's Army, 1809–14*, consisted of a series of chapters on a wide variety of topics, many of interest to the general reader. More importantly, however, he wrote about the myriad of sources that were then available to those who wish to research the British Army of the Napoleonic Wars. In the back of the book, he lists eight pages of primary sources, chiefly memoirs and diaries of those who fought in the army. This listing is by regiment (e.g. 18th Hussars or 95th Rifles), position (staff), branch of service (e.g. engineers, artillery, or chaplains), and those who were seconded to the Portuguese or attached to the Spanish.

Although the listing is quite extensive it only covers those who served in the Peninsular War. Those who served in other theatres of the war (e.g. Bunbury) or just at Waterloo (e.g. Mercer) were not included. Unfortunately his listing is also eighty-five years old and does not include the memoirs that have been published since 1913. To assist the researcher, I have kept the same basic format as Oman, but have included the publisher when available. I have annotated most books with brief notes that list the years and campaigns that each book covers and other pertinent information. Additionally, when a soldier served in several units, the book is listed under each of the units. I was also able to track down the authors of several of the books that Oman lists as having no author. Many of the books listed have different bibliographic information than what is in Oman. This is because they have been reprinted multiple times. I have tried to list the most current edition that I could find.

The books are catalogued under the following headings:

General Officers
The Staff
Artillery
Cavalry (by regiment)
Engineers
Infantry (by regiment)
The King's German Legion (by unit)
Officers in Portuguese Service
Commissariat
Medical Department
Rank-and-File Memoirs
Miscellaneous

British Memoirs of the Napoleonic Wars: a Bibliography

GENERAL OFFICERS

Anglesey, Marquess of. *One-Leg: The Life and Letters of Henry William Paget First Marquess of Anglesey K.G. (1768–1854)*. Oxford: Reprint Society of London, 1961. 428 pages.
    Notes: Heavily annotated, but contains numerous letters. Pages 41–154 cover Coruña, Walcheren, and Waterloo Campaigns.

Baird, David. *The Life of General, the Right Honourable Sir David Baird*. Theodore Hook (ed.), 2 volumes; 1832. 448 & 442 pages.
    Notes: Includes India, Egyptian, Copenhagen 1807, and Coruña Campaigns.

Blayney, Andrew T. *Narrative of a Forced Journey through Spain and France, as a Prisoner of War, in the Years 1810 to 1814*. London: E. Kirby, 1814. 2 vols.

Cole, Lowry. *Memoirs of Sir Lowry Cole*. Cole, Maud L. (ed.) Cambridge: Ken Trotman; 2003. 271 pages.
    Notes: Actually are letters written to various people between 1792 and 1831. First 200 pages concern the Napoleonic Era.

Colville, John. *A Portrait of a General: a Chronicle of the Napoleonic Wars*. Salisbury: M. Russel, 1980. 246 pages.

Combermere, Mary W. *Memoirs and correspondence of Field Marshal Viscount Combermere*. London: Hurst and Blackett, 1866. 2 vols.
    Notes: Papers of Stapleton Cotton.

Fullom, S. W. *The Life of General Sir Howard Douglas, from His Notes, Conversations, and Correspondence*. London: J. Murray, 1863. 440 pages.

Graham, Thomas. *A Contemporary Account of the 1799 Campaign in Germany and Italy*. George Nafziger (ed.), 4 vols. 2001–2002. 553 pages.

Graham, Thomas. *A Contemporary Account of the 1799 Campaign in Holland*. George Nafziger (ed.), 2002. 180 pages.

Halkett, Colin. in *With the 69th in the Waterloo Campaign*. Darlington: Napoleonic Archive, n.d. 36 pages.
    Notes: Primarily an account written by the regimental colour bearer, Ensign George Ainslie. Has General Colin Halkett's account of Quatre-Bras.

Hill, Rowland. *Lord Hill's Letters from the Peninsula*. Darlington: Napoleonic Archive; (no date, probably 2003). 40 pages.
    Notes: Taken from Edwin Sidney's *Life of Lord Hill*. Over 60 letters. Several letters on Talavera, good descriptions of Arroyo Molinas and Almaraz.

Jones, John T. *The Military Autobiography of Major General John T. Jones, Royal Engineers*. Privately Printed; 1853.
    Notes: Only 12 copies printed.

Le Marchant, John. *Memoirs of the Late Major General Le Marchant*. Denis Le Marchant (ed.), Staplehurst: Spellmount; 1997. 337 pages.
    Notes: Full name was John Gaspard Le Marchant; Holland 1793; Peninsula 1811–1812.

Long, Robert B. *Peninsular Cavalry General (1811–13): The Correspondence of Lieutenant General Robert Ballard Long*. T. H. McGuffie (ed.) London: George G. Harrap; 1951. 304 pages.

MacKinnon, Henry. *A Journal of the Campaign in Portugal and Spain, containing Remarks on the Inhabitants, Customs, Trade, and Cultivation, of Those Countries, from the Year 1809 to 1812*. Cambridge: Ken Trotman; 1999. 103 pages.
    Notes: Major General; commanded 1st Brigade of the 3rd Division. Killed at

Ciudad Rodrigo. This journal was published by Ken Trotman in 1999 under the title: *Two Peninsular War Journals.*

Money, John. *An English General in the Army of Revolutionary France: 1792.* West Chester: George Nafziger; 2001. 84 pages.

Moore, John. *The Diary of Sir John Moore.* J.F. Maurice (ed.), London: E. Arnold, 1904. 2 vols.

Ompteda, Christian von. *In the King's German Legion: Memoirs of Baron Ompteda, Colonel in the King's German Legion during the Napoleonic Wars.* Von Ompteda, Louis (ed.), Cambridge: Ken Trotman; 1987. 328 pages.

    Notes: Full name Christian von Ompteda; 1793–1815; commanded 1st Light Battalion 1812; 5th Line Battalion 1813; Brigadier 1815.

Paget, Edward. *Letters and Memorials of General Sir Edward Paget.* Eden Paget (ed.), Privately printed in 1898. 189 pages.

    Notes: Only 50 copies were printed. Covers Flanders, the Mediterranean, Egypt, the Peninsula, Ceylon, and India.

Pakenham, Edward. *The Pakenham Letters from the Peninsula.* Darlington: Napoleonic Archive; n.d. 39 pages.

    Notes: Extracted from *Pakenham Letters 1800 to 1815.*

Picton, Thomas. *Memoirs of Lieutenant General Sir Thomas Picton.* H. Robinson (ed.), London: Richard Bentley; 1835. 2 vols. 404 and 436 pages.

    Notes: Are letters by General Picton from 1797–1815. They contain much editorial comment and other material, including letters from associates of Picton.

Stewart, William. *The Cumloden Papers.* Edinburgh: Privately published; 1881. 335 pages.

    Notes: Only 50 copies published. Includes preface, correspondence with Lord Nelson, official correspondence with Wellington, and Journal of the Baltic Expedition in 1801.

Vivian, Richard H. *Richard Hussey Vivian: A Memoir.* Claud Vivian (ed.), Cambridge: Ken Trotman; 2003. 342 pages.

    Notes: Was commissioned in the 20th Foot, but exchanged to the 54th Regiment in 1793; exchanged into the 28th Regiment in 1794 and saw extensive service in Flanders. In 1798, he exchanged into the 7th Hussars; in 1804 into the 25th Light Dragoons, then back into the 7th Hussars. Led the regiment in the Coruña Campaign and then back to the Peninsula with them in 1813, where he became the brigade commander. Commanded a cavalry brigade in the Waterloo Campaign.

Whittingham, Samuel F. *A Memoir of the Services of Lieutenant general Sir Samuel Ford Whittingham.* London: Longmans, 1868. 531 pages.

    Notes: Served with Spanish troops.

Wilson, Robert T. *General Wilson's Journal, 1812–1814.* Brett-James, Antony (ed.), London: Kimber; 1964. 240 pages.

THE STAFF

Anonymous. *An Account of the Battle of Waterloo.* Upton: Gosling Press; 1993.

Boutflower, Charles. *The Journal of an Army Surgeon during the Peninsular War.* Staplehurst: Spellmount; 1997. 193 pages.

    Notes: With 40th Regiment 1809–1812; served as the 4th Division (Hill's Division) surgeon from November 1812–May, 1813.

Bradford, William. *Sketches of the Country, Character, and Costume, in Portugal and Spain, Made during the Campaign, and on the Route of the British Army, in 1808 and 1809.* London: J. Booth; 1812. 381 pages.

Browne, Thomas H. *The Napoleonic War Journal of Captain Thomas Henry Browne:*

1807–1816. Roger N. Buckley (ed.). London: Army Records Society; 1987. 388 pages.
   Notes: 23rd Fusiliers until 1812; served in Adjutant General's Office, attached to 4th Division.

Buckham, E. *Personal Narrative of Adventures in the Peninsula during the War in 1812–13.* Cambridge: Ken Trotman; 1995. 339 pages.
   Notes: Was an officer in the Staff Corps Regiment of Cavalry, yet his duty was primarily as a commissary officer. Great descriptions of Almeida and buying cattle for the army.

Bunbury, Henry. *Narratives of Some Passages in the Great War with France: 1799–1810.* London: Peter Davies; 1927. 324 pages.
   Notes: Holland and Mediterranean; never in the Peninsula; great detail on the Egypt Campaign – where he never served; Maida 1806; and served as Under-Secretary for War, 1809–16.

Carr-Gomm, Francis. *Letters and Journals of Field Marshal Sir William Maynard Gomm from 1799 to Waterloo 1815.* London: John Murray; 1881. 390 pages.
   Notes: Holland, 1799; Hanover, 1806; Copenhagen; Stralsund, 1808; Roliça; Vimeiro; Coruña; Walcheren; Peninsula 1810–1814 where he was attached to 5th Division; Waterloo.

Cocks, Edward C. *Intelligence Officer in the Peninsula: Letters & Diaries of Major the Hon. Edward Charles Cocks 1786–1812.* Julia Page (ed.), New York: Hippocrene Books; 1986. 255 pages.
   Notes: 1808–1812; served also with 16th Light Dragoons and 79th Infantry.

Daniel, John Edgecombe. *Journal of an Officer in the Commissariat Department: 1811–1815.* Cambridge: Ken Trotman; 1997. 503 pages.
   Notes: Peninsula 1811–1814; Waterloo. On the Army staff; transferred to 3rd Division in early 1813.

D'Urban, Benjamin. *The Peninsular War Journal: 1808–1817.* London: Greenhill Napoleonic Library; 1988. 385 pages.
   Notes: Staff officer to Robert Wilson; as QMG to Marshal Beresford; commanded brigade of Portuguese Cavalry in 1812.

Fane, John. *Memoir of the Early Campaigns of the Duke of Wellington in Portugal and Spain by an Officer Employed in His Army.* London: John Murray; 1820. 234 pages.
   Notes: Aide-de-Camp to Wellington 1808–1810. Succeeded his father as 11th Earl of Westmorland in 1841; best known by his courtesy title of Lord Burghersh. Married Wellington's niece in 1811.

Fitzclarence, George. 'The British Campaign of 1809 under Sir A. Wellesley' published in William Maxwell's *Peninsular Sketches; by Actors on the Scen*e Cambridge: Ken Trotman; 1998. 2 vols. 389 & 399 pages.
   Notes: vol. 1; pp. 64–217. The illegitimate son of William, Duke of Clarence and Mrs Jordan, grandson of George III. Created Earl of Munster 1831 when his father became William IV. Served as ADC to Charles Stewart, the Adjutant General 1809–11.

Frazer, Augustus S. *Letters of Colonel Sir Augustus Simon Frazer Commanding the Royal Horse Artillery in Army under the Duke of Wellington.* Uckfield: Naval and Military Press; 2001. 664 pages.
   Notes: One hundred and eighty-one letters covering from November 1812–July 1815. Peninsula and Waterloo.

Gordon, Alexander. *At Wellington's Right Hand: the Letters of Lieutenant Colonel Sir Alexander Gordon, 1808–1815.* Rory Muir (ed.), Phoenix Mill: Sutton; 2003. 458 pages.

Notes: Served on the staff of General David Baird in the Coruña Campaign and as Aide-de-Camp to Wellington from 1809–1815. Killed at Waterloo.

Gronow, Rees H. *Captain Gronow: His Reminiscences of Regency and Victorian Life: 1810–60.* Hibbert, Christopher (ed.), London: Kyle Cathie; 1991. 332 pages.

Notes: 2nd Battalion 1st Foot Guards in Peninsula 1813–1814; ADC to Picton during Waterloo Campaign.

Hay, Andrew Leith. *A Narrative of the Peninsular War.* London: John Hearse; 1850. 445 pages.

Notes: ADC to his uncle, General Leith.

Jones, Rice. *An Engineer Officer under Wellington in the Peninsula.* Cambridge: Ken Trotman; 1986. 128 pages.

Notes: Staff engineer in Light Division; letters from 1793–1812.

Laing, Samuel. *The Autobiography of Samuel Laing of Papdale: 1780–1868.* R.P. Fereday (ed.), Kirkwall, Orkney: Bellavista Publications; 2000. 326 pages.

Notes: Laing served as an ensign in the Royal Staff Corps from 1805–1809. Roliça, Vimeiro, and Coruña. Pages 95–130 cover his time in the army.

Larpent, George. *The Private Journal of F.S. Larpent, Judge Advocate General of the British Forces in the Peninsula Attached to the Headquarters of Lord Wellington During the Peninsular War from 1812 to its Close.* Staplehurst: Spellmount; 2000. 600 pages.

Notes: This is from the 3rd Edition which was printed in 1854. Little on military justice, but much on life in the British Army and Wellington's HQ.

MacCarthy, John E.C. *Recollections of the Storming of the Castle of Badajoz by the Third Division.* Staplehurst: Spellmount; 2001. 118 pages.

Note: Lieutenant MacCarthy was serving as a volunteer assistant engineer on General Picton's staff during the siege.

Napier, George. *The Early Military Life of General Sir George T. Napier.* William Napier (ed.). London: John Murray; 1886. 254 pages.

Notes: Sweden 1808; on staff of Sir John Moore at Coruña; in 52nd Regiment in Peninsula from 1809–1812; lost arm at Ciudad Rodrigo & invalided home; rejoined regiment in 1814 in France; transferred to 71st Infantry as commander through rest of Peninsular War; transferred to command company of 3rd Guards, but does not mention Waterloo.

Pierrepoint, Charles A. *The Coruña Journal of Captain C. A. Pierrepoint AQMG.* Huntingdon: Ken Trotman; 2005. 52 pages.

Notes: Was on the staff of Paget's Reserve Division.

Porter, Robert Ker. *Letters from Portugal and Spain, Written during the March of the British Troops under Sir John Moore.* Cambridge: Ken Trotman; 1985. 336 pages.

Notes: Years 1808–1809; served on Moore's staff.

Shaw-Kennedy, James. *A Private Journal of General Craufurd's Outpost Operations on the Coas and Agueda in 1810.* Printed in Frederick Fitzclarence's *A Manual of Outpost Duties.* London: Parker, Furnivall and Parker; 1851. 233 pages.

Notes: Shaw-Kennedy was the Aide-de-Camp to Craufurd.

Shaw-Kennedy, James. *Notes on the Battle of Waterloo.* Staplehurst: Spellmount; 2003. 213 pages.

Notes: 43rd Light, but served on the Quartermaster-General's staff of the 3rd Division at Waterloo (Alten's).

Smith, Harry. *The Autobiography of Sir Harry Smith: 1787–1819.* London: Constable; 1999. 333 pages.

Notes: Was in 1/95th Rifles; Buenos Aires, Copenhagen, Coruña, Peninsula

1809–1814; Washington, New Orleans; Brigade-major for Lambert's Brigade at Waterloo.

Sorell, Thomas S. *Notes on the Campaign of 1808–1809, in the North of Spain: in Reference to Some Passages in Lieutenant Colonel Napier's History of the War in the Peninsula, and in Sir Walter Scott's Life of Napoleon Bonaparte.* London: J. Murray; 1828. 53 pages.

Thornton, James. *Your Most Obedient Servant: James Thornton Cook to the Duke of Wellington.* Exeter: Webb & Bower; 1985. 120 pages.

> Notes: With Wellington 1811–1820; is an interview rather than memoirs.

Vere, Charles Broke. *Marches, Movements, and Operations, of the 4th Division of the Allied Army, in Spain and Portugal, in the Years 1810, 1811, & 1812.* Ipswich: R. Deck; 1841. 44 pages.

> Notes: Was a major in the 5th Regiment 4 February 1808; made brevet lieutenant colonel 27 April 1812; Assistant quartermaster-general 4th Division from 7 February 1811. Last entry is 28 November 1812.

Warre, William. *Letters from the Peninsula: 1808–1812.* Staplehurst: Spellmount; 1999. 231 pages.

> Notes: Aide to General Ferguson at Roliça and Vimeiro; aide to Marshal Beresford 1809–1812.

ARTILLERY

Dansey, Charles C. *The Peninsular Letters of 2nd Captain Charles Dansey Royal Artillery.* Godmanchester: Ken Trotman; 2006. 50 pages.

> Notes: 1806–1813; Greek islands and the Peninsula.

Dickson, Alexander. *The Dickson Manuscripts: Being Diaries, Letters, Maps, Account Books, with Various Other Papers of the Late Major General Sir Alexander Dickson.* Leslie, John H. (ed.). 5 vols.; Cambridge: Ken Trotman; 1987. 1190 pages total.

> Notes: Years 1809–1813. Served with Portuguese Artillery before becoming chief of Wellington's siege-trains.

Dyneley, Thomas. *Letters Written by Lieutenant-General Thomas Dyneley While on Active Service Between the Years 1806 and 1815.* London: Ken Trotman; 1984. 68 pages.

> Notes: Maida and the Siege of Scylla; Peninsula with E Troop RHA as 2nd Captain from 1811–1813; Quatre-Bras and Waterloo.

Frazer, Augustus S. *Letters of Colonel Sir Augustus Simon Frazer Commanding the Royal Horse Artillery in Army under the Duke of Wellington.* Uckfield: Naval and Military Press; 2001. 664 pages.

> Notes: One hundred and eighty-one letters covering from November 1812–July 1815; Peninsula and at Waterloo.

Hayter, Alethea (ed.). *The Backbone: Diaries of a Military Family in the Napoleonic Wars.* Edinburgh: Pentland Press; 1993. 343 pages.

> Notes: John Henry Slessor's diary; lieutenant colonel 1814. Served in Royal Irish Artillery in Ireland.

Hough, Henry. 'The Journal of Second Lieutenant Henry Hough, Royal Artillery, 1812–3.' *The Journal of the Royal United Service Institution.* vol. 61, November 1961. pp. 840–81.

> Notes: In Captain Baynes' brigade until August 1812 when he joined Captain Douglas's brigade. Good description of the Siege of Burgos.

Ingilby, William B. 'Diary of Lieutenant Ingilby, RA, in the Peninsular War.' *Minutes of the Proceedings of the Royal Artillery Institution.* vol. 20; 1893. Pp. 241–62, 315–23.

> Notes: In Captain Lawson's Battery July 1810–April 1814. Joined Gardiner's

RHA troop in May 1815 and served with it at Waterloo.

Light, Henry. *The Expedition to Walcheren 1809.* Huntingdon: Ken Trotman; 2005.
Notes: Light was in the Royal Horse Artillery.

Mercer, Cavalié. *Journal of the Waterloo Campaign Kept Throughout the Campaign of 1815 by the Late General Cavalié Mercer.* New York: Praeger; 1970. 402 pages.
Notes: Commanded Dickson's troop Royal Horse Artillery.

Mercer, Cavalié. *Reminiscences of Waterloo: Correspondence between Henry Leathers and Alexander Mercer of G Troop RHA.* Cambridge: Ken Trotman; 2004. 36 pages.

Miller, Benjamin. *The Adventures of Serjeant Benjamin Miller Whilst Serving in the 4th Battalion of the Royal Regiment of Artillery 1796–1815.* Dallington: Naval & Military Press; 1999. 43 pages.
Notes: Served in Egypt and in the Coruña Campaign.

Swabey, William. *Diary of Campaigns in the Peninsula for the Years 1811, 12 and 13.* London: Ken Trotman; 1984. 217 pages.
Notes: In MacDonald's troop Royal Horse Artillery.

Wall, Adam. *Diary of the Operations in Spain under Sir John Moore.* Godmanchester: Ken Trotman, 2005. 18 pages.
Note: Commanded a brigade of six-pounders.

Webber, William. *With the Guns in the Peninsula: the Peninsula War Journal of Captain William Webber, Royal Artillery.* Richard Wollocombe (ed.). London: Greenhill; 1991. 196 pages.
Notes: 2nd Captain in Captain Maxwell's 9-pounder battery; August 1812–June 1813.

CAVALRY (BY REGIMENT)

1st Life Guards

James, Haddy. *Surgeon James' Journal: 1815.* Jane Vansittart (ed.). London: Cassell; 1964. 175 pages.
Notes: First name was Haddy; was assistant surgeon.

2nd Life Guards

Playford, Thomas. *A Lifeguardsman at Waterloo.* Godmanchester: Ken Trotman; 2006. 90 pages.
Notes: Was a private; joined 2nd Life Guards 1810.

1st Royal Dragoons

Burroughs, George Frederick. *A Narrative of the Retreat of the Army from Burgos in a Series of Letters with an Introductory Sketch of the Campaign of 1812 and Military Character of the Duke of Wellington.* Cambridge: Ken Trotman Military Monographs; 2004. 59 pages.
Notes: Was assistant surgeon.

Heathcote, Ralph. *Letters of a Young Diplomatist and Soldier During the Time of Napoleon.* London: John Lane; (date *circa* 1910). 326 pages.
Notes: Copenhagen; Peninsula 1809–1813.

2nd Royal North British Dragoons (Scots Greys)

Dickson; Corporal. *Scots Greys at Waterloo.* Darlington: Napoleonic Archive; n.d. 39 pages.

Notes: Primarily the account of Corporal Dickson of F Troop (Captain Vernon's troop). A great description of the charge of the Union Brigade.

3rd King's Own Dragoons

Cassels, Simon (ed.). *Peninsular Portrait 1811–1814: the Letters of Captain William Bragge.* London: Oxford University Press; 1963. 167 pages.

7th Hussars

Daniel, John Edgecombe. *Journal of an Officer in the Commissariat Department: 1811–1815.* Cambridge: Ken Trotman; 1997. 503 pages.
    Notes: Peninsula 1811–1814; Waterloo. On army staff; 3rd Division 1813; assigned to 7th Hussars 1815 Campaign.
Hodge, Edward. *With the 7th Hussars in the Peninsula: the Diary of Edward Hodge.* Darlington: Napoleonic Archive; n.d. 59 pages.
    Notes: Coruña Campaign.
Verner, William. *Reminiscences of William Verner (1782–1871) 7th Hussars.* London: Society for Army Historical Research; 1965. 60 pages.
    Notes: Coruña; Peninsula 1813–1814; Waterloo; Army of Occupation in France.
Vivian, Richard H. *Richard Hussey Vivian: A Memoir.* Claud Vivian (ed.). Cambridge: Ken Trotman; 2003. 342 pages.
    Notes: 7th Hussars 1798–1804.

9th Light Dragoons

Morland, Charles. *Letters from Egypt & Spain.* Huntingdon: Ken Trotman; 2005. 26 pages.
    Notes: One letter from 1812; Morland commanded 9th Light Dragoons in Spain.
Schaumann, A.L.F. *On the Road with Wellington: the Diary of a War Commissary in the Peninsular Campaigns.* Anthony Ludovici, (ed.). London: Greenhill Books; 1998. 440 pages.
    Notes: Author was August Ludolf Friedrich Schaumann; 9th Light Dragoons 1812.

10th Hussars

Taylor, Thomas W. *Letters of Captain Thomas William Taylor of the 10th Hussars, during the Waterloo Campaign from April 20th to August 2nd, 1815.* Cambridge: Ken Trotman; 2002. 43 pages.

11th Light Dragoons

Farmer, George. *The Light Dragoon.* Cambridge: Ken Trotman; 1999. 2 vols. 309 and 327 pages.
    Notes: Peninsula 1811, captured on 22 June. Served 2 1/2 years as a groom to Count Goldstein, the commander of the 1st Berg Lancers. Was in Dusseldorf in 1814, when Russians and Prussians occupied it; escaped to England in 1814; Waterloo. Great account of looting battlefield after Waterloo.

12th Light Dragoons

Hay, William. *Reminiscences 1808–1815 under Wellington.* Cambridge: Ken Trotman; 1992. 319 pages.
    Notes: Exchanged into 12th Dragoons 1812.

Morland, Charles. *Letters from Egypt & Spain.* Huntingdon: Ken Trotman; 2005. 26 pages.
Notes: Was a lieutenant; Egypt 1801.

14th Light Dragoons

Brotherton, Thomas. *A Hawk at War: The Peninsular War Reminiscences of General Sir Thomas Brotherton.* Bryan Perrett (ed.). Chippenham: Picton Publishing; 1986. 84 pages.
Notes: 1801–1814; Egypt and the Peninsula.

Hall, Francis. *Recollections in Portugal and Spain during 1811 and 1812.* Cambridge: Ken Trotman; 2003. 53 pages.
Notes: Cornet; Peninsula February, 1811. Participated in the pursuit of Masséna from Santarem to Sabugal and fought at Fuentes d'Oñoro. Wounded at Carpio 25 September 1812 and invalided to England in late 1812.

Hanley, William. 'Capture of the Enemy's Picquet at Blanchez Sanchez' published in William Maxwell's *Peninsular Sketches; by Actors on the Scene.* Cambridge: Ken Trotman; 1998. 2 vols. 389 & 399 pages.
Notes: vol. 2; pp. 380–388. Author was an NCO.

Hawker, Peter. *Journal of a Regimental Officer during the Recent Campaign in Portugal and Spain under Lord Viscount Wellington.* London: Ken Trotman; 1981. 143 pages.
Notes: Campaign of 1809 only.

15th Hussars

Anonymous. 'British Cavalry on the Peninsula' published in William Maxwell's *Peninsular Sketches; by Actors on the Scene.* Cambridge: Ken Trotman; 1998. 2 vols. 389 & 399 pages.
Notes: vol. 2; pp. 97–132. Covers 1813.

Anonymous. *Jottings from My Sabretasch.* Godmanchester: Ken Trotman; 2005. 292 pages.
Notes: Coruña Campaign; Peninsula 1813–1814; Waterloo.

Gibney, William. *Eighty Years Ago or the Recollections of an Old Army Officer.* London; 1896.
Notes: Was an assistant surgeon; 1814–15; Waterloo.

Gordon, Alexander. *A Cavalry Officer in the Coruña Campaign: 1808–1809.* Tyne & Wear: Worley Productions; 1990. 252 pages.
Notes: Contains music and words to Ballad 'Sahagun' and regimental call.

Griffiths, Edwin. *From Coruña to Waterloo: The Letters and Journals of Two Napoleonic Hussars, 1801–1816.* Glover, Gareth (ed.). London: Greenhill; 2006. 240 pages.
Notes: Major Edwin Griffiths and his nephew, Lieutenant Frederick Phillips; Coruña, Peninsula 1813–1814; Waterloo.

Thackwell, Joseph. *The Military Memoirs of Lieutenant General Sir Joseph Thackwell.* London: John Murray; 1908. 438 pages.
Notes: Captain; Coruña; Peninsula 1813–1814; Waterloo.

16th Light Dragoons

Cocks, Edward C. *Intelligence Officer in the Peninsula: Letters & Diaries of Major the Hon. Edward Charles Cocks 1786–1812.* Page, Julia (ed.). New York: Hippocrene Books; 1986. 255 pages.
Notes: 1808–1812.

Tomkinson, William. *The Diary of a Cavalry Officer in the Peninsular War and Waterloo:*

1809–1815. London: Frederick Muller; 1971. 366 pages.
    Notes: Peninsula 1809–1813; Quatre-Bras and Waterloo.

18th Hussars
Hunt, Eric. *Charging against Napoleon: Diaries & Letters of Three Hussars.* Barnsley: Leo
    Cooper; 2001. 313 pages.
    Notes: Includes the diaries of three officers – James Hughes, Arthur Kennedy, and
    George Woodberry; Coruña 1808–1809; Peninsula 1813–1814; Waterloo; heavily
    edited.
Schaumann, A.L.F. *On the Road with Wellington: the Diary of a War Commissary in the
    Peninsular Campaigns.* Ludovici, Anthony (ed.). London: Greenhill Books; 1998. 440
    pages.
    Notes: Author was August Ludolf Friedrich Schaumann; 18th Hussars
    1812–1813.

23rd Light Dragoons
Blathwayt, George. *Recollections of My Life including Military Service at Waterloo.*
    Cambridge: Ken Trotman; 2004. 32 pages.
    Notes: Commissioned 1814; lieutenant at Waterloo.

York Hussars
Howard, Thomas P. *The Haitian Journal of Lieutenant Howard, York Hussars, 1796–1798.*
    Roger N. Buckley, (ed.). Knoxville: University of Tennessee Press; 1985. 250 pages.
    Notes: Full name is Thomas Phipps Howard; regiment disbanded 1802.

ENGINEERS

Boothby, Charles. *Under England's Flag from 1804 to 1809.* London: A. & C. Black; 1900.
    285 pages.
Jones, Harvey. 'Seven Weeks Captivity in ST Sebastian, in 1813' published in William
    Maxwell's *Peninsular Sketches; by Actors on the Scene.* Cambridge: Ken Trotman;
    1998. 2 vols. 389 & 399 pages.
    Notes: vol. 2; pp. 286–311.
Jones, John T. *Account of the War in Spain, Portugal, and the South of France.* London:
    Edgerton; 1821. 2 vols.
Jones, Rice. *An Engineer Officer under Wellington in the Peninsula.* Cambridge: Ken
    Trotman; 1986. 128 pages.
    Notes: Staff engineer in Light Division; letters from 1793–1812.
Landmann, George. *Recollections of My Military Life.* Godmanchester: Ken Trotman;
    2005. 623 pages.
    Notes: Two volumes in one. First volume 1806–1808; 2nd volume 1808. At Roliça
    and Vimeiro.
MacCarthy, John E.C. *Recollections of the Storming of the Castle of Badajoz by the Third
    Division.* Staplehurst: Spellmount; 2001. 118 pages.
    Note: Lieutenant; volunteer assistant engineer on Picton's staff.
Wrottesley, George. *Life and Correspondence of Field Marshal Sir John Burgoyne.* London:
    Richard Bentley; 1873. 318 pages. 1st Volume only.
    Notes: Egypt 1806; Stralsund; 1808; Coruña; Peninsula 1809–1814; New Orleans.

INFANTRY (BY REGIMENT)

1st Foot Guards

Batty, Robert. *Campaign of the Left Wing of the Allied Army, in the Western Pyrenees and South of France in the Years 1813–1814.* London: Ken Trotman; 1983.

    Notes: Is a campaign study and contains little information on daily life and activities.

Beech, H. Eva. *Joseph Boulcott of the Grenadier Guards: Baggage Master to the Duke of Wellington.* Privately published. No date. 29 pages.

    Notes: This contains a short history of the Guards in the Napoleonic wars, one letter from Joseph Boulcott to his mother dated 9 October 1815, and miscellaneous information on his life.

Collett, John. *John Collet and the Company of Foot Guards.* Barbara Chambers (ed.). Letchworth Garden City: Barbara Chambers; 1996. 2 vols.

    Notes: 1803–1823; was a private; about 15 per cent of the book is his diary.

Gronow, Rees H. *Captain Gronow: His Reminiscences of Regency and Victorian Life: 1810–60.* Christopher Hibbert (ed.). London: Kyle Cathie; 1991. 332 pages.

    Notes: 2nd Battalion; Peninsula 1813–1814; ADC to Picton at Waterloo.

2nd Foot Guards (Coldstream)

Brown, Robert. *An Impartial Journal of a Detachment from the Brigade of Foot Guards, Commencing 25th February 1793 and Ending 9th May 1795.* Godmanchester: Ken Trotman; 2006. 280 pages.

    Notes: Was a corporal.

Mills, John. *For God and Country: The Letters and Diaries of John Mills, Coldstream Guards 1811–1814.* Ian Fletcher (ed.). Staplehurst: Spellmount; 1995. 297 pages.

    Notes: Peninsula 1811–1814.

Rous, John. *A Guards Officer in the Peninsula: the Peninsula War Letters of John Rous, Coldstream Guards, 1812–1814.* Ian Fletcher (ed.). Tunbridge Wells: Spellmount; 1992. 144 pages.

3rd Foot Guards

Aitchison, John. *An Ensign in the Peninsular War: the Letters of John Aitchison.* W.F.K. Thompson, (ed.). London: Michael Joseph; 1981. 349 pages.

    Notes: 1808–1813.

The following three are from William Maxwell's *Peninsular Sketches; by Actors on the Scene.* Cambridge: Ken Trotman; 1998. 2 vols. 389 & 399 pages.

Anonymous. 'Military Retribution' vol. 2; Pages 349–356.

Anonymous. 'Outpost Anecdotes' vol. 2; Pages 332–336.

Anonymous. 'Reminiscences of Bayonne' vol. 2; Pages 163–186.

    Notes: Light Company 1st Battalion; a good description of the bridging of the Adour and the action around Bayonne in 1814.

Clay, Matthew. *Narrative of the Battle of Quatre-Bras & Waterloo With the Defence of Hougoumont.* Godmanchester: Ken Trotman; 2006. 43 pages.

Clay, Matthew. *With the Guards at Hougoumont.* Darlington: Napoleonic Archive. n.d. 20 pages.

    Notes: Private in Light Company 2nd Battalion; great description of Quatre-Bras and the defence of Hougoumont; covers 15–18 June 1815.

Cowell, J. Stepney. *Leaves From the Diary of an Officer of the Guards.* Cambridge: Ken Trotman; 1994. 306 pages.

    Notes: 1809–1812; Oman gives name as Stepney Cowell. Ian Fletcher gives name as John Stepney Cowell.

Napier, George. *The Early Military Life of General Sir George T. Napier.* William Napier (ed.). London: John Murray; 1886. 254 pages.

    Notes: Commands company of 3rd Guards in 1815, but does not mention Waterloo.

Stevenson, John. *A Soldier in Time of War, or the Military Life of Sergeant John Stevenson.* London, 1841.

    Notes: Oman lists this as *Twenty-one Years in the British Foot Guards.*

Stothert, William. *A Narrative of the Principal Events of the Campaigns of 1809, 1810, & 1811 in Spain and Portugal.* Cambridge: Ken Trotman; 1997. 288 pages.

    Notes: Captain and adjutant.

1st Foot

Douglas, John. *Douglas's Tale of the Peninsula & Waterloo: 1808–1815.* Stanley Monick (ed.). London: Leo Cooper; 1997. 133 pages.

    Notes: Sergeant; Walcheren, Peninsula (1809–1814), Waterloo.

3rd Foot

Bunbury, Thomas. *Reminiscences of a Veteran, being Personal and Military Adventures in Portugal, Spain, France, Malta . . . and India, etc.* London: C.J. Skeet; 1861. 3 vols.

    Notes: Spent 1808–1809 in 3rd Foot.

5th Foot

Anonymous. 'The Storming of Badajoz' published in William Maxwell's *Peninsular Sketches; by Actors on the Scene.* Cambridge: Ken Trotman; 1998. 2 vols. 389 & 399 pages.

    Notes: vol. I; pp. 288–292; 2nd Battalion.

Dayes, John. *Memoir of the Military Career of John Dayes, late Paymaster Sergeant of the 5th Regiment of Foot.* Cambridge: Ken Trotman; 2004. 26 pages.

    Notes: Holland 1799; Buenos Aires 1806; Coruña; Peninsula 1812–1814.

Morley, Stephen. *Memoirs of a Sergeant of the 5th Regiment of Foot, containing an Account of His Service, in Hanover, South America, and the Peninsula.* Cambridge: Ken Trotman; 1999. 123 pages.

    Notes: Buenos Aires 1806; Peninsula 1808–1809; Roliça, Vimeiro, Coruña Campaign where he was captured. Escaped and made his way to Portugal. Assigned to 2nd Battalion of Detachments. Returned to England October 1809; Peninsula 1812. Was invalided from retreat of 1812, returned to England 1813.

Ridge, Henry. 'Affair of El Bodon' published in William Maxwell's *Peninsular Sketches; by Actors on the Scene.* Cambridge: Ken Trotman; 1998. 2 vols. 389 & 399 pages.

    Notes: vol. 1; pp. 218–224. Was battalion commander.

Ridge, Henry. 'Private Letter' *Eyewitness Accounts of the Storming of Ciudad Rodrigo.* Cambridge: Ken Trotman; 2004. Pages 6–9.

    Notes: 2nd Battalion. Ridge led one of the assault columns. Contains the original order given to the battalion for the assault. Superb account of the assault.

Vere, Charles Broke. *Marches, Movements, and Operations, of the 4th Division of the Allied*

Army, in Spain and Portugal, in the Years 1810, 1811, & 1812. Ipswich: R. Deck; 1841. 44 pages.

> Notes: Major in 5th Regiment 4 February 1808; brevet lieutenant colonel 27 April 1812; assistant quartermaster-general 4th Division 7 February 1811. Last entry is 28 November 1812.

7th Fusiliers

Cooper, John S. *Rough Notes of Seven Campaigns: 1809–1815.* Staplehurst: Spellmount Library; 1996. 160 pages.

> Notes: Sergeant. All of the major battles of Peninsula, plus New Orleans.

Knowles, Robert. *The War in the Peninsula: Some Letters of a Lancashire Officer.* Staplehurst: Spellmount; 2004. 109 pages.

> Notes: Covers 1811–1813. Killed at Roncesvalles.

9th Foot

Cameron, Sir John. *The Memoirs and Letters of Colonel Sir John Cameron 9th Foot 1809–13.* Godmanchester: Ken Trotman; 2006. 50 pages.

> Notes: Cameron commanded 9th Foot; 1809–1813; mostly on Siege of San Sebastian.

Dent, William. *A Young Surgeon in Wellington's Army: the Letters of William Dent.* Old Woking: Unwin Brothers; 1976. 68 pages.

Gomm, William M. *Letters and Journals of Field Marshal Sir William Maynard Gomm from 1799 to Waterloo 1815.* Francis Carr-Gomm (ed.). London: John Murray; 1881. 390 pages.

> Notes: Holland, 1799; Hanover, 1806; Copenhagen; went to staff college and served on Army Quartermaster General staff for rest of service; Stralsund, 1808; Roliça; Vimeiro; Coruña; Walcheren; Peninsula 1810–1814; Waterloo.

Hale, James. *The Journal of James Hale: Late Serjeant in the Ninth Regiment of Foot.* Windsor: IX Regiment; 1998. 139 pages.

> Notes: Royal North Gloucester Regiment 1801; volunteered for the 9th 1807; Roliça, Vimeiro, and Walcheren; Peninsula from 1810–1813; wounded at San Sebastian, invalided home.

12th Foot

Bayly, Joseph. *The Diary of Colonel Bayly, 12th Regiment, 1796–1830.* Uckfield: Naval and Military Press; 2003. 282 pages.

> Notes: India.

19th Foot

Calladine, G. *Colour-Sergeant Calladine.* Darlington: Napoleonic Archive; n.d.

> Notes: Derbyshire Militia 1805; 19th Foot 1811. Ceylon 1814–1816.

20th Foot

Steevens, Charles. *Reminiscences of My Military Life from 1795 to 1818.* Winchester: Warren & Son; 1878. 144 pages.

23rd Fusiliers

Browne, Thomas H. *The Napoleonic War Journal of Captain Thomas Henry Browne: 1807–1816.* Roger N. Buckley (ed.). London: Army Records Society; 1987. 388 pages.

Notes: Copenhagen & Martinique; Peninsula 1810–1812 with regiment; Adjutant General's Office in Wellington's HQ.

24th Foot

Anderson, Joseph. *Recollections of a Peninsular Veteran.* Darlington: Napoleonic Archive; *circa* 2003. 29 pages.

Notes: Lieutenant; Peninsula 1809–1811; Talavera, Busaco, and Fuentes d'Oñoro; description of Beresford's investiture as a knight in the Order of the Bath 1810.

Ward, Harriet. *Recollections of an Old Soldier. A Biographical Sketch of the Late Colonel Tidy, C.B., 24th Regiment, with Anecdotes of His Contemporaries.* London, 1849. 285 pages.

27th Foot (Inniskilling)

Cassidy, Martin. *Marching with Wellington: with the Inniskillings in the Napoleonic Wars.* Barnsley: Leo Cooper; 2003. 232 pages.

Notes: Contains the diary of Lieutenant Charles Crowe, who was in the 2nd Battalion until mid–1813, then 3rd Battalion; in rear areas on medical leave much of 1813–1814, joined the 3rd Battalion for final campaigns of 1814; fantastic description of the Battle of Toulouse from the company officer level. Takes over command of the 5th Company during the battle.

Emerson, J. 'Recollections of the Late War in Spain and Portugal' published in William Maxwell's *Peninsular Sketches; by Actors on the Scene.* Cambridge: Ken Trotman; 1998. 2 vols. 389 & 399 pages.

Notes: vol. 2; pp. 205–242. Covers 1811: Badajoz and Albuera.

Simcoe, Francis. *Our Young Soldier: Lieutenant Francis Simcoe 6 June 1791–6 April 1812.* Mary Fryer (ed.). Toronto: Dundurn Press; 1996. 190 pages.

Notes: Commissioned in 1808 in Ireland; Peninsula 1809–1812; missed Talavera; Busaco; killed at Badajoz.

28th Foot

Blakeney, Robert. *A Boy in the Peninsular War.* London: Greenhill Books; 1989. 382 pages.

Notes: 1808–1815; Coruña, Barossa, Arroyo Molinos, but not Waterloo.

Cadell, Charles. *Narrative of the Campaigns of the Twenty-eighth Regiment, since Their Return from Egypt in 1802.* London: Whittaker; 1835. 301 pages.

Keep, William T. *In the Service of the King: the Letters of William Thornton Keep at Home, Walcheren, and in the Peninsula, 1808–1814.* Staplehurst: Spellmount; 1997. 214 pages.

Notes: 28th Regiment in 1811; Peninsula 1813–1814.

O'Neil, Charles. *The Military Adventures of Charles O'Neil.* Staplehurst: Spellmount; 1997. 269 pages.

Notes: Rank and file; Peninsula 1811–1814; Waterloo.

Vivian, Richard H. *Richard Hussey Vivian: A Memoir.* Claud Vivian (ed.). Cambridge: Ken Trotman; 2003. 342 pages.

Notes: 28th Regiment 1794; saw extensive service in Flanders.

29th Foot

Anonymous. 'The Twenty-Ninth at Albuera' published in William Maxwell's *Peninsular Sketches; by Actors on the Scene.* Cambridge: Ken Trotman; 1998. 2 vols. 389 & 399 pages.
>
> Notes: vol. 2; pp. 321–331.

Hay, Andrew Leith. *A Narrative of the Peninsular War.* London: John Hearse; 1850. 445 pages.
>
> Notes: ADC to his uncle, General Leith.

Leslie, Charles. *Military Journal of Colonel Leslie, K.H., of Balquhain whilst Serving with the 29th Regiment in the Peninsula, and the 60th Rifles in Canada, &c., 1807–1832.* Aberdeen University Press, 1887. 332 pages.

30th Foot

Carter, John V. *The 1812 Diary of Ensign Carter 30th Foot.* Godmanchester: Ken Trotman; 2006. 25 pages.
>
> Notes: Only 1812; died of sunstroke 23 July 1812.

31st Foot

L'Estrange, George B. *Recollections of Sir George B. L'Estrange.* London: Sampson, Low, Marston, Low, & Searle; no date.
>
> Notes: Peninsula late 1812–1814. Officer in the light company.

32nd Foot

Ross-Lewin, Harry. *With the Thirty-Second in the Peninsular and Other Campaigns.* Cambridge: Ken Trotman; 2000. 368 pages.
>
> Notes: West Indies, Copenhagen, Roliça, Vimeiro, Coruña, & Walcheren; Peninsula in 1811–1814; Quatre-Bras & Waterloo.

33rd Foot

Pattison, Frederick Hope. *Personal Recollections of the Waterloo Campaign.* Upton: Gosling Press; 1992. 48 pages.
>
> Notes: Quatre-Bras and Waterloo.

34th Foot

Bell, George. *Soldier's Glory: Being Rough Notes of an Old Soldier.* Tunbridge Wells: Spellmount; 1991. 325 pages.
>
> Notes: 1811–1814.

Sherer, Moyle. *Recollections of the Peninsula.* Staplehurst: Spellmount; 1996. 273 pages.
>
> Notes: 1809–1813.

35th Foot

Austin, Thomas. *'Old Stick-Leg' Extracts from the Diaries of Major Thomas Austin.* New York: Dial Press; date unknown but at least 1947. 206 pages.
>
> Notes: Holland 1813–1814.

Hayter, Alethea (ed.). *The Backbone: Diaries of a Military Family in the Napoleonic Wars.* Edinburgh: Pentland Press; 1993. 343 pages.
>
> Notes: John Henry Slessor's diary; lieutenant colonel 1814; 35th Infantry in 1806; served at Gibraltar, Sicily, Egypt, governor of the island of Zante, the Adriatic Campaigns, Northern Italy; in 4th Division at Waterloo.

36th Foot
Anonymous. *Buenos Aires 1807: A Personal Narrative by an Officer of the 36th Foot.* El Dorado Books; 1994. 104 pages.

40th Foot
Boutflower, Charles. *The Journal of an Army Surgeon during the Peninsular War.* Staplehurst: Spellmount; 1997. 193 pages.
    Notes: August 1809–November 1812.
Lawrence, William. *A Dorset Soldier: The Autobiography of Sergeant William Lawrence 1790–1869.* Hathaway, Eileen (ed.). Tunbridge Wells: Spellmount; 1993. 176 pages.
    Notes: Buenos Aires; Peninsula 1808–1814; New Orleans; Waterloo.
Stretton, S. 'The Pyrenees, in 1813' and 'The 40th Regiment in the Pyrenees' published in William Maxwell's *Peninsular Sketches; by Actors on the Scene.* Cambridge: Ken Trotman; 1998. 2 vols. 389 & 399 pages.
    Notes: vol. II, pp. 343–349.

42nd Highlanders
Anonymous. *Personal Narrative of a Private Soldier in the 42nd Highlanders.* Cambridge: Ken Trotman; 1996. 289 pages.
    Notes: In 1st and 2nd Battalions; Coruña, Walcheren, Peninsula 1812–1814; wounded at Toulouse.
Anton, James. *Retrospect of a Military Life.* Cambridge: Ken Trotman; 1991. 395 pages.
    Notes: Rank and file; 1813–1815.
Malcolm, John. *Reminiscences of a Campaign in the Pyrenees and South of France in 1814.* Cambridge: Ken Trotman; 1999. 74 pages.
    Notes: 1813–1814; published in 1999 by Ken Trotman in *Two Peninsular War Journals.*

43rd Light
Anonymous. *Memoirs of a Sergeant Late in the Forty-third Light Infantry Regiment previous to and during the Peninsular War.* Cambridge: Ken Trotman; 1998. 278 pages.
    Notes: Copenhagen 1806; Peninsula: Coruña Campaign; returned to Peninsula in June, 1809; River Coa; seriously wounded at Badajoz; returned to England 1812.
Brumwell, John. *With the 43rd in the Peninsula: the Letters of Lieutenant John Brumwell.* Darlington: Napoleonic Archive; n.d. 31 pages.
    Notes: Coruña; 1st Battalion on outpost lines vicinity of Ciudad Rodrigo and Almeida 1810; action on the Coa; killed at Badajoz.
Cooke, John H. *A True Soldier Gentleman: the Memoirs of Lieutenant John Cooke 1791–1813.* Hathaway, Eileen (ed.). Swanage: Shinglepicker; 2000. 266 pages.
    Notes: 2nd Battalion at Walcheren; 1st Battalion Peninsula 1811–1813.
Cooke, John H. *A Narrative of Events in the South of France and of the Attack on New Orleans in 1814 and 1815.* London: T. & W. Boone; 1835. 319 pages.
Cooke, John H. 'A Sketch of the Storming of Ciudad Rodrigo: a Letter by an Officer Engaged' *Eyewitness Accounts of the Storming of Ciudad Rodrigo.* Cambridge: Ken Trotman; 2004. Pages 1–6.
The following were published in William Maxwell's *Peninsular Sketches; by Actors on the Scene.* Cambridge: Ken Trotman; 1998. 2 vols. 389 & 399 pages.
Cooke, John H. 'The Battle of Vitoria' vol. 2; pp. 28–54.
Cooke, John H. 'The Storming of Badajoz' vol. 1; pp. 267–288.

Cooke, John H. 'The Battle of Salamanca' vol. 1; pp. 321–346.

Hamilton, Anthony. *Hamilton's Campaign with Moore and Wellington during the Peninsular War*. Staplehurst: Spellmount; 1998. 164 pages.

   Notes: 2nd Battalion Peninsula 1808–1813. In 1st Battalion of Detachments. Captured at San Sebastian 1813.

Hennell, George. *A Gentleman Volunteer: The Letters of George Hennell from the Peninsular War 1812–1813*. Glover, Michael (ed.). London: Heinemann; 1979. 190 pages.

Shaw-Kennedy, James. *Notes on the Battle of Waterloo*. Staplehurst: Spellmount; 2003. 213 pages.

   Notes: Was in the 43rd, but served on the Quartermaster-General's staff of the 3rd Division (Alten's).

45th Foot

Brown, William. *With the 45th at Badajoz, Salamanca, and Vitoria*. Darlington: Napoleonic Archive; n.d. 44 pages.

   Notes: 1st Battalion; Peninsula 1809–1814; Busaco, Ciudad Rodrigo, Badajoz (great descriptions of the assault and pillage of the city), Salamanca (superb description of being ridden down by French cavalry), the 1812 retreat, and Vitoria and the subsequent looting of the French baggage train. Also served as an officer's servant. Fantastic descriptions of the daily life of a soldier on campaign.

47th Foot

Harley, John. *The Veteran, or Forty Years in the British Service: Comprising Adventures in Egypt, Spain, Portugal, Belgium, Holland, and Prussia*. London: (Privately published); 1838. 2 vols.

49th Foot

Fitzgibbon, James. *A Veteran of 1812: the Life of James Fitzgibbon*. Mary A. Fitzgibbon (ed.). London: R. Bentley & Son; 1894. 347 pages.

50th Foot

MacCarthy, John E.C. *Recollections of the Storming of the Castle of Badajoz by the Third Division*. Staplehurst: Spellmount; 2001. 118 pages.

   Note: Was volunteer assistant engineer on Picton's staff.

Napier, Charles J. *Life and Opinions of General Sir Charles James Napier*. William Napier (ed.). London: James Murray; 1854. 4 vols.

   Notes: Volume 1 covers the Peninsula.

Patterson. 'Leaves from the Journal of a Veteran' published in William Maxwell's *Peninsular Sketches; by Actors on the Scene*. Cambridge: Ken Trotman; 1998. 2 vols. 389 & 399 pages.

   Notes: vol. I; pp. 21–51; Coruña Campaign.

Patterson. 'Arroyo de Molino' published in William Maxwell's *Peninsular Sketches; by Actors on the Scene*. Cambridge: Ken Trotman; 1998. 2 vols. 389 & 399 pages.

   Notes: vol. II; pp. 312–320.

Patterson, John. *The Adventures of Captain John Patterson with Notices of the Officer, etc. of the 50th, or Queen's Own Regiment, from 1807 to 1821*. London: T. and W. Boone; 1837. 436 pages.

Patterson, John. *Camps and Quarters; Scenes and Impressions of Military Life, Interspersed with Anecdotes of Various Well-known Characters Who Flourished in the War.* London: Saunders, 1843. 2 vols.

51st Foot

Blainey, William. *Bonaparte versus Blainey.* Union Springs: Tallcot Bookshop; 1988. 48 pages.

> Notes: Sergeant; Walcheren; Peninsula 1811–1814.

Mockler-Feryman, A.F. *The Life of a Regimental Officer during the Great War 1793–1815 Compiled from the Correspondence of Colomel Samuel Rice.* London: William Blackwood; 1913. 341 pages.

> Notes: Is a biography with many letters interspersed throughout the book. Rice commanded 51st at Waterloo.

Wheeler, William. *The Letters of Private Wheeler.* B.H. Liddell Hart (ed.). Boston: Houghton Mifflin; 1952. 350 pages.

> Notes: Full name William Wheeler; Walcheren; Peninsula 1811–1814; Waterloo.

52nd Foot

Colborne, John. *The Life of John Colborne, Field Marshal Lord Seaton: . . . Compiled from His Letters, Records of His Conversations, and Other Sources.* G.C. Moore Smith (ed.). New York: Dutton; 1903. 449 pages.

Dobbs, John. *Recollections of an Old 52nd Man.* Staplehurst: Spellmount; 2000. 101 pages.

> Notes: Commissioned in 2nd Battalion 1808; Swedish expedition 1808; Coruña; Walcheren; Peninsula 1810–1814. Commanded company of 5th *Caçadores* 1813; claims to be the last British officer wounded in the Peninsula War, 14 April 1814.

Hay, William. *Reminiscences 1808–1815 Under Wellington.* Cambridge: Ken Trotman; 1992. 319 pages.

> Notes: 52nd Infantry until late 1811.

Napier, George. *The Early Military Life of General Sir George T. Napier.* William Napier (ed.). London: John Murray; 1886. 254 pages.

> Notes: Peninsula 1809–1812; lost arm at Ciudad Rodrigo & invalided home; rejoined regiment 1814 in France.

53rd Foot

Glover, Gareth. *Wellington's Lieutenant, Napoleon's Gaoler: the Peninsula letters & St Helena Diaries of Sir George Ridout Bingham 53rd Foot 1809–21* Barnsley: Pen & Sword; 2005. 310 pages.

> Notes: Lieutenant Colonel, commander 2nd Battalion; Peninsula April 1809–December 1813.

54th Foot

Vivian, Richard H. *Richard Hussey Vivian: A Memoir.* Claud Vivian (ed.). Cambridge: Ken Trotman; 2003. 342 pages.

> Notes: 1793–1794.

56th Foot

Surtees, William. *Twenty-five Years in the Rifle Brigade.* London: Greenhill; 1996. 480 pages.

> Notes: 56th Regiment; Holland 1799.

61st Foot

Pearson, Andrew. *The Soldier Who Walked Away: The Autobiography of Andrew Pearson a Peninsular War Veteran.* Arthur H. Haley (ed.). Liverpool: Bullfinch Publications; *circa* 1991. 130 pages.

Notes: Egypt; Maida; Gibraltar; Peninsula 1809–1812. Deserted and was never caught.

65th Foot

Harness, William. *Trusty and Well Beloved: the Letters Home of William Harness, an Officer of George III.* Caroline Duncan-Jones (ed.). London: SPCK; 1957. 223 pages.

Notes: Egypt and India.

66th Foot

Henry, Walter. *Surgeon Henry's Trifles: Events of a Military Life.* Pat Hayward (ed.). London: Chatto & Windus; 1970. 281 pages.

Notes: First name was Walter; Peninsula 1811–1814; Saint Helena 1817–1821.

68th Foot

Green, John. *The Vicissitudes of a Soldier's Life or a Series of Occurrences from 1806 to 1815.* Wakefield: EP Publishing; *circa* 1965. 239 pages.

Notes: Rank and file; Walcheren; Peninsula 1810–1813; wounded at San Sebastian.

69th Foot

With the 69th in the Waterloo Campaign. Darlington: Napoleonic Archive; n.d. 36 pages.

Notes: Primarily an account written by the regimental colour bearer, Ensign George Ainslie; has General Colin Halkett's account of Quatre-Bras, plus letters from the regimental commander Lieutenant Colonel Charles Morice (who was killed at Waterloo), Captain Charles Cuyler, and Ensign William Bartlett.

70th Foot

Leach, Jonathan. *Rough Sketches of the Life of an Old Soldier.* Cambridge: Ken Trotman; 1986. 442 pages.

Notes: 1801–1806; stationed in the West Indies.

71st Highland Light Infantry

Anonymous. *Vicissitudes in the life of a Scottish Soldier.* London: Henry Colburn; 1827. 357 pages.

A Soldier of the Seventy-First: The Journal of a Soldier of the Highland Light Infantry 1806–1815. Christopher Hibbert (ed.). Warren: Squadron/Signal Publications; 1976. 121 pages.

Notes: Author's name probably James Todd; Buenos Aires; Walcheren; Peninsula; Waterloo.

Gavin, William. *The Diary of William Gavin, Ensign and Quartermaster 71st Highland Regiment, 1806–1815.* 1921.

Napier, William. *The Early Military Life of General Sir George T. Napier.* William Napier (ed.). London: John Murray; 1886. 254 pages.

Notes: Exchanged to 71st Infantry as commander, 1814; through rest of Peninsula War; exchanged to command company of 3rd Guards, 1815.

73rd Foot

Morris, Thomas. *The Napoleonic Wars: Thomas Morris.* John Selby (ed.). Hamden: Archon Books; 1968. 151 pages.
>Notes: 1813–1817; North German Campaign, and Waterloo.

77th Foot

Anonymous. 'The Capture of Ciudad Rodrigo' published in William Maxwell's *Peninsular Sketches; by Actors on the Scene.* Cambridge: Ken Trotman; 1998. 2 vols. 389 & 399 pages.
>Notes: vol. I; pp. 236–256.

C.J.T.S. 'Recollections of the Storming of Cuidad Rodrigo—On a Comparison with Recent Accounts' *Eyewitness Accounts of the Storming of Ciudad Rodrigo.* Cambridge: Ken Trotman; 2004. Pages 10–20.
>Note: This is the same account as the one above.

Keep, William T. *In the Service of the King: The Letters of William Thornton Keep at Home, Walcheren, and in the Peninsula, 1808–1814.* Staplehurst: Spellmount; 1997. 214 pages.
>Notes: Walcheren; with the regiment until 1811.

79th Highlanders

Cocks, Edward. *Intelligence Officer in the Peninsula: Letters & Diaries of Major the Hon. Edward Charles Cocks 1786–1812.* Julia Page (ed.). New York: Hippocrene Books; 1986. 255 pages.
>Notes: 1808–1812; served with 16th Light Dragoons and as an intelligence officer for Wellington's headquarters.

Eadie, Robert. *On Campaign with the 79th Cameron Highlanders: Through Portugal and Spain.* Darlington: Napoleonic Archive; n.d. 47 pages.
>Notes: Rank and file; Peninsula 1809–1813, when he was invalided out of the service. Interesting description of Busaco and the Chelsea Hospital.

Vallence, Dixon. *At Waterloo with the Cameron Highlanders.* Darlington, Napoleonic Archive; n.d. 44 pages.
>Notes: Vallence was in the 6th Company and was severely wounded at Waterloo. Superb descriptions on what it was like to be a private at Quatre-Bras and Waterloo; includes memorable sketches of camp life (especially using a French cuirass as a frying pan after Quatre-Bras), to stand under intense artillery fire, and to be in the front rank (kneeling) of a square being charged by cavalry.

82nd Foot

Wood, George. *The Subaltern Officer: a Narrative.* Cambridge: Ken Trotman; 1986. 263 pages.
>Notes: Peninsula 1808–1814; did not take part in Coruña Campaign; 2nd Battalion of Detachments.

85th Light

Bourne, George. *My Military Career by Lieutenant George Bourne 85th Foot 1804–18.* Godmanchester: Ken Trotman; 2006. 90 pages.

Gleig, George R. *The Subaltern: A Chronicle of the Peninsular War.* London: Leo Cooper; *circa* 1970. 388 pages.
>Notes: 1813–1814.

Gleig, George R. *A Subaltern in America: Comprising the Narrative of the Campaigns of the British Army at Baltimore, Washington, etc. during the Late War.* Philadelphia: E. A. Carey and A. Hart; 1833. 266 pages.

87th Foot

Knox, Wright. *At Barossa with the 87th: the Diary of Lieutenant Wright Knox.* Darlington: Napoleonic Archive; n.d. 52 pages.
> Notes: Seriously wounded at Talavera; Cadiz 1810–1812; Barossa and Siege of Tarifa; in Skerritt's brigade 1812; Vitoria and the Pyrenees.

Rait, Robert S. *The life and campaigns of Hugh, first Viscount Gough, Field Marshal.* Westminster: A. Constable, 1903. 2 vols.

88th Foot (Connaught Rangers)

The following two accounts were published in William Maxwell's *Peninsular Sketches; by Actors on the Scene.* Cambridge: Ken Trotman; 1998. 2 vols. 389 & 399 pages.

Anonymous. 'Events Subsequent to the Battle and Advance from Salamanca' vol. I; pp. 349–389.

Anonymous. 'The Storming of Badajoz' vol. I; pp. 292–303. Possibly Lieutenant Parr Kingsmill.

Dansey, George H. *Letters from an Officer in the 'Devils Own,' the Peninsular letters of Captain George Henry Dansey.* Godmanchester: Ken Trotman; 2006. 30 pages.
> Notes: 1804–1814; the Peninsula.

Grattan, William. *Adventures with the Connaught Rangers: 1809–1814.* London: Greenhill Books (Napoleonic Library); 1989. 362 pages.

92nd Highlanders

Hope, James. *The Iberian and Waterloo Campaigns: The Letters of Lt James Hope 1811–1815.* Heathfield: Naval and Military Press; 2000. 362 pages.
> Notes: Peninsula November 1811–1814; Quatre-Bras; wounded at Waterloo; in France until late 1815. Is listed as *Letters from Portugal, etc., during the Campaigns of 1811–14 by a British Officer* in Oman.

Nicol, Daniel. *With Abercrombie and Moore in Egypt.* Gibbs, Peter and Watkins, David (Editors). Bridgnorth: First Empire; 1995. 40 pages.
> Notes: Rank and File.

Robertson. *Spanish Adventures.* Gibbs, Peter and Watkins, David (Editors). Bridgnorth: First Empire; 1995. 40 Pages.
> Notes: Memoirs of Coruña and Arroyo dos Molinos.

94th Highlanders

Anonymous. 'The Capture of Ciudad Rodrigo' published in William Maxwell's *Peninsular Sketches; by Actors on the Scene.* Cambridge: Ken Trotman; 1998. 2 vols. 389 & 399 pages.
> Notes: vol. I; pp. 225–236.

Donaldson, Joseph. *Recollections of the Eventful Life of a Soldier.* Staplehurst: Spellmount; 2000. 499 pages.
> Notes: Peninsula 1809–1814. Sergeant when discharged.

95th Rifles

Costello, Edward. *The Peninsular and Waterloo Campaigns.* Hamden: Archon Books; 1968. 194 pages.

> Notes: 1st Battalion; 1809–1815. Wounded at Quatre-Bras; missed Waterloo.

Fernyhough, Thomas. *Military Memoirs of Four Brothers.* Staplehurst: Spellmount; 2002. 294 pages.

> Notes: After serving as Royal Marine Officer, Robert transferred to 3rd Battalion 95th Rifles 1811; Badajoz, Salamanca, and was captured by the French for a short period. Sickness prevented him from seeing much action after that.

Green, William. *Where Duty Calls Me: The Experiences of William Green of Lutterworth in the Napoleonic Wars.* John and Dorothea Teague (eds.). West Wickham: Synjon Books; 1975. 72 pages.

> Notes: Joined 95th 1805; Germany, 1805; Copenhagen, 1807; Coruña; 1st Battalion in Peninsula from 1809–1812; wounded at Badajoz and invalided home. Was company bugler.

Harris, John. *The Recollections of Rifleman Harris.* Christopher Hibbert (ed.). London: Leo Cooper; 1970. 140 pages.

> Notes: 1806–1809; 2nd Battalion; Copenhagen, Coruña, and Walcheren.

Kincaid, John. *Adventures in the Rifle Brigade in the Peninsula, France, and the Netherlands from 1809–1815.* Staplehurst: Spellmount; 1998. 352 pages.

> Notes: 1st Battalion; Walcheren; Peninsula 1810–1814; Quatre-Bras and Waterloo.

Kincaid, John. *Random Shots from a Rifleman.* Staplehurst: Spellmount; 1998. 368 pages.

Leach, Jonathan. *Rough Sketches of the Life of an Old Soldier.* Cambridge: Ken Trotman; 1986. 442 pages.

> Notes: 1/95th Rifles 1806; Copenhagen 1806, Peninsula 1808–1814; Quatre-Bras and Waterloo.

Leach, Jonathan. *Rambles along the Styx. Being 'Colloquies between old soldiers who are supposed to have met in the Stygian Shades'* London; 1847. 142 pages.

Simmons, George. *A British Rifleman: Journals and Correspondence during the Peninsular War and the Campaign of Wellington.* London: Greenhill; 1986. 416 pages.

> Notes: 1810–1815; 1st Battalion; Waterloo.

Smith, Harry. *The Autobiography of Sir Harry Smith: 1787–1819.* London: Constable; 1999. 333 pages.

> Notes: 1st Battalion; Buenos Aires, Copenhagen, Coruña, Peninsula 1809–1814; Washington, New Orleans; Brigade-major General Lambert's brigade at Waterloo.

Surtees, William. *Twenty-five Years in the Rifle Brigade.* London: Greenhill; 1996. 480 pages.

> Notes: 2/95th Rifles in 1805; Germany 1805, Copenhagen 1806, Peninsula 1808–1814; New Orleans; Quartermaster 3rd Battalion from 1810–1814.

96th Foot

Le Couteur, John. *Merry Hearts Make Light Days: the War of 1812 Journal of Lieutenant John Le Couteur, 104th Foot.* Donald E. Graves (ed.). Ottawa: Carleton University Press; 1994. 320 pages.

> Notes: 1811 in 96th Regiment, which was garrisoned on Jersey Island.

104th Foot

Le Couteur, John. *Merry Hearts Make Light Days: the War of 1812 Journal of Lieutenant John Le Couteur, 104th Foot.* Donald E. Graves (ed.). Ottawa: Carleton University Press; 1994. 320 pages.

  Notes: 104th Regiment in 1811.

1st Battalion of Detachments

Hamilton, Anthony. *Hamilton's Campaign with Moore and Wellington during the Peninsular War.* Staplehurst: Spellmount; 1998. 164 pages.

  Notes: 2/43rd Infantry in the Peninsula from 1808–1813.

Nicol, Daniel. *With Abercrombie and Moore in Egypt.* Gibbs, Peter and Watkins, David (Editors). Bridgnorth: First Empire; 1995. 40 pages.

  Notes: Memoirs of Daniel Nicol 1808–1809; includes Oporto and Talavera.

2nd Battalion of Detachments

Morley, Stephen. *Memoirs of a Sergeant of the 5th Regiment of Foot, containing an Account of His Service, in Hanover, South America, and the Peninsula.* Cambridge: Ken Trotman; 1999. 123 pages.

  Notes: 2nd Battalion of Detachments until after Talavera. Returned to England October 1809.

Wood, George. *The Subaltern Officer: a Narrative.* Cambridge: Ken Trotman; 1986. 263 pages.

  Notes: 82nd Foot in Peninsula from 1808–1814.

Militia Regiments

Calladine, G. *Colour-Sergeant Calladine.* Darlington: Napoleonic Archive; n.d.

  Notes: Derbyshire Militia in 1805–1811.

Dobbs, John. *Recollections of an Old 52nd Man.* Staplehurst: Spellmount; 2000. 101 pages.

  Notes: Armagh Militia 1806–1808.

Green, William. *Where Duty Calls Me: The Experiences of William Green of Lutterworth in the Napoleonic Wars.* John and Dorothea Teague (eds.). West Wickham: Synjon Books; 1975. 72 pages.

  Notes: Leicester Militia 1803–1805.

Hale, James. *The Journal of James Hale: Late Serjeant in the Ninth Regiment of Foot.* Windsor: IX Regiment; 1998. 139 pages.

  Notes: Royal North Gloucester Regiment 1801–1807.

Ross-Lewin, Harry. *With the Thirty-Second in the Peninsular and Other Campaigns.* Cambridge: Ken Trotman; 2000. 368 pages.

  Notes: Rank and file volunteer in Limerick Militia; ensign 1793–1794.

KING'S GERMAN LEGION (BY UNIT)

1st KGL Hussars

Hering, John Frederick. *Journal of an Officer in the King's German Legion.* Cambridge: Ken Trotman; 2000.

  Notes: Was a medical officer. 1st KGL Hussars 1809–1811.

Schaumann, A.L.F. *On the Road with Wellington: the Diary of a War Commissary in the Peninsular Campaigns.* Anthony Ludovici, (ed.). London: Greenhill Books; 1998. 440 pages.

  Notes: In 1st KGL Hussars 1810. Peninsula 1808–1813

5th Line Battalion

Ompteda, Christian von. *In the King's German Legion: Memoirs of Baron Ompteda, Colonel in the King's German Legion during the Napoleonic Wars.* Von Ompteda, Louis (ed.). Cambridge: Ken Trotman; 1987. 328 pages.

  Notes: Full name Christian von Ompteda; 1793–1815; commanded 5th Line Battalion 1813.

Wheatley, Edmund. *The Wheatley Diary: A Journal and Sketchbook Kept during the Peninsular War and the Waterloo Campaign.* Christopher Hibbert (ed.). London: Longmans, Green and Co.; 1964. 111 pages.

  Notes: Peninsula 1813–1814, not at Vitoria; at Waterloo.

7th Line Battalion

Hering, John Frederick. *Journal of an Officer in the King's German Legion.* Cambridge: Ken Trotman; 2000.

  Notes: Medical officer. Served in Sicily with 7th KGL Battalion from 1811–1815.

Maempel, Johann C. *Adventures of a Young Rifleman, in the French and English Armies, during the War in Spain and Portugal, from 1806 to 1816.* London: Henry Colburn; 1826. 371 pages.

  Notes: Captured in 1811. Enlisted in KGL in 1812.

Schaumann, A.L.F. *On the Road with Wellington: the Diary of a War Commissary in the Peninsular Campaigns.* Anthony Ludovici, (ed.). London: Greenhill Books; 1998. 440 pages.

  Notes: Peninsula 1808–1813; 7th KGL Infantry in 1811.

1st Light Battalion

Ompteda, Christian von. *In the King's German Legion: Memoirs of Baron Ompteda, Colonel in the King's German Legion during the Napoleonic Wars.* Von Ompteda, Louis (ed.). Cambridge: Ken Trotman; 1987. 328 pages.

  Notes: Full name Christian von Ompteda; commanded 1st Light Battalion 1812.

OFFICERS IN PORTUGUESE SERVICE

Blakiston, John. *Twelve Years' Military Adventure in Three-Quarters of the Globe.* London: Henry Colburn; 1840. 2 volumes.

  Notes: Java, 1810; 17th Portuguese Line Regiment 1813–1814.

Bunbury, Thomas. *Being Personal and Military Adventures in Portugal, Spain, France, Malta . . . and India, etc.* London: C.J. Skeet; 1861. 3 vols.

  Notes: Portuguese 20th Regiment 1810–1813; 5th *Caçadores* 1813–1814.

Dickson, Alexander. *The Dickson Manuscripts: Being Diaries, Letters, Maps, Account Books, with Various Other Papers of the Late Major General Sir Alexander Dickson.* John H. Leslie (ed.). 5 vols.; Cambridge: Ken Trotman; 1987. 1190 pages.

  Notes: Years 1809–1813. Served with Portuguese Artillery before becoming chief of Wellington's siege-trains.

Dobbs, John. *Recollections of an Old 52nd Man.* Staplehurst: Spellmount; 2000. 101 pages.

  Notes: Commanded a company of the 5th *Caçadores* in 1813; claims to be the last British officer wounded in the Peninsula War, 14 April 1814.

D'Urban, Benjamin. *The Peninsular War Journal: 1808–1817.* London: Greenhill Napoleonic Library; 1988. 385 pages.

  Notes: Staff officer to Robert Wilson; Quartermaster General for Marshal Beresford; commanded brigade of Portuguese Cavalry 1812.

Elder, George. 'The Storming of Badajoz' published in William Maxwell's *Peninsular Sketches; by Actors on the Scene.* Cambridge: Ken Trotman; 1998. 2 vols. 389 & 399 pages.

> Notes: vol. I; pp. 304–320. Commander of 3rd *Caçadores.*

Mayne, William and Lillie. *A Narrative of the Campaigns of the Loyal Lusitanian Legion during the Years 1809, 1810 & 1811.* Cambridge: Ken Trotman; 1986. 358 pages.

> Notes: Good account of the Battle of Alcantara.

Warre, William. *Letters from the Peninsula: 1808–1812.* Staplehurst: Spellmount; 1999. 231 pages.

> Notes: Aide to General Ferguson at Roliça and Vimeiro; aide to Marshal Beresford 1809–1812.

COMMISSARIAT

Buckham, E. *Personal Narrative of Adventures in the Peninsula during the War in 1812–13.* Cambridge: Ken Trotman; 1995. 339 pages.

> Notes: In Staff Corps Regiment of Cavalry; primary duty was as a commissary officer; great descriptions of Almeida and buying cattle for the army.

Chesterton, George Laval. *Peace, War, and Adventure: an Autobiographical Memoir of George Laval Chesterton.* London: Longman, Brown, Green & Longmans; 1853. 2 vols.

> Notes: Volume 1 covers war in Catalonia in 1812–1814.

Dallas, Alexander. *Felix Alvarez, or, Manners in Spain Containing Descriptive Accounts of Some of the Prominent Events of the Late Peninsular War.* New York: J. Eastburn; 1818. 2 vols.

Daniel, John Edgecombe. *Journal of an Officer in the Commissariat Department: 1811–1815.* Cambridge: Ken Trotman; 1997. 503 pages.

> Notes: Peninsula 1811–1814; Waterloo. On the Army staff; 3rd Division 1813.

Graham, William. *Travels through Portugal and Spain, during the Peninsular War.* London: Richard Phillips; 1820. 92 pages.

Henegan, Richard. *Seven Years Campaigning in the Peninsula and the Netherlands, from 1808–1815.* London: H. Colburn; 1846. 2 vols.

Schaumann, A.L.F. *On the Road with Wellington: the Diary of a War Commissary in the Peninsular Campaigns.* Anthony Ludovici, (ed.). London: Greenhill Books; 1998. 440 pages.

> Notes: Peninsula 1808–1813; 1st KGL Hussars 1810; 7th KGL Infantry 1811; 9th Light Dragoons 1812; 18th Hussars 1812–1813.

MEDICAL DEPARTMENT

Anonymous. 'Marshal Beresford' published in William Maxwell's *Peninsular Sketches; by Actors on the Scene.* Cambridge: Ken Trotman; 1998. 2 vols. 389 & 399 pages.

> Notes: vol. 2; pp. 337–343. Provided medical assistance to Marshal Beresford at Salamanca.

Boutflower, Charles. *The Journal of an Army Surgeon during the Peninsular War.* Staplehurst: Spellmount; 1997. 193 pages.

> Notes: 40th Regiment August, 1809 November 1812; 4th Division surgeon November 1812 May–1813.

Bradley, James B. 'A Night in the Peninsular War' published in William Maxwell's

Peninsular Sketches; by Actors on the Scene. Cambridge: Ken Trotman; 1998. 2 vols. 389 & 399 pages.

    Notes: vol. 2; pp. 187–204. Assigned to a hospital in Castello Branco.

Burroughs, George Frederick. *A Narrative of the Retreat of the Army from Burgos in a Series of Letters with an Introductory Sketch of the Campaign of 1812 and Military Character of the Duke of Wellington.* Cambridge: Ken Trotman; 2004. 59 pages.

    Notes: Assistant surgeon, Royal Dragoons.

Dent, William. *Letters to His Parents from Colchester, Peninsula, North America, France, West Indies, 1808–1824.* Old Woking: Unwin Brothers; 1976. 68 pages.

Henry, Walter. *Surgeon Henry's Trifles: Events of a Military Life.* Pat Hayward (ed.). London: Chatto & Windus; 1970. 281 pages.

    Notes: First name was Walter; Peninsula 1811–1814; Saint Helena 1817–1821.

Hering, John Frederick. *Journal of an Officer in the King's German Legion.* Cambridge: Ken Trotman; 2000.

    Notes: Was a medical officer. Served in Hanover, the Baltic, Peninsula 1809–1811, with 1st KGL Hussars; Sicily with the 7th KGL Battalion 1811–1815.

James, Haddy. *Surgeon James' Journal: 1815.* Jane Vansittart (ed.). London: Cassell; 1964. 175 pages.

    Notes: Assistant Surgeon; 1st Life Guards.

McGrigor, James. *Sir James McGrigor: the Scalpel and the Sword.* Dalkeith: Scottish Cultural Press; 2000. 320 pages.

Neale, Adams. *Letters from Portugal and Spain; Comprising an Account of the Operations of the Armies under Their Excellencies Sir Arthur Wellesley and Sir John Moore from the Landing at Mondego Bay to the Battle of Coruña.* London: Phillips, 1809. 2 vols.

Wooldridge, John M. *Letters from Spain: being Some Correspondence from John Mogg Wooldridge of Cholwell in Somerset, Surgeon in the Army of the Duke of Wellington during the Wars in Spain 1809–1814.* Bristol: Merchant Venturers'Technical College School of Printing; 1941. 16 Pages.

RANK-AND-FILE

Anonymous. *Jottings from My Sabretasch.* Godmanchester: Ken Trotman; 2005. 292 pages.

    Notes: 15th Hussars; Coruña Campaign; Peninsula 1813–1814; Waterloo.

Anonymous. *Memoirs of a Sergeant Late in the Forty-third Light Infantry Regiment previous to and during the Peninsular War.* Cambridge: Ken Trotman; 1998. 278 pages.

    Notes: Copenhagen 1806; Peninsula: Coruña; Peninsula June, 1809; good account of River Coa; wounded Badajoz; returned to England 1812.

Anonymous. *A Soldier of the Seventy-First: The Journal of a Soldier of the Highland Light Infantry 1806–1815.* Christopher Hibbert (ed.). Warren: Squadron/Signal Publications; 1976. 121 pages.

    Notes: Author's name was probably Thomas Howell; Buenos Aires; Walcheren; Peninsula; Waterloo.

Anton, James. *Retrospect of a Military Life.* Cambridge: Ken Trotman; 1991. 395 pages.

    Notes: 42nd Highlanders 1813–1815.

Blainey, William. *Bonaparte versus Blainey.* Union Springs: Tallcot Bookshop; 1988. 48 pages.

    Notes: Sergeant; 51st Regiment; Walcheren; Peninsula 1811–1814.

Brown, Robert. *An Impartial Journal of a Detachment from the Brigade of Foot Guards,*

Commencing 25th February 1793 and Ending 9th May 1795. Godmanchester: Ken Trotman; 2006. 280 pages.

Notes: Was a corporal.

Brown, William. *With the 45th at Badajoz, Salamanca, and Vitoria.* Darlington: Napoleonic Archive; n.d. 44 pages.

Notes: 1st Battalion; Peninsula 1809; Busaco, Ciudad Rodrigo, Badajoz (great descriptions of the assault and pillage of the city), Salamanca (great description of being ridden down by French cavalry), the 1813 retreat, and battle for Vitoria and the subsequent looting of the French baggage train. Also served as an officer's servant. Fantastic descriptions of the daily life of a soldier on campaign.

Clay, Matthew. *With the Guards at Hougoumont.* Darlington: Napoleonic Archive; n.d. 20 pages.

Notes: Light Company 2/3rd Foot Guards. Great description of Quatre-Bras and the defence of Hougoumont.

Collett, John. *John Collet and the Company of Foot Guards.* Barbara Chambers (ed.). Letchworth Garden City: Barbara Chambers; 1996. 2 vols.

Notes: 1st Foot Guards; 1803–1823; private; about 15 per cent of book is his diary.

Cooper, John S. *Rough Notes of Seven Campaigns: 1809–1815.* Staplehurst: Spellmount Library; 1996. 160 pages.

Notes: Sergeant; 7th Fusiliers. In all major battles of Peninsula, New Orleans.

Costello, Edward. *The Peninsular and Waterloo Campaigns.* Hamden: Archon Books; 1968. 194 pages. SBN: 208–00630–3.

Notes: 1/95th Rifles; 1809–1815. Wounded at Quatre-Bras; missed Waterloo.

Dayes, John. *Memoir of the Military Career of John Dayes, late Paymaster Sergeant of the 5th Regiment of Foot.* Cambridge: Ken Trotman; 2004. 26 pages.

Notes: Holland 1799; Buenos Aires 1806; Coruña Campaign; returned to the Peninsula in 1812.

Dickson, Corporal. *Scots Greys at Waterloo.* Darlington: Napoleonic Archive; n.d. 39 pages.

Notes: Primarily the account of Corporal Dickson of F Troop (Captain Vernon's troop). A great description of the charge of the Union Brigade.

Donaldson, Joseph. *Recollections of the Eventful Life of a Soldier.* Staplehurst: Spellmount; 2000. 499 pages.

Notes: Joined 94th Highlands 1809; Peninsula 1809–1814; sergeant when discharged.

Douglas, John. *Douglas's Tale of the Peninsula & Waterloo: 1808–1815.* Stanley Monick (ed.). London: Leo Cooper; 1997. 133 pages.

Notes: Sergeant by 1814; 1st Foot; Walcheren; Peninsula 1809–1814; Waterloo.

Eadie, Robert. *On Campaign with the 79th Cameron Highlanders: Through Portugal and Spain.* Darlington: Napoleonic Archive; n.d. 47 pages.

Notes: Peninsula 1809–1813, when he was invalided out of the service. Interesting description of Busaco and the Chelsea Hospital.

Green, John. *The Vicissitudes of a Soldier's Life or a Series of Occurrences from 1806 to 1815.* Wakefield: EP Publishing; circa 1965. 239 pages.

Notes: 68th Regiment; Walcheren; Peninsula 1810–1813; wounded San Sebastian.

Green, William. *Where Duty Calls Me: The Experiences of William Green of Lutterworth in the Napoleonic Wars.* John and Dorothea Teague (eds.). West Wickham: Synjon Books; 1975. 72 pages.

Notes: Leicester Militia 1803; 95th 1805; Germany, 1805; Copenhagen, 1807; Peninsula 1808–1812; wounded Badajoz; invalided home; company bugler.

Hale, James. *The Journal of James Hale: Late Serjeant in the ninth Regiment of Foot.* Windsor: IX Regiment; 1998. 139 pages.
　　Notes: Royal North Gloucester Regiment 1801; 9th in 1807; Roliça, Vimeiro, Coruña, and Walcheren; Peninsula 1810–1813; wounded at San Sebastian and invalided home.

Hamilton, Anthony. *Hamilton's Campaign with Moore and Wellington during the Peninsular War.* Staplehurst: Spellmount; 1998. 164 pages.
　　Notes: 2/43rd Foot; Peninsula 1808–1813; 1st Battalion of Detachments. Captured at San Sebastian 1813.

Hanley, William. 'Capture of the Enemy's Picquet at Blanchez Sanchez' published in William Maxwell's *Peninsular Sketches; by Actors on the Scene.* Cambridge: Ken Trotman; 1998. 2 vols. 389 & 399 pages.
　　Notes: vol. 2; pp. 380–388. Sergeant, 14th Light Dragoons.

Harris, John. *The Recollections of Rifleman Harris.* Christopher Hibbert (ed.). London: Leo Cooper; 1970. 140 pages.
　　Notes: 1806–1809. 2/95th Rifles; Copenhagen; Coruña; Walcheren.

Lawrence, William. *A Dorset Soldier: The Autobiography of Sergeant William Lawrence 1790–1869.* Eileen Hathaway (ed.). Tunbridge Wells: Spellmount; 1993. 176 pages.
　　Notes: 40th Regiment; Buenos Aires; Peninsula 1808–1814; New Orleans; Waterloo.

Miller, Benjamin. *The Adventures of Serjeant Benjamin Miller Whilst Serving in the 4th Battalion of the Royal Regiment of Artillery 1796–1815.* Dallington: Naval & Military Press; 1999. 43 pages.
　　Notes: Egypt; Coruña Campaign.

Morley, Stephen. *Memoirs of a Sergeant of the 5th Regiment of Foot, containing an Account of His Service, in Hanover, South America, and the Peninsula.* Cambridge: Ken Trotman; 1999. 123 pages.
　　Notes: Buenos Aires 1806; Peninsula 1808–1813; Roliça, Vimeiro, Coruña Campaign where he was captured. Escaped and made his way to Portugal. Assigned to 2nd Battalion of Detachments until after Talavera; returned to England in October 1809; Peninsula in 1812; invalided after retreat of 1812 and returned to England 1813.

Morris, Thomas. *The Napoleonic Wars: Thomas Morris.* John Selby (ed.). Hamden: Archon Books; 1968. 151 pages.
　　Notes: 73rd Regiment 1813–1817; North German Campaign and Waterloo.

Nicol, Daniel. *With Abercrombie and Moore in Egypt.* Peter Gibbs and David Watkins (eds.). Bridgnorth: First Empire; 1995. 40 pages.
　　Notes: 92nd Highlanders; 1st Battalion of Detachments.

O'Neil, Charles. *The Military Adventures of Charles O'Neil.* Staplehurst: Spellmount; 1997. 269 pages.
　　Notes: 28th Regiment; Peninsula 1811–1814; Waterloo.

Pearson, Andrew. *The Soldier Who Walked Away: The Autobiography of Andrew Pearson a Peninsular War Veteran.* Arthur H. Haley (ed.). Liverpool: Bullfinch Publications; *circa* 1991. 130 pages.
　　Notes: 61st Regiment; at Egypt; Maida; Gibraltar; Peninsula 1809–1812.

Playford, Thomas, *A Lifeguardsman at Waterloo.* Godmanchester: Ken Trotman; 2006. 90 pages.
　　Notes: Was a private; joined 2nd Lifeguards 1810.

Robinson. *Spanish Adventures.* Peter Gibbs and David Watkins (eds.). Bridgnorth: First Empire; 1995. 40 pages.
　　Notes: 92nd Highlanders; Coruña and Arroyo dos Molinos.

Surtees, William. *Twenty-five Years in the Rifle Brigade.* London: Greenhill; 1996. 480 pages.

Notes: 56th Regiment, Holland in 1799; 2/95th Rifles 1805; Germany 1805, Copenhagen 1806, Peninsula 1808–1814; New Orleans; Quartermaster by 1812.

Vallence, Dixon. *At Waterloo with the Cameron Highlanders.* Darlington, Napoleonic Archive; n.d. 44 pages.

Notes: Vallence was in the 6th Company and was severely wounded. Superb descriptions on what it was like to be a private at Quatre-Bras and Waterloo; includes memorable sketches of camp life (especially using a French cuirass as a frying pan after Quatre-Bras), to stand under intense artillery fire, and to be in the front rank (kneeling) of a square being charged by cavalry.

Wheeler, William. *The Letters of Private Wheeler.* B.H. Liddell Hart (ed.). Boston: Hoghton Mifflin; 1952. 350 pages.

Notes: 51st Regiment; Walcheren; Peninsula 1811–1814; Waterloo.

MISCELLANEOUS

Glover, Gareth. *Letters from the Battle of Waterloo: Unpublished Correspondence by Allied Officers from the Siborne Papers.* London: Greenhill; 2004. 352 pages.

Operations of the Fifth or Picton's Division in the Campaign of Waterloo. Cambridge: Ken Trotman; 2001. 34 pages.

Siborne, H.T. *Waterloo Letters.* London: Greenhill; 1993. 464 pages.

Select Bibliography

Adjutant General's Office. *General Regulations and Orders for the Army.* London: G. Roworth; 1804.

——. *General Regulations and Orders for the Army, 12th August, 1811. To which are added such Regulations as have been issued to the 1st January 1816.* Facsimile edition London: Frederick Muller Ltd; 1970.

Anonymous. *'Advanced Principles of Military Justice: Subcourse IS1804; edition B.'* Charlottesville, VA: Judge Advocate General's School, U.S. Army; 2001.

——. *British Parliamentary Papers.* vol. i of the 'Military and Naval' series of the Irish University Press edition; 1969.

——. 'Description of the Pontoon Train in the Peninsula,' *Royal Engineer Journal.* Issue III, 2 January 1870.

——. *Essay on the Art of War: in which the General Principles of All the Operations of War in the Field are fully Explained. The Whole Collected from the Opinions of the Best Authors.* London: A. Millar; 1761.

——. *Further Strictures on Those Parts of Colonel Napier's History of the Peninsular War Which Relate to the Military Opinions and Conduct of General Lord Viscount Beresford G.C.B., &c. &c. &c. To Which is Added A Report of the Operations in the Alemtejo and Spanish Estremadura, During the Year of 1811. By M. General Sir Benjamin D'Urban.* Reprinted Chapelgarth, Sunderland: Mark Thompson Publishing; 1995. Originally published London; 1832.

——. *The Little Bombardier and Pocket Gunner.* London: T. Egerton; 1801.

——. *A Military Dictionary, Explaining and Describing the Technical Terms, Phrases, Works, and Machines, used in The Science of War, Embellished with Copper-Plates of All Common Works used in Military Architecture: as well as the Utensils employed in Attacks and Defence; with References for their Explanation; and an Introduction to Fortification.* London: G. Robinson, and Fielding and Walker; 1778.

——. *The Perfection of Military Discipline, After the Newest Method; as Practiced in England and Ireland, &c. or, The Industrious Souldier's Golden Treasury of Knowledge in the Art of making War . . .* 2nd edition. Facsimile reprint n.p., n.d. Originally published London: W. Wild for Nicholas Boddington; 1691.

——. *The Personal Narrative of a Private Soldier in the 42nd Highlanders, for Twelve Years, During the Late War.* Facsimile reprint Cambridge: Ken Trotman Ltd, 1996. Originally published 1821.

——. *The Royal Military Calendar or Army Service and Commission Book Containing the Services and Progress or Promotion of the Generals, Lieutenant Generals, Major Generals, Colonels, Lieutenant Colonels, and Majors, of the Army, According to Seniority: with Details of the Principal Military Events of the Last Century.* 3rd edition, 5 vols. Facsimile reprint Uckfield: Naval & Military Press, Ltd; n.d. Originally published London: A.J. Valpy; 1820.

——. *The Royal Military Chronicle; or, The British Officer's Monthly Register, Chronicle, and Military Mentor.* 2nd edition; issues for November 1810–April 1811. London; 1813.

——. *A System of Camp-Discipline, Military Honours, Garrison Duty, And other Regulations for the Land Forces. Collected by a Gentleman of the Army. In which are included Kane's Discipline for a Battalion in Action. With a Map of the Seat of War, Lines and Plans of Battles, and above Sixty Military Schemes, finely engraved from the Originals of the most eminent Generals, &c. To which is added, General Kane's Campaigns of King William and the Duke of Marlborough, Improved from the late Earl of Craufurd's and Colonel Dunbar's Copies, taken from General Kane's own Writing. With His Remarks on the several Stratagems by which every Battle was won or lost, from 1689 to 1712.* 2nd edition. Facsimile reprint USA: The Nova Anglia Press; n.d. Originally printed London; 1757.

——. *Strictures on Certain Passages of Lieutenant-Colonel Napier's History of the Peninsular War Which Relate to the Military Opinions and Conduct of General Lord Viscount Beresford, G.C.B. &c., &c.* Reprinted Chapelgarth, Sunderland: Mark Thompson Publishing; 1995. Originally published London; 1831.

Anglesey, Marquis of. *One-Leg.* London: Jonathan Cape; 1961.

Anton, James. *Retrospect of a Military Life, During the Most Eventful Periods of the Last War.* Facsimile reprint Cambridge: Ken Trotman Ltd; 1991. Originally published Edinburgh; 1841.

Atkinson, C.T. 'The Battalions of Detachments at Talavera,' *Journal of the Society for Army Historical Research.* vol. 15; 1936.

——. 'The Composition and Organization of the British Forces in the Peninsula, 1808–1814,' *English Historical Review.* No. LXVII; July, 1902.

Barnes, Major R. Money. *A History of the Regiments and Uniforms of the British Army.* London: Sphere Books Ltd; 1972.

Barthorp, Michael. *Wellington's Generals.* Men-At-Arms Series #84. London: Osprey Publishing; 1978.

Bateson, Gregory. *Mind and Nature: A Necessary Unity.* New York: Bantam Books; 1980.

Batty, Robert. *Campaign of the Left Wing of the Allied Army, in the Western Pyrenees and South of France, in the Years 1813–14.* London: Ken Trotman; 1983.

Beamish, N. Ludlow. *History of the King's German Legion.* 2 vols. London: Buckland and Brown; 1993. First published 1832–37.

Bell, Douglas. *Wellington's Officers.* London: Collins; 1938.

Bell, George. *Soldier's Glory: Being 'Rough Notes of an Old Soldier.'* Tunbridge Wells: Spellmount; 1991.

Beresford, General Lord Viscount. *Refutation of Colonel Napier's Justification of His Third Volume.* Reprinted Chapelgarth, Sunderland: Mark Thompson Publishing; 1996. Originally published London; 1834.

Bland, Lieutenant-Colonel Humphrey. *A Treatise of Military Discipline: In which is Laid down and Explained the Duty of the several Branches of the Service.* 2nd edition. London: Sam Buckley; 1727. (The 1st edition was published earlier in 1727.)

—— (Lt-General). *A Treatise of Military Discipline: In which is Laid down and Explained the Duty of the several Branches of the Service.* 9th edition. Reprint Cambridge: Ken Trotman, Ltd; 2001. Originally published London: R. Baldwin, J. Richardson, T. Longman, S. Crowder and Co., & H. Woodgate; 1762.

Brett-James, Anthony. *Life in Wellington's Army.* London: Tom Donovan Publishing; 1994.

Brownrigg, Beatrice. *The Life and Letters of Sir John Moore.* Oxford: Basil Blackwell; 1923.

Bruce, H.A. *Life of General Sir William Napier.* 2 vols. London: John Murray; 1864.

Buckham, E. *Personal Narrative of Adventures in the Peninsula.* Cambridge: Ken Trotman; 1995.

Buckley, Roger N., ed. *The Napoleonic War Journal of Captain Thomas Henry Browne: 1807–1816.* London: Army Records Society; 1987.

Bueno, José. *Uniformes Militares Españoles: El Ejercito y la Armada en 1808,* Malaga, Spain; 1982.

Burgoyne, John. *Life and Correspondence of Field Marshal Sir John Burgoyne.* London: Richard Bentley; 1893.

Butler, Lt-Colonel Lewis, *The Annals of the King's Royal Rifle Corps.* London: John Murray; 1923.

—— (Captain). *Wellington's Operations in the Peninsula 1808–1814.* 2 vols. Uckfield, England: Naval & Military Press Ltd, in association with Firepower, The Royal Military Museum, Woolwich; England; n.d. Originally published 1904.

Carew, Tim. *How the Regiments got their Nicknames.* London: Leo Cooper; 1974.

Carr-Gomm, Francis Culling, ed. *Letters and Journals of Field Marshal William Maynard Gomm, G.C.B., Commander-in-Chief of India, Constable of the Tower of London &c. &c. From 1799 to Waterloo 1815.* Facsimile edition Elibron Classics, 2003. Originally published London: John Murray; 1881.

Cassidy, Martin. *Marching with Wellington: With the Inniskillings in the Napoleonic War.* Barnsley, S. Yorks: Leo Cooper, Pen & Sword Books; 2003.

Castlereagh, Lord. *Correspondence, Dispatches and other Papers of Viscount Castlereagh, Second Marquess of Londonderry.* Edited by his brother, Charles William Vane, Marquess of Londonderry. 12 vols. London: William Shoberl; 1848–1853.

Chichester, Henry Manners & Burges-Short, George. *The Records and Badges of the British Army,* London: Frederick Muller Ltd; 1970.

Clark-Kennedy, A.E. *Attack the Colour! The Royal Dragoons in the Peninsula and at Waterloo.* London: Research Publishing; 1975.

Connelly, Owen. *Napoleon's Satellite Kingdoms.* New York: Free Press; 1965.

Connelly, T. W. J. *The History of the Corps of Royal Sappers and Miners.* 2 vols. London: Longman, Brown, Green & Longmans; 1855.

Cooper, John Spencer. *Rough Notes of Seven Campaigns: 1809–1815.* Staplehurst: Spellmount Ltd; 1996. First published 1869.

Cope, Sir William H. *History of the Rifle Brigade.* London: Chatto & Windus; 1877.

Costello, Edward. *The Peninsular and Waterloo Campaigns.* Hamden: Archon Books; 1968.

Creevey, Thomas. *The Creevey Papers.* Edited by Sir Herbert Maxwell. London: John Murray; 1923.

Csartoryski. *Memoirs of Prince Adam Csartoryski.* Edited by Adam Gielgud. 2 vols. London: Remington; 1888.

Dalbiac, Colonel P.H. *History of the 45th: 1st Nottinghamshire Regiment (Sherwood Foresters).* Facsimile reprint Cambridge: Ken Trotman; 2000. Originally published London: Swan Sonnenschein & Co., Ltd; 1902.

Dalton, Charles. *The Waterloo Roll-Call.* New York: Hippocrene Books; 1971.

Delavoye, Alex. M. *Life of Thomas Graham Lord Lynedoch.* London: Richardson & Co.; 1880.

Dickinson, H., *Instructions for forming a regiment of infantry for parade exercise, together with the eighteen manoeuvres, as ordered to be practised by His Majesty's infantry forces, accompanied by explanations and diagrams,* London, 1798.

Dickson, Alexander. *The Dickson Manuscripts.* Edited by Major John Leslie. 2 vols., Woolwich: R. A. Institute; 1905. Also reprinted in 5 vols., Cambridge: Ken Trotman; 1987.

Dodge, Theodore Ayrault. *Hannibal: A History of the Art of War Among the Carthaginians and Romans Down to the Battle of Pydna, 168 b.c., with a Detailed Account of the Second Punic War.* New York: Da Capo Press; 1995. Originally published Boston; 1891.

Donaldson, Joseph. *Recollections of the Eventful Life of a Soldier.* Staplehurst: Spellmount; 2000.

Douglas, Howard. *An Essay on the Principles and Construction of Military Bridges and the Passage of Rivers in Military Operations.* 2nd edition. London: Thomas and William Boone; 1832.

Douglas, Corporal John. *Douglas's Tale of the Peninsula and Waterloo.* Edited by Stanley Monick. London: Leo Cooper; 1997.

Duncan, Major Francis. *History of the Royal Regiment of Artillery.* 3rd edition, 2 vols. London: John Murray; 1879.

Dundas, Colonel David. *Principles of Military Movements, Chiefly Applied to Infantry. Illustrated by Manœuvres of the Prussian Troops and by An Outline of the British Campaigns in Germany, During the War of 1757. With An Appendix, Containing a Practical Abstract of the Whole . . .* Reprinted Cambridge: Ken Trotman, Ltd; 2002. Originally published London: T. Cadell; 1788.

Dunn-Pattison, R. P. *The History of the 91st Argyllshire Highlanders.* Edinburgh: Wm. Blackwood & Sons; 1910.

D'Urban, Benjamin. *The Peninsular Journal of Major General Sir Benjamin D'Urban.* Edited by I. J. Rousseau. New York: Longmans, Green and Co.; 1930.

Esdaile, Charles J. *The Peninsular War. A New History.* London: Allen Lane; 2002.

——. *Fighting Napoleon. Guerrillas, Bandits and Adventurers in Spain, 1808–1814.* New Haven: Yale University Press; 2004.

Fletcher, Ian, ed. *The Peninsular War: Aspects of the Struggle for the Iberian Peninsula.* Staplehurst: Spellmount Ltd; 1998.

——, ed. *Voices from the Peninsula: Eyewitness Accounts by Soldiers of Wellington's Army 1808–1814.* London: Greenhill Books; 2001.

Fortescue, J. W. *The British Army 1783–1802: Four Lectures Delivered at the Staff College and Cavalry School.* London: Macmillan and Co., Ltd; 1905.

——. *A History of the British Army. Vols. i–x.* London: Macmillan and Co., Ltd; 1906–1920.

Fosten, Bryan. *Wellington's Infantry.* vol. i. London: Osprey; 1981.

Foy, Le Générale [Maximilian]. *Histoire de la Guerre de la Péninsule sous Napoléon.* 4 vols. and *Atlas.* Paris: Baudouin Frères, Éditeurs; 1827.

Fraser, Edward. *The Soldiers whom Wellington Led.* London: Methuen; 1913.

Frederick, J. M. B. *Lineage Book of the British Army.* Cornwallville, NY: Hope Farm Press; 1968.

Fuller, J.F.C. *British Light Infantry in the Eighteenth Century (An Introduction to 'Sir John Moore's System of Training').* London: Hutchinson & Co.; 1925.

Furse, Colonel George Armand. *The Art of Marching.* London: William Clowes & Sons, Ltd; 1901.

Gardyne, Lieutenant-Colonel C. Greenhill. *The Life of a Regiment: The History of the Gordon Highlanders from its Formation in 1794 to 1816.* vol. i. Facsimile reprint Uckfield, England: Naval & Military Press; n.d. Originally published Edinburgh: Douglas; 1901–3; then reprinted London: The Medici Society; 1929.

Garwood, F.S. 'The Royal Staff Corps: 1800–1837,' *Royal Engineer Journal.* vol. 57; 1943.

Gates, David. *The British Light Infantry Arm, c1790–1815.* London: Batsford; 1987.

Geike, Archibald. *Life of Sir Roderick I. Murchison . . .* 2 vols. London: John Murray; 1875.

George III. *The Later Correspondence of George III.* Edited by A. Aspinall. 5 vols. Cambridge University Press; 1962–70.

George IV. *Correspondence of George, Prince of Wales.* Edited by A. Aspinall. 8 vols. London: Cassell; 1963–71.

Gibbs, Peter & Watkins, David, eds. 'Daniel Nicol's with the First Battalion of Detachments,' *Spanish Adventures.* Bridgnorth: First Empire Publishing; 1996.

Glover, Gareth. *Wellington's Lieutenant Napoleon's Gaoler: the Peninsula Letters & St Helena Diaries of Sir George Ridout Bingham.* Barnsley: Pen and Sword; 2005.

Glover, Michael. *Britannia Sickens,* London: Leo Cooper; 1970.

——, ed. *A Gentleman Volunteer: The Letters of George Hennell from the Peninsular War, 1812–13.* London: Heinemann Ltd; 1979.

——. *The Peninsular War 1808–1814.* London: David & Charles; 1974.

——. *Wellington as Military Commander.* Sphere Books; 1973.

——. *Wellington's Army in the Peninsula 1808–1814.* New York: Hippocrene Books; 1977.

Glover, Richard. *Peninsular Preparation: The Reform of the British Army 1795–1809.* Cambridge: Ken Trotman Ltd; 1988.

Grattan, William. *Adventures with the Connaught Rangers, 1809–1814.* London: Greenhill Books; 1989.

Green, John. *The Vicissitudes of a Soldier's Life or a Series of Occurrences from 1806 to 1815; with an Introductory and Concluding Chapter: the Whole Containing, with Some Other Matters, a Concise Account of the War in the Peninsula, From its Commencement to its Final Close.* Republished Cambridge: Ken Trotman Ltd,; 1996. First published London: J. and J. Jackson; 1827.

Gurwood, Lt-Colonel, ed. *The General Orders of Field Marshal the Duke of Wellington, K.G., &c. &c. &c. in Portugal, Spain, and France, From 1809 to 1814; in the Low Countries and France, in 1815; and in France, Army of Occupation, From 1816 to 1818; Compiled alphabetically from the several printed volumes, which were originally issued to the General and Staff Officers and Officers commanding regiments in the above campaigns.* London; 1837.

Guy, Alan J. *Oeconomy and Discipline: Officership and administration in the British Army 1714–63.* Manchester: Manchester University Press; 1985.

——, ed. *The Road to Waterloo: The British Army and the Struggle Against Revolutionary and Napoleonic France, 1793–1815.* London: National Army Museum; 1990.

Hale, James & Catley, Peter, eds. *The Journal of James Hale: Late Serjeant in the ninth Regiment of Foot.* Windsor, Berkshire: IX Regiment; 1998.

Hall, Christopher D. *British Strategy in the Napoleonic War, 1803–1815.* Manchester University Press; 1992.

——. *Wellington's Navy. Sea Power and the Peninsular War, 1807–1814.* London: Chatham; 2004.

Hall, John A. The Biographical Dictionary of British Officers Killed and Wounded 1808–1814. [vol. viii: *The History of the Peninsular War.*] London: Greenhill Books; 1998 .

Hamilton, Anthony. *Hamilton's Campaign with Moore and Wellington During the Peninsular War.* Staplehurst: Spellmount; 1998. Originally published Troy, N.Y.; 1847.

Hamilton, Lt-General Sir F. W. *The Origin and History of the First or Grenadier Guards.* London: John Murray; 1874.

Hancock, J. T. 'It Was Not His Day,' *The Royal Engineers Journal.* vol. 90, September, 1976.

Hawker, Peter. *Journal of a Regimental Officer During the Recent Campaign in Portugal and*

Spain Under Lord Viscount Wellington. With a Correct Plan of the Battle of Talavera. Facsimile edition published London: Ken Trotman; 1981. Originally published London; 1810.

Hawks, Major John. *Orderly Book and Journal of Major John Hawks on the Ticonderoga-Crown Point Campaign, Under General Jeffery Amherst: 1759–1760.* Published by the Society of Colonial Wars in the State of New York, through the Historian and Committee on Historical Documents, New York; 1911.

Haythornthwaite, Philip J. *The Armies of Wellington.* London: Arms and Armour Press; 1994.

——. 'The Battalions of Detachments in 1809.' *Empires, Eagles, and Lions.* #69; 15 January 1983.

——. *Wellington's Specialist Troops.* London: Osprey; 1988.

——. *Who Was Who in the Napoleonic Wars.* London: Arms and Armour; 1998.

Hennell, George. *A Gentleman Volunteer: The Letters of George Hennell from the Peninsular War, 1812–13.* Edited by Michael Glover. London: William Heinemann Ltd; 1979.

Herodotus. *The History.* Translated by David Grene. Chicago: University of Chicago Press; 1987.

Hibbert, Christopher, ed. *Captain Gronow: His Reminiscences of Regency and Victorian Life 1810–60.* London: Kyle Cathie; 1991.

——. *Coruña.* London: Pan Books; 1972.

——, ed. *A Soldier of the Seventy-First: The Journal of a Soldier of the Highland Light Infantry 1806–1815,* UK: Book Club Edition of Purnell Book Services Ltd; 1975. Based on the 2nd Edition, originally published as *Journal of a Soldier of the 71st or Glasgow Regiment, Highland Light Infantry from 1806 to 1815;* 1819.

——, ed. *The Wheatley Diary: A Journal and Sketchbook Kept during the Peninsular War and the Waterloo Campaign.* London: Longmans, Green and Co.; 1964.

Hill, Rowland. *Lord Hill's Letters from the Peninsula.* Darlington: Napoleonic Archive; n.d. [2003?]

Homer. *The Iliad.* Translated by Robert Fagles. New York: Penguin Books; 1990.

Hood, Lieutenant Nathaniel. *Elements of War: or Rules & Regulations of the Army in Miniature: Shewing The Duty of a Regiment in every Situation.* 3rd edition. London; 1804.

Horward, Donald D. *The French Campaign in Portugal 1810–1811: An Account by Jean Jacques Pelet.* Minneapolis: University of Minnesota Press; 1973.

——. *Napoleon and Iberia. The Twin Sieges of Ciudad Rodrigo and Almeida, 1810.* Tallahassee: Florida State University; 1984.

Hough, Henry. 'The Journal of Second Lieutenant Henry Hough, Royal Artillery, 1812–13,' *Journal of the Royal United Service Institution.* #444, vol. LXI; 1916.

Houlding, J.A. *Fit for Service: The Training of the British Army 1715–1795.* Oxford: Clarendon Press; 1981.

House of Commons. *British Sessional Papers.* 1808, 1809, 1810.

Hyden, Captain John S. 'The Sources, Organization and Uses of Intelligence in the Anglo-Portuguese Army 1808–1814,' *Journal of the Society for Army Historical Research.* vol. 62; 1984.

James, Charles. *A New and Enlarged Military Dictionary, in French and English: in which are Explained the Principal Terms, with Appropriate Illustrations, of All the Sciences that are, more or less, Necessary for an Officer and Engineer.* 2 vols. London: T. Egerton; 1810.

Jennings, Louis J., ed. *The Croker Papers, The Correspondence and Diaries of the late Right Honourable John Wilson Croker.* 3 vols. London: John Murray; 1884.

Jomini, Baron de. *The Art of War.* Translated by Captain G.H. Mendell & Lieutenant W.P. Craighill. Reprinted (Book Club edition) Westport, CT: Greenwood Press; n.d. Based on edition by J.B. Lippincott & Co.; 1862.

Jones, John. *Journal of the Sieges Carried on by the Army under the Duke of Wellington in Spain.* 2nd edition, 2 vols. London: T. Egerton; 1826.

Langley, Sergeant Thomas, *The eighteen manoeuvres, as practised by His Majesty's Infantry, with a copper-plate engraving to each, shewing the different posts of the Commissioned and Non-Commissioned Officers, Privates, etc., together with the words of command, cautions and instructions,* London n.d. (c. 1794?).

Larpent, George, ed. *The Private Journal of F. S. Larpent.* 3 vols. London: Richard Bentley; 1853.

Lawrence, Sergeant William. *The Autobiography of Sergeant William Lawrence: A Hero of the Peninsular and Waterloo Campaigns.* Uckfield: Naval & Military Press Ltd; n.d. Originally published London; 1886.

Laws, Lt-Colonel M. E. S. *Battery Records of the Royal Artillery.* Woolwich: Royal Artillery Institute; 1952.

Leach, Jonathan. *Rough Sketches of the Life of an Old Soldier: During a Service in the West Indies; at the Siege of Copenhagen in 1807; in the Peninsula and the South of France in the Campaigns from 1808 to 1814, with the Light Division; in the Netherlands in 1815; including the Battles of Quatre-Bras and Waterloo: with a Slight Sketch of the Three Years Passed by the Army of Occupation in France, &c. &c. &c.* Facsimile reprint Cambridge: Ken Trotman Ltd; 1986. Originally published London; 1831.

Lee, Sidney, ed. *Supplement to the Dictionary of National Biography.* London: Smith, Elder and Co.; 1901.

Leith Hay, Andrew. *A Narrative of the Peninsular War.* 2 vols. London: John Hearse; 1850.

Leslie, Colonel. *Military Journal of Colonel Leslie, K.H., of Balquhain, whilst serving with the 29th Regiment in the Peninsula, and the 60th Rifles in Canada, &c.: 1807–1832.* Aberdeen: Aberdeen University Press; 1887.

Leslie, Major John H. *The Services of the Royal Regiment of Artillery in the Peninsular War 1808–1814.* London: Hugh Rees Ltd; 1908.

Leslie, N. B. *The Battle Honours of the British and Indian Armies 1695–1914.* London: Leo Cooper; 1970.

Lloyd, E.M. *A Review of the History of Infantry.* Reprinted Westport, CT: Greenwood Press; 1976. Originally published London & New York: Longmans, Green, and Co.; 1908.

Londonderry, Lt-General Charles William Vane, Marquis of. *Narrative of the Peninsular War, from 1808 to 1813.* London: Henry Colburn; 1828.

Mackesy, Piers. *British Victory in Egypt, 1801: The end of Napoleon's conquest.* New York: Routledge; 1995.

Malmesbury. *A Series of Letters of the First Earl of Malmesbury, His Family and Friends, from 1745 to 1820.* Edited by the Earl of Malmesbury. 2 vols. London: Richard Bentley; 1870.

Mathews H. C. G., & Harrison, Brian, eds. *Oxford Dictionary of National Biography.* Oxford University Press; 2004.

Maxwell, Sir Herbert, ed. *The Lowland Scots Regiments.* Glasgow: James Maclehose and Sons; 1918.

Maxwell, W.H. *Peninsular Sketches; by Actors on the Scene.* 2 vols. Cambridge: Ken Trotman; 1998. Originally published London: Henry Colburn; 1844.

McGuffie, T.H., ed. *Peninsular Cavalry General (1811–13): The Correspondence of Lieutenant General Robert Ballard Long.* London: George G. Harrap & Co. Ltd; 1951.

Mills, John. *For King and Country: The Letters and Diaries of John Mills Coldstream Guards, 1811–1814.* Staplehurst: Spellmount; 1995.

Moore, James. *A Narrative of the Campaign of the British Army in Spain Commanded by his Excellency Lieutenant General Sir John Moore.* 3rd edition. London: J. Johnson; 1809.

Moore, Sir John. *The Diary of Sir John Moore.* Edited by Maj-General Sir J.F. Maurice. 2 vols. London: Edward Arnold; 1904.

Moore Smith, G. C. *The Life of John Colborne, Field Marshal Lord Seaton.* London: John Murray; 1903. Also facsimile reprint by Elibron Classics; n.d.

Moorsom, W. S. *History of the Fifty-Second Regiment 1755–1816,* Tyne & Wear: Worley Publications; 1996, from the 1890 edition.

Morley, Stephen. *Memoirs of a Sergeant of the 5th Regiment of Foot.* Cambridge: Ken Trotman; 1999.

Muir, Howie. 'Observations on Deployment at Salamanca, 1812,' *First Empire Magazine.* Issue 49, November/December, 1999.

Muir, Rory. *Britain and the Defeat of Napoleon, 1807–1815.* New Haven: Yale University Press; 1996.

——. *Tactics and the Experience of Battle in the Age of Napoleon.* New Haven: Yale University Press; 1998.

——. *Salamanca, 1812.* New Haven: Yale University Press; 2001.

Myatt, Frederick. *Peninsular General, Sir Thomas Picton 1758–1815.* Devon: David & Charles (Publishers) Ltd; 1980.

Napier, Sir, W.F.P. *History of the War in the Peninsula and in the South of France from a.d. 1807 to a.d. 1814.* Both 5 & 6 volume editions. New York: W.J. Widdleton; 1862. Also New York: AMS Press; 1970. [In view of the many and varied formats of Napier's work, his 'Book' and 'Chapter' are also cited in notes to aid locating the reference in different editions.]

Napoleon. *The Confidential Correspondence of Napoleon Bonaparte with his Brother Joseph.* 2 vols. New York: D. Appleton and Co.; 1856.

Neave-Hill, Lt-Colonel W B R. 'The Rank Titles of Brigadier and Brigadier General,' *JSAHR.* vol. 47; 1969.

Oman, Carola. *Sir John Moore.* London: Hodder & Stoughton; 1953.

Oman, Sir Charles. *A History of the Peninsular War.* 7 vols. Reprint New York: AMS; 1980. Originally published Oxford; 1902–1930.

Oman, Charles. *Studies in the Napoleonic Wars.* London: Greenhill Books; 1989.

Oman, Charles. *Wellington's Army, 1809–1814.* London: Greenhill Books; 1986.

Page, Julia. *Intelligence Officer in the Peninsula: Letters & Diaries of Major the Hon. Edward Charles Cocks: 1796–1812.* New York: Hippocrene Books; 1986.

Palmer, Alan. *Alexander I: Tsar of War and Peace.* London: Weidenfeld and Nicolson; 1974.

Partridge, Richard & Oliver, Mike. *Battle Studies in the Peninsula.* London: Constable; 1998.

Patton, George S. Jr. *War as I Knew It.* Boston: Hougton Mifflin Co.; 1947.

Polybius. *Histories.* Translated by Fridericus Hultsch & Evelyn S. Shuckburgh. Reprinted Bloomington: Indiana University Press; 1962. Originally published New York: Macmillan; 1889.

Porter, Major General Whitworth. *History of the Corps of Royal Engineers.* 2 vols. London: Longmans Green and Co.; 1889.

Redgrave, T. M. O. 'Wellington's Logistical Arrangements in the Peninsular War, 1809–1814.' Unpublished PhD thesis presented to the University of London, n.d. [c1979].

Reid, Stuart. *Highlander.* London: Military Illustrated, Publishing News Ltd; 2000.

——. *Wellington's Army in the Peninsula 1809–14.* Battle Orders Series. Oxford: Osprey Publishing Ltd; 2004.

——. *Wolfe: The Career of General James Wolfe from Culloden to Quebec.* Rockville Centre, NY: Sarpedon; 2000.

Reide, Captain Thomas. *A Treatise on the Duty of Infantry Officers and the Present System of British Military Discipline with an Appendix.* London: n.p.; 1795.

Rigaud, Major-General Gibbes. *Celer et Audax A Sketch of the Services of the Fifth Battalion Sixtieth Regiment (Rifles) During the Twenty Years of their Existence.* Reprinted Cambridge: Ken Trotman Ltd; 2002. Originally published Oxford: E Pickard Hall & J.H. Stacy; 1879.

Robson, Martin. 'British Intervention in Portugal, 1793–1808,' *Historical Research.* vol. 76, 2003.

Rodrigues, Manuel A. Ribeiro (text) & Santos, Carlos Alberto (ills.). *Guerra Peninsular (1): Infantaria 1806–1815.* Lisbon: Destarte, Representações e Edição, Lda.; 2000.

Rogers, H.C.B. *The British Army of the Eighteenth Century,* London: George Allen & Unwin Ltd, 1977.

Ross-Lewin, Harry, *With the Thirty-Second in the Peninsula,* Cambridge: Ken Trotman Ltd, 2000; originally published as *With 'The Thirty-Second' in the Peninsular and other Campaigns,* Dublin: Hodges, Figgis & Co., Ltd; 1904.

Sabine, Edward. *Letters of Colonel Sir Augustus Simon Frazer, Commanding the Royal Horse Artillery in the Army under the Duke of Wellington.* Uckfield: Naval & Military Press; 2001.

Schroeder, Paul W. *The Transformation of European Politics, 1763–1848.* Oxford: Clarendon Press; 1994.

Shaw, W. E. *The Knights of England.* Baltimore: Genealogical Publishing Co.; 1971.

Sherer, Moyle. *Recollections of the Peninsula.* Staplehurst: Spellmount; 1996. First published 1824.

Sherwig, John M. *Guineas & Gunpowder: British Foreign Aid in the Wars with France, 1793–1815.* Harvard University Press; 1969.

Siborne, H.T. *Waterloo Letters.* London: Greenhill Books; 1993.

Sidney, Sir Edwin. *The Life of Lord Hill Late Commander of the Forces.* London: John Murray; 1845.

Simes, Thomas. *The Military Guide for Young Officers.* 2 vols. Philadelphia; 1776.

——. *The Military Medley: Containing the 'Most Necessary Rules and Directions for Attaining a Competent Knowledge of the Art' To which is added an Explanation of Military Terms, Alphabetically Digested.* 2nd edition. Facsimile reprint Oldwick, New Jersey: The King's Arms Press & Bindery; n.d. Originally published London; 1768.

——. *A Treatise on the Military Science, which Comprehends the Grand Operations of War, and General Rules for Conducting an Army in the Field, Founded upon Principles for the Improvement of the same, with Occasional Notes: to which is added, The Manner of Attacking and Defending of Military Posts, Villages, Church-Yards, Mills, Houses, &c.* London; 1780.

Simmons, George. *A British Rifleman.* London: Greenhill; 1986.

Smith, Sir Harry. *The Autobiography of Lieutenant General Sir Harry Smith,* Edited by G.C. Moore Smith. One-volume edition, John Murray, London; 1903 & 1910.

Stanhope, Philip Henry, Earl. *Notes of Conversations with the Duke of Wellington 1831–1851.* London: Prion; 1998. First privately published in 1886, publicly in 1888.

Stephen, Leslie & Sidney, Lee, eds. *The Dictionary of National Biography.* 22 vols. Oxford: Oxford University Press; 1921–22.

Stewart, Lieutenant Charles. *A Journal of the Various Services of His Majesty's 28th or North Gloucester Regiment of Foot During The Campaigns Of 93, 94 & 95, Until the Recall of the British Infantry from Germany in May 1795 Under The Earl Of Moira, His Royal Highness The Duke, and Count Walmoden.* Edited and presented by Lt-Colonel R. M. Grazebrook in 'The Campaign in Flanders of 1793–1795: Journal of Lieutenant Charles Stewart, 28th Foot,' in *JSAHR.*, vol. xxix; no.117; Spring, 1951.

Stothert, Captain William. *A Narrative of the Principal Events of the Campaigns of 1809, 1810, & 1811, in Spain and Portugal; Interspersed with Remarks on Local Scenery and Manners.* Republished Cambridge: Ken Trotman Ltd; 1997. Originally published London: P. Martin; 1812.

Surtees, William. *Twenty-Five Years in the Rifle Brigade.* London: Greenhill Books; 1996.

Swiney, Colonel G. C. *Historical Records of the 32nd (Cornwall) Light Infantry.* London; 1893.

Swinson, Arthur. *A Register of the Regiments and Corps of the British Army.* London: Archive Press; 1972.

Tacitus. *Complete Works of Tacitus.* Translated by Alfred John Church & edited by William Jackson Brodribb. New York: Random House, Inc.; 1942. (Includes both *The Annals* and *The History.*)

Teffeteller, Gordon, L. *The Surpriser, The Life of Rowland, Lord Hill.* Newark: Associated University Press, Inc.; 1983.

Thompson, Mark S. *The Fatal Hill: The Allied Campaign under Beresford in Southern Spain in 1811.* Chapelgarth, Sunderland: Mark Thompson Publishing; 2002.

Thompson, W.F.K., ed. *An Ensign in the Peninsular War: The Letters of John Aitchison.* London: Michael Joseph Ltd; 1981 & 1994.

Thorne, R. G., ed. *The House of Commons 1790–1820.* 5 vols. London: Secker and Warburg; 1986.

Tomkinson, William. *The Diary of a Cavalry Officer: 1809–1815.* London: Frederick Muller; 1971. Originally published 1894.

Urban, Mark. *The Man who Broke Napoleon's Codes. The Story of George Scovell.* London: Faber and Faber; 2001.

——. *Rifles. Six Years with Wellington's Legendary Sharpshooters.* London: Faber and Faber; 2003.

Vann, J. A. 'Habsburg Policy and the Austrian War of 1809,' *Central European History.* vol. 7, 1974.

Various. *Grande Enciclopédia Portuguesa E Brasileira.* Lisbon: Editorial Enciclopédia, Limitada; n.d.

Vere, Charles Broke, *Marches, Movements, and Operations of the 4th Division of the Allied Army in Spain and Portugal, in the Years 1810, 1811 & 1812,* Ipswich; 1841.

——. *The Times.* The newspaper, various issues, 1808 & 1809.

Verner, Willoughby. *The History and Campaigns of the Rifle Brigade: 1800–1813.* London: Buckland and Brown; 1912–19.

Vichness, Samuel E. 'Marshal of Portugal: the Military Career of William Carr Beresford, 1785–1814.' Unpublished PhD thesis. Florida State University; 1976.

Ward, S.G.P. 'The Peninsular Commissary,' *JSAHR.*, vol. 75, 1997.

——. 'The Portuguese Infantry Brigades, 1809–1814,' *JSAHR.*, vol. 53, Summer 1975.

——. *Wellington's Headquarters: A Study of the Administrative Problems in the Peninsula 1809–1814.* Oxford: Oxford University Press; 1957.

War Office. Army Lists, London: C. Roworth; for various years.

——. *Rules and Articles for the Better Government of His Majesty's Forces.* Facsimile reprint

Oldwick, N.J.: King's Arms Press and Bindery; n.d. Originally published London: George Eyre and Andrew Straman; 1807. [Referenced as *Articles of War.*]

——. *General Orders and Observations on the Movements and Field Exercise of the Infantry.* London: T. Egerton; 1804.

——. *General Orders: Spain and Portugal.* Vols. i–v, for 1809–1813, London: T. Egerton, 1811–1814.

——. *Rules and Regulations for the Formations, Field-Exercise, and Movements, of His Majesty's Forces.* London; 1803. (The 1793, 1806 and 1808 printings also consulted.)

Warre, William. *Letters from the Peninsula, 1808–1812.* Staplehurst: Spellmount; 1999.

Webber, William. *With the Guns in the Peninsula: The Peninsula War Journal of Captain William Webber, Royal Artillery.* London: Greenhill Books; 1991.

Webster, C. K. *The Foreign Policy of Castlereagh, 1812–1815.* London: G. Bell; 1931.

Webster, Graham. *The Roman Imperial Army of the First and Second Centuries A.D.* 3rd edition. Totowa, New Jersey: Barnes & Noble Books; 1985.

Wellington. 'A Missing Letter from the Duke of Wellington,' *The Athenaeum.* No. 3209, 27 April 1889.

Wellington, Duke of. *The Dispatches of Field Marshal the Duke of Wellington, During his Various Campaigns in India, Denmark, Portugal, Spain, the Low Countries, and France, from 1799 to 1818.* Edited by Lieutenant-Colonel John Gurwood. 13 vols. London: John Murray; 1834–9. [Referenced as 'WD'.] The 'New Edition,' published 1837–39, also by John Murray in 13 volumes [cited as 'WD (new ed.)'], revised the early volumes of the original edition, while there was only one printing of the last four volumes, being the same for both editions. In 1844, an 'Enlarged Edition' in 8 vols. was published by Parker, Furnivall and Parker [cited as 'WD (enlarged ed.)'] which contained much new material, and with, of course, completely different pagination from the original edition; and a 'New and Enlarged Edition,' also in 8 vols. published by John Murray in 1852, seemed to share the pagination of the 1844 edition.

——. *Supplementary Dispatches, Correspondence, and Memoranda of Field Marshal Arthur Duke of Wellington, K.G.* Edited by the 2nd Duke of Wellington. Vols. vi–xiv. London: John Murray; 1860–1871. [Referenced as 'WSD'.]

Williamson, John. *The Elements of Military Arrangement and of the Discipline of War; Adapted to the Practice of the British Infantry.* 3rd edition, 2 vols. Whitehall: T. & J.Egerton, Military Library; 1791.

Wood, Captain George. *The Subaltern Officer: A Narrative.* Cambridge: Ken Trotman Ltd; 1986. Originally published London; 1825.

Worley, Colin, ed. *An Atlas of the Peninsular War 1808–1814: A collection of 131 maps and plans from various sources.* Felling, Tyne and Wear: Worley Publications; 2000.

Wyld, James, ed. *Maps and Plans showing the Principal Movements, Battles & Sieges, in which the British Army was engaged during the War from 1808 to 1814 in the Spanish Peninsula and the South of France.* London: James Wyld; 1841. [Referenced simply as Atlas.]

——. *Memoir annexed to an Atlas containing the principal Battles, Sieges and Affairs in which the British Troops were Engaged During the War in the Spanish Peninsula and the South of France from 1808 to 1814.* London: James Wyld; 1841.

Acknowledgements

Although my three co-authors provided much advice and many suggestions, there were numerous others who willingly assisted in hunting down obscure references and information: Tom Holmberg, librarian extraordinaire, who has always been able to track down almost any book on the planet; Tony Broughton, who opened his incredible library for our use and could find any image I have ever requested from him; the immense knowledge of Mark Thompson and Rod MacArthur on the Royal Engineers; Gareth Glover on British memoirs and diaries; Vic Powell and the Portsmouth Napoleonic Society, who provided much background information on the British Army; Lewis Orans and John White of the Association of Friends of the Waterloo Committee. I would be remiss in not thanking Fons Libert, who, as father of the Napoleon Series, brought the co-authors and I together and was thus indirectly responsible for this book. And of course to my wife, Denah, who over the years has visited numerous battlefields, museums and bookstores with me! I would also like to thank Captain John Borer, Assistant Secretary of the Institution of Royal Engineers, for permission to use many of the bridging images in the chapter on bridges. These images first appeared in the *Journal of the Institution of the Royal Engineers*, which owns the copyright. Further, I would like to thank Roz and Richard Brown of Ken Trotman Books, for permission to use Alexander Dickson's sketch of the bridge of boats over the Tagus at Villa Velha.

Robert Burnham

Foremost, I want to thank my friends and co-authors: Rory Muir, for his many valid comments and valued advice; Robert Burnham, for his suggestions on making the text easier to understand; and Howie Muir, for his recommendations on clarifying what I meant to say in the text. I also wish to thank Andy Remisch for translations of German text; Paul Remisch, for reading the text over and over again, and correcting my grammar; Tony Broughton, for kindly supplying all of the generals' portraits; João Centeno, for supplying information on the Portuguese officers; Michael-Andreas Tänzer, for supplying information on the Hanoverian officers, and his kind assistance with the King's German Legion (see his excellent website at www.kgl.de); Colm McLaughlin of the National Library of Scotland, for his painstaking work in searching for and providing obscure General Orders; Mrs. M. Harding of the National Army Museum, for finding and providing two General Orders; and Major Colin Robins OBE,

FRHistS, for his kind assistance with information relating to the Royal Artillery – a topic outside his usual 'era' of research; the Arquivo Histórico Militar, Lisboa; the Bodleian Library, Oxford; the British Library, London; the Central Library, London Ontario; the D. B. Weldon Library of the University of Western Ontario, London; The Gordon Highlanders Museum, Aberdeen; the Hartley Library University of Southampton; the King's Own Royal Regiment Museum, Lancaster; the National Army Museum, London UK; Niedersächsisches Hauptstaatsarchiv, Hannover Germany; The Regimental Museum of the Queen's Own Highlanders, Inverness; the Royal Artillery Institution, Woolwich; the Soldiers of Gloucestershire Museum, Gloucester; Toronto Reference Library, Toronto Ontario; University of Guelph, Guelph Ontario; Windsor Public Library, Windsor Ontario; and especially, the late Michael Glover. Also, a Sincere Thank You to the Trustees of the National Library of Scotland, Edinburgh, for permission to use information from their manuscript collection of the Murray Papers. Finally, my special thank you to my wife Debbie and my children Shannon and Ian for their continued support and understanding.

Ron McGuigan

My research was greatly facilitated and clarified by the generous assistance of Ron McGuigan, whose grasp of rank, promotions, and customs of seniority in British service is seemingly boundless. Further appreciation goes to David McCracken, a retired infantry sergeant major in the Canadian Forces, for patient explanations of the technicalities, terminology and concepts of drill and military etiquette. Meanwhile, Rory Muir's practical experience in the field of military history was a bottomless well of solutions and wise perspectives, as was his wide array of resources he shared. Also, my thanks to the following for their editorial suggestions – as well as to Bob Burnham, for inviting my participation in the project – to Bill Haggart, for gamely bouncing ideas about; to Sam Wilson Jr., for intellectual challenges; and to David Commerford, for helpful nuggets of information and sanity checks. I am also grateful to the Nevada County Library (California), for their remarkable success in unearthing books difficult to obtain or access. Not least, my thanks to the many and varied participants on the Napoleon Series Discussion Forum, who have, over the years, demonstrated the power and joy of international collegiality on the internet, and who have shared with me – and one another – a broad range of information and insight. Any errors in the application of guidance and advice from these and other helpers, however, are my entirely my own – darn!

Howie Muir

My essay for this book is based on many years' work, primarily directed at other projects, and all the help I have received in working on them has also assisted me here. It is impossible to disentangle and acknowledge all the assistance I have received, but I would like to thank the staff at all the libraries and archives at which I have worked, and in particular, those at the Archives and Special Collections of the Hartley Library, University of Southampton, and the staff of the Barr Smith Library, University of Adelaide. Throughout the time I have been working on the essay I have continued to be a Visiting Research Fellow at the Department of History, University of Adelaide: a position that has offered me perfect conditions to pursue my researches. Of the many correspondents and friends who have shaped my ideas over the years, I should especially wish to thank Prof. Charles Esdaile of the University of Liverpool, S. G. P. Ward, Julia Page, the late David Elder, Mark Urban, Mark Thompson, Dr Christopher Woolgar, and all the participants in the Napoleon Series Discussion Forum. My fellow contributors have been a constant source of advice, encouragement and enthusiasm, on topics both broad and esoteric: they have enriched not just this essay, but all my work.

Rory Muir

Index

Page numbers in *italics* indicate information appearing in illustrations or other graphics, while significant discussion appearing in notes is indicated at the end of a topic, signalled by a shorthand for the chapter and note number (e.g., 'Ch2 n155', for note 155, appearing at the end of Chapter 2).

Abercromby (Abercrombie), Alexander, 90, 146, *147*
Abercromby, Ralph, 35, 100
Abrantes, 53–4, 64, 69
Acland, Wroth Palmer, 41, 43–4, 47–52, *111–12*
Adour River, 246–62, *249, 250, 259, 261*
Agueda River, 227, 239–41, *241*
Albuera, battle of, 20, 90, 126, 134, 137, 139–49, *142–4, 147*, Ch2 n155, n172, 193, 196
Alcantara, 53, 237, 241–6, *243, 244, 245, 246*
Allies, role of Continental Powers, 10–11, 21, 33–4
Almeida, 52, 64, 137
Almeida, João Lobo Brandáo de, 196
Alten, Charles Baron: 42, 49, 51–3, 55, 59, 61, 139, *142–3*, 144, *152*, 190, 194–6
Alten, Victor Baron, 187–8
Alva River, See Ponte de Murcella
Alyling, John, 74, 82
Amarante, Conde de, see Silveira
Andalusia, French Conquest, 15
Anson, George, 122–3, *130–1*, 188, 192
Anson, William, 58, 152, 155, *155*, 178, 192
Anstruther, Robert, 41, 43, 47–53, 55, 59–60, *111, 113*
Arentschildt, Frederick de, 188
Arentschildt, Victor de, 69
Army, British (general): artillery, 31, 40;

character 19, 28, 31; commissariat, 5, 15; size, 2; tactics, 28–30 – infantry, 28–30, 39–40; cavalry, 30–1, 39; waggon train, 40
Army, British, Organisation:
(i) Corps, Army, 84, 100–2, 134, 139, 151–3, 181, 187–90, 192–4, 196
(ii) Divisions, Army (under Moore): 100, 112, *113*
Cavalry Division, 59
Infantry – 1st Division, 58; 2nd Division, 58; 3rd Division, 59; Reserve Division, 59, 112
(iii) Divisions, Army (under Wellesley/Wellington; see also under individual officers' names), 84, 100–1, *113*, 120, *121*, 122, 123, 150, Ch2 n86, n92, n117, n149, n193, n202:
Anglo-Allied Cavalry, 90, 186 – 1st Division, 187; 2nd Division, 187–8, 190
Anglo-Allied Infantry – 1st Division, 98, 100–2, 107, 110, *110, 121–2*, 122, *125*, 126–8, *126, 129*, 130, *127–31*, 134, 137, 139, Ch2 n56, n131, n157, 188–9, 196; 2nd Division, 89–90, 101, *121*, 122, *122, 125*, 126, *126–31*, 128–30, 132–4, *134*, 137, 139, 141, *142–4*, 145–6, *147*, 148–9, *150*, 151–2, *151, 153*, Ch2 n56, n143, n155,

n172–3, 187–90, 194, 196; 3rd
Division, 84, 89, 110, *110*, *121*,
122, *122*, *125–7*, 128–9, *128–30*,
131–2, *131*, 135, 137–8, 151, *152*,
Ch2 n68, n126, 190, 192, 194–5;
4th Division, 89–91, 110, *121*,
122–3, *122*, *125–31*, 126–7, 129,
135, 137, 141, *142–4*, 148–9,
151–4, *152*, *155*, Ch2 n190, n192,
191–3, 195; 5th Division, 101, 110,
110, 137–8, Ch2 n56, n157, 188,
190–1, 192–4; 6th Division, 101,
137–8, 151–4, *152*, *155*, 156, Ch2
n190, 191–3; 7th Division, 101,
110, *110*, 137–9, 178, 190–2,
193–4, 196; Light Division, 84,
100–1, 135, 137, 152, *152*, Ch2
n151, n157, 191, 195

(iv) Brigades (for others, see under
individual officers' names):
Flank (under Moore) – Alten, 59; R
Craufurd, 59
Guards Brigade(s), 54, 56, 99, 101,
115, *119*, 121–2, *121–2*, 128, *128*,
130–1, 132, 137, 183, 188–9, Ch2
n86, n88, n92;
Independent Brigades, 138, 168 n158,
196;
Portuguese, 197

(v) Royal Engineers, 40, 43, 47, 51, 66,
175, 183; at Badajoz, 22–3
(vi) Royal Sappers and Artificers Corps,
40, 252
(vii) Royal Staff Corps, 40, 227, 229–31
(viii) Artillery, 40, 48, 62, 68, 175, 182:
Royal (foot) – 40–6, 48, 52–3, 56,
58–60, 62–5, 67, 69, *107*
Royal Horse – 54, 56–60, 69, *151*
(ix) Regiments, Guards and Line:
Cavalry – Royal Horse Guards: 54; 1st
Dgn Gds, 60; 2nd Dgn Gds, 54;
3rd Dgn Gds, 54, 60, 67–9, *115*,
142, *144*; 4th Dgn Gds, 60; 1st
Dgns, 60, 67; 2nd Dgns, 54; 3rd
Dgns, 60; 4th Dgns, 54, 60, 67–9,
115, *142*, *144*; 7th Lt Dgns (Hus),
54, 56–9, *155*; 10th Lt Dgns (Hus),
54, 56–9, *155*; 13th Lt Dgns, *142*;
14th Lt Dgns, 54, 57, 60, 63–6, 68,
115, 125, *130*; 15th Lt Dgns (Hus),

56–9, *115*, *155*; 16th Lt Dgns, 54,
60, 67–8, *130*; 18th Lt Dgns (Hus),
43–4, 48–9, 51, 53, 55, 59; 20th Lt
Dgns, 40, 43, 45–7, 49, 52, 61–6,
68, *107*, *115*; 23rd Lt Dgns, 69,
130, 133
Infantry – 1st Foot Guards, 56–8, *113*,
114, *130*, Ch2 n38; Coldstream
Foot Guards, 65–6, 68, 114, *115*,
130; 3rd Foot Guards, 65–6, 68,
114, *115*; Guards Flank Bn, 57–8;
(4th Royal Veteran Bn, 40, 42,
45;) 1st Foot, 56–8, 61, *113*, Ch2
n156; 2nd Foot, 41, 43, 47, 49,
51–3, 55, 59, 61–2, *113*, *155*; 3rd
Foot ('Buffs'), 44, 48–9, 54, 57,
61–6, 68, *113*, *115*, *130*, *134*,
142–3, 145–6, *147*, *151*; 4th Foot,
41, 43, 48–9, 51–3, 55, 58, *113*; 5th
Foot, 40, 44–5, 47, 49, 51–3, 55,
59, 104, *105*, *107*, *109*, *111*, *113*;
6th Foot, 44, 46–7, 49, 51–2, 54–5,
59, *105*, *107*, *109*, *111–13*, Ch2
n68; 7th Foot, 66, 68, *115*, *130*,
142, *144*, *155*; 9th Foot, 40, 41,
44–5, 47, 49, 51–3, 55, 59, 61–5,
67–8, 104, *105*, *107*, *109*, *111*, *113*,
115, Ch2 n156; 11th Foot, 153,
155, Ch2 n68, n156; 14th Foot,
55–9, *113*; 20th Foot, 41, 44, 47,
49, 51–5, 59–2, *111*, *113*, *155*; 23rd
Foot, 56–9, *113*, *142*, *144*, *155*,
Ch2 n23; 24th Foot, 67–9, *115*,
130; 26th Foot, 55–8, *113*; 27th
Foot, 56–7, 62–6, 68, *115*, 152,
155; 28th Foot, 41, 43, 48–9, 51–3,
55, 59, *113*, *142–3*, *147*, *150*; 29th
Foot, 41, 44, 46–7, 50, 61–6, 68,
105, *107*, *109*, *111–12*, *115*, *130*,
132–3, *134*, 141, *142–3*, 146, *147*,
Ch2 n182; 30th Foot, 66–9, *115*;
31st Foot, 56–7, 62–6, 68, *115*,
130, *142–3*, 145–6, *147*, *150*, *151*;
32nd Foot, 41, 44, 46–7, 49, 51–3,
55, 59–60, *105*, *107*, *109*, *111–13*,
153, *155*; 34th Foot, *142*, *143*, 145,
147, *155*; 36th Foot, 42, 44–6, 47,
49, 51, 53, 55, 59, 104, *105*, 106–7,
107, *109*, *111–13*, 153, *155*, Ch2
n63; 38th Foot, 40, 44–6, 47, 49,

51–3, 55, 59, 104, *105, 107, 109,
111, 113*, Ch2 n156; 39th Foot,
142, 143, 147, 150, Ch2 n155; 40th
Foot, 40, 44–5, 47, 50, 61, 63–5,
67–9, 104, *105*, 106, *107, 109,
111–12*, 123, *130, 131, 155*; 42nd
Foot, 30, 44, 48–9, 51–3, 55, 58,
60, *113*, 153, 154, *155*, 156; 43rd
Foot, 41, 43, 47, 49, 51–3, 55–9,
61, 69, *111, 113*, 116, 136; 45th
Foot, 42, 44–7, 49, 54, 61, 63–6,
68, 104, *105*, 106–7, *107, 109, 111,
115, 130*, Ch2 n63, n66; 48th Foot,
62, 66, 68, *115, 130*, 132, *134*, 141,
142–3, 145, 146, *147, 155*, Ch2
n170, n182; 50th Foot, 41, 44,
46–7, 50, 54–5, 57–8, 61–2, *105*,
106, *107, 109, 111, 113, 150;* 51st
Foot, 56–9, *113*; 52nd Foot, 30,
41–3, 47–9, 51–3, 55, 59, 69, *111*,
116, 136; 53rd Foot, 66, 68, *115,
130, 155*, Ch2 n86; 57th Foot, *142,
143*, 146, *147, 150*, Ch2 n155,
n180, n182; 59th Foot, 56–9, *113*;
60th Foot, 30, 40, 43, 45–9, 51–7,
63–6, 68, 104, *104–5, 107, 109,
111*, 112, *112, 115*, 116–18, *126,
130, 150*, 153, *155*, Ch2 n63, n69,
n82, n139, n166; 61st Foot, 62,
130, 153, *155*; 66th Foot, 66, 68,
115, 130, 133, *134, 142–3*, 145–6,
147, 150, Ch2 n155; 71st Foot, 40,
44–6, 47, 49, 51, 53, 55, 59, 104,
105, 106, *107, 109, 111–13, 150,
151–2*, Ch2 n63, n68; 76th Foot,
56–9, *113*; 79th Foot, 41, 44, 48,
50–3, 55, 59, *113*, 153–4, 156, *155*;
81st Foot, 56–8, *113*; 82nd Foot,
41, 44, 46–7, 49, 54–55, 59, 61,
63–4, *105, 107, 109, 111–12, 131*;
83rd Foot, 60, 65–6, 68, *115, 130*;
87th Foot, 60, 65–6, 68, *115, 130*;
88th Foot, 60, 65–6, 68, *115, 130*;
91st Foot, 40, 44–7, 49, 51–53, 55,
59, 104, *105*, 106, *107, 109, 111,
113*, 153, *155*, 156; 92nd Foot, 41,
44, 48–9, 51, 53, 55, 59, *113, 150*;
95th Foot ('Rifle Corps'), 30,
40–3, 45–53, 55–9, 69, 104, *104–5,
107, 109, 111, 113*, 116, 136–7,

Ch1 n53, Ch2 n63, n69; 97th Foot,
41, 44, 47–9, 54, 61, 63–6, 68, *111,
115, 130*
(x) King's German Legion (KGL), 98,
98, 114, *115*, 116, 118, *119*, 120, 122,
127–8, 130, *130–1*, 132–3, 137–9,
141, 145, 175, 183, 188–189, Ch2
n92, n139, n146:
Artillery companies – 41, 42, 44, 48,
62–5, 67, 69
Cavalry regiments – 1st Lt Dgns
(Hus), 60, 67, 69, *130*, 133; 2nd Lt
Dgns (Hus), 60; 3rd Lt Dgns
(Hus), 42–3, 48–9, 51, 53, 55, 59,
61, 63–6, 68, *115*
Infantry battalions – 114, 116; 1st
Light, 42–3, 48–9, 51–3, 55, 59,
116, 118, *142*; 2nd Light, 42–3,
48–9, 51–3, 55, 59, 116, 118, *142*;
Light detachments, 65–6, 68, *115*,
116; 1st Line, 41, 44, 48–9, 61–6,
68, *115*, 116, *130*, Ch2 n92; 2nd
Line, 41, 44, 48–9, 61–6, 68, *115*,
116, *130*, Ch2 n92; 5th Line, 42,
44, 48–9, 61–6, 68, *115*, 116, *130*,
131, Ch2 n92, 138; 7th Line, 42,
44, 48–9, 61–6, 68, *115*, 116, *130*,
131, Ch2 n92
Garrison company – 42, 48, 61, 63–6,
68–9
(xi) Other Foreign Corps in British
Service: Brunswick-Oels Jägers, *115*,
118, *142, 155*, 175, Ch2 n166;
Chasseurs Britanniques, *115*
(xii) Battalions of Detachments, 202–10:
1st Battalion, 65–6, 68, *115*, 116, *130*,
131, 132, *134*, 202 – commander,
203; Douro Campaign, 204–5;
Talavera Campaign, 206–8; units
comprising, 203–4
2nd Battalion, 65–6, 68, *115, 130, 131*,
204 – commander, 204; Talavera
Campaign, 205, 208; units
comprising, 203; assessment,
209–10; disbandment, 209; Douro
Campaign, 204–5; formation, 202;
Talavera Campaign, 205–8;
Wellington's view of, 209
(xiii) Provisional Battalions, 216–9: 1st
Provisional Battalion, *150*, 216–8;

2nd Provisional Battalion, *155*, 217–8; 3rd Provisional Battalion, 218; 4th Provisional Battalion, 218; 5th Provisional Battalion, 218; justification for forming, 216, 218; resistance to disbanding, 219
(xiv) Militia Battalions, British, 196, 221–3; 1st Provisional Militia Bn, 221; 2nd Provisional Militia Bn, 221; 3rd Provisional Militia Bn, 221; as Brigade, 194; description of deployment, 222–3; Wellington's opposition to, 222
Army, Portuguese, Organisation:
  (i) Division, 101, 134, *142–3,* 150, 151, *151, 153,* 189–90, 196
  (ii) Artillery, 69–70, *151*
  (iii) Cavalry: regiments – 1st Cav, 69, *142*; 4th Cav, 70; 5th Cav, *142*; 6th Cav, 46, 69; 7th Cav, 70, *142*, *155*; 8th Cav, *142*; 11th Cav, 46; 12th Cav, 46, 69; Cavalry of the Police, 46
  (iv) Infantry: *caçador* battalions, 30 – 1st, 70; 3rd, 70; 4th, 70, *150*; 5th, 70, *142*; 6th, 46, 70, *109*, *150*; 7th, *142*, *144*; 9th, *155*; 10th, *150*; regiments – 1st Line, 69, 70; 2nd Line, 69, *142*, *150*; 3rd Line, 70; 4th Line, 70, *142*; 5th Line, *142*; 6th Line, 69, *150*; 7th Line, 69; 8th Line, *155*; 9th Line, 69; 10th Line, 69, *115*, *142*, *150*; 11th Line, 69, *142*, *144*, *155*; 12th Line, 46, 70, *109*, *155*; 13th Line, 70; 14th Line, 69, *142*, *150*; 15th Line, 70; 16th Line, 69, *115*; 18th Line, 69, *150*; 19th Line, 69; 21st Line, 46, *109*; 23rd Line, *142*, *144*, *155*; 24th Line, 46, 70, *109*; 1st Grenadiers, 69, *115*; Militia – Bragança, 70; Chaves, 70; Covilhã, 70; Miranda, 70; Moncorvo, 70; Santarem, 70; Thomar, 70; Vila Real, 70
  (v) Legion, Loyal Lusitanian – infantry, *142*, *144*, 149; artillery, *126*
Ashworth, Charles, *150–1*, 190, Ch2 n155, n157
Auberge, Ange, 74
Aylmer, Matthew, Lord Aylmer, 139, 179, 182, 196

Bacellar, Manoel Pinto de Morais, 69, 197
Badajoz, 20, 22–3, 101, 139, 141, *142–3*
Baird, David, 50, 54–8, 60–3, *113*
Ballesteros, Francisco, *142–3*
Baradiu, Pierre, 74
Barbaçena, Francisco de Mendonça, 7th Visconde de, 188
Bárcenas, Pedro de la, *152*
Barclay, Robert, 196
Barnard, Andrew, 196, Ch5 n78
Barnes, Edward, 152, *150–1*, 190–91, 193–4
Barréto, Luiz de Rego, 193
Barsse, Adolphus Baron, 198
Bathurst, James, 42, 45, 47
Battalions, Flank, 117
Battle-Array, see Order of Battle
Bayley, Edward, 221
Bayly, Henry, 196
Beckwith, Thomas Sydney, 136, 196
Beevor, Robert, 56–8, 60
Benevante, Battle of, 60
Bentinck, Lord William, 43, 49–3, 55, 58, 60, 67, 69, *113*, 177, 180–1, 185, 197
Beresford, William, 3–4, 6–9, 17, 20, 25, 44, 48–55, 59–60, 69, 84, 102, 110, *110*, *113*, 139–41, *142–3*, 145, 148, 151–4, *152, 155*, 172, 180–1, *184*, 186–7, 190, 194, Ch2 n159, n182
Berington, John, 221
Bingham, George, 217, Ch2 n86
Blake, Joaquín, 140–1, *142–3*, Ch2 n159, n161
Blanckley, Henry, 74
Bland, Humphrey, 98–9, 124–6, Ch2 n119
Blunt, Richard, 69, 197
Bock, George Baron, 186, 188
Borthwick, William, 182
Boteler, Richard, 40
Bowes, Barnard, 45–7, 50, *105, 106, 107,* 109, *109, 111–12,* 192–3, 197, Ch2 n68
Bradford, Thomas, *110*, 197, Ch2 n157
Bridges, *viii*: Adour River, 246–62, *249, 250, 259, 261*; Agueda River, 227, 239–41, *241*; Alcantara, 237, 241–6, *243, 244, 245, 246*; Coa River, 234–6, *235, 236, 237*; Guadiana, 229; Ponte de Murcella, 232–4, *233*; Tietar, 231–2, *232*; Villa Velha, 236–9, *238, 239*
Brisbane, Thomas, 138, 191

British Government and Wellington, 4–5,
    11–12, 18, 24, 35
Brodrick, John, 51, 54, 57
Brooke, William, 179
Brown, George, 208
Buchan, John, *150–1*, 196–7
Bunbury, William, 203
Burgoyne, John Fox, 183, 230, 238–9, 247,
    253
Burne, Robert, 193
Burrard, Harry, 42, 43, 47, 50–52, 57, 60–2
Burrows, John, 74, 82
Busaco, Battle of, 17, 126, 148, Ch2 n155,
    n157
Byng, John, *150–1*, 190

Cadiz, 64–5, 139, 180–1, 189, 197
Cairnes, Robert, 265
Calcraft, Granby, 179, 187
Cameron, Alan, 41, 45, 50, 54, 61, 63–8,
    115, 119, 120, *121*, 122, *122, 127, 130*,
    183, 189, Ch2 n92
Campbell, Alexander, 66–8, *115, 119,
    121–2, 127–8, 130–1*, 183, 191–3, Ch2
    n86, n92, n131
Campbell, Archibald, *142–3*, 196–7
Campbell, Colin (Lt. Gov. of Gibraltar),
    180
Campbell, Henry, 54, 65–8, *115, 130*, 183,
    188–9, Ch2 n92
Campbell, James, 198
Campbell, John, 188
Campbell, William, 70, 197
Canning, George, 3–5, 11, 35
Carew, Robert, 204
Carey, Thomas, 61
Cartagena, 197
Cartwright, William, 60
Castaños, Francisco Xavier, 140, *143*
Castlereagh, Robert Stewart, Viscount, 1,
    4, 5, 12, 39, 42, 57, 62, 116, 120, 131
Champalimaud, José, 191
Chasse-marées, 247, 251–2, 258, 260–1
Cheney, Robert, 58
Cheshire, John, 258, 261
Cheynee, George, 257
Chowne, Christopher see Tilson,
    Christopher
Ciudad Rodrigo, 22
Clinton, Henry, 41, 43, 50–1, *184*, 193, 195

Clinton, William, *152, 155*, 177, 190–4, 198
Coa River, 135, 234–6, *235, 236, 237*
Cocks, Charles, 74, 76–9, 82, 133
Colborne, John, 90, 141, *142–3*, 145–6,
    147, 148, 216, Ch2 n155, n173
Cole, Galbraith Lowry, 89–91, 134, 135,
    137, 140–1, *142–4*, 148–9, *152, 155*,
    184, 191–2, Ch2 n166
Coleman, Francis, 194
Collins (Lieutenant RN), 258–60
Collins, Richard, *142*, 194, 197
Colville, Charles, 138, 176, *184*, 190–4,
    Ch2 n68
Command Tenure, 89–90, 137–8: assume
    (a command), 88–90, 122, *122, 144*,
    Ch2 n155, n193; assumptive, 89–91,
    100, 122, 135, Ch2 n155; incumbent,
    89–91, 94, 100, 122, 134–8, *144*, Ch2
    n149, n155, n193; incumber (a
    command), 134–6; interim, 89–91, 100,
    134–5, 137–8
Connolly, Tomás, 74
Cooke, George, 197
Cookson, George, 56–58, 60
Copson, Edward, 204, 209
Cork, 40, 42, 45, 55, 57, 66–7, 104, 106–7
Coruña (Corunna), 3, 50, 57, 61, 65: Battle
    of, 60, 112, *113*
Costa, Antonio Hippólyto, *150–1*, 196
Costa de Atiade Teive, Christovâo da, 188
Costello, Edward, 213–5
Cotton, Charles, 1, 2
Cotton, Stapleton, 54, 63–8, *115*, 120, 122,
    130–1, 183, *185*, 186–9, Ch2 n92
Cox, William, 197
Cradock, John, 4–5, 60, 62–5, 67, 112, 116,
    Ch2 n86
Craufurd, James Catlin, 40, 43–7, 50–3, 55,
    59, 104, *104–5*, 106, *107*, 108, *109, 111*,
    113, 148, 190, Ch2 n66, n124, n155
Craufurd, Robert, 51, 54, 56–9, 61, 69,
    100, 117, 135, 172, 190–1, 196, Ch2
    n150, n157
Cuesta, Gregorio Garcia de la, 12–15, 123,
    125–6, *130*

Dalhousie, George Ramsay, 9th Earl of,
    194
Dalrymple, Hew, 42, 43, 47–8, 50
Darroch, Duncan, 63

Daubrawa, Beirimhof, 74
Debenham, John, 247, 257, 260
de Bernewitz, John, 194
de Grey, George, *142, 144*, 188
De Lancey (de Lancey), William Howe, 182
Dickson, Alexander, 114, 116, 182–3, 237–8, 245, 264, 267
Dilkes, William, 197
Disney, Moore, 51, 54–5, 59, *113*, 197
Division, Army (in general): 85, 136; command of, 88–91, 100–1, 122, 134–5; organisational evolution, 91, 96, 100, 112, 114, 120, 134–5, 138, Ch2 n17; spatial arrangement (of and within), 96, 98, 100–1, 120, 133, 136–7, 158, Ch2 n144; terminological evolution, 100, 120
Donkin, Rufane, 61, 63, 67, *121–2, 126, 130–1*, 131, 191, 198, Ch2 n139
Dorrien, John, 54
Douglas, James, 153, 193
Douro (Oporto) Campaign, 6, 114, 118, 120, 122, 126, Ch2 n126
Doyle, John, *155*, 194
Drieberg, George de, 42, 61, 63–8, *115*, 183
Drummond, George, 137, 196
Dumaresq, Henry, 241
Dundas, Robert, 230
Dunlop, James, 137, 193–4
D'Urban, Benjamin, 3, 141, *143*, 188
Dyott, William, 61, 177

Eben, Frederick Baron, 193
Éblé, Jean Baptiste, 229
Ellis, Henry Walton, *155*
Elphinstone, Howard, 183, 230, 248, 251, 266, Ch5 n37
Elvas, 53, 64
Encampment ('Castrametation'), 124–5, 166, Ch2 n115
English, Frederick, 266–9
Erskine, James, 60, 67, 69, 122, 130, 183, 188
Erskine, William, 101, 186–9, 193, 196
España, Carlos José de, *110, 142–3*

Falmouth, 50, 56, 67
Fane, Henry, 40, 43–7, 49–53, 55, 59–61, 67–9, 104–5, *104–5, 107*, 108, *109, 111,*
113, 115, 120, 183, 186–8, 194, Ch2 n63, n66, n92
Ferguson, Ronald, 42–7, 49–51, 54, 57, 61, 104, *104–5*, 106, *107*, 108–10, *109, 111–12*, 197, Ch2 n60
Fermor, Thomas, 179, 189, Ch2 n20
Fisher, George, 66–7, 69, 182
Fletcher, Richard, 43, 47, 51, 66, 183, *184*
Fonseca, Antonio Luiz da, *142*, 196
Fortescue, John, 90, 109, 112, 128, 130, 133, 141, 145, 152–3, 158, Ch2 n65, n82, n92, n131, n137–9, n143–4, n151, n166, n191
Framingham, Hoylet, 66–7, 182
Fraser, Alexander Mackenzie, 41, 43–4, 48–50, 52–3, 55, 59, *113*
Frazer, Augustus, 253, 264
French Army: strength in Peninsula, 2, 11, 20, 21, 32–4; resilience, 19
Freyre, Manuel, 151, *152, 155*
Fuentes de Oñoro, 19–20, 163 n68, 168 n157

Garonne River, 267–9
Garrisons, British, 39
George III, 5, 18
Gibraltar, 40, 42, 44–5, 48, 50, 62, 67, 106, 163 n68, 179–180
Goldfinch, Henry, Ch5 n37
Goldie, Alexander, 179
Gordon, James Willoughby, 182
Gower, John Leveson, 63
Graham, Thomas, 101–2, 110, *110*, 180–1, *185*, 186, 188–9, 197, Ch2 n 56, n157
Grant, Colquhoun (cavalry brigadier), 188
Grant, Colquhoun (observing officer), 73–5, 77, 80–2
Grant, John, 74, 80, 82
Grenville, Richard, 221
Grey, Samuel, 74
Griffiths, Charles, 179
Gurwood, John, 101

Halkett, Colin, 139, 189
Hamilton, Alexander, 218
Hamilton, John, 8, *142–3*, 196
Hanover, 98, 100, 116, Ch2 n146
Harding, John, 48, 50, 53, 59–60, 62
Hardinge, Henry, 190
Hartmann, Julius, 42, 48, 62, 64–5, 67

Harvey, William, 90, *142, 144*, 192
Harwich, 40–42, 56
Hay, Andrew, 58, 137, 193
Hay, Andrew Leith, 74–7, 79, 81–2
Head, Michael, 144, 179
Hennell, George, 214, Ch2 n154
Hill, Rowland, 5, 40, 43–7, 49–53, 55,
    59–60, 66–8, 89–90, 101–2, 104, *105*,
    106, *107, 109, 111, 113, 115, 119*, 120,
    121, 122, *122, 127*, 128–30, *128–31*,
    132, 134, *134*, 139, *143, 150*, 151, *151,
    153*, 172, 183, *184*, 186–7, 189–90, 194,
    196, Ch2 n56, n68, n86, n92, n110,
    n143, n155, n158
Hillier, George, 74
Hinde, Samuel, 60, 193
Hinüber, Henry de, 189
Hoghton, Daniel, 90, *142–3*, 146, *147*, 190,
    197, Ch2 n70, n182
Homer, 85, 159 n3
Honstedt, Augustus, 198
Hope, John (1st Division), 41, 43, 49–51,
    53, 55, 58, 60, 102, *113*, 181, *184*,
    188–9, 193
Hope, John (7th Division), 194
Houston, William, 90–1, *144*, 177, 192, 194
Howard, Kenneth, 168 n155, 188–90
Howorth, Edward, 66–8, 182–3
Hulse, Richard, 192–3
Hulse, William, 221
Hutchinson, William, 179
Inglis, William, 194, Ch2 n20, n155, n180

Ipswich, 67

Jersey, 56, 67
Jones, James, 74

Keane, John, 191
Kelly, William, 218
Kemmis, James, 64, 90, 123, *130–1*, 135,
    137, 141, *142, 144*, 192, Ch2 n166
Kempt, James, 138, 191, 196

Lacenda, A de L P de, 3
Lambert, John, 153, *155*, 179, 193, 198
Langwerth, Ernest Baron, 41, 61, 63–8,
    115, 116, *130*, 183, 189, Ch2 n92
Lardizábal, José de, *142*

Larpent, Francis, 247, 267
Lecor, Carlos-Frederico, 70, *150*, 151,
    151–2, 194, 196–7
Leith, Alexander, 217
Leith, James, 26, 28–9, 51, 54, 57–9, 177,
    113, 138, 189–90, 192–3, *184*, Ch2 n22,
    n156
Leith Hay, Andrew, see Hay, Andrew
    Leith
Le Marchant, John, 188
L'Estrange, Guy G. C., *147*
Light Infantry, 29–30, 104–5, 116, 118,
    138, 158, *117*, Ch2 n92: *caçadores*, 118,
    134, Ch2 n151; light battalion (ad
    hoc), 117–8, 149, Ch2 n60; light
    brigade, *105*, 106, 108, 191; light
    company, 105, 117–18, *144, 147, 151*;
    light regiment, 136; rifle company,
    106, 118, Ch2 n82, n166; riflemen, 112,
    118
Lightburne, Stafford, 191–92
Lisbon, 48, 50, 57, 61–2, 64–5, 67, 69,
    116–7, 122, 183, 192, Ch2 n155
Liverpool, Robert Jenkinson Lord
    Liverpool, 18
Long, Robert, 51, 60, *142*, 187–8, 194
Löw, Sigismund Baron, *121*, *130*, Ch2 n92
Loy, Casimiro, *142*, 189
Lumley, William, 90, *142–4*, 148, 187, 190,
    Ch2 n155
Lyra, HMS, 251, 257

Maceira Bay, 47–48
Macfarlane, Robert, 177, 193
Mackenzie, Alexander, 40, 42
MacKenzie, John, 198
Mackenzie, John Randoll, 45, 56–7, 61–70,
    114, *115, 119*, 120, *121*, 122, *122*, 126,
    126, 127, 128, *128, 130*, 131–2, 131,
    183, 190–1, Ch2 n131
Mackenzie, Kenneth, 197
Mackinnon, Henry, 135, 137–8, 191
Madden, George, 142, 188, 192–3
Madeira, 44, 48
Maitland, Frederick, 198
Manningham, Coote, 51, 54–8, *113*
Marcilla, Antonio Garcés de, *152*
Marialva, See Agueda River
Marmont, Auguste, 20, 24–7

Masséna, André, 16–20
Martial, HMS, 251, 257–8
Martial Temper, 94, *95*, *127*
McLeroth, Robert, 197
McMahon, Thomas, 192, 197
Meade, Robert, 177
Melhuish, Samuel, 252, 260
Mellish, Henry, 74, 82
Millar, Charles, 197
Mills, John, 238
Mondego Bay, 45, 47, 104
Moore, John, 2–3, 29, 35, 41–4, 47–51, 54–5, 57–8, 60–2, 64, 100, 112, *113*, 158, Ch2 n68, n92
Morillo, Pablo, 151, *152*
Mosinho, Manoel de Brito, 3, 70
Munro, Thomas, 203
Murray, George, 41, 43, 50–1, 67, 182–3, *184*
Murray, John, 8, 41, 43–4, 48, 49, 61–3, 65–8, *115*, 120, 122, 183, 186, 198, Ch2 n92
Myers, William, 90, *142, 144*, 146, Ch2 n166

Napoleon: could he have won? 20–1; orders attack on Valencia, 21–2
Navy, Royal, 34–5
Napier, Charles, 127, *128*, 140, Ch2 n159, n182, n190
Napier, William, 211, 215
Nightingall, Miles, 41, 43–4, 46–7, 50–1, 54, *105*, 106, *107*, 108, *109*, *111–12*, 163 n67, 177, 188–89
Nicol, Daniel, 204–8, 210

Oakes, Hildebrand, 180
Obidos, skirmish at, 47, 107, Ch2 n71, n73
Observing Officers: accomplishments, 80–1; casualties, 82; mode of operations, 74–5; obtaining information, 75–6; reports, 77–9; transmission of reports, 79–80; types of missions, 76–7
O'Callaghan, Robert, 190
O'Loghlin, Terence, 188
Oman, Charles, 112, 130, 132–3, 141, 152–4, 158, Ch2 n66, n92, n138, n151, n158, n166

Oporto, 6, 54, 63, 183
Order of Battle (Battle Order, Battle-Array), 84–5, 87–92, 98–9, 104, *104–5*, 106–8, *107*, *109*, 110–12, *112–13*, 114, *115*, 116, *117*, 118–20, *119, 121*, 124, *126*, 129–30, *129–31*, 132, 134–6, 139, 141, 146, 148–50, 152, *152–3*, 154, *155*, 156–9, Ch2 n63, n92, n115, n117, n155, n182, n185: inversion, 96, *97*; 'natural order', 96, *97*, 107, 129, 133, 148, Ch2 n37; as pattern, 84–7, 92, 94, 157; 'reverse order', 96, 102, 116, 128, 130, 132–3, *143*, 149, 152, 154
Order of March, 84, 109, 124–6, *125–6*, 141, 149, 158, Ch2 n71
O'Reilly, Dowell, 28, 31, 252, 257
O'Ryan, José, 74
Oswald, John, 190, 193–94, Ch2 n157
Otway, Loftus, *142*, 188

Pack, Denis, *110*, 153–6, *155*, 179, 193, 197, Ch2 n157
Paget, Edward, 42–3, 48, 50–3, 55, 59, 67, 69, *113*, 118, *119*, 120, 122, 180–1, 183, 185, 188–9, Ch2 n92
Paget, Henry Lord Paget, 43–4, 50, 54, 57–9, 178
Pakenham, Edward, 176, 182, 189, 191–3, 196
Palmeirim, Luiz, 191, 194
Payne, William, 54, 61, 67, 69, 118, 120, 122, *130*, 180, 183, 185–8, Ch2 n92
Peacocke, Warren, *121*, 122, *122*, *130–1*, 192
Pearson, Thomas, *144*
Penrose, Charles, 247–8, 250, 257–8
Penne-Villemur, Count Luis (Louis), *142*
Pereira, José Clemente, 74
Perry, Samuel, 244–5
Picton, Thomas, 89, 110, *110*, 134–5, 137–8, *152*, 172–3, 177, *185*, 190–1, 194, Ch2 n157
Pinhel, See Coa River
Piper, Robert, 266
Polybius, 124
Ponsonby, William, 188
Ponte de Murcella, 232–4, *233*
Pontoons, 252–6, 262–4

Pontoon Train, 262–9: composition of train, 263; crossing the Garonne, 267–9; description of pontoons, 262–4; draft animals, 263–5; equipment, 263–4; personnel, 266; problems with carriages, 264–5; problems with pontoons, 264

Porcupine, HMS, 259

Portsmouth, 40, 43–5, 48, 56–7, 61, 67

Portugal: role in the war, 1–5, 9, 16, 34; reform of army, 3–5, 7–9; army in Oporto Campaign, 6–7; see also Army, Portuguese

Post of honour, 86, 98–9, 104, 106, *110*, 125, 129, 141, 151, 154, *155*, Ch2 n161; first, 85, 94, 106, 129, 141, *142*; second, 86, 94, 96, 100, *111*, 129, 141, *142*, 151, 158–9, Ch2 n144; third, 100; fourth, 100

Power, Manley, 191, 196–7

Precedence, 87, 89, 91, 94, 98, 139, Ch2 n201: artillery, 96; brigade, 101, 106, 130, 136–8, 141, 148, Ch2 n155; cavalry, 96, 133; command (brigade, division, army corps), 89–91, 99, 102, 136, 152; company, 94; divisional, 101, 129, 135, 152; foreign corps, 98; guards, 96, 114; Hanoverian, 116; international, 125–6, *131*, 140–1, Ch2 n159; lifeguards, 96; militia, 98, Ch2 n44; rank and seniority, 84, 87–9, 91, 94, 102, 138, Ch2 n7, n18; regimental, 96, 98–9, 136, 154; spatial, 86, 94, 96, 98, 128

Prevost, George, 180

Pringle, William, *150–1*, 190, 193, Ch2 n155

Ramsgate, 40–42, 56

Rank, Nature of: brevet, 87–8, 99, 173–4; commissions at a, 87–9, 94, Ch2 n7, n11, n18; dual, 175; local, 174–5, 180, 186; substantive, 87–9, 173–4; temporary, 175

Rebow, Francis, 188

Regency crisis, 18

Reid, William, 252, 260, 269

Rezende, Luiz de Castro, Conde de, 193

Richmond and Lennox, Charles Lennox 4th Duke of, 181

Rivers, Charles, 252, 260

Robe, Alexander, 252

Robe, William, 40, 45–7, 62, 64–5, 67, 182

Robinson, Frederick, 193

Rockets, 254–5

Roliça, Battle of, 47, 106–8, *109*, 110, 112, 126, 158, Ch2 n59

Ross, Andrew, 197

Ross, Robert, 52–3, 55, 60, *155*, 179, 192, Ch2 n20, n192, n193

Rumann, Lewis, 74

Russians in the Peninsula, 219–21

Sacavem, 64

Sahagun, Battle of, 60

St Pierre, Battle of, 139, *150–1*

Salamanca, 53–5, 110, *110*: Battle of, 25–9, 31, Ch2 n185; Campaign of, 24–5, 149

Sampaio, Manuel de Lusignano 2nd Conde de, 70, 188

Santarem, 64, 69

Saunders, John, 179

Savage, Henry, 252

Scott, Charles, 233–6

Sebastiani, Horace Comte, on British musketry, 14

Second-in-Command in the Peninsula, 101, 106, *111*, 122, 179–81, 186

Seddon, Daniel, 188

Seniority, 85–7, 89–91, 102, 111, 136: army rank, 87–9, 90; of brigades, 89–91, 99–100, 106–7, 114, 116, 136–8, 153, Ch2 n155; of companies, 94, *95*; within companies, *93*, 94; of divisions, 89–91, 100–1, 135, 152; of grand divisions, 94, *95*; of the guards, 98, 114; international, 125, Ch2 n159; regimental rank, 87–8, 94; of regiments, 89, 99, 132–3, 136–7, Ch2 n21

Sequencing, 85, 96, 107–9, 114, 118, 150, 157: of brigades, 90–1, 100–1, 106, 109, *122*, 136–7, 148, Ch2 n190; of cavalry, 139; of companies, 94, *95*, 96, 136, Ch2 n41; of divisions, 91, 101; of foreign corps, 98, 114, *131*; of grand divisions, 94, *95*; of the guards, 114, Ch2 n92; of light infantry, 104, 106, 149; of regiments, 96, 106, 109, 132–3, 141, 148–9, 154, 156; reverse

sequencing (from the left), 96, 101, 106, 108, *108*, 132–3, 141, *155*, 158, Ch2 n144
Seville, 64–65, 67, 69
Sheldrake, John, 56, 58
Sherbrooke, John, 61, 65, 67, 70, 118, 120, *121*, 122, *122*, 127–30, *128*, *130–1*, 132, 180, 183, 185–6, 188–9, Ch2 n92, n131
Sicily, 41, 54, 62, 116, 177, 192–4, 197
Sieges, Wellington's, 22–3
Silveira, Francisco Pinto da Fonseca Teixeira da, 6, 70, 196
Skerrett, John, 137, 139, 179, 192, 196–7
Slade, John, 54, 56–9, 186–8
Slade, William, 252, 260
Smith, Harry, 214
Smith, Haviland, 198
Somerset, Lord Edward, *155*, 179, 188
Sontag, John, 42, 43, 62–67, 69, *115*, *119*, 120, *121*, 122, 183, 194, 197, Ch2 n92
Soult, Nicholas Jean, 5, 6, 14, 32–4
Sousa, José Lopes de, 69, 197
Spain: east coast, 189–91, 194, 197–8; guerrillas, 9–10; regular army, 10; role in war, 1, 9–10, 15, 34
Spanish Recruits, 210–5: conditions of service, 211–2; discharged, 215; how recruited, 213–4; numbers authorized, 212–3; number recruited, 214; performance, 214–5; units that recruited them, 214; why recruited, 211
Specie, Shortage of, 12
Spencer, Brent, 1, 41–5, 47, 49–50, 101, *105*, 106, *107*, *111*, 116, 180–81, 185–6, 188, Ch2 n60, n66, n68, n70
Spry, William, 193
Staveley, William, 232
Stewart, Charles (Londonderry), 9, 43–4, 47, 49–51, 53, 55, 59, 67, 126, *127*, *131*, 133, 182–3, 187, Ch2 n102
Stewart, Richard, 2, 41, 43, 49, 62–8, *115*, *119*, 120, *121*, 122, *122*, 130, *130*, 132–3, *134*, 148, 183, 190, Ch2 n92, n143, n155
Stewart, William, 90, 117, 141, *142–3*, 145–6, *147*, 148–9, *150–1*, *153*, 188–90, 197, Ch2 n173
Stirling, James, 60, 189, 193
Stopford, Edward, *144*, 189, 192

Stubbs, Thomas, 192
Sturgeon, Henry, 230, 239–46, 248, 253, 269
Surtees, William, 213
Sutton, Charles, 191

Tagus River, 60, 64, 69; Bridging of, See Alcantara and Villa Velha
Talavera, Battle of, 13–14, 19, 117, 123–33, *127–31*, *134*, Ch2 n155; Campaign of, 12–13, 125–6
Thornhill, Robert, 60
Tietar River, 231–2, *232*
Tilson, Christopher, 61, 65–68, 114, *115*, *119*, 120, *121*, 122, 130, *130–1*, 132–3, *134*, 183, 186, 189–90, Ch2 n22, n110, n143, n155
Tinling, George, 252, 260
Tod, Alexander, 230, 232, 235, 248, 259, 261–2, 269
Torres Vedras, 194; Lines of, 15–16
Toulouse, Battle of, 84, 139, 150–4, *152–3*, *155*, 156–7
Trant, Nicholas, 46, 108, *109*, *111*, 197
Tucker, George, 42, 45, 47
Tulloh, Alexander, *151*

Vandeleur, John, 137, 188, 196
Vasconcel(l)os e Sá, José de, *155*, 192
Vichness, Samuel E., 3
Victoria, Antonio da, 197
Vigo, 57, 61, 64
Vimeiro, Battle of, 47–48, *111*, 112, *112*, 116, Ch2 n82, n123
Viney, James, 40, 45–6, 52–3, 60
Vitoria, 33
Vivian, Richard Hussey, 188
Walcheren Expedition, 12
Walker, George, *150–1*, 190, 193–4, 197, Ch2 n155
Wallace, Alexander, 191, 252, 260
Waller, Charles, 183
Walsh, Anthony, 69
Warde, Henry, 51, 54, 56–8, *113*
Warre, William, 3
Waters, John, 72–5, 80, 82, 182
Webber, William, 245
Wellesley, Henry, 15
Wellesley, Richard Lord Wellesley, 15

Wellington, Arthur Wellesley, 1st Duke of, 39, 172, *185*, Ch2 n13, n20: and the Portuguese army, 2–9; and Perceval's government, 18; and sieges, 22–3; tactical skill, 27–8; use of light infantry, 29–30, 104–5, 112, 116–18, *104*, *117*; artillery, 31; nurtures army, 31–2, 35; reluctance to advance into France, 34; role in allied victory, 34–5; commanding South American Expedition 1808, 40; appointed commander of the force Portugal 1808, 42; superseded in command 1808, 42; at Vimeiro, 47; returns home 1808, 50; appointed to Moore's army, 50; to Ireland as Chief Secretary, 54; appointed commander of the force Portugal 1809, 67; orders advance of his army, 70; preparations and battle-array at Toulouse, 84, 150–2, *152–3*, *155*; general use of battle-array, 85–6, 157–9; discontinues numbering brigades, 91; but informal practice continues, 136; manipulates the correlation of rank and command, 91, 100, 135–7, 176, Ch2 n150; maintaining brigade precedence in divisions, 137–9; first organises divisions in June 1809, 100, *121*, 122, 185; use of army corps, 101–2, 139, 181; the 1808 Campaign, 104; first provisional order of battle, 104–5, *104*, Ch2 n63, n65, n66, n68; remodelled order of battle, *105*, 106–7, *107*; preparations and battle-array at Roliça, 107–10, *109*; preparations and battle-array at Vimeiro, *111*, 112, *113*, Ch2 , n82; evolution to divisional organisation, 114, *115*, 116–20, *119*, *121*, Ch2 n86, n92, n126; policy against flank battalions, 117; policy of keeping colonels with their regiment's

brigade, 123, 177, Ch2 n112; preparations and battle-array at Talavera, 123–33, *125–31*, Ch2 n108, n110; integrating the Portuguese into divisional organisation, 134–6, 197; creating the Light Division, 135–7; preparations and battle-array for Albuera, 139–41; promotion to Field Marshal, 173; local general, 176; comments on his generals, 181–2, 187, 189, 190–1, 196; on health of generals, 177; on second-in-command, 179–80; on absences of generals, 176, Ch2 n150; requests generals, 177; complains about lack of generals, 178; on recalling generals, 178; on employing generals, 178; as Marshal General of the Portuguese Army, 180; choosing his artillery commander, 182–3; comment on Light Division, 195; responsibilities expanded, 197; final comment on his Peninsular army, 198

West, George, 252
Westmacott, John, 231, 238
Wheatley, William, 189, 197
Wilson, George, 190, Ch2 n155
Wilson, John, 197
Wilson, Robert, 70, 197
Wood, George (82nd Foot), *131*, 205, 208–9
Wood, George (RA), 42, 48, 52–3, 60
Woodlark, HMS, 251, 257
Wright, Peter, 267–8
Wynch, James, 52–3, 196
Wynne, Watkin, 221
York, HRH Frederick Duke of, 187; as commander-in-chief, 4, 5, 35, 42, 44, 173–4, 176, 177, Ch2 n65
Young, William, 221
Zayas, José, *142*